I Saw the World End

If I now fare no more
to Valhalla's fortress,
do you know whither I go?
From the land of desire I depart,
the land of illusion I flee for ever;
  the open gates
  of eternal becoming
I close behind me:
  to the desire-free, illusion-free
  holiest chosen land,
the goal of world-wandering,
redeemed from rebirth,
she who understands now departs.
  The blessed end
  of all things eternal,
do you know how I reached it?
  Deepest suffering
  of grieving love
opened my eyes:
I saw the world end.

(Lines rejected from the closing scene of
The Twilight of the Gods
but printed in the definitive text of 1872.)

I Saw the World End

A study of Wagner's *Ring*

Deryck Cooke

London

Oxford University Press

New York   Melbourne

1979

Oxford University Press, Walton Street, Oxford OX2 6DP

OXFORD LONDON GLASGOW NEW YORK
TORONTO MELBOURNE WELLINGTON CAPE TOWN
IBADAN NAIROBI DAR ES SALAAM TOKYO
KUALA LUMPUR SINGAPORE JAKARTA HONG KONG
DELHI BOMBAY CALCUTTA MADRAS KARACHI

ISBN 0 19 315318 1

© Jacqueline Cooke 1979

First published 1979

Text set in 9/10½ pt VIP Palatino, printed by photolithography, and bound in Great Britain at The Pitman Press, Bath

Preface

Deryck Cooke's death in October 1976 deprived us of over half of his monumental study of *The Ring* – not only the entire second volume, dealing with the music, but also the detailed study of the sources, texts, and action of both *Siegfried* and *The Twilight of the Gods*. But what was completed at the time of his death is of such importance for Wagner studies that its publication was essential.

In his 'Introduction' to the Decca recording of *The Ring* (a spoken commentary, with music examples, on three records), Deryck Cooke said that:

[Wagner's] themes – or leading motives as they have come to be called – are not mere identification tags; nor is the score a simple patchwork made up by introducing each motive at the appropriate point in the stage-action . . . Wagner's motives have, in reality, a fundamentally psychological significance, and his score is a continuous symphonic development of them, reflecting the continuous psychological development of the stage action. In consequence, a comprehensive analysis of *The Ring* would be an enormous task. It would involve clarifying the psychological implications of all the motives, and tracing their changing significance throughout the whole of their long and complex development.

This was the 'enormous task' that Deryck Cooke set himself, and which would have constituted the second volume. But, fortunately, the introductory section of the first volume goes into considerable musical detail, so that the basis of the second volume is at least present, even if its loss is thus the more acutely felt.

In editing the text of this book most of the forward references to unwritten sections have been retained, though it has been necessary to omit a few which are not self-explanatory; one or two other similar adjustments have also had to be made, but otherwise nothing has been changed. The 'Second summing-up' – the conclusion of the section on *The Valkyrie* – has, however, been omitted as too fragmentary.

It should perhaps be stressed that, in considering the texts of *The Ring*, Deryck Cooke was not attempting to follow the chronological sequence of their compilation (i.e. from *Siegfried's Death* backwards). This he considered to have been adequately covered by other commentators, and to be largely irrelevant to this study.

Colin Matthews

Grateful acknowledgement is due to the Society of Authors, on behalf of the Bernard Shaw Estate, for permission to quote from George Bernard Shaw's *The Perfect Wagnerite*, and to Faber and Faber Ltd and St. Martin's Press, Inc. for permission to quote from Robert Donington's *Wagner's Ring and Its Symbols*.

Contents

The unsolved problem

1. *The puzzle of* The Ring

At this late stage in the history of Wagner studies, any would-be interpreter of *The Ring* faces the immediate question: 'Is your interpretation really necessary?' Perhaps we have interpreted and reinterpreted this masterpiece until we are in danger of interpreting it out of all recognition. Perhaps it is time to leave it alone, and let it speak for itself.

Wagner himself would certainly have agreed with this view. In 1850, he wrote in *Opera and Drama*:

At a performance of a dramatic work of art, nothing should remain for the synthesising intellect to search for: everything presented in it should be so conclusive as to set our feeling at rest about it: for in this setting at rest of feeling, after it has been aroused to the highest pitch in the act of sympathetic response, resides that very repose which leads us towards an instinctive understanding of life. In drama, we must become *knowers* through *feeling*.[1]

And again, the following year, in *A Communication to my Friends*:

The artist addresses himself to feeling, not to [intellectual] understanding: if he is answered in terms of [intellectual] understanding, it means that he has not been [instinctively] understood.

Wagner was referring to himself, of course, and to the *musico-dramatic* works he himself intended to create – *The Ring*, *Tristan*, *The Mastersingers*, and *Parsifal* – and especially to *The Ring*, for which *Opera and Drama* was essentially a blueprint, and of which he had already begun the text. Yet strangely enough, *The Ring* is the one work amongst these for which his dicta do not hold good. With the others, we do find that our feeling is set at rest, that nothing remains for the intellect to search for, that our instinctive understanding of life is enriched, and that we become 'knowers through feeling'. But there has always been puzzlement over *The Ring*, right from the moment when Wagner's friend and fellow-

---

[1] Wagner's italics, as in all the quotations from his own writings, unless stated otherwise.

revolutionary August Röckel, after reading the first version of the text immediately on its private publication in 1853, wrote to him asking: 'Why, since the Rhinegold is restored to the Rhine, do the gods still perish?' Wagner found himself unable to answer this question, and in his reply of 25 January 1854 he fell back on his appeal to feeling:

I believe that, at a good performance, the most simple person will be quite satisfied on this point. Certainly the gods' downfall does not arise out of the dramatic counterpoints. These could be turned, twisted and interpreted in any way – it would only need a juristic politician to take on the job; no, the necessity of this downfall springs from our innermost feeling, as it does with Wotan.

This was only the text, of course. By now Wagner had completed the composition-sketch of *The Rhinegold*, and he offered a legitimate counter to Röckel's question:

I have now come to realize again how much there is, owing to the whole nature of my poetic aim, that only becomes clear through the music.

Yet even when, after long delay, the whole music was ready, and *The Ring* was produced at Bayreuth in 1876, there was still puzzlement, not only over the point raised by Röckel, but over many others as well. As we know, commentary after commentary appeared, aiming to disentangle the 'dramatic counterpoints', with or without the aid of the so-called 'leading motives', some of them aspiring to the status of 'interpretations' by aiming to elucidate the 'inner meaning' of the work. And these commentaries, by answering Wagner's 'address to feeling' in 'terms of intellectual understanding', showed only too clearly that in this work he had 'not been understood'. Evidently, *The Ring* had not set feeling at rest, and plenty remained for the intellect to search for. Worse still, the intellect found itself incapable of discovering the objects of its search. The extreme difficulty of doing so became manifest in the fact that the commentaries and interpretations conflicted, and none was found sufficiently convincing to be accepted as definitive. Questions always remained, and have remained to the present day, some of them arising from the music as much as from the text.

To be absolutely clear how baffled we have been by *The Ring*, let us consider a single one of these questions. When Siegmund, in Act 1 of *The Valkyrie*, grasps the sword to pull it from the tree, and invokes 'Holiest love's deepest need', why does he sing the theme associated with the *renunciation* of love by Alberich in *The Rhinegold*? (See Ex. 1 – the theme's original form, sung by Woglinde to Alberich – and Ex. 2 – the same form, sung by Siegmund.)

Ex. 1

Ex. 2

It might be tempting to adopt the attitude indicated at the beginning of this chapter, and say that if we leave the work alone, and let it speak for itself, the theme works magnificently, on both its appearances, as immediate musico-dramatic expression, and why should we worry further? Indeed, many people no doubt follow this course in the theatre, being so absorbed in the musico-dramatic excitement at this point of the work that they fail to notice the identity of the actual theme altogether (which they have not heard since the previous evening, anyway); and they would seem to be reacting as Wagner intended them to, since their feeling is eventually set at rest, and they experience no need to search for anything with their intellects.

But in fact this is only because their feeling, in the first place, is not, as Wagner intended it to be, 'aroused to the highest pitch in the act of sympathetic response': they are not reacting to the very disturbing implications which he deliberately wove into the score at this point. Even on the simple story-line level, Siegmund's singing of this theme relates his action crucially to everything that has gone before. In Act 1 of *The Valkyrie*, the scene, the characters, and the events are so completely different from those in *The Rhinegold* that this second drama is dangerously disconnected from the first; and Wagner was only able to succeed with such an oblique procedure through his own peculiar method of constantly introducing musical reminiscences to evoke dramatic reminiscences, and thereby to preserve dramatic coherence and continuity. Already, various thematic references to *The Rhinegold*, especially to the ideas associated with Valhalla and the sword, have hinted that two of the new characters, Siegmund and Sieglinde, are children of Wotan; and now, the entry of the theme associated with Alberich's renunciation of love indicates the wider and less glorious implication of their love-idyll. This is that Siegmund is drawing the sword from the tree, not only to win Sieglinde for his bride, as it seems to him, but also, unwittingly, to regain for Wotan the ring of absolute power which was originally made by Alberich at the cost of renouncing love. Unless we notice the musical reminiscence, and remember Alberich and his ring, we shall miss this vital implication altogether.

On the story-line level, in fact, this musical reminiscence presents no difficulty. But Wagner's musical reminiscences go far beyond the mere business of preserving the coherence of the plot. They are powerfully emotive – this one is no exception – and they normally establish profound emotional and psychological connections between events and characters. Once we notice the musical reminiscence sung by Siegmund, and respond with our own dramatic reminiscence, we seem invited to feel some emotional and psychological connection between his situation and that of Alberich. But renouncing love is evidently the farthest thing from Siegmund's intentions at this moment; and so here, immediately, there is something for the intellect to search for. We may set it aside for the moment, to prevent it from disturbing our response to the closing stages of Act 1; but during the interval we look back and realize that our feeling has not been set at rest on this point, and we feel forced to bring intellect to bear on the problem. Since we can feel no immediate emotional or psychological connection between Siegmund's action and Alberich's, the connection intended by Wagner must presumably be a symbolic one – but what is it? Thus we are compelled to start interpreting, whether we like it or not, to try and discover some meaningful symbolic connection between the Nibelung's renunciation of love, in order to forge a ring that will bring him mastery of the world, and the

Volsung's drawing of a sword from a tree, in order to win himself a bride (and, unknown to himself, to regain Alberich's ring for Wotan).

So far, no convincing connection has been established. Nearly all the commentators have either overlooked this reminiscence, or have evaded the question of its implications; and the few explanations offered are patently far-fetched. We may consider the treatment that this difficult problem received in the only three really ambitious commentaries in English[2] on *The Ring* – those of Bernard Shaw (*The Perfect Wagnerite*), Ernest Newman (in *Wagner Nights*), and Robert Donington (*Wagner's 'Ring' and its Symbols*).

Shaw's book is an interpretation of the work in terms of his own theories of socialism and creative evolution, and he has no music examples: he contents himself with a short and quite superficial chapter on 'The Music of the Ring', in which he describes a small number of the more pictorial musical ideas, and indicates their aptness from the point of view of tone-painting and characterization. In this chapter he makes no mention of the theme associated with Alberich's renunciation of love, and so it is impossible to tell whether he noticed the musical reminiscence in question or not. If he did, he must have dismissed the idea of bothering about such a minor detail (as it would have seemed to him) in a work concerned essentially with social and political allegory. The result, in any case, is that the reminiscence is ignored at the relevant point in his commentary. The closing stages of Act 1 of *The Valkyrie* are swiftly disposed of; Shaw ignores Siegmund's invocation of 'Holiest love's deepest need' and passes straight on to the naming of the sword:

Hailing the sword by the name of Nothung (or Needed), he plucks it from the tree as [Sieglinde's] bride-gift, and then, crying 'Both bride and sister be of thy brother; and blossom the blood of the Volsungs!', clasps her as the mate the Spring has brought him.

Newman's chapters on *The Ring* in *Wagner Nights* are simply commentary, with only a modicum of interpretation to help out in awkward moments, but with many musical examples. He both noticed and tried to explain our puzzling musical reminiscence, but his explanation is no more than an evasion:

[2] See pp. 38–62 for comments on the German authorities (especially the footnote to p. 38).

When Siegmund sings:

> Holiest love's
> most mighty need,
> passionate longing's
> feverish need,
> brightly burns in my breast,
> drives to deed and death,

it is to the strain of . . . the motive to which, at its first appearance in the *Rhinegold*, the commentators have all attached the label of 'Renunciation of Love', because it is to this melody that Alberich avows the renunciation that had won him the gold. Manifestly there can be no 'renunciation' of love implied in the episode in the *Valkyrie* at which we have now arrived; rather is it an assertion of love. Here is yet another warning of the danger attending the labelling of a Wagnerian motive, however convenient it may be for us to do so, according to the words or the situation in connection with which it makes its first appearance in the opera. For the composer, the range of psychological reference of a motive was far wider, and the terms of reference far subtler, than our ready-made tickets can provide for: the musical idea came from a psychical complex within him that may take on an infinity of nuances in the course of the drama. It becomes clear to us now that when [this motive] first appears in the *Rhinegold* it should be taken as signifying not so much Alberich's renunciation of love as the Love itself, universal, omnipotent, which the gnome, in his lust for power, has decided to renounce.

What Newman says about the danger of labelling a Wagnerian 'motive' is true enough – though the 'motives' in *The Ring* have far more concrete and consistent identities than those in, say, *Tristan* or *Parsifal*. But his interpretation of the one in question goes all against its manifest expressive character. This is quite obviously no love-theme (in any case, Wagner himself used, as we shall see later, a very particular kind of melodic line for love-music): it is charged with an ominous feeling, both when it first appears in connection with the possible renunciation of love, and when Siegmund sings it as he grasps the sword. We cannot evade the problem of a puzzling reminiscence by trying to take a theme as expressing something it cannot and does not express; even less can we realize, at some recurrence of a theme, that it did not originally express what we felt it to express, but the opposite. A theme expresses what it does express, at any time, and cogitation on the matter cannot change its character.

This is taken as an axiom by Donington, whose book is an interpretation of *The Ring* in Jungian terms. Like Newman, he has music examples, and he both notices and tries to explain the reminiscence in question; furthermore, he accepts the dark character of the theme itself, and he indicates a symbolic connection between Alberich's situation and that of Siegmund. But unfortunately, he is only able to do this by transforming the characters and their actions into something which, in the actual work as we experience it in the theatre, they are not.

Donington's whole interpretation is so complex and ramifying that a summary of any single point is liable to oversimplify his argument. However, the ultimate explanation, and its degree of fidelity to the drama as we experience it, are the final test. Donington first admits that

> What Wagner, according to his published account of the matter, supposed Alberich to be renouncing by the act of forswearing love was that very principle of sympathy and compassion by which Wagner, by no means mistakenly, believed the world to be knit together.

But then, after discussing Wagner's own relationships with women, and concluding that they were 'surcharged with unconscious mother-longing', he interprets the Rhinemaidens as representing 'seduction by infantile fantasies', and says that 'this might suggest a more positive interpretation of Alberich's renunciation of love, to set alongside the negative interpretation which has certainly to be put on it in the first place'. And so

> On this level of interpretation, the essence of what Alberich renounced was not the love of woman. It was an undue dependence on the love of woman. He renounced the infantile fantasy of being mothered through life by one woman after another . . .

Hence, on this level, Alberich's act becomes a partly praiseworthy one:

> Alberich has certainly the courage to follow the implications of his nature to their lonely conclusion, and we respect him for it even while we hate and fear him in his new-found power.

And the interpretation of the 'renunciation' theme is as follows:

> The Rhinemaidens tell[3] Alberich the secret of their gold in the words: 'Only he that renounces the power of desire (*Minne*), only he that foregoes the delights of love (*Liebe*), only he gains the magic to enforce the gold into a ring'. This is sung to a motive . . . not harsh and forbidding, as might on the face of it be expected, but of a singularly sad, moving and resigned

[3] Should be: 'Woglinde tells'.

nobility. The acceptance of an unsought and undesired but ultimately creative destiny, simply because it is destiny and therefore real and inescapable, could not be more truthfully matched in the mood of the music.

All this brings Alberich nearer to Siegmund; and in the commentary on *The Valkyrie*, Siegmund is brought nearer to this view of Alberich. Much use is made of Jungian interpretation of myth-symbolism in discussing the incest-relationship between Siegmund and Sieglinde, and we are told that

> The retrogression symbolised by incest can lead to a regressive entanglement in escapist infantile fantasies; or it can lead on to a regenerative reliving of infantile situations, in such a way as to give them a more progressive outcome than occurred in actual infancy . . . It may well be counted a prefiguration of rebirth for Siegmund if he can win his manhood under the symbolism of pulling his father's sword out of a tree related, as this tree undoubtedly is related, to the mother-world of nature.

And so we reach the explanation of the reminiscence of the 'renunciation' theme:

> We feel sure that Siegmund is going to pull the sword out when first we catch sight of the gleaming hilt . . . when he does pull it out, we shall hear, in its original dark key of C minor, a full statement of the 'renunciation' motive . . . first heard when the Rhinemaidens were describing to Alberich the condition on which their gold could be pulled away. The words sung by the Rhinemaidens to this wonderful motive, which is at once so deeply sad and so nobly resigned, are: 'Only he that renounces the power of desire, only he that foregoes the delights of love, only he gains the magic to enforce the gold into a ring'. The words sung by Siegmund to the same motive are: 'Holiest desires, highest need,[4] yearning love's compelling need, burns bright in my breast, urges to deed and death'. In this Siegmund shows the intuitive foreknowledge often attributed by the Sagas to heroic characters . . . the deed will be the begetting of Siegfried on Sieglinde; the death will be Siegmund's own. This is not renouncing love; it is accepting a destiny shaped by love even at the price of death. But it is renouncing escapist fantasies. Renouncing escapist fantasies and accepting the full impact of one's destiny are two descriptions for the same act of courage. [The motive] might just as well be called the 'acceptance' motive as the 'renunciation' motive.

In this typically Jungian way, a union of incompatible opposites is effected through manipulation and transformation. What Wagner himself unequivocally represented as 'renunciation of love' is first accepted as such, but then, with the aid of a

---

[4] Should be: 'Holiest desire's highest need'.

tendentious translation of the word 'Minne',[5] it is transformed into 'renunciation of infantile fantasies'. How can this 'positive' interpretation be 'set alongside' the basic negative one? – the two are incompatible. Again, although Alberich is at first admitted to be the chief villain of the drama, he is then ennobled into a courageous accepter of an unsought destiny; while Siegmund, who is patently noble anyway, is provided gratuitously with 'escapist infantile fantasies' to renounce, in order to 'win his manhood'. These fantasies are found for him, by the way, not only by Jungian interpretation of the incest-relationship but by illegitimate conjecture outside the text of the drama:

> We have no direct evidence as to the quality of the mothering Siegmund and his sister received . . . but it may not have been so good as we are inclined on romantic grounds to assume.

Without any justification in Wagner's text we can assume nothing either way; we are simply faced with Siegmund himself who, having spent most of his youth fighting in the company of his father, has clearly 'won his manhood' already, and has no discernible 'escapist infantile fantasies' at all. However satisfying this kind of interpretation may be to those who accept Jung's theories, to others it can only appear to contradict the overt meaning of the drama as we experience it in the theatre. It seems impossible to recognize Wagner's actual Alberich and Siegmund in these curious Jungian guises.

As regards the 'renunciation' theme itself, Donington is quite right in describing it as being 'of a singularly sad, moving and resigned nobility'. Or at least, this is a perfectly accurate description of its expressive quality on its first appearance, when sung by the Rhinemaiden Woglinde – a quality which is entirely appropriate here, since renunciation of love is presented merely as a tragic possibility (which is nevertheless, unknown to her, destined to become reality). But when Alberich sings a powerful compressed version of it, in making his actual renunciation of love, it has, as Donington says, 'a harsh twist to it which it did not have before.' What he does not mention is that when Siegmund sings the theme (surely in startling contradiction of all our musico-dramatic expec-

---

[5] 'Desire' is a limiting translation of 'Minne', which means the kind of love felt by lovers, which *includes* sexual desire. Both Siegmund and the Rhinemaiden Woglinde use 'Minne' and 'Liebe' in a way which clearly indicates parallelism; English can only offer 'love' in both cases, if it wishes to be accurate.

tations), it strikes in with such dynamic emphasis and conclusive force that it loses its original sense of resignation and acceptance, and realizes to the full its potential for expressing pure tragedy – the tragedy inherent, as Wagner's overt musico-dramatic symbolism compels us to infer, in the renunciation of love.

If we ask why, then we have to admit that no convincing explanation has been forthcoming. This is only an isolated example, admittedly, but it is an important one, and there are many others in *The Ring*, all of which lead away from their immediate dramatic contexts to the whole involved story, and to its complex tangle of symbols, which seems intended to bring some great revelation but has always eluded our understanding. As early as 1899, Newman, in *A Study of Wagner*, declared that in creating *The Ring* Wagner 'was not contributing one iota to the wisdom or the knowledge of mankind'. This was in spite of Shaw's interpretation, published the year before; and even now, despite Donington's interpretation, it has to be said that no one has yet proved Newman wrong.

Faced with the fact that Wagner was unable to communicate his intentions clearly, how are we to account for his failure? Why did it happen in this particular work, and not in *Tristan*, *The Mastersingers*, or *Parsifal*?

Two main reasons offer themselves, both inherent in the work's dramatic content. As is well known, Wagner drew mainly on mythology for his music-dramas, rather than on history or romantic fiction, since he believed myths to be humanity's intuitive expression, in symbolic form, of the ultimate truths about its own nature and destiny. His intention, in re-creating them in musico-dramatic form, was to set forth on the stage pure symbols of those fundamental elements of human life which underlie all particular cases and instances. And in support of his procedure he adduced the cogent example of the ancient Greek dramatists. As he said in *Opera and Drama*:

> The [Greek] tragic poet merely imparted the content and essence of myth in the most conclusive and intelligible way, and [Greek] Tragedy is nothing else but the artistic completion of myth itself, while myth is the poem of a life-view held in common.

In one important particular, however, the parallel was not exact: myths had ceased to be the living reality that they were to the Greeks. They were no longer 'poems of a life-view held in common', and this meant that Wagner's 'imparting' of them need not necessarily be 'conclusive and intelligible' at all. With the love-story of *Tristan* there was no difficulty since (as Debussy said) the two lovers became simply 'he and she', and the characters in *Parsifal* are only a little less self-explanatory; *The Mastersingers* is of course a straightforward tale of Wagner's own, woven around the historical figure of Hans Sachs. But in the case of *The Ring*, the gods and the other supernatural beings whom Wagner drew from Teutonic[6] mythology are for many people obscure and puzzling figures. For Wagner himself, naturally, they were as much a living reality as Apollo and Athene were for Aeschylus: he had devoured every available source-book, and relived the whole cycle of myths. But despite a general resurgence of interest in this long-forgotten material, in German intellectual circles, from about 1800 onwards, Wagner was idealizing the situation in expecting an immediate response to the ancient Teutonic gods from a modern audience.

It is one thing to respond to Tristan, Isolde, and King Mark, or to Parsifal, Amfortas, and Kundry, or even to the saga-characters Siegmund, Sieglinde, and Hunding in *The Valkyrie* (significantly, the long-established favourite of the four parts of *The Ring*); but responding to Wotan, Donner, and Loge is another matter. They come trailing long-forgotten symbols – a spear, a hammer, magic fire – which no longer evoke a flash of recognition. Those who have been familiar with Teutonic mythology since childhood are best placed to respond; others, who have not, can manage to accept these characters for what they are, even if they find them rather strange; but many people are actually put off *The Ring* because they find them frankly ridiculous.

The chief trouble is that the actions of these characters are not immediately intelligible in ordinary human terms. When Wotan, for example, gets two labourers to build him a castle, to help him establish his mastery of the world, the payment he offers them is his own sister-in-law; and the world he seeks to master is a curious one anyway, made up of gods, giants, water-nymphs, and dwarfs, with at first no human beings in sight at all. The castle Valhalla functions as a pure symbol of world-power, without any recognizable human reality in the drama to correspond to it.

[6] One has to use this word, in spite of its unfortunate overtones, since it is the accepted term. But it should be remembered that 'Teutonic' is not a racial, but a *linguistic* term: it signifies the peoples whose languages belong to one particular group of the Indo-European family: Icelandic, Norwegian, Swedish, Danish, Frisian, Dutch, Flemish, German – and English.

This brings us to the second and more important reason for Wagner's failure to communicate his intentions clearly: the nature of the subject he used the myths to expound. In taking the legend of Tristan and Isolde as the basis of a music-drama on the theme of romantic love, he was doing a perfectly natural thing, since not only is the legend itself concerned entirely with love, but the emotions arising from love are particularly susceptible to musical expression; and the same is true of the legend of Parsifal and the theme of sin and redemption. But as we shall see, Wagner's original intention in creating *The Ring* (however much he may have expanded and modified this intention later) was to set forth the evils of modern civilization and adumbrate a possible amelioration of them; and this was a most unusual undertaking for a musical dramatist. The connection between the Teutonic myths and modern civilization is far from obvious; and to indicate it, Wagner had to deal, not only in emotions, but in concepts – renunciation of love, mastery of the world, law by contract, and so on – which are not expressible in music, but only in words. What puzzles us about Siegmund's reminiscence of Alberich's renunciation theme, as we have seen, is not the musical character of the theme itself but the intellectual associations that are attached to it: it is the concept that gets in our way.

The truth is that in *The Ring*, the text is important to the understanding of the whole in a way that it is not in *Tristan* or *Parsifal*: we have to comprehend and connect the concepts expressed by the text before we can give ourselves spontaneously to the musical expression of the emotions which lie behind these concepts. *The Ring* is unique amongst great musical stage-works in having at the core of its emotional music-drama a text which is almost as much a 'play of ideas' as a work by Ibsen or Shaw. This is, of course, one of the things that makes it so many-sided and inexhaustible; yet the fact that this 'play of ideas' has proved opaque to our intellects makes the tetralogy fall short of being a perfect work of art, since we are always still puzzling over its meaning when we leave the theatre.

But we should not therefore dismiss it as ultimately a musico-dramatic failure, which is only redeemed by its magnificent music; for in that case we should have to pass a similar kind of judgement on *Hamlet* or Goethe's *Faust*, since with these also the sense of illumination experienced in the theatre gives way afterwards to intellectual uncertainty. It would be more just to place *The Ring*, together with these two dramas, in the category of 'problematic' works – works in which their creators have attempted to delve so deep into the springs of human action that they have been unable to make their findings absolutely clear. It would be more profitable, too, since there is always the hope, with problematic works, that the intellect may be able to solve the problems and leave our feeling free play.

But what real hope of success is there, when even Wagner confessed himself unequal to the task? In one of his letters to Röckel (23 August 1856) he wrote:

How little can an artist expect to find his intuitive perceptions perfectly reproduced in others, when he himself, in the presence of his work of art, if it is a genuine one, stands faced by a riddle, concerning which he might fall into the same illusions as anyone else?

Nevertheless, he went on to admit that he had been helped to a clearer intellectual understanding of what he had been about, in creating *The Ring*, through reading Schopenhauer, who provided him with 'the concepts perfectly corresponding to my intuitive perceptions'. We need not doubt that Wagner had always known intuitively what *The Ring* was about; indeed, his greatness lay in just this intuitive insight, which had produced the work, not in his powers of conceptual analysis. He was no better fitted than any other artist to give a conceptual explanation of the findings of his intuition; others may easily be more successful.

Yet if so many commentators have failed in the task, what chance remains of success? It must be admitted that absolute success is unlikely with this well-nigh infinitely complex work; but at least a start can be made by following two hopeful paths of investigation – the two *main* paths, in fact – which have not been taken by any commentator yet. These are (1) as complete an objectivity as possible in the matter of interpretation; and (2) as comprehensive a musico-dramatic method as possible in the matter of analysis. What these two ideas imply will become clear as we proceed; we must now consider the first of them.

2. *Objectivity in interpretation*

Anyone who undertakes to interpret *The Ring* has to decide what conceptual terms are best suited to the purpose. It might be thought that his choice will be inevitably determined by his own personal way of looking at the world (Shaw was a Socialist and Creative Evolutionist, Donington is a Jungian), and it certainly goes without saying that in interpretation, as in anything to do with art, a considerable subjective element is unavoidable. But there is more to it than that.

No interpreter of any dramatic work, if he is genuinely intent on elucidating its inner meaning, can afford to be entirely subjective. It is clearly not enough to identify certain features of it which correspond to one's own view of things, and then to ignore or coerce any recalcitrant elements which do not fit in with that view. This is simply to insist on making the work mean what one wants it to mean. An interpreter should surely begin by paying full respect to the objective side of interpretation: he should adopt a realistic humility towards the artist's own avowed intentions in creating the work, and towards the manifest intentions of the work itself, before putting his own construction on these.

After all, the question is not 'What meaning can *we* find in *The Ring*?', but 'What did *Wagner* really *mean* by *The Ring*?'; and any attempt to answer this question obviously entails fulfilling the following four conditions:

(1) Every single intention which Wagner avowed in creating the work must be taken into full account, and the interpretation must either absorb it, or else give very good reasons for rejecting it.

(2) The overt meaning of each element in the drama must be accepted as what it is, and not explained away or made to mean something else.

(3) The degree of emphasis placed by Wagner on each element of the drama must be faithfully reflected by the interpretation, with nothing exaggerated, or minimized, or omitted.

(4) The interpretation should be such that it merely clears the way for an unhindered reaction to the work in the theatre, and

leaves it to speak for itself there: it should not put ideas into the reader's head which he cannot possibly relate to his experience of the work in performance.

If we consider now Shaw's *Perfect Wagnerite*, we find that, brilliant and often extremely penetrating as it is, it fulfils only one of these conditions – the second. It does (almost entirely) accept the overt meaning of each element in the work without distortion – Shaw's innate realism prevented him from doing otherwise. But the peculiar limitations of his genius led him to fulfil the other conditions only partly, or not at all. The fundamental weakness of his interpretation is its failure to fulfil the first condition: he accepted only one of the various intentions Wagner avowed in creating *The Ring* – the basic original one of setting forth the evils of modern civilization and adumbrating a possible amelioration of them.

Wagner, in his famous letter to Röckel of 1854, said that Wotan

resembles us to a hair. He is the sum of the intelligence[1] of the present, whereas Siegfried is the man of the future whom we wish for and will to arrive, and yet cannot create – who must create himself by means of *our annihilation*.

Thus spake Wagner the meliorist, the revolutionist, even the creative evolutionist, before his time; and it was this aspect of the work which fascinated Shaw. In his interpretation, Wotan is 'Godhead . . . lawgiver . . . Pontiff and King' – in other words, the civilizing type of ruler, the established authority of the modern state; Alberich is 'the wielder of the Plutonic power . . . the sworn plutocrat' – otherwise the capitalist; Siegfried is 'a born anarchist, the ideal of Bakoonin,[2] an anticipation of the "overman"[3] of Nietzsche'.

Such ideas were undeniably part of Wagner's basic original intention. We should not smile at Shaw's comment on Nibelheim:

This gloomy place need not be a mine: it might just as well be a match-factory, with yellow phosphorus, phossy jaw, a large dividend, and plenty of clergymen shareholders. Or it might be a whitelead factory . . . or any other of the places where human life and welfare are daily sacrificed . . .

[1] Sc: *political* intelligence.
[2] Usually spelt 'Bakunin': the Russian anarchist with whom Wagner and Röckel were associated in the 1849 Dresden uprising.
[3] 'Uebermensch', usually translated 'superman'.

Wagner himself had such things on his mind during the gestation of the text of *The Ring*. In 1849, he wrote in *Art and Revolution*:

> . . . our modern factories offer us the miserable spectacle of the deepest degradation of man: perpetual soul- and body-destroying toil, without joy or love, often almost without aim.

Again, as regards the superseding of the established authority of the state by some kind of superman, Wagner had written a few months earlier, in a newspaper article headed *Man and Existing Society*, this heavily italicized passage:

> *In 1848 the fight of Man against existing society began . . . the determination of Man is to achieve, through ever greater perfecting of his spiritual, moral and physical powers, a higher, purer happiness.*

And that this end could only be attained by the actual overthrow of existing society was proclaimed by Wagner in another article soon afterwards, headed *Revolution*, in which he imagined the mass of humanity listening to

> the greeting of the Revolution: 'I am life, the ever-renewing, the ever-creating! . . . I destroy what exists, and wherever I turn, new life bursts forth from the dead rock . . . I will destroy the order of things . . . which makes millions the slaves of a few, and those few the slaves of their own power, of their own riches.

We may recall the words of Alberich when he curses the ring after Wotan has robbed him of it in Scene 4 of *The Rhinegold*: 'The ring's master [shall be] the ring's slave'.

Wagner's social and political prose (unlike his writings on music, and his music itself) may often be naive in thought and unreal in tone. Nevertheless, he did play an active, practical part in the Dresden uprising of 1849; he had to flee the country to avoid being imprisoned like his friend Röckel, and he spent many years in exile. The connection between his revolutionary ideas and the text of *The Ring* is inescapable; and Shaw's analysis of the social and political aspect of the work is firmly rooted in Wagner's basic original intention.

But Wagner avowed other intentions as well. Two of them, concerned with 'renunciation of the will' and with 'redemptive love', can be found in that same letter to Röckel of 1854:

> Wotan rises to the tragic height of *willing* his own destruction . . . The creative achievement of this supreme self-sacrificing will is to bring into existence at last a *fearless* human being, who never ceases to love: *Siegfried*

. . . Even Siegfried alone (man alone) is not the complete 'human being': he is merely the half; only together with Brünnhilde does he become the redeemer . . . suffering, self-sacrificing woman becomes at last the true, conscious redeemer – for love is in reality 'eternal womanhood' [*das ewig Weibliche*].

To consider the question of love first, it is hardly surprising that Shaw was not impressed by this intention of Wagner's, as he made clear in some special chapters on the subject. However, he did not try to manipulate it, and make it mean something else, but simply gave his own reasons for rejecting it. In a section headed 'The Love Panacea', he says that 'Wagner, only mortal after all, succumbed to the panacea mania when his philosophy was exhausted, like any of the rest of us'. And he compares *The Ring* with Shelley's *Prometheus Unbound*, seeing the same weakness in both:

Both works set forth the same conflict between humanity and its gods and governments, issuing in the redemption of man from their tyranny by the growth of his will into perfect strength and self-confidence; and both finish by a lapse into panacea-mongering by the holding-up of love as the remedy for all evils and the solvent of all social difficulties.

This might be all very well if Wagner had not conceived of love, from the very beginning, as the all-important factor in 'the growth of man's will into perfect strength and self-confidence'. In 1849, the year of the political extracts quoted earlier, he wrote *The Art-Work of the Future*, and in this he said:

The life-need of humanity's life-needs is the *need of love* . . . but the satisfaction of his *need of love* is only attained through *giving*, and indeed, through the *giving of the self* to other human beings, and at the highest point *to all humanity*.

And in *Art and Climate*, written a year later, when the text of *The Ring* was still in its early stages, he pointed to the origin of this universal love in the love between the sexes:

The mediator between power and freedom, the redeemer without which power remains violence and freedom caprice, is therefore – *love* . . . that *love* which proceeds from the *power* of true and undistorted human nature; which in its origin is nothing else but the most active expression of this nature, that proclaims itself in pure delight in sensuous existence, and, starting from sexual love, strides forward through love of children, brothers, and friends, to *universal love of humanity*.

So when Wagner, in his letter to Röckel, said that Siegfried was 'merely the half', he was clearly not 'succumbing to the panacea mania when his philosophy was exhausted', but only going a little deeper into the conception of 'universal love' he had held all along. And in that same letter to Röckel he goes a little deeper still:

> Love in its fullest reality is only possible between the sexes: only as *man* and *woman* can we human beings truly love. Every other love is merely derived from this, arisen from it, connected with it, or artificially modelled on it.

Shaw tries to wave this aside, using an argument which is in fact very true, and of cardinal importance for understanding the part played by love in *The Ring*, though it does not dispose of Wagner's intention in the slightest:

> Wagner sought always for some point of contact between his ideas and his senses, so that people might not only think or imagine them in the eighteenth-century fashion, but see them on the stage, hear them from the orchestra, and feel them through the infection of passionate emotion . . . Now he could apply this process to poetic love only by following it back to its alleged origin in sexual passion . . .

For Wagner, Shaw's curious term 'poetic love' could have had no meaning, but he certainly represented the growing ascendancy of *universal love* over repressive law and tyrannous power by symbolizing it as sexual passion – the love of Siegmund (the rescuer of the oppressed and helpless) for Sieglinde, the love of Siegfried (who eventually meets his end through loving human beings too indiscriminately) for Brünnhilde. But in doing so, he was not only seeking 'some point of contact between his mind and senses' to give concrete expression to things which might be taken wrongly as abstractions: he was remaining faithful to his own intuitive awareness of the sexual origin of all love, as expressed in *Art and Climate* and again in his letter to Röckel.

Shaw, of course, would have none of this; hence his phrase about the *alleged* origin of 'poetic love' in 'sexual passion'. Here we are confronted with his sexual inhibition, his basic puritanism, which finds compulsive expression in his treatment of the love-scenes. The above quotation continues (referring back to the comparison with Shelley's *Prometheus Unbound*):

> . . . sexual passion, the emotional phenomenon of which he [Wagner] has expressed with a frankness and forcible naturalism which would possibly have scandalised Shelley. The love duet in the first act of The Valkyrie is brought to a point at which the conventions of our society demand the precipitate fall of the curtain . . .

And later, of the final scene of *Siegfried*:

> Certainly it is clear enough that such love as that implied by Siegfried's first taste of fear as he cuts through the mailed coat of the sleeping figure on the mountain, and discovers that it is a woman; by her fierce revolt against being touched by him when his terror gives way to ardor; by his manly transports of victory; and by the womanly mixture of rapture and horror with which she abandons herself to the passion which has seized on them both; is an experience which it is much better, like the vast majority of us, never to have passed through, than to allow it to play more than a recreative holiday part in our lives.

Scared off by the frankly sexual character of this scene, Shaw did not even consider that it might have wider implications. The verbal text of it was already written in 1851, while Wagner was still entirely committed to his revolutionary ideals, so there is no justification for Shaw's statement that it represents a later 'succumbing' to the 'panacea mania'. The sexual basis of love is certainly brought out even more strongly here than in Act 1 of *The Valkyrie*, and treated more fully, yet the symbolism is still that of love for humanity gaining the ascendancy over repressive law and tyranny: Siegfried's first action, after leaving Brünnhilde and meeting Gunther in Act 1 of *The Twilight of the Gods*, is to give friendship and service. But Shaw could see only the sex in the *Siegfried* scene, and it blinded him to other considerations.

The result is that although he faithfully accepted the overt meaning of the love-element, the reasons he gave for rejecting it are not good enough. And in consequence he failed to satisfy the third condition of a realistic interpretation – although he actually claimed, in one of his prefaces, to have fulfilled it meticulously:

> The story as told in this book has its centres of gravity where Wagner has placed them in his score. What Wagner made much of, I have made much of . . . what he passed lightly over, I have passed lightly over.

But the fact is that Wagner's emphasis is pretty constant everywhere, and is nowhere more weighty than in the love-scenes, which Shaw passes over very lightly indeed.

Worse still, he passes over altogether the revelation which comes to Brünnhilde when she realizes what Siegmund's love for Sieglinde means to him – when he rejects a hero's glorious immortality in Valhalla because Sieglinde cannot accompany him to this purely male paradise. Shaw's account of Brünnhilde's state of mind at this moment is unenlightening:

How can Brynhild, being what she is, choose her side freely in a conflict between this hero and the vassal of Fricka? By instinct she at once throws Wotan's commands to the winds . . .

In fact she does so, not by some unspecified instinct, as Shaw suggests, but, as she herself explains to Wotan later, by her sudden realization of the meaning of love. Shaw actually glosses over this whole tremendous scene between Brünnhilde and Wotan, with its far-reaching implications for the development of the drama: unbelievably, their altercation and their gradual reconciliation are simply omitted. The commentary passes straight on from 'he is left alone with Brynhild', through some abstract explanation of the social implications of their separation, to 'Wotan, with a breaking heart, takes leave of Brynhild, throws her into a deep sleep . . .'.

Shaw's blindness to the significance of the love-element in the drama crippled his interpretation, and even left him at a loss in face of the extraordinary fact that Wagner himself eventually repudiated the idea of the supremacy of love. In the original 1853 version of the text of *The Ring*, Brünnhilde's final monologue, in *The Twilight of the Gods*, contained a passage exalting love as the only valid thing in life:

> *Not goods, not gold,*
> *nor godly pomp;*
> *not house, not court,*
> *nor lordly splendour;*
> *not shady bargains'*
> *deceiving bonds,*
> *nor two-faced customs'*
> *rigid laws;*
> *blesséd in joy and grief,*
> *let there be only – Love.*

But in his 1856 letter to Röckel, Wagner described how dissatisfied he had become with these lines:

I remember that finally, once and for all – but once only – I brought out powerfully my [original] intention: to wit, in the tendentious closing phrases addressed by Brünnhilde to those around her, in which she points away from the evils of possession to all-redeeming love, without (unfortunately!) making absolutely clear the nature of that love, which we have seen, in the course of the myth, to have appeared fundamentally destructive.

Shaw's comment on Wagner's change of mind is completely misleading:

It is highly significant of the extent to which this uxorious commonplace lost its hold of Wagner (after disturbing his conscience, as he confesses to Röckel, for years) that it disappears in the full score of Night Falls on The Gods, which was not completed until he was on the verge of producing Parsifal, twenty years after the publication of the poem. He cut the homily out, and composed the final scene with a flagrant recklessness of the old intention.

In fact, as Wagner's letter of 1856 to Röckel makes clear, it was as early as that year, only *three* years after the text had been published, and *sixteen* years before the final act of *Twilight of the Gods* was composed, that he had decided to cut the passage; so his decision must be taken, not as a last-minute change of mind, but as an early modification of the 'old intention'.

Shaw might have been more interested in the implications of this change of intention, if it had not gone hand in hand with the central transformation of the whole original conception, which Wagner also stated in this same letter to Röckel:

I shaped it [the text of *The Ring*] at a time when I had built up in my conceptual thought a hellenistic-optimistic world, the realization of which I held to be entirely possible, if only men wanted it – though I rather ingeniously pushed away the problem why they actually didn't want it. I remember that I worked out the personality of my Siegfried in this premeditated way, with the desire to represent an existence free from pain; and I thought to express myself even more clearly in the presentation of the complete Nibelung myth, by showing the original injustice from which a whole world of injustice arose and therefore fell to ruins, so as to – well – teach us a lesson how to recognize injustice, tear it out by the roots, and establish a just world in its place. But I hardly noticed that, in carrying out my plan – indeed, even in laying it down – I was unconsciously following a quite different, much deeper intuition, and instead of conceiving a phase in the development of the world, I had conceived the essence of the world itself and recognized its nothingness; from which it naturally followed that, since I had been faithful to my intuition and not to my conceptual ideas, something different came to light from what I actually thought.

Then, after telling Röckel of his decision to cut the passage exalting love from Brünnhilde's final monologue, Wagner continued:

Strangely enough, this passage was a continual torment to me, and it needed a complete revolution of my conceptual thought, brought about eventually through Schopenhauer, to reveal the reason for my torment, and to provide me with a really adequate keystone to my poem, consisting of a frank recognition of the true, profound relationships of things, without anything in the least tendentious.

This 'really adequate keystone' took the form of a new passage to replace Brünnhilde's exaltation of love – a passage expressing a renunciation of the material world altogether as an illusion, and a dissolution into a state of non-being: Wagner had been led on by Schopenhauer to the ideas of Buddhism. But this passage, too, was eventually omitted (at the last moment, just before the final scene was composed, on the advice of Cosima, who thought it 'rather artificial') and Wagner left the final scene to speak for itself, as musical drama, without any moralizing at all.

Nevertheless, he had this rejected passage printed as a footnote to the scene in the publication of the final version of the text in 1872; and he added a comment which shows that he had not excised it because he no longer held by what it said, as was the case with the passage it had replaced. He said that it had 'fallen out' because 'its meaning is already expressed with the greatest precision in the effect of the musically-sounding drama [in der Wirkung des musikalisch ertönenden Dramas]'. The lines that Brünnhilde was to have sung are as follows:

> *If I now fare no more*
> *to Valhalla's fortress,*
> *do you know whither I go?*
> *From the land of desire I depart,*
> *the land of illusion I flee for ever;*
> *the open gates*
> *of eternal becoming*
> *I close behind me:*
> *to the desire-free, illusion-free*
> *holiest chosen land,*
> *the goal of world-wandering,*
> *redeemed from rebirth,*
> *she who understands now departs.*
> *The blessed end*
> *of all things eternal,*
> *do you know how I reached it?*
> *Deepest suffering*
> *of grieving love*
> *opened my eyes:*
> *I saw the world end.*

Shaw could make nothing of all this, nor did he want to. The metaphysical idea of renouncing the material world was anathema to him – 'the doctrine of Pessimism' he called it. Again he tried to explain away this intention of Wagner's by stressing the contradictions of his nature:

When he had exhausted himself in the character of the most pugnacious, aggressive, and sanguine of reformers, he rested himself as a Pessimist and a Nirvanist . . . Wagner was not a Schopenhauerite every day of the week, nor even a Wagnerite . . . if The Ring says one thing and a letter written afterwards says that it said something else, The Ring must be taken to confute the letter just as conclusively as if the two had been written by two different hands.

The truth is that, as Wagner himself said in his letter of 1856, his study of Schopenhauer had only made clear to him what he had felt intuitively all along, or at least very early on. Already, between February 1849, when the text of *Siegfried's Death* was completed, and May 1849, Wagner had changed the nature of Brünnhilde's address to the gods in her final monologue. Whereas originally she was to have led Siegfried to Valhalla in triumph, and called on the gods to rejoice in him, she now simply proclaimed to them 'blessed atonement', and before the spring of 1851, he changed the passage again, making Brünnhilde bring them 'blessed death-redemption from their anxious fear'. Also, as we have seen, Wagner was already talking of Wotan 'willing his own destruction' in his letter to Röckel of 25 January 1854 – which was several months before he was introduced to the writings of Schopenhauer. So Shaw's theory of Wagner's vacillation cannot be substantiated. When he says that 'Wagner was, when he wrote *The Ring*, a most sanguine revolutionary meliorist', one can only answer: 'No, not when he wrote *The Ring*, but when he began the *text* of it; as he *completed* the text and wrote the *music* he changed his mind and modified the nature of the work'.

Clearly, Wagner began the text of *The Ring* with the intention of making it say one thing only, and gradually completed the whole music-drama so that it went on to say other and opposite things as well. Shaw unconsciously admits as much, in fact, since after interpreting the work as a social and political allegory up to the end of the scene between Wotan and Siegfried in Act 3 of *Siegfried*, he finds himself unable to continue: he heads the next section 'Back to Opera Again', and after merely describing the events of the final scene of *Siegfried*, and of the whole of *The Twilight of the Gods*, he adds an epilogue headed 'The Allegory Collapses'. He could simply make nothing of the other things *The Ring* came to say, and so he rejected them as meaningless.

The result is that his interpretation stands as an exaggeration of the social and political aspect of the work, bringing it as near as possible to a Shavian 'play of ideas'. And as such, it fails to fulfil the fourth condition of a realistic interpretation: it sends the reader into the theatre with a number of concepts which cannot be related to his experience of the actual drama, and with others which, even though they can be related to it, miss the deeper meaning. Shaw's interpretation of Nibelheim, quoted earlier, is certainly apposite, but when Alberich makes himself invisible by means of the Tarnhelm, and thrashes Mime, we read:

> This helmet is a very common article in our streets, where it generally takes the form of a tall hat. It makes a man invisible as a shareholder, and changes him into various shapes, such as a pious Christian, a subscriber to hospitals, a benefactor of the poor, a model husband and father, a shrewd, practical, independent Englishman, and what not, when he is really a pitiful parasite on the commonwealth, consuming a great deal and producing nothing, feeling nothing, knowing nothing, believing nothing, and doing nothing except what all the rest do, and that only because he is afraid not to do it, or at least pretend to do it.

This brilliant Shavian invective is all very effective and entertaining in itself; but the fact remains that the Alberich of the drama is no hypocrite, is not at all afraid to do things opposite to 'what the rest do', and has no characteristics which bear the slightest resemblance to any of those which Shaw lists. We simply cannot see Alberich as a smug, fake-Christian shareholder, respectable in a top hat. Here, as so often in the Fabian Shaw's writings, the essential sadism of the tyrant has been overlooked.

Again, we may accept, as an accurate interpretation, Shaw's view of Wotan as the civilizing type of ruler, which he calls 'Godhead', and of Brünnhilde as 'that soul in itself [i.e. in the civilizing power] which cares only to make the highest better and the best higher'. But his interpretation of Wotan's punishment of Brünnhilde eventually plunges into a mass of political abstractions which are surely far from our minds when we witness the scene in the theatre:

> Godhead [Wotan] has now established its dominion over the world by a mighty church [Valhalla] compelling obedience through its ally the Law [Fricka] with its formidable State organisation of arms [the heroes in Valhalla] and cunning of brain [Loge]. It has submitted to this alliance to keep the Plutonic power [Alberich] in check – built it up primarily for the sake of that soul in itself which cares only to make the highest better and the best higher; and now here is that very soul [Brünnhilde] separated from it and working for the destruction of its indispensable ally the lawgiving State. How is the rebel to be disarmed? Slain it cannot be by Godhead,

since it is still Godhead's own very dearest soul. But hidden, stifled, silenced it must be, or it will wreck the State and leave the Church defenceless.

True as much of this is as an abstraction of the social implications of the scene, we find, by the time we come to that 'defenceless Church', that we have finally lost all contact with Wagner's profoundly moving father-and-daughter scene between Wotan and Brünnhilde – with both its emotional content and its clash between the two opposed principles of power and love.

Shaw, of course, by the very nature of his genius, could have written no other kind of interpretation of *The Ring*. We have to admire his honesty – his explanation of as much as he could make sense of, and his rejection of the rest without any distortion of it to fit his thesis. Above all, we should by no means underestimate the accuracy of his interpretation as a map of the work's social implications. But as with so much in his own plays, it takes us into a realm of pure concepts, divorced from the existential realities of human psychology – aggression, sex, love, compassion – and from all metaphysical implications.

Donington dismisses Shaw's interpretation as 'a one-sided study which does full justice to the economic issues but to very little else'. This is hardly fair, since, as can be seen in the last extract quoted, Shaw is concerned not with mere economics, nor even with mere politics, but with the force of creative evolution working through the development of human civilization towards something higher. And I find it hard to be fair, myself, to Donington's own interpretation, since I am totally out of sympathy with the entirely introverted theories of Jungian psychology, and even more with the idea of applying them wholesale to a work with such manifest social implications as *The Ring*. Nevertheless, I can only consider his book in relation to the four necessary conditions, given earlier, for a realistic interpretation; and this forces me to the conclusion that he does justice to none of the issues in *The Ring*, but only to the theories of Jung.

As always with Jungian interpretation, all the characters, events, and objects of the drama are treated as symbols of elements in the 'psyche' of a single individual, and the various crucial events are understood as phases in the internal psychological development of that individual. With Donington, moreover, these phases are related to the psychology of Wagner himself, as well as to that of everyman. Seen from this viewpoint, there is no outside world in *The Ring* at all, no sense of society, but only psychological transformations happening inside a single unconscious. Hunding, for example, is not an oppressor from whom Sieglinde has to be rescued; he is Siegmund's own 'shadow', and therefore one of the manifestations of the 'shadow' of the single 'psyche' portrayed by *The Ring* (the 'shadow' being that repressed, disreputable side of a man's character which he does not want to face). And it is obvious that such an approach entails a failure to fulfil the first condition of a realistic interpretation, since it necessitates the repudiation of all Wagner's avowed intentions in creating the work.

Donington's method, in fact, with regard to Wagner's avowed intentions, is to state them and then immediately discount them. Taking the basic original one first – the meliorist intention – he quotes the passage from Wagner's 1854 letter to Röckel about Wotan being 'the sum of the intelligence of the present' and Siegfried being 'the man of the future' who 'must create himself by means of our annihilation', and then simply contradicts it:

> But, of course, Siegfried is not the man of the Future: not even in the *Ring*, where he soon comes to an untimely end. The man of the Future is a symbol for our own state after a sufficient growth in our character has taken place; and he is shaped, if at all, not by our annihilation but by our transformation.

Not the *actual* man of the future, no. Wagner himself eventually came to realize that the 'man of the future' was a figment of the over-heated imaginations of idealistic revolutionaries, including himself. Already in 1849, as we have seen, he scrapped the original ending of *The Ring*, in which Siegfried, after his death, was to have been led to Valhalla in triumph by Brünnhilde. And there is always the awkward fact that Siegfried, even as a *symbolic* projection of regenerate man, is a very curious figure. Nevertheless, such was Wagner's original conception of him; and it remains inextricably embedded in the final work, until it vanishes with everything else in the ultimate holocaust. No other conception of Siegfried ever took its place: from the purely objective point of view, this character, with the enormous build-up he is given, remains Wagner's projection of a future regenerate type of man to supersede the corrupt Wotans, Alberichs, and Mimes of existing society; and part of the manifest meaning of *The Ring* is that Wagner finally cancelled this projection. There is no justification at all, on the other hand, for Donington's interpretation of Siegfried as a symbol of a certain stage in the psychological development of everyman, except that this is the way that Jungian interpretation is obliged to function.

Wagner's intentions with regard to the love-element in the drama are partly transformed by Donington into Jungian terms, and partly ignored altogether. In the first place, the basic love between man and woman is again interiorized into an element in everyman's psychological development. Man and woman become those disembodied Jungian concepts, the animus and the anima; the love between Siegfried and Brünnhilde, for example, is equated with the 'Mystical Union' in the writings of St Thomas Aquinas, which, says Donington, 'can in one aspect be described as a union of the complementary masculine and feminine principles within the psyche'. This kind of interpretation can of course be applied to any ideal love-situation in any drama, and is no doubt valid on one level, whatever mystical or psychological phraseology one may use to describe it; but it does not take us very far in the matter of understanding the particular situation in the drama concerned. Certainly, in the case of *The Ring*, this totally introverted view can find no place for Wagner's wider conception of love as a social force.

The treatment of Siegmund, for example, is extremely puzzling. We have already seen Donington providing this character with 'escapist infantile fantasies': to support this view, he interprets him mainly in his aspect of unwelcome outlaw – the man who brings troubles on his own head – and he links him closely with Wagner himself in this respect. He says of Siegmund:

> Half his troubles, including the one from which he is now in flight, are of his own making . . . As often as he intervened in a good cause, and with the best of intentions, he only found that no-one, not even the victim he had rushed in to save, took the same view as he did of the rights and wrongs of the quarrel . . . He could find no settled place for himself in human society anywhere . . . The indications which this history gives us with regard to Siegmund's character correspond strikingly enough with what we know of Wagner's . . .

This generalized account of Siegmund's history is true, being a résumé of part of his own narrative, but it is anything but the whole truth. The one crucial piece of information is unaccountably omitted – the actual *nature* of the trouble 'from which he is in flight' – which is the only concrete case Wagner gives us of his behaviour as an outlaw. In fact he has been trying to rescue a girl from the same kind of forced marriage that Sieglinde has been made to undergo with Hunding; and it seems inescapable that Wagner was intentionally symbolizing here the emergence of a fierce compassion amidst a brutal, repressive society – a compassion which becomes merged in family and sexual love when the latest woman in distress that Siegmund encounters turns out to be his own long-lost sister, and he falls in love with her.

The comparison with Wagner's own case is a false one. Siegmund's troubles must inevitably be 'of his own making' if he is a bold exponent of compassion in a primitive society run by Hundings and Neidings, whereas the troubles which Wagner brought on his own head, in the civilized society of his time, were not the product of any attempt to rescue those in distress, but rather of his exploitation of others in the interests of furthering his own cause. What he put into Siegmund, as in the case of all his great male figures, was something of his *ideal* self: the symbolic significance of the character is to be found, not in Wagner's unfortunate real life, but in his original intentions in creating *The Ring*. His avowed conception, in his writings, of a universal love, rooted in family and sexual love, as the central force making for a regeneration of society, could not be more unequivocally symbolized than here, in Act 1 of *The Valkyrie*, where it figures as a first decisive break with the loveless, power-ridden world of Wotan and Alberich in *The Rhinegold*. But this conception can find no place in Donington's interpretation, since the characters have been arbitrarily interiorized as components of the Jungian 'psyche'.

Wagner's final intention – the one concerned with 'renunciation of the will' and withdrawal into a mystic state of non-being, is likewise transformed into Jungian terms. Donington quotes from Wagner's 1856 letter to Röckel,[4] and then says:

> Wagner believed that he had found, in Schopenhauer, a philosophy to fit his intuitions. Schopenhauer's 'explanation of the universe' is summed up by Wagner in this letter as depending on 'the high tragedy of renunciation, the deliberate, reasoned, ultimately necessary negation of the will, in which alone is salvation'. Wagner felt that he had always intuitively 'discerned the nature of the universe itself in all its conceivable phases and had recognised its nothingness'. But whatever either Schopenhauer or Wagner may have supposed, these are explanations not of the outer but of the inner universe.

[4] See p. 20–1.

With this last categorical (and completely unverifiable) statement, Wagner's metaphysical intention is neatly reduced to a purely psychological one. And again, after mentioning the 'Buddhistic' lines of Brünnhilde which were printed as a footnote to the final version of the text, Donington counters with:

> I do not know, and I doubt if Wagner knew, what Buddhist thought really expresses under the symbol of annihilation. I do know that none of Wagner's images in the *Ring*, whatever his reason may have had to say about it, actually points to annihilation as our own Western thought conceives it. One after another of them points to rebirth in the sense of transformation.

No one knows, of course, what 'negation of the will' or 'annihilation' or 'non-being' really means – such phrases are mere verbal constructions groping towards some metaphysical reality which is ungraspable, and inexpressible in words; but again, this was how Wagner stated his final intention, and it is here turned into its direct opposite. Remembering the tremendous doom-filled images at the end of *The Ring* – not to mention Brünnhilde's explicit phrase 'redeemed from rebirth', which although not set to music was printed as a gloss in the final publication of the text – one wonders whether any artist could possibly create an image of annihilation which Jungian thought could not interpret as an image of rebirth and transformation. One after another of Wagner's images – including such drastic ones as Wotan's sacrifice of Siegmund and Hagen's murder of Siegfried – is certainly *taken* as a symbol of rebirth and transformation, in Donington's book; but this seems the central weakness of Jungian interpretation. Anything and everything is enclosed within the narcissistic magic circle of the individual psyche, into which no image of irrevocable external catastrophe can enter without being gelded of its manifest meaning, so that black becomes white, and all is always for the best.

Inevitably, then, Donington does not fulfil the second condition of a realistic interpretation – that of accepting the overt meaning of each action in the drama without distorting it. We have seen that Alberich's renunciation of love becomes renunciation of 'escapist childish fantasies'; likewise the text's 'accursèd ring' of tyrannical world-domination becomes the Jungian concepts of 'libido' – the energy of life – and the 'spread of consciousness' (simply because it is golden). And in order to accommodate such interpretations, the third condition has to remain unfulfilled, too – the faithful reflection of the degree of emphasis laid by Wagner on the various elements in the drama. To take only one example: since Alberich's act of forging the ring, at the cost of renouncing love, is ennobled into a 'renunciation of escapist fantasies' in a search to discover the 'self', his expression of his aggressive intention of making everyone pay for his renunciation is minimized, and even in places ignored. One such case is his ferocious threat to Wotan in Nibelheim, in Scene 3 of *The Rhinegold*:

> *Beware! Beware!*
> *For once you men*
> *are under my power,*
> *your pretty women,*
> *who despise my wooing,*
> *shall serve the pleasure of the dwarf,*
> *though love smiles not on him!*

This utterance is given a whole paragraph of interpretation by Shaw, who describes it as 'horrible and sinister', and Newman sees Alberich here as 'an impressive figure, the incarnation of envy and hatred and evil will'; but the passage is simply omitted from Donington's interpretation altogether. He passes straight on from the moment when Alberich notices the presence of Wotan and Loge to the moment when Loge starts to trick him:

Alberich next sees his visitors, and hurries Mime and the other dwarfs off-stage before confronting the two gods, which he does with all possible suspicion. [Here Alberich's outburst is ignored.] He is nevertheless soon trapped, by one of Loge's most cunning wiles. I can scarcely believe, says Loge, that you can really transform yourself as you claim. In the twinkling of an eye Alberich has turned himself by means of Tarnhelm into a vast writhing snake . . .

The final result is that, even more than with Shaw, the fourth condition is not fulfilled: the reader is sent into the theatre with conceptions which he cannot relate to his experience of the work in performance. We have seen how hard it is to recognize, in Donington's Jungian dress, Wagner's love-renouncing and tyrannous Alberich, and his heroic and compassionate Siegmund; and it is even more difficult to recognize the giants Fasolt and Fafner, or Fafner the dragon. In the commentary on Scene 2 of *The Rhinegold* we read:

The giants come pounding after Freia . . . Our earliest experience of such towering figures, with whose mere walk we can scarcely keep pace at the run, is of our parents . . . Has Wotan been turning on to a problem of adult life the brutal aspect of parental authority as it may be experienced in childhood?

And in the commentary on Act 2 of *Siegfried*:

> In Fafner the dragon, Siegfried the hero meets the Terrible Mother.

Again, Donington's interpretation of the scene between Wotan and Brünnhilde in Act 3 of *The Valkyrie* finally takes us as far away from the actual conflict of principles between the two as Shaw's does. He speaks of

> . . . the hard wilfulness of Wotan in his entrenched capacity as ego and the compassionate responsiveness of Brynhilde in her developing capacity as that aspect of the anima which stands for warmth of feeling.

And he says that Wotan

> . . . is projecting his own hostile intentions on to the other person instead of seeing them in himself: this enables him to accuse the other person most self-righteously of the very offence he is himself committing . . . One of the ways in which we can describe a man who is in this blind state of self-righteous certainty at the very height of his own folly is by saying that he is possessed adversely by his anima . . . Such anima-possessed moods range from a mere passing sulkiness or touchiness to much graver follies . . . Casting Brynhilde off is tantamount to Wotan thrusting his anima out of sight; and leaving Brynhilde exposed to the first stranger to find is tantamount to Wotan leaving his anima at the mercy of his own shadow, since no part of the psyche is so strange yet so near at hand as our own dark component of unacknowledged disreputability.

No less than Shaw's 'defenceless Church', Donington's 'anima-possession' and 'leaving one's anima at the mercy of one's own shadow' are abstractions which finally separate us from the actual clash of principles between Wagner's intensely human characters.

The fatal defect of Jungian interpretation is that it simply imposes its own categories on the work interpreted. Sieglinde and Brünnhilde have to be anima-figures, Hunding and Hagen have to be representations of the shadow, the dragon has to be the Terrible Mother, because these are the only categories available. Just so, in *Hamlet*, say, Ophelia would have to be Hamlet's anima, Claudius his shadow, and Gertrude the Terrible Mother, and the whole work would have to be treated as a therapeutic development of the psyche; likewise, the last stage would have to be nobody's actual death, but a general rebirth, except for the shadow, which would disappear, leaving the psyche in one final healthful state of transformation – and the peculiar quality of the masterpiece *Hamlet* unilluminated.

The Jungian argument, of course, is that if a dramatist traffics in lovers and villains and mother-figures and death, he is inevitably, whether he realizes it or not, dealing in the archetypes of the anima, the shadow, the Terrible Mother, and transformation; and the way he deals in them tells us much of value about his own psychology and that of everyman. And for those who accept the theories of Jung, an interpretation of this kind is doubtless illuminating. So perhaps the fairest thing to say about Donington's book is that it is 'a Jungian interpretation of *The Ring*' – just as there can be a Jungian interpretation of any other dramatic work of art – which nevertheless does not explain what *The Ring* is actually about.

Donington's justification of his approach is that there are different 'levels' in *The Ring*: he admits that there is an 'economic' level, explored by Shaw, and claims that his own interpretation concentrates on the underlying psychological one. That there are different levels of meaning in *The Ring* is of course true – but it is exactly this which constitutes the work's peculiar greatness, and it should be the business of any interpreter who is intent on demonstrating that greatness to try to indicate and clarify all of them. The trouble with concentrating on one level only, and ignoring the others, is that so much of the meaning of *The Ring* is left out of account, and even the level the interpreter does examine is attenuated by being reduced to the abstractions belonging to one particular conceptual system. As a result, the reader is offered, not a clarification of the work in all its many-sidedness, which will help him towards a richer experience of it in the theatre, but an intellectual argument in one particular field which tends to *replace* the actual work, and is naturally *incommensurate* with it.

The truth is that many of the symbols in *The Ring* work on all levels at once, and to interpret them on one level only is to impoverish them; on the other hand, one here and there does work on one level only, and if that is not the level the interpreter is examining, his attempt to transfer it to that level can only make nonsense of it. Shaw reduces all that he can to social abstractions, and rejects the rest; Donington tries to reduce absolutely everything – including such manifest social elements as the castle-building giants – to Jungian psychological abstractions. Nor can it be said that the two interpretations are complementary, since they contradict each other in a way which admits of no reconciliation, and they both ignore the existential and metaphysical levels.

The only way the pitfall of one-sidedness can be avoided is to approach the work from the all-embracing standpoint of (to employ the phrase that Wagner used over and over again in connection with it) – 'the purely human'. If it be asked what this involves, one can do no better than take an example from Wagner himself. For in *Opera and Drama* he offered his own interpretation of a great dramatic work of art – the *Antigone* of Sophocles, in which the clash between the princess Antigone and her uncle Creon, King of Thebes, is very similar to that between Brünnhilde and her father Wotan.

Antigone's two brothers, Eteocles and Polynices, leading opposite armies in a civil war, have killed each other. Creon issues a command that Eteocles (who has defended the city) shall be given honourable burial as a hero, while the body of Polynices (who has attacked the city) shall be left to rot in ignominy; and that anyone trying to bury the body will incur the penalty of death. Antigone disobeys Creon, and buries her brother's body; Creon has her immured in a cave, and she hangs herself. The outcome is that Creon's son Haemon, who was in love with Antigone, kills himself by falling on his sword; Haemon's mother (Creon's wife Eurydice) stabs herself to death; and Creon is utterly broken. Wagner's interpretation (much condensed) is as follows:

> Creon had become ruler . . . and with this command he slapped humanity in the face, and cried 'Long live the State!' . . . Antigone knew nothing of politics: *she loved*. Did she seek to invoke law to exonerate Polynices? . . . No, she loved him. Did she love him because he was her brother? Wasn't Eteocles her brother? . . . She loved Polynices because he was unfortunate, and only the greatest power of love could save him from his curse. What was this love, which was neither sexual love nor family love? It was the highest bloom of all . . . *pure human love* . . . And behold! – *the love-curse of Antigone destroyed the State!* . . . *Holy Antigone! I call on you! Let your banner wave aloft, that beneath it we may destroy and redeem!*

Wagner saw Antigone as a symbol of the imminent (as he hoped) revolt of natural human love against State oppression; and he clearly had his own Brünnhilde in mind (he had drawn up the prose-sketch of *The Ring* two years earlier, and was to write the prose-sketch of *The Valkyrie* a year later). We have seen how Shaw and Donington interpret the conflict between Brünnhilde and

Wotan, and we can see how much more comprehensive, in its more basic human approach, is Wagner's interpretation of the conflict between Antigone and Creon. Like Shaw, Wagner pinpoints the social content, but unlike Shaw, he emphasizes the sheer brutal aggression in the tyrant's decree; and unlike either Shaw or Donington, he concentrates on the motivation of compassionate love behind the heroine's disobedience. That this latter motivation was all-important to Wagner in his own work is shown by the fact that it was one of the only two important elements he added to this part of the original myth,[5] and by his exaltation of it in the music of Brünnhilde's passionate outburst to Wotan:

> *You who breathed*
> *this love into my heart,*
> *you whose will*
> *allied me with the Volsung –*
> *inwardly faithful to you,*
> *I disobeyed your command.*

Here, on the woodwind, Wagner first introduces the soaring theme (Ex. 3) which later glorifies the reconciliation between Wotan and Brünnhilde – their long, loving embrace.

Ex. 3

Rather broad

Der die-se Lie — — be mir in's Herz ge —haucht

Ww. *p dolce*

[5] Or at least, developed from the merest hints. In the myth, Brynhild (Brünnhilde) gives victory to Agnar by killing Hjalmgunnar, whom Odin has favoured, and her reason is given as follows:

She . . . told how two kings warred with each other: one was called Hjalmgunnar, an old man and the greatest warrior, and Odin [Wotan] had promised him the victory; and the other was Agnar, the brother of Auda – there was no one willing to shield him.

It was Wagner who, apart from tying this incident closer to the story of the Volsungs by replacing Agnar and Hjalmgunnar with Sigmund (Siegmund) and Hunding, amplified the hint of Brynhild's sympathy for the underdog into Brünnhilde's motivation of compassionate love for Siegmund. (His other important addition, or amplification, was Brünnhilde's attitude of reproach and defiance.)

It is from this wide human standpoint that the present interpretation is undertaken, in an attempt to operate on all levels at once. The basic level is of course the social one, built into the work ineradicably by Wagner himself; and here some of Shaw's ideas will be accepted, though they will be developed on broader, non-ideological lines. Indissolubly fused with this is what I call the 'existential' level (the characters' immediate motivations of aggression, sex, love, and compassion) to distinguish it from the 'psychological' level of Donington, on which the characters' motivations are explained in terms of the Jungian unconscious. Finally, there is the metaphysical level: words are, of course, completely at a loss here, but even so, some attempt will be made to come to terms with the work from this point of view.

Furthermore, the four conditions given earlier for a realistic interpretation will be kept continually in mind, with a view to absorbing Wagner's own intention concerning any given element, before putting any personal construction on it. (1) Wagner's own avowed intentions in creating *The Ring* – social, existential, and metaphysical – will be accepted for what they are, as he expressed them in his letters, and as they are illuminated by his contemporary prose writings. (2) The overt meanings of all the elements in the drama will also be accepted for what they are, and will be shown in the clearest possible light by an investigation of Wagner's considerable manipulations and alterations of the original myths, whereby he adapted them to his own creative purposes (this whole subject will be dealt with at length in later chapters). (3) Every single element in the drama will be taken into full consideration, with nothing minimized, exaggerated, or omitted. (4) An attempt will be made to carry out the interpretation in such a way as to lead back to the work itself, by leaving the characters as characters and not replacing them with abstractions which can only evaporate in the opera house. For example, Fricka will not be treated as 'the Law' (Shaw) or as 'part of Wotan's inner femininity' (Donington), nor even as (what would seem to be a more accurate and comprehensive abstraction for her) 'Wotan's super-ego'. She will remain Fricka, the jealous, outraged, nagging wife of the ruler of the world of *The Ring* – who simply *recalls* him to one side of his inner self, as she puts forward the claims of the existing law and of all the other obsolescent ideals of his super-ego, which were the original basis of their mutual attraction, and from which Wotan is struggling to liberate himself.

But a realistic approach to the verbal text of the drama can be of no use at all unless an equally realistic approach is made to the music. *The Ring* is, after all, not a verbal drama, but a musical drama; and this brings us to a consideration of the second neglected main path towards a clarification of the work's meaning, mentioned earlier – an absolutely comprehensive musico-dramatic method of analysis.

3. *Comprehensiveness in musico-dramatic analysis*

All the commentaries on *The Ring* that have ever been published have one fatal defect: they concentrate on the text, which is only the conceptual framework, at the expense of the music, which carries Wagner's ultimate meaning.[1] Page after page is devoted to narration, explanation, and interpretation of the verbal drama, and only a sentence or a paragraph here and there touches on the musical expression, while a mere hundred or two hundred short music examples quote the main 'leading motives'. Shaw, as said earlier, has no music examples at all, and devotes only a short chapter to 'The Music of the Ring'; but even Newman and Donington are not free from this defect. Newman has 198 examples, but few of his 255 pages of text contain more than factual references to the appearance of a 'motive' here and there, and fewer still discuss the dramatic and psychological significance of these appearances: in fact he sometimes gives the impression that Wagner did not know what he was about, owing to his own failure to examine in depth what Wagner was actually doing. Donington has only 113 examples (grouped under 90 headings), and although he always gives Wagner full credit for knowing what he was about, and occasionally indicates the transformation of a 'motive' for some dramatic or psychological purpose, his 273-page interpretation contains little detailed discussion of the music.

Naturally, this is very much a problem of space. A full account of the plot of *The Ring*, coupled with explanation and interpretation, takes up a good many pages, and a full account of the score would take so many more that the result would be a very large book. But it must be said that, if *The Ring* is to be given an adequate interpretation, from any point of view and on any level, then only a very large book will suffice, since unless the music is examined in at least as much detail as the text, the meaning of the work will be

---

[1] See the passage referring to the newly-completed composition-sketch of *The Rhinegold*, in Wagner's letter to Röckel of 25 January 1854, already partly quoted on p. 2: 'I have now come to realize again how much there is, owing to the whole nature of my poetic aim, that only becomes clear through the music: *I now simply cannot look at the uncomposed poem any more.*' (My italics.)

only half-understood, or misunderstood completely. It might not matter so much if a commentator had carried out such a detailed examination of the music, and used his findings as the basis of his interpretation, without actually setting them out in full. But this would, in practice, be scarcely possible; and the unfortunate truth is that none of the commentators has studied the score in the depth that it demands.

Ultimately, it is all the fault of Baron Hans Paul von Wolzogen, the friend of Wagner's who, in 1878, two years after the first production of *The Ring* at Bayreuth, wrote the first commentary on the work.[2] Or rather, it is the fault of those who followed Wolzogen, for not developing his pioneer-work beyond its inevitable limitations. His little book remains basic in the field, in that it established the identity of many of the main musical ideas of the work, and indicated Wagner's method of reintroducing them continually as reminiscences; but being written so early, it was naturally far from definitive. First of all, it established an unfortunate pattern by having for its music examples a large number of short ideas and nothing else, thereby creating the impression that the score was an intermittent patchwork of such ideas, bound together by a large amount of music with no recognizable function beyond that of filling out the time between their appearances and reappearances. None of the later commentators went beyond this elementary scheme: however much some of them may have known and said that the facts were otherwise – that the score is a unified symphonic fabric, built up by development, fragmentation, variation, and transformation of these ideas – their practice has been to follow Wolzogen in simply indicating the ideas themselves, and some of their reappearances, and leaving the rest of the score to look after itself.[3]

---

[2] *Führer durch die Musik zu Richard Wagners Der Ring des Nibelungen*, Leipzig, 1878.

[3] There is, of course, the exhaustive analysis of the *form* of *The Ring* by Alfred Lorenz – Part 1 of his monumental four-part work *Das Geheimnis der Form bei Richard Wagner* (1924–33), the other three parts dealing with *Tristan*, *The Mastersingers*, and *Parsifal*. But the fact that this is an essentially structural analysis, coupled with the encyclopedic and well-nigh mathematical appearances of so many of its pages, has inevitably limited its circulation compared with the commentaries – and especially for English readers, as it has never been translated (though Gerald Abraham gives a clear résumé of Lorenz's analysis of Act 1 of *The Valkyrie*, in his book *A Hundred Years of Music*). Lorenz is almost entirely free from the defects of the commentators, which we are concerned with in this chapter: some of his findings will be referred to as the chapter proceeds.

This was only the first of the several shortcomings of Wolzogen's book. The second was the terminological one of using the word *Leitmotive* (leading motives, sing. *Leitmotiv*) to designate the main musical ideas of *The Ring* – though Wolzogen may have been led into it by Wagner himself, who did apply the term *Hauptmotiv* (principal motive) to certain of the main musical ideas in *Tristan*. '*Motiv*', or 'motive', in the true sense of the word, means the shortest significant thematic idea; but very few of the ideas in *The Ring* are of such brevity (the 'Nibelung Motive', Ex. 4, is a rare example). Most of them are full symphonic themes (that of the Rhinemaidens, Ex. 5), or thematic phrases (the one attached to the ring, Ex. 6), or chord-sequences (that associated with the Wanderer, Ex. 7), or cadences (the second of the two ideas connected with the renunciation of love, Ex. 8), and so on.

Ex. 4

Ex. 5

Ex. 6

Ex. 7

Ex. 8

In fact, many of the 'motives' which appear in the commentaries are merely the first phrases of extended symphonic themes, with the remainders left unquoted. The use of this single misleading term, handed down by Wolzogen and continued by everybody else, adds to the impression of bittiness, and is also responsible for the faintly comical character that attaches to all Wagner exegesis. Only with this composer do we talk exclusively of 'motives', never of themes or phrases; and the continual reiterations of the names – the Curse Motive, the Annunciation of Death Motive, and so on – creates an esoteric and rather ludicrous effect. In the present book, except in reference to Wolzogen and his followers, the word 'motive' is used in its correct sense only.

The third failing of Wolzogen's book was that his actual tally of 'motives' was far from complete; and little work has been done since to make a more comprehensive one. Much of the apparent space between the appearances and reappearances of the 'motives' is in fact occupied by the appearances and reappearances of 'motives' which Wolzogen overlooked. While, for example, he could hardly miss the purely pictorial 'Rainbow-Bridge Motive' near the end of Scene 4 of *The Rhinegold* (Ex. 9) – though in fact it does not function as a 'leading motive' at all, since it is never heard again after this scene – he completely failed to notice many really important recurrent ideas, such as those connected with the aggressive nature of Alberich (Exs. 10, 11, and 12), the purpose of the sword (Exs. 13, 14, and 15), or the emotion of fear which Siegfried finds so hard to learn (Exs. 16, 17, and 18). Nor did any later commentator discover them after him; and the outcome has been to make the score seem of even less thematic density than Wolzogen's original approach already suggested.

Ex. 9

Ex. 10   Alberich clambers up into the Rhine

Ex. 11   Alberich scolds Wellgunde

Ex. 12   Alberich drags Mime along by his ear

Ta–pfer ge—zwickt   Sollst du mir sein,

Ex. 13   Wotan hails the fortress with the sword

Rather slow

So   grüss' ich die   Burg,   si–cher vor Bang' und   Grau'n!

Ex. 14   Siegmund remembers the sword his father promised him

Moderately slow

Ein Schwert ver-hiess mir der Va—ter   ich fänd'es in höch-ster Noth.

Ex. 15   Siegmund remembers again as he goes to draw the sword

Very fast

Wäl — se   ver—hiess mir   in   höch ——— ster   Noth

fänd' ich   es   einst;

Ex. 16   Mime thinks about Fafner's fearful size

Moderate speed

. . . .   . . mit des furcht-ba—ren Lei—bes Wucht

Tubas *pp* 8ves

Ex. 17   Wanderer to Mime: 'Only he who never felt fear . . .'

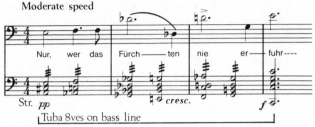

Ex. 18   Mime tells Siegfried he can learn fear from Fafner

A fourth weakness of his book is its neglect of all but the most obvious cases of interrelationship between the 'motives'. Wolzogen largely ignored Wagner's continual transformation of existing 'motives' into new ones – or rather his evolution of nearly all of them out of a few original basic ones to create a few large families, each concerned with the progressive psychological development of one of the central symbols of the drama. For example, Wolzogen did notice the transformation of the Rhinemaidens' cry of 'Rhinegold! Rhinegold! Heiajaheia! Heiajaheia!' (Ex. 19) into the theme associated with the tyrannical power of the ring (Ex. 20) and he explained the nature of the transformation accurately, saying that Ex. 20

shows itself to be formally related to the third Rhinegold motive [i.e. Ex. 19], being a combination of its two parts, which meanwhile have grown into two entirely Nibelungish motives of Servitude [Ex. 21] and Forging [Ex. 22].

But he ignored the more subtle transformation of this theme of the power of the ring (Ex. 20) into the one associated with Hagen's determination to possess the ring during his Watch-Song in Act 1 of *The Twilight of the Gods* (Ex. 23, which is not even quoted by Wolzogen).

Wagner himself, in an essay written a year after the publication of Wolzogen's book, referred to the identity of Exs. 19 and 23 as something quite self-evident. In this essay (*On the Application of Music to the Drama*, 1879), he was intent on maintaining that his

Ex. 19

Ex. 20

Ex. 21   'Servitude' (*upper line*);
Ex. 22   'Forging' (*lower line*)

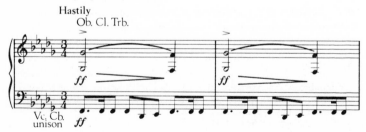

Ex. 23

own particular kind of dramatic transformation of themes had opened up a new radical way of developing musical material, which he thought was impossible in absolute music. He said he was surprised that no one had tried to analyse this aspect of his works, and he referred briefly to Wolzogen:

This path, as far as I know, has never been taken; I have only to remember one of my younger friends, who, in his detailed consideration of the characteristics of what he calls my 'leading motives' has seen them rather in the light of their dramatic significance than in that of their bearing on musical construction (since the specific art of music lay outside the author's province).

Then, later on, Wagner quoted in music-type the first two bars of Ex. 19 (the double cry of 'Rhinegold!'), and, referring to (as he conceived it) the possibilities of radical thematic transformation open to dramatic music alone, he said:

On this point, some real insight could be gained from a meticulous examination of the reappearances of the motive of the Rhinedaughters which I have quoted, provided it were pursued through all the changing passions of the four-part drama, down to Hagen's Watch-Song in the first act of *The Twilight of the Gods* [Ex. 23].

Wagner may have been confining himself to purely musical analysis (and incidentally propounding a theory which the subsequent development of musical history has proved false); but he was also, without realizing it, throwing out a hint as to how his works should be interpreted, which no commentator has ever taken. Only if the transformations of each 'motive' are pursued carefully 'through all the changing passions of the four-part drama', can the drama's true significance be made clear.

Donington alone, amongst the commentators, has attempted a comprehensive account of thematic relationships; but unfortunately many of the similarities which he indicates are beside the point, having nothing to do with the actual process of the symphonic transformation of themes whereby the drama's meaning is conveyed; and in any case, his list is less comprehensive than most. With regard to the above-mentioned case, for instance, he quotes only the first two bars of Exs. 19 and 20, relating the first to the second, certainly, but also relating Ex. 20, factitiously, to the thematic phrase associated with the end of the gods (Ex. 49, p. 62); and he does not even quote Ex. 23. Moreover, he includes Ex. 20 under the same heading as the quite subsidiary Ex. 24 – Alberich's outcry after being rejected by the third Rhinemaiden – instead of simply relating it back to its manifest source, the absolutely basic Ex. 19.[4]

Ex. 24

Moderate tempo

We — he!   ach   we — he!

---

[4] This is curious, since, as we have seen, Wolzogen at least indicated the identity of Exs. 19 and 20; and this was pointed out again by Aylmer Buesst in his book *The Nibelung's Ring* (London, 1932). However, this identity (along with several others which Wolzogen indicated) was ignored by Newman, who has been the most highly-regarded of modern commentators on Wagner's works, and has had the field largely to himself; and this may explain Donington's failure to carry over Wolzogen's discoveries and build on them. The truth is that Buesst's book is by far the best of all 'straight' commentaries on *The Ring* in respect of a thorough and detailed listing of the 'motives'. He obviously absorbed Wolzogen's list and occasionally corrected and added to it, whereas Newman and Donington paid little attention to Wolzogen (or to Buesst), and consequently quite a number of Wolzogen's most important basic findings are absent from their commentaries.

The effect of the inadequate treatment of the thematic interrelationships in *The Ring* has been to enhance further the false impression of an arbitrary patchwork of multitudinous unconnected short ideas, without any real thematic or symphonic unity. It all makes sadly ironic reading of something that Wagner said in his letter to Röckel of 25 January 1854, concerning the newly-completed composition sketch of *The Rhinegold*:

It has grown into a tightly interwoven unity: the orchestra has hardly a bar which is not developed out of preceding motives.

The foregoing criticism is not simply in the interests of absolute musical accuracy and comprehensiveness (though these in themselves might be thought desirable): it directly concerns the whole essential meaning of *The Ring*. If Donington, for example, had built on Wolzogen's discovery and, starting from the bright innocent song of the Rhinemaidens in Scene 1 of *The Rhinegold* (Ex. 19), had traced its progressive distortion through Scene 2 (in Loge's narration) into the baleful theme connected with the power of Alberich's ring in Scene 3 (Ex. 20); moreover if he had noticed the grotesque motive hinting at the aggressive nature of Alberich in Scene 1 (Exs. 10 and 11), and its ferocious reappearance when he drags Mime along by his ear in Scene 3 (Ex. 12); if he had noticed the motive of Alberich's self-pitying cry 'Die dritte so traut', after being rejected by the third Rhinemaiden in Scene 1 (Ex. 25), and its violent sequential development as an expression of his burning lust for revenge in the interlude between Scenes 2 and 3 (Ex. 26); – if he had dealt as meticulously with these crucial musico-dramatic elements as he did with the mytho-psychological connotations of dwarfs and water-nixies, he might have found it less easy to turn this whole aspect of Wagner's overt meaning inside out – to ennoble Alberich into some kind of hero, by playing down his sheer brutal malevolence, and to degrade the Rhinemaidens into representatives of 'escapist infantile fantasies', by playing up their roles as seductive enchantresses.

Ex. 25

die   drit—te, so traut,   be — trog sie mich auch?

Ex. 26

Again, Shaw might have thought twice about interpreting the final scene of *The Valkyrie* in purely social and political terms, and ignoring the all-important motivation of compassionate love behind Brünnhilde's defiance of Wotan, if he had taken account of the eventual transformation of the reproachful theme she sings when she begins to defy Wotan (Ex. 27) into the soaring love-theme which accompanies her avowal of the revelation of love which led her to disobey his orders (Ex. 3, p. 34). As it is, neither of these themes is even mentioned in his short chapter on 'The Music of The Ring'.

Ex. 27

Most important of all, every commentator might have been saved from taking an entirely lop-sided view of *The Ring* – from failing to identify one of the two central musico-dramatic symbols of the work – if he had not followed unquestioningly Wolzogen's complete misunderstanding of the function of one single musical idea. Here we come to the final defect of Wolzogen's book, the really fatal one: the inaccurate and misleading title which he gave to one of the 'motives'. This was the label of '*Fluchtmotiv*' (Flight Motive) which he attached to the second part of the swift agitated minor theme first heard when Freia runs on in *The Rhinegold*, pursued by the giants (Ex. 28B). A small point, it may seem; yet it is, in fact, absolutely crucial to our understanding of what Wagner was getting at in *The Ring*. Wagner's musical symbolism will be examined in detail in Volume 2, but Freia's theme may be dealt with here, to indicate how essential it is to apply a really comprehensive musico-dramatic method of analysis when interpreting a work by Wagner.

Ex. 28

The whole theme is manifestly attached to Freia, just as Loge's music is attached to him when he first enters, some time later. And again, just as Loge's music continues to reappear from *The Valkyrie* onwards, when he himself has vanished from *The Ring*, recalling his symbolic function as both god of fire and god of mind, so does Freia's theme continue to reappear when she has vanished, recalling her symbolic function as goddess of love.[5] And once more like Loge's music, Freia's theme splits into its component parts, which appear separately – in this case, its two quite different halves. Wolzogen noticed this, but for some reason best known to himself, he retained the title 'Freia Motive' only for the first part (Ex. 28A), and gave the title of 'Flight Motive' to the second (Ex. 28B).

As Wolzogen indicated, the first part soon (in Loge's narration) loses its agitated character and takes on a slow sinuous major form (Ex. 29); this is associated with love in its sexual aspect, returning later in connection with Siegmund and Sieglinde (Ex. 30) and with Siegfried when he climbs to the mountain-top to find Brünnhilde (Ex. 31). But in fact exactly the same thing happens to the second part of the theme. It soon (when Fasolt imagines Freia as his wife) takes on a slow sinuous major form (Ex. 32); and this is associated with love in its totality, later becoming attached to Siegmund and Sieglinde as their main love-theme (Ex. 33) and to Siegfried and Brünnhilde (Exs. 34, 35, and 36). In both cases, it would seem

[5] For those who are well-informed about modern research into the old northern mythology, it may be as well to say here immediately that Wagner relied on the authoritative work of his own time, Jacob Grimm's *Deutsche Mythologie*, for his understanding of the natures of the various gods and goddesses. He followed Grimm in taking Loki (Loge) to be the god of *fire* as well as of mind, and equating Freyja (Freia) with the Roman Venus, as goddess of *love* – two of Grimm's interpretations which have been much disputed since. (See pp. 171–2, and 154–5.)

obvious, an idea first associated with Freia as goddess of love in
The Rhinegold recurs quite naturally throughout *The Ring* in connection with lovers, one idea representing sexual love, the other love
in its totality.

Ex. 29

Ex. 30   Siegmund to Sieglinde: 'Most blest of women!'

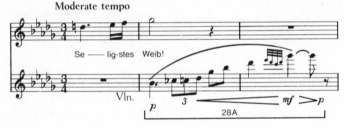

Ex. 31

Ex. 32

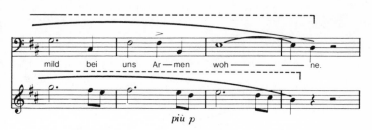

mild   bei   uns   Ar—men   woh————ne.

più p

Ex. 33

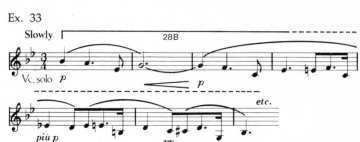

Slowly   28B

Vc. solo *p*

p

etc.

più p

pp

Ex. 34   Brünnhilde to Siegfried: 'Yours will I ever be'

Animated   28B

Dein————   werd' ich e————wig   sein!

Ob. Cl. *f*   Cl. *dim.*   *p*

Ex. 35   Brünnhilde waves goodbye to Siegfried

Swiftly   28B

ff

Vln. Ww.

etc.

Ex. 36 Brünnhilde praises the dead Siegfried's purity in love

But the two ideas differ greatly in importance. The first, representing sexual love, remains a subsidiary idea, recurring rarely, practically always in the same form (Ex. 29), and hardly ever being

Ex. 37 Siegfried longs to love like the birds and beasts

developed symphonically. But the second idea, representing love
in its totality, is one of the central and most fertile ideas in *The Ring*:
it recurs as often as any, in more different forms than most, and
undergoes a great deal of symphonic development. It appears in
the major and in the minor, slow and fast, soft and loud, and in
every possible combination of these, to represent different aspects
of love: its longing (Ex. 37), its frustration (Ex. 38), its fulfilment
(Ex. 39), its ecstasy (Ex. 40), and so on.

Ex. 38   Siegmund despairs of possessing Sieglinde

Ex. 39   Sieglinde to Siegmund: 'You are the spring'

Ex. 40   Siegmund embraces Sieglinde with furious ardour

What probably misled Wolzogen was that this second part of
Freia's theme, unlike the first, often reappears in its original
agitated swift minor form, in various rhythmic guises, as a basis for
symphonic development portraying lovers in a state of agitation
and/or distress. In Act 2 of *The Valkyrie*, for example, it pictures (in
the prelude) Siegmund and Sieglinde on their arduous journey
away from Hunding's home (Ex. 41), and later it accompanies
Sieglinde as she runs madly onwards in a state of shame and

Ex. 41

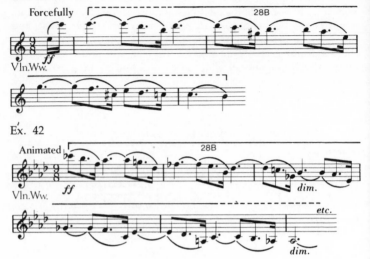

remorse while Siegmund follows and tries to comfort her (Ex. 42) –
just as it originally accompanied Freia, the goddess of love, as she
fled in terror from the giants (Ex. 28B).[6]

It must have been such powerful recurrences of this original
swift minor form of the idea, associated with lovers' agitation, that
caused the confusion in Wolzogen's mind – coupled with his
blindness to the significance of its identity with the love-theme of
Siegmund and Sieglinde (Ex. 33), and his failure to notice any of
the other transformations of the idea. As a result, although he
found it easy to take the right course of retaining the original title of
'Freia Motive' for the first part of Freia's theme, he could find
nothing but the idea of 'flight' to attach to its second part, and so
this became for him the 'Flight Motive'. As for Ex. 33, which could
not be taken for anything else but a love-theme, its obvious
identity with the 'Flight Motive' had to be explained by some very
special pleading:

[6] The one apparent exception to this interpretation – the passage near the beginning
of the 'Descent to Nibelheim' in *The Rhinegold* (Ex. 26), where lovers are not involved
(though neither is 'flight' for that matter) – is a complex case which will be dealt with
in Volume 2. [see p. 71.]

For the Volsung twins, it is also a matter of flight: out of this trouble grows their love, and their love lives by this trouble.

Intellectually very plausible, no doubt, but Wolzogen's bracketing of the first four bars of this long-drawn love-theme as 'Flight', and of only the remainder as 'Love', is a patent musico-emotional absurdity.

And other absurdities are bound to arise from accepting the label of 'Flight Motive'. For example, when the idea occurs swiftly in the major at the very end of Act 1 of *The Valkyrie* (Ex. 40), it will be assumed to indicate that Siegmund and Sieglinde are about to run away from Hunding's hut immediately, in flight; indeed, it must have been this misapprehension that has caused so many producers of the work to make the lovers run out through the door, although the stage-direction is simply 'He draws her to him with furious ardour'. Presumably, since Hunding is in a drugged sleep, and Wagner asks for the curtain to fall swiftly, the lovers consummate their union and beget Siegfried then and there (rather than out in the forest somewhere on a chilly Northern spring night!).[7] Again, when the idea bursts out passionately in the Prelude to *The Twilight of the Gods*, as Siegfried leaves Brünnhilde in search of new adventures (Ex. 35), the label 'Flight Motive' suggests that Wagner meant him to be in some abstruse sense fleeing from her, whereas his stage-direction indicates that he intended the idea to express Brünnhilde's unbounded love for Siegfried as she watches him go. The stage-direction, at the very point where the idea strikes in, reads: 'Now she again sees Siegfried in the valley; she waves to him with rapturous gestures'.

Anyone can make a mistake; but it seems strange that all the subsequent commentators should have accepted almost without question the messy and confusing state of affairs handed down to them owing to this fatal mistake of Wolzogen's. It might have been expected that someone would rectify it, for three separate reasons. In the first place, we never find Wagner detaching a segment of a theme introduced in connection with a central symbol of the drama, for the purpose of using it as a mere figuration portraying a physical activity. And then, in any case, the swift minor form of this idea has an intensely emotional character, which lifts it far

---

[7] Shaw certainly saw this clearly, as we have seen, in saying that 'the love-duet in the first act of The Valkyrie is brought to the point at which the conventions of our society demand the precipitate fall of the curtain'.

above the level of mere 'hurry music'.[8] Finally, and even more to the point, the idea itself, in all its possible forms, is a basic term of Wagner's musical vocabulary, which he used throughout his whole life's work *exclusively in association with love and lovers*.

If this seems a large claim to make, let us consider a few examples, outside *The Ring*. The first piece of music by Wagner to reveal something of his true personality is an operatic 'insert' he composed at the age of twenty – a new closing section for the tenor aria 'Wie ein schöner Frühlingsmorgen' in Marschner's opera *Der Vampyr*.[9] And this already contains, as its salient thematic element, the idea which Wolzogen, faced with its appearance in *The Ring*, labelled the 'Flight Motive'. The hero of Marschner's opera, Aubry, is in a terrible predicament: his sweetheart, Malwina, is being compelled by her father to marry the rich Lord Ruthven, and Aubry alone knows that this nobleman is in fact the mysterious Vampire; but unfortunately, he once took a vow never to reveal this secret, and so his lips are sealed. In the opening section of Marschner's aria (slow, soft, major, nostalgic), he ruefully remem-

[8] As so often, Lorenz, in his monumental structural analysis of *The Ring*, shows much deeper insight on this point that the commentators. Although he was not concerned with interpreting the symbolic meaning of the work as a drama, he had, of course, to use Wolzogen's names for its multitudinous musical ideas, for the purpose of easy reference; and he found some of them unacceptable – especially the label 'Flight Motive'. He described it as 'too narrow', and suggested that the most reasonable name would be *'Notmotiv'* – *'Not'* being a complex German word meaning 'need', 'trouble', and 'distress'. He offered, as an explanation of this view, a division of the theme's basic motive into two separate intervals – a falling one and a rising one; and he fancifully set two words to them – *'Wehe! Warum?'* (Alas! Why?). Moreover, to cover all possible appearances of the motive he set out the result as a music example with neither tempo marking nor exact pitch:

We — he! Wa–rum?

This view does take account of the intensely emotional character of the motive; but unfortunately it ignores the many different expressive effects it can have, according to whether it appears as major or minor, loud or soft, quick or slow. Certainly, the slow, loud, minor version, played on the orchestra when Siegmund despairs of possessing Sieglinde (Ex. 38), conveys need, trouble, and distress, and could be taken as saying 'Alas! Why?'; but, for example, the fast loud major version, used when they are actually united (Ex. 40), expresses the exact opposite.

[9] It was written to please his elder brother Albert, who was singing the leading tenor role in a production of the opera at Würzburg in 1833. Albert, finding that this all-important aria never 'brought the house down', as it was obviously intended to do, decided that Marschner's closing section was to blame, and asked young Richard to write a more effective one.

bers his happy days of love with Malwina; but in the closing section – an agitated stretto (fast, loud, minor, frenzied) – he despairs of his love, and cries out that he is threatened by the powers of Hell with madness or death. We are not concerned with Marschner's own closing section; but in Wagner's substitute one – which draws on none of Marschner's material, and is completely new – we find the first appearance of the musical idea he was to use from then on as a frequent motivic basis of much of his operatic love-music. Here it appears (keeping Marschner's general atmosphere) at top speed, loud, and in the minor, portraying the anguish of one whose love seems doomed to total annihilation (Ex. 43).

Ex. 43

In the 'early Wagner' operas, the most notable appearance of this love-motive is in *Lohengrin*. Strange as it may seem, it occurs as one of the phrases of the slow, soft major theme attached to the Holy Grail, of which the knight Lohengrin is the saintly champion: the theme is the whole basis of the orchestral prelude to the opera (Ex. 44a). But Lohengrin is also, of course, the champion of Elsa, the 'lady in distress': when he first appears, early in Act 1, to defend her against the calumny levelled at her, he eventually asks her if she will be his wife – and it is only at this point that the phrase of the Grail theme which is in fact Wagner's love-motive detaches itself decisively from the theme, comes to the fore, and is developed. The phrase, as it occurs in the Grail theme which begins the orchestral prelude, is bracketed in Ex. 44a; its first appearance as a motive in its own right, and its development, is shown in Ex. 44b – and it has remained entirely latent since its unobtrusive appearance as a mere part of the Grail theme of the orchestral prelude. The other phrases of the prelude's Grail theme have already been developed on their own – especially the one connected with the sacred swan that has drawn the boat bringing Lohengrin to Elsa; but now, the holiness of human love emerges from the holiness of divine love, in the form of Wagner's basic love-motive, slow, soft, and in the major.

Ex. 44a

Ex. 44b

In Wagner's mature music-dramas, apart from *The Ring*, his love-motive occurs in both *Tristan* and *The Mastersingers*. In Act 2 of *Tristan*, while Isolde is waiting for Tristan to come to her, she tells her maid Brangaene, with suppressed excitement, that it was not the love-potion that awakened her fatal love for him, but 'Frau Minne', an ancient German folk-figure representing love. Here, a new theme enters on the orchestra – fast, soft, in the major – which is to be developed right up to the climax just before Isolde extinguishes the torch as a signal to Tristan to come to her; and this theme incorporates Wagner's love-motive, which in *The Ring* he attached to the ancient Scandinavian goddess of love, Freia. The theme is shown in Ex. 45a, with the love-motive bracketed; but soon, the motive is detached from the theme and developed on its own (Ex. 45b), until it generates that great climax when Isolde proclaims the bewitching power of Frau Minne, who demands the darkness of night for the celebration of her rites.[10]

Ex. 45a

Ex. 45b

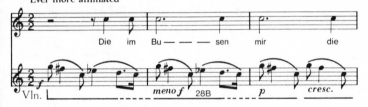

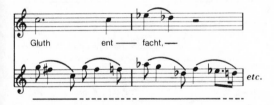

In *The Mastersingers*, Wagner's love-motive forms part of Walther's Prize Song – which is about his love for Eva (Ex. 46); but it appears most noticeably in connection with Hans Sachs' love for Eva. She is to be given in marriage by her father to the winner of the Mastersingers' song-contest, and, afraid that her beloved Walther will never win it, she hates the idea of being forced to marry someone else. But there is always the wise and lovable old

[10] This may seem to conflict with the earlier statement that the motive expresses love in its totality, not merely sexual love (p. 49ff); but in *Tristan*, sexual love and love in its totality are so fused as to be indistinguishable.

Ex. 46

Ex. 47

Ex. 46

Moderate tempo
28B
denn, gleich zwei'n Son — nen rein-ster Won — nen, der
hehr-sten Au — gen Paar — nahm' — ich da wahr.

Ex. 47

Moderate tempo
SACHS
Lieb' Ev — — chen, mach'st du blau-en
Cl.
Vln.
28B
EVA
Dunst? Nicht ich, ihr seid's ihr macht mir Flau-sen! Ge-steht nur,
Vln.
dass ihr wan-del-bar. Gott weiss, wer euch jetzt im Her-zen mag hau-sen!
poco cresc.
etc.

shoemaker Hans Sachs, himself a Mastersinger: he is a widower and, as she well knows, is very sweet on her. In Act 2, she cajoles him, pleading with him to enter the contest, and to win it; and the way she makes up to him stirs his susceptible heart painfully. At this point he reproaches her, with the question 'Sweet Eva, are you trying to ensnare me?'; and Wagner's love-motive strikes in immediately, spinning itself out at great length as a troubled melodic line (Ex. 47) – flowing uneasily and quietly, mingling major and minor inextricably.

These examples should be sufficient to establish that the second part of Freia's theme in *The Ring* is no 'Flight Motive' but a theme built entirely out of the idea which Wagner used, from work to work, as his basic love-motive.

The failure to correct Wolzogen's unhappy error had a crippling effect on the three main commentaries we have been considering. Shaw, of course, made no mention of Freia's theme in his short chapter on 'The Music of The Ring', just as he ignored every single one of the other themes connected with the love-element of the drama. Newman did quote it, and actually jibbed at the label 'Flight Motive' for its second part; moreover he was vaguely aware that the idea was a basic term of Wagner's musical vocabulary; but he could find no more satisfactory solution to the problem than another of his evasions. After quoting the whole of Freia's theme (Ex. 28), he adds a comment, in parentheses, to the effect that its second part (Ex. 28B)

has been a source of much trouble to the analysts. They have dubbed it the motive of Flight, because it occurs now and later in some sort of connection with this idea. But we meet with it also in Wagner in quite other connections, and the truth seems to be that it was a musical *tic* into which he was inclined to fall on various occasions, sometimes, as here, with a specific purpose, sometimes without any.

Thus the main love-theme of *The Ring*, and its prodigious development and transformation throughout the whole tetralogy, is reduced to a mere affliction with a musical *tic*; and Wagner is made to appear careless and confused through the carelessness and confusion of the commentator. In fact Newman continues to refer to this quick minor version of the idea as the 'Flight Motive'; and when he comes to the main love-theme of Siegmund and Sieglinde (Ex. 33), he does not even mention its identity with that 'motive', nor even with that supposed 'musical *tic*'.

Donington, to whom I privately put forward my view of the true function of the idea, briefly incorporated my explanation in a paragraph of his book, acknowledging the debt; but he could not develop all its implications into one main basis of his interpretation, since, as we have seen, the love-element of the drama, considered as such, did not seem of cardinal importance to him. And in his list of motives, the original confusion is replaced by a worse one. The whole of Freia's theme is quoted, and is headed 'agitation, but including both passion and compassion'; also it is misleadingly said to be derived from Alberich's cry of 'Wehe! ach wehe!' (Ex. 24), instead of from his cry of 'Die dritte so traut' (Ex. 25), which is its true source. The slow major form into which the first part settles down (Ex. 29) is listed as a quite separate 'motive' on its own, with the heading 'Freia as young love', and is related back to its distant progenitor, the thematic phrase associated with the Rhine (Ex. 48), instead of to its manifest immediate source, the first part of Freia's theme in its original form (Ex. 28A). Finally, as regards the slow major form of the second part which enters in Act 1 of *The Valkyrie* (Ex. 33 – which is headed correctly 'Love of Siegmund and Sieglinde'), its identity with its original swift minor form is explained in terms which are accurate enough, as far as they go, but they do not go far enough.

. . . the notes . . . in various rhythms may convey almost any sort of 'involvement' from fearful agitation, through urgent passion, to profound compassion.

Finally, this Siegmund-and-Sieglinde version is related back, again quite factitiously, to the thematic phrase associated with the end of the gods (Ex. 49).

Ex. 48

With calm and joyful movement

Ex. 49

Slowly

The result of all this confusion, in the case of every commentator, has been to obscure completely one of the two central musico-dramatic symbols of the work. For the simple truth is that in Freia, her theme and its development, Wagner presented the symbol of that love, growing from sexual love into love for humanity, which he laid such stress on in his letters and essays as the all-important factor in the regeneration of mankind, and the representation of which he avowed as one of his main intentions in creating *The Ring*. Moreover, the central conflict of the whole work is between this love and the enemy it is up against – repressive, unloving, political power, symbolized by Wotan's spear, with its authoritarian descending scale (Ex. 50),[11] and Alberich's ring, with its dissonant, contracted, self-enclosed thematic phrase (Ex. 51).

Ex. 50

Moderate tempo

Ex. 51

Rather slow

Indeed, owing to the overall failure to understand the true nature of the second part of Freia's motive, her very function as goddess of love has passed unnoticed, or at least uninterpreted.[12]

[11] Generally known to the commentators as the 'Treaty', 'Contract', or 'Bargain' Motive – another unfortunate misnomer of Wolzogen's (*Vertragsmotiv*), which was at last set right by Buesst.

[12] Wolzogen called her 'the goddess of youth and beauty'; Buesst's description is 'the goddess of love', but he adds, curiously, 'and of domestic happiness', and he does not give Freia any special significance in his commentary. More recently, Kurt Overhoff (*Die Musikdramen Richard Wagners*, Salzburg, 1967) calls Freia boldly 'the goddess of love' and interprets her as such; but he sees the central conflict of *The Ring*, not as between political power and love, but as between two more abstract ideas – necessity and freedom – and he still refers the second part of Freia's theme to the idea of flight.

For Shaw, she is simply 'Fricka's sister, Freia', who, in her function as the price Wotan has agreed to pay for Valhalla, stands simply for 'Woman' – Loge's word for her, which might actually have given Shaw a clue to her real identity, had he not been such an inveterate scoffer at the idea of love between man and woman. Newman's description of her is 'the Goddess of youth and beauty and health and charm' – which is a case of hitting the nail on the head without actually driving it home. Donington gets as far as 'goddess of youth and youthful love'; but his adjective 'youthful' is a depreciative qualification, since he goes on to describe youthful love as a passing, if inevitable and valuable phase of human life, and nowhere does he equate Freia with the principle of love itself.

Any apparent loose ends here – such as the curious characterlessness of Freia herself, or the origin of the second part of her theme (Ex. 28B) in a vocal utterance of Alberich's (Ex. 25) – must await tying up until later. The point of this preliminary discussion of Freia's theme is to make clear that no commentator can hope to get to the heart of the complex symbolism of Wagner's drama unless he examines the music in detail with the utmost care. Freia herself, in the text, might be taken to stand for a number of things, especially since she vanishes from *The Ring* after *The Rhinegold*, and is scarcely mentioned again; but since the two parts of her theme continue to recur in conjunction with love and lovers, and the second part – a basic term of Wagner's musical vocabulary, always associated with love – becomes the central love-theme of the whole work, she can only have been intended to function as the goddess of love, as indeed Wagner understood her to be, relying on the interpretation of the Scandinavian goddess Freyja by Jacob Grimm.

This is only the worst instance of the general mistake made by all the commentators – that of approaching *The Ring* as though it were a *verbal* drama *illustrated* by music. They have interpreted the text according to their own view of things, and fitted the 'motives' into their interpretations as best they could, without taking care to identify all the motives, or to understand their correct functions, or to discover what happens to them afterwards. Perhaps Wagner himself was responsible for their wrong-ended approach, in his insistence that his works should be regarded as *dramas*. In 1851, while the text of *The Ring* was in its early stages, he wrote, in *A Communication to my Friends*:

I shall never write any more *operas*: as I have no desire to invent an arbitrary name for my works, I shall call them *dramas*, since this will at least indicate as clearly as possible the standpoint from which what I offer must be accepted.

Then, in 1853, when the first text of *The Ring* was complete, he had it published as a 'poem', as though it were a complete work of art in itself. And many years later, in 1872, when he had nearly completed *The Ring*, he wrote an essay *On the Term 'Music-Drama'* in which he rejected, on dubious linguistic grounds, both this term and its possible alternative, 'musical drama'. The double-noun formulation 'music-drama', he maintained, could only mean 'drama for the purpose of music', which was actually an accurate description of the old hack type of opera-libretto he had so decisively rejected; the adjective-noun formulation 'musical drama', on the other hand, could only convey the absurd idea of 'a drama that made music itself, or was good for making music, or even understood music'; he himself would finally settle for the term *Bühnenfestspiel* (stage festival play).

This old terminological battleground, which has been fought over so often to so little purpose, need not be entered again here. That Wagner's greatest works – *The Ring*, *Tristan*, *The Mastersingers* and *Parsifal* – are genuine dramas, as opposed to certain artificial old recitative-and-set-number operas which were a mere vehicle for entertaining music and vocal display, is now quite obvious. The same is true, of course, in a general sense, of any great opera by any composer; but the fact that Wagner wrote his own texts, full of a unique kind of dramatic symbolism, and that he set them to music in such a way as to confer on the finished works a quite incomparable richness and density of dramatic and symbolic texture, sets them completely apart from the genus 'opera', and places them in a category of their own. Nevertheless, the word 'drama' alone is always used to mean 'verbal drama'; and so, *pace* Wagner, the best description of his unique type of work is either 'music drama' or 'musical drama' (a drama of which the ultimate expressive medium is music) on the analogy of 'poetic drama' (a drama of which the ultimate expressive medium is poetry).

All that really matters is that the ultimate meaning of a Wagner 'drama' is achieved through the music, as Wagner himself was perfectly well aware. After publishing the text of *The Ring*, he soon came to realize that it would only mislead the reader by itself; as we have seen, once he had composed the music of *The Rhinegold*, he confessed to Röckel that he could not 'look at the "uncomposed poem" any more'. In fact, it is not a 'poem' at all, since a poem is a self-sufficient work of art; it is only a conceptual dramatic framework, which is why I have been careful to describe it as the 'text'. All that it provides is the overt meaning of the drama – the characters and their actions, some of their thoughts, and a rough indication of some of their emotional states; and these things, taken in isolation, can be interpreted as symbols of almost anything, given a skilful enough argument. The actual work of art is this conceptual framework *as realized definitively in music*; and this can only be taken to mean what Wagner intended it to mean, provided that the musical realization is given detailed consideration throughout.

Even where the overt meaning of the text seems straightforward enough, and in need of no symbolic interpretation at all, the music provides it with a rich and complex symbolism of its own; and if the commentator leaves this out of account, his overall interpretation of the whole work will inevitably be thrown off target. A single example will suffice. When Wotan is finally defeated in his argument with Fricka, in Act 2 of *The Valkyrie*, he gives vent to his feelings in the following seven lines of the text:

> O heilige Schmach!
> O schmählicher Harm!
> Götternot!
> Götternot!
> Endloser Grimm!
> Ewiger Gram!
> Der Traurigste bin ich von Allen!

or, in an English approximation:

> O divinity's disgrace!
> O shameful wrong!
> Gods' distress!
> Gods' distress!
> Unending wrath!
> Eternal grief!
> I am the unhappiest of all beings!

The English lacks the force of the original, with its crudely effective use of the power of certain German root-words, and those clanging accentuated alliterations which are so suited to musical setting; but even Wagner's original is no more than a generalized indication of thought and feeling, conveying nothing in itself as to the essential nature of Wotan's self-disgust, rage, and despair, or the wider implications of them. If this passage of the text were offered at such a crucial moment in a poetic drama, we should rightly regard it as so much empty mouthing: we should expect a more masterly use of language, peculiar to the character concerned, expressing his state of mind and feeling in a much more complex way, and setting up all kinds of resonances backwards and forwards throughout the drama.

In fact, we are offered just such an experience by this brief passage, which is one of the supreme moments in *The Valkyrie*, but the language used to provide it is the language of music. The setting of the lines is pure 'Wotan music', of the particularly mighty and majestic kind given to this character throughout *The Ring*, and to no other; and the resonances backwards and forwards are set up by the development and transformation of previous musical ideas, in the orchestra and in the voice. The peculiarly Wotan-like character of the music can perhaps be left to speak for itself, since it is immediately unmistakable; but the development and transformation of previous musical ideas is a subtle and complex process, which should be the main concern of the commentator at this point.

The whole passage begins with a ferocious new thematic idea rising from the depths of the orchestra (Ex. 52); this is an inverted transformation of the gloomy phrase recently introduced to express Wotan's sense of frustration at the thwarting of his will by Fricka (Ex. 53), which is itself a broken, twisted form of the imperious descending scale associated with the spear which symbolizes his will (Ex. 50, p. 63). The new idea finds a natural continuation in the thematic phrase attached to the curse which Alberich has put on the ring (Ex. 54) – and here the harmonic texture rises to a new high level of dissonance for *The Ring*, and indeed for all Wagner's music up to this moment: the moment is marked with an asterisk in Ex. 55 – a dominant minor ninth on the flat submediant of F minor (that is, on D flat), *over a dominant pedal* (that is, over a pedal-note C). Then the whole thematic and harmonic complex is repeated, a perfect fourth higher, bringing an even higher level of dissonance – this time a dominant minor ninth on the *flat supertonic* (G flat), still over the dominant pedal (C). Meanwhile, at the end of the first statement of the complex, the voice has entered: Wotan delivers the first two lines of the text to free declamation – a falling octave and a falling seventh a semitone higher – oppressive intervals which in the harmonic context convey a terrible feeling of frustration. The sense of his whole being revolting against the frustration of his will, and against his entanglement in the curse on the ring, which he himself has coveted, is expressed with a power which no words could achieve.

Ex. 52

Ex. 53

Ex. 54

Ex. 55

The musical allusion to the ring, through the phrase attached to the curse on it, now becomes explicit – not through a statement of the idea attached to the ring itself, but in a more all-encompassing way. The new idea starts off for a third time (another tone higher), but now, instead of continuing with the phrase associated with the

curse on the ring, as before, it leads straight into the sequence of
two chords symbolizing the tyrannical power of the ring (the first
two bars of Ex. 20, p. 44). This is stated twice, the second time a
tone higher, and after each statement there strikes in the beginning
of the theme recently attached to the contumacious Fricka: the first
time it breaks off after five notes, the second time after two, greatly
heightening the tension (Ex. 56). Again, the dissonance is extreme:
over the continuing pedal-note of C, we have first a chord of E
major, and then a chord of G flat major.

Ex. 56

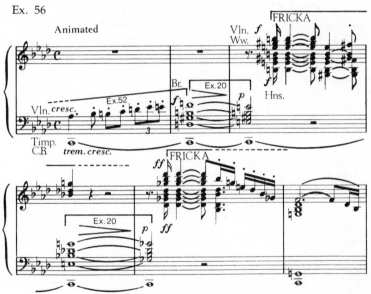

During these bars, Wotan sings the repeated 'Götternot!' (gods'
distress), still to oppressive falling sevenths, but with greater
rhythmic agitation; and this leads to the high point of the whole
passage. The new idea rises once again, now no longer in the
depths, and while it soars to the heights, the voice arrives at its
highest note (baritone top F), taking over the thematic development from the orchestra, and making a climactic statement. Wotan
sings the words 'Unending wrath, eternal grief' to a long-drawn,
grief-stricken minor version of the second part of Freia's theme
(Ex. 57 – cf. Ex. 28B, p. 49); and then, as the orchestral agitation

ceases, he follows them with the words 'I am the unhappiest of beings' to the melancholy falling cadence associated with the renunciation of love (Ex. 58 – cf. Ex. 8, p. 40).

Ex. 57

This musical climax tells us what the words do not (and more directly and profoundly than any words could): what is eating Wotan's heart out is his realization that he is unloved and unloving. The second part of Freia's motive, in this long-drawn minor form, has already expressed Siegmund's sense of the hopelessness of his love for Sieglinde (Ex. 38, p. 53), and before that it had poured out its powerful lament as the newly love-bereft Alberich raced back to Nibelheim (interlude between scenes 2 and 3 of *The Rhinegold*) to forge his ring of absolute power (Ex. 59).

Ex. 59

Earlier, in its quicker form, it has of course portrayed the plight of Freia herself, goddess of love (Ex. 28b, p. 49), whom Wotan promised to barter away in exchange for the power-symbol of Valhalla, and was actually prepared to, in exchange for the ring itself; and first of all it was the despairing cry of the original love-seeking Alberich after his final rejection by the third Rhinemaiden (Ex. 25, p. 47). Finally, in Wotan's outburst, the sorrowful cadence associated with the renunciation of love speaks for itself, and sets its seal on the whole. Fricka's humiliation of Wotan has brought home to him that the splendid world he has built up, and hopes to maintain by regaining the ring through the agency of Siegmund, is no less rooted in the lust for power and the rejection of love than would be the dreadful world that Alberich might make of it, if he were given the chance; yet that new ferocious thematic phrase that begins the whole passage (Ex. 52) holds out little hope that Wotan will consider the claims of love yet awhile.

All of which throws a clear light on the important words uttered by Wotan when, a little later, he begins his confession to Brünn-hilde with a superb piece of pure recitative (one of the very few in the whole of *The Ring*) without any thematic reference at all:

> *When youthful love's*
> *pleasure grew pale,*
> *my spirit longed for power.*

As can be seen, the whole meaning of Wotan's tremendous outburst is in the music, not in the words, which merely sketch a general mood of shame, distress, rage, and despair. But the commentators have been prevented from even attempting to interpret this passage through the music by their unthinking acceptance of Wolzogen's incomplete and partly inaccurate list of motives. Of the six musical ideas used by Wagner here, only three are identified correctly in Wolzogen's book – the 'Curse Motive', the 'Power of the Ring Motive', and the 'Variant of the Renunciation of Love Motive'; the new idea which begins the passage is ignored, so is Fricka's theme, and the second part of Freia's theme is of course labelled 'Flight Motive'. Of later commentators, only Buesst identified the new idea, calling it 'Godly stress' – but he did not notice its derivation; nearly everyone noticed Fricka's theme, but this was an obvious oversight of Wolzogen's anyway; the second part of Freia's theme remained the 'Flight Motive', of course, for everyone except Newman, who regarded it as a mere *tic* of Wagner's, and Donington, who regards it as conveying 'almost any sort of involvement'. Add to this that Wolzogen's correct identification of the cadence attached to the renunciation of love was obscured by later commentators with such labels as 'Powerlessness' or 'Futility'; that Newman failed to mention it throughout his whole commentary; and that Donington regards it as representing 'Destiny accepted' (which is surely the last phrase to describe Wotan's state of mind at this moment) – and it is hardly surprising that this crucial passage receives completely inadequate treatment from our three main commentators.

Shaw ignores the passage completely – no doubt he regarded it as no more than a magnificent piece of Wagnerian rhetoric with no bearing on the main argument of *The Ring*; and Newman merely gives an abbreviation of the text, with a single adjective indicating the general character of the music:

His [Wotan's] brooding ends with a terrible cry of 'O shame! O distress! Gods' extremity! Wrath and Grief without end! The saddest am I of all living!'

And for Donington the passage merits no more than one short sentence:

His [Wotan's] outburst of despair torments her [Brünnhilde].

Yet this is an all-important moment in Wotan's development: Lorenz, although he was concerned with form, not content, describes the passage as expressing 'the moment of tragic guilt'. And he points out what none of the commentators has noticed, that it recurs twice with shattering effect – first when Brünnhilde temporarily rejects Siegfried in the final scene of *Siegfried*, and again when she refuses to give up the ring to Waltraute in Act 1 of *The Twilight of the Gods*.

This single example will suffice to indicate why a large book is necessary for a really adequate interpretation of *The Ring*. The interpretation undertaken in the present two-volume book is an attempt to elucidate Wagner's intentions throughout the whole work, by considering the simple overt meaning of each passage of the text as it is given its full and complex symbolic significance by its musical setting. But before going on to the musico-dramatic interpretation, it is necessary to consider the overt meaning of the text itself in detail, and to examine more closely the nature of Wagner's musical language. And since Wagner himself had to begin by writing the text – even though he wrote it entirely with his own kind of musical realization in mind – we will turn to that first; it will occupy us for the remainder of Volume 1.

The text and the sources

1. *The nature of the text*

To say that the text of *The Ring* is not a poem, as Wagner insisted on calling it, but only a conceptual framework for the creation of a musical drama, is not to deny its superb efficacy for its purpose: it still stands as the most prodigious 'opera libretto' ever written. It compresses into thirty-seven scenes, with the most decisive dramatic clarity and point, a story of phenomenal intricacy, involving thirty-four characters, sixteen of them main ones, each of whom has a sharply defined individuality and uses such vivid and succinct language that a wealth of overt meaning is packed into the whole text, in spite of a number of passages which mainly refer back to events already set forth.

Turning to the language first, it stands unique in Wagner's *œuvre*, in that it is conceived in the style of the ancient alliterative verse – known in German as *Stabreim* – which was used for the earliest Teutonic poetry, including the old Norse lays and ballads that Wagner drew on as one of the main sources of *The Ring*. This Teutonic poetry included Anglo-Saxon, and its successor early English, the finest example of the latter being the fourteenth-century religious poem *Piers the Plowman*, by William Langland. A characteristic short passage from this work – the one in which Conscience refuses to marry Meed (Reward, or Bribery) – will show the concentrated power of which the medium was capable:

> Quoth Conscience to the King: Christ it me forbid!
> Ere I wed such a wife, woe me betide!
> She is frail of her faith, fickle of her speech,
> and maketh men misdo, many score times.

This was one of the two main forms of alliterative verse – a line of four stresses, divided into two symmetrical halves of two stresses each, and having either two or three of the stresses emphasized by using the same initial sound for the different words (all vowels counting the same). The other form alternated lines of this kind with lines of three stresses only, having no division, and with up to all three of the stresses emphasized by alliteration. An example of this is the old Norse *Sigrdrifumol* (Ballad of the Victory-Bringer),

which was one of Wagner's sources for the final scene of *Siegfried*.
In this poem, the words of the awakening Valkyrie are as follows:

> Heill dagr! Heilir dags synir!
>   Heil nott oc nipt!
> Oreiðom augom litið ocr þinig
>   oc gefit sitjondom sigr!
>
> Heilir Aesir! Heilar Asynjar!
>   Heil sia in fjolnyta fold!
> Mal oc manvit gefit ocr maerom tveim
>   oc laecnishendr meðan lifom!
>
> Lengi ec svaf, lengi ec sofnoð vask,
>   long ero lyda lae.
> Oðinn þvi veldr er ec eigi mattac
>   bregða blundstofom.

Or in English:

> Hail, day! Hail, day's sons!
>   Hail night, and the daughter of night!
> With gracious eyes grant to us
>   the victory we await!
>
> Hail, gods! Hail, goddesses!
>   Hail earth, with its fruitful fields!
> Counsel and wisdom wish on us lovers,
>   and hands that heal, while we live.
>
> Long I slept, long did I slumber,
>   long are the woes of life.
> Odin's will was that I might not
>   burst the bonds of sleep.

The words of Wagner's awakening Brünnhilde preserve something of these ancient verses, which he knew in German translation.[1] He himself set out his text for publication with the four-stress
lines divided into two lines of two stresses each; but when set out
in the old way, the passage reads:

> Heil dir, Sonne! Heil dir, Licht!
>   Heil dir, leuchtender Tag!
> Lang' war mein Schlaf; ich bin erwacht:
>   wer ist der Held, der mich erweckt'?
>
> Heil euch, Götter! Heil dir, Welt!
>   Heil dir, prangende Erde!
> Zu End' ist nun mein Schlaf; erwacht seh' ich:
>   Siegfried ist es, der mich erweckt!

---

[1] He did in fact study old Norse to the extent of being able to follow the original texts
with the aid of annotated German translations.

Or in English:

> Hail, sun! Hail, light!
>   Hail, luminous day!
> Long was my sleep; I am awake:
> Who is the hero who wakened me?
>
> Hail, gods! Hail, world!
>   Hail, glittering earth!
> At an end is my sleep; awake, I see:
> Siegfried it is who wakened me!

As can be seen, Wagner is free in his interweaving of the two different kinds of line, and in his carrying over of the alliteration from one line to the next; but even so, the whole main effect is retained. This kind of verse, with its short simple phrases hammered home by alliteration, is perfectly suited to the heroic world of *The Ring* – that is, to the heroic kind of musical setting for which it was conceived. And it is also responsible for the extraordinary succinctness of most of the text, as for example the opening utterance of Wotan in Act 2 of *The Valkyrie* (the passage is set out this time as Wagner himself had it published, in lines of two and three stresses only);

> Nun zäume dein Ross,
> reisige Maid!
> Bald entbrennt
> brünstiger Streit:
> Brünnhilde stürme zum Kampf,
> dem Wälsung kiese sie Sieg!
> Hunding wähle sich,
>   wem er gehört;
> nach Walhall taugt er mir nicht.
> Drum rüstig und rasch
> reite zur Wahl!

These eleven short lines plunge us swiftly into the whole new situation which opens the second act of the drama: they present immediately Wotan in his new role of War-Father, granting Siegmund the victory in his forthcoming fight with Hunding, and the entirely new character of Brünnhilde, who as chief Valkyrie is made responsible for carrying out this decision. Moreover, the explosive consonants, especially the repeated r, b, and br, set the whole violent, war-like atmosphere – which is, of course, definitively conveyed by the violent music to which the passage is set, with the alliterative consonants accentuating the two heavy beats of each broad six-eight bar. The lines have at least one characteristic of genuine poetry, in that a translation matching sound and sense is out of the question: the force of the German consonants and their continual interweaving into cross-alliterations cannot be transferred into English. The sense is as follows:

> Now bridle your horse,
> cavalry maid:
> soon will blaze
> furious strife.
> Brünnhilde, storm to the fight,
> to the Volsung victory give.
> Let Hunding choose
> where he belongs;
> in Valhall he's no use to me.
> Then ready and swift,
> ride to the fray.

Elsewhere, not only succinctness, but a kind of genuine poetic compression emerges from Wagner's *Stabreim* – for instance in Brünnhilde's defiant statement to Wotan in the final scene of *The Valkyrie*:

> *S*ieg oder *T*od
> mit *S*iegmund zu *t*eilen –
> dies nur er*k*annt' ich
> zu *k*iesen als Los!

– which loses everything in translation:

> Victory or death
> to share with Siegmund –
> this was the lot
> that alone I could choose!

At times, too, the *Stabreim* takes on a fascinatingly grotesque quality, as in the splutterings of Alberich when he clambers up the rock in the Rhine:

> *G*arstig *gl*atter
> *gl*itschriger *Gl*immer!
> Wie *gl*eit ich aus! . . .
> *F*euchtes *N*ass
> *f*üllt mir die *N*ase;
> ver*f*luchtes *N*iesen!

– to which English can get a little nearer:

> Nasty slippery
> slithery slate!
> How I keep slipping! . . .
> Clammy moisture
> fills my nostrils;
> curse this sneezing!

Nor is tenderness out of reach of the medium, as we find when Sieglinde remembers having heard Siegmund's voice long ago in her childhood:

> O *st*ill! *l*ass' mich
> der *St*imme *l*auschen:
> mich dünkt, ihren *K*lang
> hört' ich als *K*ind . . .

– the effect of which vanishes altogether in translation:

> O hush! Let me
> listen to your voice:
> its sound, I'm sure,
> I heard as a child . . .

For all its purely literary faults – the worst of which are a tendency to overuse superlatives ('Holiest love's deepest need') and a too-easy reliance on well-worn euphoric adjectives such as *selig* (blessed), *wonnig* (delightful), and *herrlich* (splendid) – the verbal language of *The Ring* has a kind of raw poetry about it which conveys Wagner's overt meaning vividly throughout. Also, while giving strength to the music through its sound, it gains back from the music an enormous strengthening of its own meaning; and it thus fuses with the music's full symbolic expression without any incongruity. No other medium could have served Wagner's purpose.

Even more successful than the text's language is its dramatic structure – the way that certain really decisive events of a complex mass of mythology are singled out and placed so as to give them the maximum dramatic impact, as in ancient Greek tragedy. Wagner has been ridiculed for his pretensions to a knowledge of Greek, and in particular for his claim to an intimate acquaintance with the *Oresteia* of Aeschylus; he has also been criticized as a dramatist for introducing so few events over such lengths of time. But whether or not he ever read the *Oresteia* in the original Greek, he certainly knew it well in German translation.[2] And the simple fact is that his dramatic method is very similar to that of Aeschylus in the *Oresteia*, which has an even greater scarcity of events. A setting-out of the six main subdivisions of Aeschylus' trilogy, with the events that occur in them, takes very little space:

Agamemnon. I. Agamemnon arrives home from the Trojan War. II. His wife Clytemnestra murders him.

Choephori. I. Orestes, Agamemnon's son by Clytemnestra, arrives home from exile. II. He kills Clytemnestra and her new husband Aegisthus.

Eumenides. I. Orestes, hounded by the Furies, takes refuge in the Athenian temple of Apollo. II. He is tried, and acquitted of guilt (and the work ends with the Panathenaic procession).

Only six events in six main subdivisions! The rest is narration of previous events; characterization; commentary; motivation; social, psychological, and metaphysical content; – all expressed, of course, through great poetry.

Now if we set out the events in the main subdivisions of Wagner's tetralogy, we need rather more space, owing to the greater length and complexity of the work,[3] but the result is still basically Aeschylean:

The Rhinegold. I. Alberich steals the Rhinegold. II. Fasolt and Fafner abduct Freia as a hostage. III. Wotan and Loge capture

[2] The personal library which Wagner had to leave behind in his Dresden house in 1849, when he fled into exile after the uprising, has survived, and it contains all the great Greek dramatists in German translation: the collected works of Aeschylus, Sophocles, Euripides, and Aristophanes. Also the collected works of Shakespeare, Molière, Hugo, Calderon, Goethe, Schiller, Lessing, and Kleist, together with two 'German Theatres' and a 'Spanish Theatre'. The library may have been depleted after he left it, of course, but even so it contains (as well as many books of history, most of the mythology connected with his own works, and the various scholarly writings on the subject) the following classics: Homer, Pindar, Xenophon, Herodotus, Thucydides, Demosthenes, Plutarch, Plato, and Aristotle; Virgil, Horace, Livy, Caesar, and Tacitus; Dante, Boccaccio, Tasso, and Ariosto; Chaucer, Gibbon, Byron; Le Sage and Rousseau; Cervantes; Hans Sachs, Hegel, Tieck, and Heine. Given all this, and the close acquaintance he shows in his writings with practically every author listed, Wagner must have been easily the most widely cultured of all the great composers. See Curt von Westernhagen: *Richard Wagners Dresdener Bibliothek 1842 bis 1849* (Wiesbaden, 1966).

[3] *Tristan* is perhaps the most Aeschylean of Wagner's dramatic constructions. I. Tristan brings Isolde from Ireland to Cornwall as a wife for King Mark, but they fall in love. II. Tristan is surprised with Isolde by one of King Mark's men and wounded. III. Tristan and Isolde die.

Alberich. IV. (a) Wotan robs Alberich of his ring; (b) he pays Fasolt and Fafner with it; (c) Fafner murders Fasolt for the ring.

The Valkyrie. I. (a) Siegmund and Sieglinde fall in love; (b) Siegmund draws the sword from the tree. II. (a) Wotan breaks Siegmund's sword with his spear; (b) Wotan kills Hunding. III. (a) Brünnhilde rescues Sieglinde; (b) Wotan punishes Brünnhilde by plunging her into a magic sleep.

Siegfried. I. Siegfried reforges his father's broken sword. II. (a) he kills the dragon Fafner; (b) he kills Mime. III. (a) he breaks Wotan's spear with his sword; (b) he awakens Brünnhilde.

The Twilight of the Gods. Prelude. (a) The Norns' thread of fate snaps; (b) Siegfried sets out in search of new adventures. I. (a) He is tricked by Hagen's potion into forgetting Brünnhilde and falling in love with Gutrune; (b) he wins Brünnhilde for Gunther. II. A double marriage takes place – between Siegfried and Gutrune, Gunther and Brünnhilde. III. (a) Hagen murders Siegfried; (b) he murders Gunther; (c) Brünnhilde immolates herself on Siegfried's funeral pyre; (d) the Rhinemaidens reclaim the ring; (e) Hagen drowns; (f) Valhalla and the gods are destroyed by fire.

Twenty-eight decisive events in fourteen main subdivisions – two in each, on average: extravagant by Aeschylean standards, but still very few. The rest is narration of previous events; characterization; motivation; social, psychological, and metaphysical content; – all expressed, of course, through great music.

Again as with Aeschylus, these decisive events are the crucial events of the mythology itself,[4] and practically all of them are placed near the end of a scene or act, as a climax towards which the whole preceding argument or conflict progresses (a procedure at once dramatic and musical). And most remarkable – again as with Aeschylus – is the way in which the action progresses towards these events through an absolutely clear-cut, logical, and inevitable interaction of the motivations of the characters.

Consider the dramatic mastery shown, for example, in Scene 2 of *The Rhinegold*. In the shortest possible space we are plunged *in*

[4] Or at least, nineteen of the twenty-eight are: the rest are Wagner's own inventions. Five of these enabled him to adapt the myths to his own symbolic purposes: Alberich's theft of the Rhinegold, Siegfried's reforging of the sword, his breaking of Wotan's spear, the snapping of the thread of fate, and the return of the ring to the Rhinemaidens. The other four helped to tidy up the plot: Wotan's killing of Hunding, Brünnhilde's rescuing of Sieglinde, Hagen's killing of Gunther, and his own death.

medias res: we are introduced to Wotan, chief of the gods, proud of the castle Valhalla just completed for him by the giants; also to his wife Fricka, horrified by the appalling contract engraved on his spear – that the giants' wage shall be her own sister Freia (goddess of love) – and scornful of his reliance on the untrustworthy Loge, god of cunning, to think of some acceptable substitute. Then immediately this desperate situation is brought home by the arrival of Freia herself, fleeing in terror from the giants, who claim her as wage; and Wotan's refusal to yield her up causes a tense impasse. In reply to her cries, her brothers Froh and Donner enter: Donner comes with the intention of killing the giants, but the contract engraved on the spear forbids the use of force, and the impasse remains. Thus the stage is prepared for the arrival of the unpunctual Loge; and he now appears, to reveal, reluctantly and ambiguously, the only way out. The single thing that anyone will give up love for is power; the dwarf Alberich has already done this, having renounced love and thereby gained the skill to forge a ring that guarantees mastery of the world; consequently, Wotan can rob Alberich of his ring and – Loge implies but does not state explicitly – pay for Valhalla with that. The giants agree, but Wotan does not – whereupon the decisive event happens: they abduct Freia as a hostage. The removal of her influence on the apples of eternal youth immediately begins to sap the gods' immortality: Wotan now has no alternative but to adopt Loge's unspoken suggestion; and so he and Loge set off to rob Alberich of his ring.

This is only an oversimplified outline, ignoring the subtle characterization and double-motivation of most of the personages concerned; but it is sufficient to show Wagner's masterly powers of intricate dramatic construction leading up to a logical climax. Everything fits perfectly into an inexorable dramatic pattern, the final result of which is a crime that was always inevitable, given the initial power-inspired actions of Wotan and Alberich. And Wagner's mastery appears the more remarkable when we remember that this dramatic construction, which would be perfectly satisfactory as the basis of a scene in a poetic drama, was laid down entirely with a view to musical realization through the exposition and development of a considerable number of thematic ideas. The clear-cut lines of the concentrated action follow a natural musical shape: the serenely confident Valhalla theme, contradicted by the ominous descending scale of Wotan's spear; the natural outcome of this in the distraught theme of Freia, the thunderous music of the giants, and a new domineering form of the scale of the spear as the wrangle begins; the dubious relief brought by the flickering, swift-minded music of Loge, followed by the sudden flowering of Freia's theme as he speaks of the near-omnipotence of love; the clouding-over again, as ideas from the previous scene return in new dark forms while he tells of Alberich's renunciation of love; and finally, the slowing-down to nearly a standstill through the music of the gods' fading immortality, in preparation for Wotan's decision and the further swift development of Loge's music as he and Wotan set off on their journey.

This again is only an oversimplified outline, which ignores the way that every shift of characterization and motivation is expressed by the symphonic web. We are dealing here with the text alone, considered purely as a dramatic framework; and now we come to its most extraordinary feature, whereby Wagner's dramatic mastery amounts to sheer genius. The fact is that this scene, like nearly all the others, is not simply a skilful dramatization of an already-existing, clear-cut myth (as is the case with Aeschylus): it is a creative fusion of elements from three quite separate myths, which, if Wagner had not written *The Rhinegold*, it would surely have never occurred to anyone to connect with one another.

In one of these, the gods do have a fortress built for them, and they do offer Freia (Freyja) as payment, on the advice of Loge (Loki), who promises to find a way out of the problem; but the solution is entirely different from that in *The Rhinegold*, and has nothing to do with the ring. In the second myth, the goddess with the apples of immortality is kidnapped by a giant, through the agency of Loki, who finds a way of getting her back; but the goddess is not Freyja, and again Loki's solution has nothing to do with the ring. In the third myth, Odin (Wotan) and Loki find themselves in desperate trouble, and have to pay their way out of it with gold and a ring, which is robbed from a dwarf by Loki; but the trouble is not caused by the building of the fortress, nor by the loss of the golden apples. In each case, the part of the myth which Wagner abandoned is a primitive and unstageable affair, involving the transformation of a character into an animal, while the part which he retained is latently intelligible from the point of view of human character, and eminently stageworthy: a perfectly practical procedure which resulted in a piece of superb symbolic drama – though it needed Wagner's genius to fit the fragments together and actually stage the result.

It is this aspect of the text – Wagner's manipulation of his mythic sources for the purpose of his own dramatic symbolism – that we are concerned with for the time being; but before going on to examine *The Ring* in detail from this point of view, it may be as well to answer the objections of those who have criticized Wagner for what they consider his temerity. These objections have been going on for a long time: as early as 1896, Jessie L. Weston[5] took Wagner to task for his misrepresentation of Alberich, of Siegmund and Sieglinde in *The Valkyrie*, and of Brünnhilde's jealousy in *The Twilight of the Gods*. More recently Brian Branston[6] has said that 'Gray, Wagner and Hitler have all played some part in misrepresenting the Old English and Old Norse conception of Woden-Odinn as a god of the dead'. And most recently of all, A. T. Hatto, in the Foreword to his new translation of the *Nibelungenlied*,[7] has complained: 'Modern poets and poetasters have often returned to its subject, prominent among them Richard Wagner with his gigantic music drama *Der Ring des Nibelungen* with which (as with his *Parsifal* and his *Tristan* – whatever their merits as modern works of art) he has ultimately harmed the cause of medieval German poetry by intruding reckless distortions between us and an ancient masterpiece.'

One can sympathize with scholars who have spent their lives studying ancient mythology or medieval poetry, trying to thread their way meticulously through confusions and contradictions in search of the true original meaning, and who then find that Wagner has taken only such elements as served his purpose, and fused them, altered them, even added to them, just as he liked. No doubt they would have preferred him to stage the myths or the poems in their original forms, or – this being obviously impossible – to leave them alone. But they fail to realize that his purpose was entirely different from theirs: he was not trying to dramatize old myths or poems for their own sake, but to interpret through his art such of their meaning as seemed to him still to have relevance for

[5] *Legends of the Wagner Dramas*, London, 1896, which offers a condensed examination of Wagner's use of his sources for all his music-dramas. It has since been replaced in this respect by Newman's *Wagner Nights*, except in the case of *The Ring*, which he practically ignored from this point of view, saying that 'It would . . . serve no really useful purpose to trace the various elements of Wagner's *Ring* to their sources in the myths'.

[6] *The Lost Gods of England*, London, 1957.

[7] *The Nibelungenlied*, Penguin Books, 1965.

his own time, and where that meaning was lacking, to supply it himself.

The detailed criticisms of Jessie L. Weston will be taken up in the complete examination of Wagner's manipulations which follows later; but the other strictures may be dismissed here as arising entirely from misconceptions. As regards Brian Branston's complaint that Wagner misrepresented 'the Old English and Old Norse conception of Woden-Odinn as a god of the dead', it can only be said that he was not concerned with that conception at all: he was concerned with the old *German* and Norse conception of *Wodan-*Odin as god of all living creatures (*Allvater, Alfödr*), as god of battle (*Heervater, Herfadir*), as god of the choice of those killed in battle (*Walvater, Valfadir*), and as the Wanderer. All these aspects are quite as much part of the original conception of the god, if not more so, and they were interpreted by Wagner according to Grimm's *Deutsche Mythologie*. The modern understanding of this figure's other aspect, as god of the dead, was of course arrived at after Wagner's time, and so it naturally plays no part in *The Ring*.

As for A. T. Hatto's contention that Wagner, in *The Ring*, intruded 'reckless distortions between us and an ancient masterpiece', one can only marvel at his assumption that Wagner's work is in any sense a dramatization of the *Nibelungenlied*. The single part of Wagner's plot which is covered by that medieval epic is *The Twilight of the Gods* (excluding the Prelude): the poem gives only sketchy information about Siegfried's earlier life, and none at all about the events covered in *The Valkyrie* and *The Rhinegold*. Wagner's main sources were of course the Norse *Volsunga saga* and *Poetic Edda*: between them they contain the whole story he used for *The Ring*, except the myths of the building of the castle and the loss of the golden apples, which he took from the Norse *Prose Edda*.

In any case, the anonymous poet of the *Nibelungenlied* may himself be accused of intruding reckless distortions between us and several ancient masterpieces, since he offers a curious medieval romance version of earlier poems about Siegfried which, altogether no longer extant, are believed to have been followed more faithfully, in certain respects, by the other main sources. In all of these, for example, Siegfried is an orphan, or semi-orphan, who is brought up by a foster-father; but in the *Nibelungenlied* he is brought up by his father and mother, Siegmund and Sieglinde, who are King and Queen of the Netherlands, and Siegmund lives on to lament Siegfried's death. Again, in all the other sources,

Siegfried falls in love with Gunther's sister when he meets her at Gunther's court, but in the *Nibelungenlied* he falls in love with her after the manner of a medieval knight-errant, before he has even set eyes on her, merely on the strength of her famed beauty.

The truth is, of course, that both Wagner and the poet of the *Nibelungenlied* were doing exactly the same thing. Each was taking the ancient myths and adapting them boldly (recklessly, if one wants to use the word) to create a work of art for his own time. It is heartening to find that at least one scholar in the field of Teutonic mythology has the breadth of view to recognize Wagner's genius in this respect. R. G. Finch, in the introduction to his edition and translation of *Volsunga saga*,[8] gets right to the heart of the matter:

> There can be few who have not heard of Sigurd (or Siegfried), his deeds of bravery, his love for Brynhild (or Brünnhilde) and his murder at the hands of those he trusted best, for Richard Wagner drew largely on the lays of the Icelandic Poetic Edda for the basic material of *Der Ring des Nibelungen*, and on *Volsunga saga* which, although containing additional material and differing in certain matters of detail, is essentially a prose retelling of the relevant Eddaic lays.

> Wagner's *Ring* cannot, however, be equated with the ancient Scandinavian legends that it seems to tell: it is by no means a modern dramatisation of *Volsunga saga* or of the Eddaic lays, and Wagner, in attempting to recreate the primitive 'myth', became an innovator on a grand scale whose genius produced an entirely new 'myth' in accordance with his poetic and musical purpose. His approach to the material was eclectic and arbitrary. For example, the shattering of Wotan's spear by Siegfried with a sword of his own forging is pure invention, as is the claim that Siegfried is the child of an incestuous union between brother and sister, although according to *Volsunga saga*, his half-brother, Sinfjotli, was indeed born of such a union. Sigurd's mother in Edda and Saga was named Hjordis, not Sigelinde who appears as his mother in the M[iddle] H[igh] G[erman] epic *das Nibelungenlied*. Odin (i.e. Wotan) is not, in the Icelandic version, solely responsible for despoiling the dwarf of his gold: moreover, the dwarf's name was Andvari, not Alberich, whom Wagner took over from the *Nibelungenlied*, where he plays a different role. In fact, the 'Rheingold' springs largely from Wagner's fertile imagination, and the idea of the inevitable conflict between lust for power, symbolised by the ring, and true love is his alone, arising in part at least, as so many of his themes, from the social and political situation of his day.

Dr Finch (who, it may be noticed, shows greater insight into *The Ring* than any of our three main Wagnerian commentators, in

[8] *The Saga of the Volsungs*, edited and translated with Introduction, Notes and Appendices, by R. G. Finch (Nelson dual-language publication, London and Edinburgh, 1965).

recognizing that the central conflict of the work is between lust for power and true love) says no more than the simple truth. Wagner's tetralogy is a great work of art in its own right, which intrudes nothing between us and anything. The Eddas, the Sagas, and the *Nibelungenlied* are always there, for anyone who wishes to read them: *The Ring* is something else. One may, however, take issue with Dr Finch from the opposite point of view: if Wagner was 'eclectic and arbitrary' in his approach to the material – as will always be the way with an artist, as opposed to a scholar – *The Ring* is none the less a committed interpretation *of* that material, as it appeared to him, based firmly *on* that material. It is not true, for example, that *The Rhinegold* 'springs largely from Wagner's fertile imagination': at least half of it, as mentioned earlier, is a creative fusion of three separate myths recounted in the *Prose Edda* – a fusion made by a fertile imagination, certainly, but by an imagination completely steeped in the whole material.

It might even be argued that *The Ring* is as valid and coherent a dramatic synthesis of the complex mythology of Northern Europe as we are ever likely to get. Each source itself, after all, represents a tradition introducing new and often contradictory material, which must originally have been the product of many a fertile imagination. Each source, in fact, represents a new artistic *interpretation* of pre-existing material, to suit the writer's purpose; and *The Ring* is a comprehensive artistic interpretation of the whole main essence of the material, undertaken by one of the greatest imaginations in human history. If Wagner, for example, invented Siegfried's breaking of Wotan's spear, he was doing no more than following the arbitrary method of the anonymous authors of the material preserved in *Volsunga saga*: in that work, Wotan (Odin) offers direct assistance to Siegfried (Sigurd), by helping him to choose a horse (see p. 113) and giving him advice as to the best way of attacking the dragon – features which are not found in any other source (and which Wagner preferred to omit).

Even the central conflict of *The Ring* could be considered a justifiable interpretation of latent implications in the original material. The ancient Wotan (Odin) is undoubtedly, in several of his aspects, a Teutonic personification of the general human will to dominate and to gain more and more power; and if this will to power is not opposed by love, in the myths, it certainly is by justice, since the gods' downfall is clearly represented as the inevitable retribution brought by fate on their dubious dealings in their quest for domination. And if Wagner preferred to counter-balance the lust for power with the emergence of love instead, it can be said that love, even if of a fierce and primitive kind, plays an important part in the original myths, especially in the Scandinavian sources; and Wagner was merely reinterpreting it in accordance with the conception of his own time. We have noticed earlier[9] the slight hint of compassion in the reason given by Brynhild (Brünnhilde) in the *Poetic Edda* for her support of the warrior whom Odin (Wotan) had condemned to die: 'He could find no one to shield him.' And in *Volsunga saga* she plights her troth with Sigurd (Siegfried) in terms which are not all that far removed from nineteenth-century phraseology:

'I should wish to marry you', she answered, 'even though I might have the choice of all the men there are'.

And we also read of Sigurd:

Embracing her, he kissed her and said: 'No woman born is lovelier than you'.

Wagner, as an artist, approached the material from the opposite point of view to that of a scholar. Whereas the scholar tries to understand the meaning of recorded mythology in relation to its period, Wagner tried to understand the inner essence of Teutonic mythology in relation to the abiding realities of human life which are common to all periods, including the modern era. As he wrote in *Opera and Drama*:

The incomparable thing about myth is that it is true for all time, and its content, however closely compressed, is inexhaustible throughout the ages. The only task of the poet is to expound it.

The truth is, Wagner was trying to remake the old Teutonic mythology in the light of the problems of the modern world, which, as he saw it, were not all that different from those of the ancient one. Just how he remade it is what we must now investigate; and we must begin by considering the nature of the sources he used.

[9] See p. 34n.

2. *The nature of the sources*

The Teutonic peoples first impinged decisively on recorded history towards the end of the second century B.C., when certain 'Teutoni' and 'Cimbri' invaded Gaul and Italy, and came in contact with the Roman armies. Half a century later, other tribes were encountered by Julius Caesar on the Rhine, and from then on, the 'Germani' as a whole began to reveal themselves as a growing threat to the Roman Empire. They were in fact a branch of the same Indo-European stock as the Romans themselves – and as the Greeks and the Sanskrit-speaking peoples of India; but they had become separated off, long before the beginnings of Indo-European civilization, and had remained barbarians, roaming Northern Europe as far as Scandinavia, and evolving the original language and religion in an entirely characteristic way of their own.

Their relationship with the other Indo-European peoples is manifest in certain linguistic survivals, notably that of the original word for 'god' – *dieus*. This came down in Sanskrit as *dyaus* and *devas*, in Greek as *Zeus* and *theos*, in Latin as *deus*, in Spanish as *dios*, in Italian as *dio*, and in French as *dieu*. With the Teutons it became the name of the supreme sky- and war-god, *Tîwaz*, in Gothic *Tius*, in Old High German *Zio*, in Anglo-Saxon *Tiw*, in Old Norse *Týr*. This god later yielded pride of place to Wodenaz (Wotan or Odin), and eventually vanished with the rest when the Teutons were converted to Christianity – though certain myths about him have been preserved, and his name still lingers on in various North European names for the third day of the week, Tuesday. More apposite to Wagner, the original word for 'to thunder', which came down in Latin as *tonare* (Italian *tuonare*, French *tonner*), and was applied to Jupiter as thunder-god (*Jupiter tonans*), became with the Teutons the name of the thunder-god himself, *Donar* (Old Saxon *Thunar*, Anglo-Saxon *Thunor*, Old Norse *Thor* – surviving in 'Thursday'). Wagner called this god Donner, after the modern German word for 'thunder', the god's name itself having survived in the German word for 'Thursday', *Donnerstag*.

However, with the passing ages, the Teutons' language and

religion had diverged completely from those of the peoples who had settled in Southern Europe and built up the Greco-Roman civilization. Exactly what their religion had become by Roman times is unknown, since they had not evolved the art of writing. The Roman historian Tacitus, in his *Germania* (A.D. 58), described certain Germanic tribes as worshipping, amongst other gods, 'Mercury' and 'Mars', and scholars have plausibly interpreted these Latin identifications as signifying Wodenaz and Tîwaz; but this is nevertheless conjecture. It was not until the twelfth century, after the Teutons' conversion to Christianity and their settling into the groups that were to become modern nations, that German and Scandinavian writers began to set down the hitherto oral tradition of their old pagan mythology; and it is a few manuscripts surviving from that period which provide us with our only comprehensive body of knowledge about it.

Although the authors were themselves Christians, they were nevertheless preserving, even if often in a confused form, pagan traditions going back for centuries. The manuscripts are so few because there had been, from the beginning, a natural Christian pressure to consign the old heathen religion to total oblivion, by forbidding mention of it or by destroying any written reference to it. Since the conversion was even more fiercely resisted in Germany than in Scandinavia, this pressure was more ruthless there; and since it also happened earlier there, German memories of the old religion were anyway dimmer by the twelfth century. In consequence, the German sources tell us nothing about the German gods, but only about the German heroes, whereas the Scandinavian sources tell us not only about the heroes, Scandinavian and German, but about the Scandinavian gods as well.

As regards *The Ring*, there are five main sources, and only one is in (Middle High) German – the anonymous epic poem *Das Nibelungenlied*; written in Austria around 1200, some four centuries after the conversion there, it recounts, amongst other things, the story of Siegfried. The second main source, the anonymous prose narrative *Thidriks saga af Bern*, is based on German material, but was compiled in Norway around 1260–70: again it deals, not with the gods, but with German heroes, including Siegfried. The other three main sources are pure Scandinavian ones, compiled between 1150 and 1270 in Iceland – then a Norwegian colony – where the conversion was comparatively smooth and very late (in 1000). They are the *Poetic Edda*, an anonymous collection of poems about gods and heroes, including Siegfried (under his Norse name of Sigurd) and his father Siegmund (Sigmund); *Volsunga saga*, an anonymous prose narrative about heroes, mainly Sigurd and Sigmund, with certain of the gods appearing, notably Odin (Wotan), Frigg (Fricka), and Loki (Loge); and the *Prose Edda*, a manual of instruction for poets by Snorri Sturluson, containing prose narratives about the gods, but once more including the story of Sigurd.

There are also some lesser sources. The only Scandinavian one is the fourteenth-century prose narrative *Norna–Gests thattr*, which contains a summary of the story of Sigurd as told in *Volsunga saga*, with one or two extra details. The rest are minor German epic poems about the heroes, of various dates, collected in the fifteenth-century *Heldenbuch* except for one, the sixteenth-century *Lied vom hürnen Seyfrid*; in these the mythology has become debased into phantasmagoric fairy-tales, but some of them nevertheless seem to contain elements of the original Siegfried myth.

Wagner drew on all these sources for the text of *The Ring*. But he also read the scholarly writings of his own time on the subject; and two of these – by the brothers Grimm, of fairy-tale fame – amount to sources in their own right. Wilhelm Grimm, in his *Deutsche Heldensage*, tried to clarify the confusion of the German sources by comparing them with one another and with the Scandinavian ones; and Jacob Grimm, in his *Deutsche Mythologie*, applied his vast erudition to reconstructing the German form of the old Teutonic religion by an exhaustive collation of the scattered traces preserved in German language, literature and folk-lore with the fairly comprehensive record of the Scandinavian form. There were also two important essays by other scholars: Karl Lachmann's *Kritik der Sage von den Nibelungen* and Friedrich Heinrich von der Hagen's introduction to his first edition of the original Icelandic text of the poems about the heroes in the *Poetic Edda*.

This makes seven main sources for *The Ring*, and several lesser ones.[1] We must now consider their various relationships to the text

---

[1] In answer to a letter from one Franz Müller, who wished to write a book about the origins of the text of *The Ring*, after its first (private) publication in 1853, Wagner listed all the above-mentioned books as his sources; and they are all in his surviving Dresden library, with three exceptions – *Volsunga saga*, *Thidriks saga*, and *Norna-Gests thattr*. As regards *Volsunga saga*, we know, from a letter Wagner wrote to Theodor Uhlig in 1851, that he had been unable to procure a copy from any Dresden bookshop, and had been obliged to study a copy in the Dresden Royal Library; and the same could well be true of *Thidriks saga* and *Norna-Gests thattr*, which were no doubt just as hard to come by.

of *The Ring* in a general way, before going on to examine just how Wagner adapted them in detail, to suit his own creative purpose.

It will be best to begin by setting forth all that scholars have reconstructed, with reasonable plausibility, of the origins and evolution of the surviving German material. And strangely enough, from a Wagnerian point of view, we have to start with Gunther, and with what is told of him outside the story of *The Ring*.

The Gunther of the sources is a legendary transformation of a historical fifth-century Burgundian king,[2] who is recorded in a Latin chronicle of the time (the *Lex Burgundiorum*) as Guntaharius, a descendant of King Gibicha (in German, Gibich, the semi-mythical founder of the royal line of the Gibichungs). Gunthaharius, or Gunther, ruled over territory around the Rhine; but in 437 he and his forces were massacred by an army of Huns – the eastern people whose leader was Attila, though he himself did not command this particular expedition. Sixteen years later, Attila died of a haemorrhage during his nuptials with a woman the Latin chronicle calls Ildico (presumably a German princess with the Germanic root-syllable 'Hild' as part of her name); and in the next century a rumour was recorded in another chronicle that she had actually murdered Attila.

Out of all this, it is believed,[3] arose a fifth-century Burgundian lay about the fall of the Burgundian royal family and the murder of Attila in revenge. In this, 'Ildico' would have been identified as Gunther's[4] sister, and possibly given the name 'Grim-hild' ('grim' meaning fierce), to form the usual alliteration of family names; or she may have been called Gutrune (Gunthrun), since the name is preserved in the Scandinavian sources as Gudrun. This lay would have told the following story. 'Grimhild', or 'Gutrune', married Attila (the German form of whose name was by now probably Etzel) and lived with him at his court in 'Hunland'. Etzel lusted after Gunther's treasure, and invited him and his brothers to visit him, which they did, despite their sister's warning – though they first hid the treasure, and took their army with them. Being seized

[2] The Burgundians of this period were of course a *Germanic* tribe: only their name survived, to become that of the French province of Burgundy, just as the name of the Germanic Franks survived, to become that of France itself.

[3] See A. T. Hatto, op. cit., pp. 370–95, from which this summary is partly derived.

[4] His Burgundian name, at this stage of the legend, was probably 'Gunthahari', but in dealing with the German sources I will give all the names as we know them from Wagner, except in cases where they are quite different.

and tortured, they refused to disclose the treasure's hiding-place, and so were murdered, and their whole army massacred by Etzel's Hunnish army. Their sister avenged them by murdering Etzel, killing her sons by him, and burning down the Hunnish palace.

At about the time of this lay, it is believed, another lay was current among the Franks. It concerned the wooing of a certain Brünnhilde and the resultant death of a famous Frankish hero, the dragon-slayer Siegfried – neither of which characters, unlike Gunther and his sister, can be traced back to an actual historical personage. This lay eventually became connected with that of the fall of the Burgundians, by having Siegfried marry into the Burgundian royal house, taking to wife Gunther's sister; and the outcome was probably the following story. Siegfried, the famous dragon-slayer, married 'Grimhild', or 'Gutrune'; and Gunther wished to marry Brünnhilde, a formidable woman of superhuman strength, who placed impossible obstacles in the way of any wooer. Gunther was helped to overcome these obstacles by the mighty Siegfried, who changed shapes with him for the purpose; Siegfried may also have had to deflower Brünnhilde for Gunther, or perhaps only neutralize her strength by grappling with her until she was exhausted, leaving Gunther to deflower his bride himself. In any case he either took or received a ring from her, and later gave it to his wife, who, during a quarrel with Brünnhilde about the status of their husbands, displayed it triumphantly. As a result, Brünnhilde demanded that Siegfried should be killed, to redeem her honour; and he was treacherously murdered by one of Gunther's men, possibly by being stabbed in his one vulnerable spot, between the shoulder-blades. Hagen may or may not have featured in this lay, as the murderer of Siegfried during a hunt.

With the dragon, the changing of shapes, and the motif of near-complete invulnerability, an element of the supernatural enters; and indeed, an aura of myth surrounds Siegfried, which makes the date of origin of the character quite uncertain – possibly way back in the pre-history of the Frankish peoples. Another Frankish lay is thought to have been current in the fifth century, concerned with his marvellous earlier life.[5] Its story would have

---

[5] See *Das Lied vom hürnen Seyfrid*, Critical Edition with Introduction and Notes by K. C. King, Manchester University Press, 1958. The *Lied* itself is a lesser sixteenth-century German source, which will be considered later; but Dr King presents a conjectural account of the earlier lays in his Introduction (pp. 40–59), on which I have drawn.

been as follows. Siegfried, the son of Siegmund and Sieglinde, grew up as an orphan, not knowing who his parents were. Brought up by a smith, who either did not care what happened to him or else actually wanted to get rid of him because of his giant strength and unmanageability, he was exposed to the onslaught of a dragon. Owing to his strength, he was able to kill it, and he tried to make himself invulnerable, either by bathing in its blood, or by burning it and smearing himself all over with its molten horn; in any case, he did not manage to cover the area between his shoulder-blades. At this same time, or afterwards, he won a great treasure – the 'Nibelung Hoard' – from some brothers, probably dwarfs; and at some point he gained possession of a wonderful sword, either from the smith, or when he killed the dragon, or from the brothers.

These three hypothetical lays are the only ones that have been plausibly reconstructed of the original German material; and the way they developed is believed to have been as follows. In later re-tellings of the story, the Burgundians of the original lay became known, confusingly, as 'the Nibelungs', probably because their original 'treasure' had now become the 'Nibelung hoard' of Siegfried, appropriated by them after his murder;[6] and about 1160, an anonymous Austrian poet worked up the lay about their downfall (or poems which had developed from it) into a comparatively short epic, *Der Nibelunge Nôt* (The Nibelungs' Last Stand). This would have recounted the same events as those in the original lay, but by this time there had been a complete reversal of the motivations of Attila (now definitely called Etzel) and his wife (now definitely called Kriemhild – a derivative of Grimhild – and not Gutrune).

This was due to the influence of the poems which had evolved from the lay about Siegfried and Brünnhilde. These maintained that Kriemhild had been married to Siegfried before she married Etzel, and that Siegfried had been treacherously killed by her own brothers; and so it now had to be she who, to avenge him, invited them to Etzel's court, and provoked the combat in which they and their army were massacred by the Huns. Likewise, the lust for the treasure was transferred from Etzel to her: since the treasure itself

[6] Here, for a moment, we have to forget Wagner altogether. His ingenious and by no means unjustifiable equating of 'the Nibelungs' with Alberich, Mime, and their fellow-dwarfs, will be examined later; for the time being, 'the Nibelungs' must be understood to refer to the Burgundians – to Gunther, his kin, and his army.

had become the 'Nibelung hoard' which Siegfried had gained during his earlier life, and which her brothers had appropriated after his death, it was now hers by right. Etzel, on the other hand, had become a benevolent figure, merely caught up in events he could not control, and left alive at the end to lament the wholesale slaughter – including that of Kriemhild herself, by a warrior disgusted at her savagery. By this time too, the dark and dominating figure of Hagen had fully emerged, as a liegeman and distant relative of Gunther: in the one tradition he featured as Siegfried's unrelenting enemy, coveting his treasure and murdering him during a hunt; in the other as the champion of the 'Nibelungs' in their last stand against the Huns, and the unrelenting enemy of Kriemhild – who herself struck him dead near the end.

It should be emphasized here that the foregoing comprehends practically all the information that came down into the German sources. They know nothing of any earlier meeting between Siegfried and Brünnhilde, or of any potion that made him forget her, or of her eventually joining him in death. Nor do they know anything of her having been a Valkyrie, punished by Wotan for disobedience, or of Siegfried's parents, the ring, or the gods: as we shall see, Wagner found all these things in the pure Scandinavian sources. On the other hand, the German tradition does have this story about what happened after Siegfried's death – which was absorbed into the Scandinavian tradition too; and since Wagner naturally ignored it (having decided to end the world with Siegfried's death, by bringing in the totally unrelated Scandinavian myth of the end of the gods), it may seem unnecessary that we should be concerned with it here. But there are two reasons: the nature of the material cannot be properly understood without reference to it, and – more important – Wagner incorporated one or two features of it, much transformed, into the plot of *The Ring*. Since we shall be concerned with these features, the reader would do well to keep the post-Siegfried part of the material in mind.

We can now leave conjecture and turn to the first surviving German source: this is the famous Middle High German epic *Das Nibelungenlied* – 'The Lay of (i.e. about) the Nibelungs'.

The *Nibelungenlied* was written at some time between 1195 and 1205 in Austria – that is, about forty years after the conjectured earlier Austrian epic *Der Nibelunge Nôt*; the anonymous author is believed to have been a minstrel-poet of semi-clerical status at one of the courts near the Danube, between Passau and Vienna. His work eclipsed the previous materials because he had the masterly idea of conflating all of them into a large, comprehensive epic, and the genius to carry out this idea by expanding and reshaping them in a way of his own. He based the first part of the poem on the material about Siegfried's arrival at Gunther's court, his marriage with Gunther's sister Kriemhild, his wooing of Brünnhilde for Gunther, his giving of Brünnhilde's ring to Kriemhild, with the consequent scandal, and his murder by Hagen during a hunt, to redeem Brünnhilde's honour. And during this part, he just touched in the story of Siegfried's earlier life, putting it into the mouth of Hagen on Siegfried's arrival: he has killed a dragon, made himself almost invulnerable by bathing in its blood, and won the 'Nibelung hoard' from two brothers, 'mighty princes'. The second part of the epic he based on *Der Nibelunge Nôt*, and it tells of the events following Siegfried's death: Kriemhild's marriage to Etzel and her removal with him to Hungary; the long journey from the Rhine to the Danube by Gunther and Hagen, at Kriemhild's invitation, with their army; the slaughter of their army by the Huns, and of Gunther and Hagen, through Kriemhild's agency; and Kriemhild's own death.

By the time of the *Nibelungenlied*, the old German alliterative verse or *Stabreim*, in which the original lays had been written, had given way to the new Romance technique of end-rhyme: the epic consists of nearly 2400 four-lined stanzas rhyming in couplets, which are divided into thirty-nine 'Aventiure', or 'events'. An idea of the ballad-like character of the verse can be gained from a fine stanza corresponding to a crucial moment in *The Ring* – Siegfried's death:

> Die bluomen allenthalben · von bluote wâren naz.
> Dô rang er mit dem tode · unlange tet er daz,
> wan des tôdes wâfen · ie ze sêre sneit.
> Dô mohte reden niht mêre · der recke küene und gemeit.

Or in an English translation preserving the rhythm of the original:[7]

> On every side the flowers · were soaking wet with blood.
> And there with death he wrestled · 'Twas not for long he could,
> now that death's own weapon · cut too deep its way.
> He could not speak any longer · the hero valiant and gay.

[7] All quotations from the *Nibelungenlied* are my own translations.

A. T. Hatto has described the *Nibelungenlied* as 'a heroic epic surpassed only by the *Iliad* of Homer'; but whatever its status as a work of art, it could obviously be of only limited use to Wagner. In the first place, it could offer him no more than the story of Siegfried, and that only from his arrival at Gunther's court; the references to his earlier life are brief and vague. But even more important than this, the poet liberally overlaid the primitive material with the attitudes of medieval chivalry, to suit the taste of his courtly audience. After all, the original lays had arisen among the Franks and Burgundians at a time when these peoples were still unconverted to Christianity; and meanwhile, something like seven centuries had passed – centuries of gradual Christianization and civilization. Anyone familiar with the primitive world re-established by Wagner in *The Ring* can only be surprised at the picture presented in the *Nibelungenlied*, as for example in these three stanzas describing Siegfried's upbringing:

> In the country of the Netherlands · down by the river Rhine,
> there was a famous princeling · born of a noble line.
> His father was called Siegmund · Sieglind his mother's name;
> they held their court in Xanten · a city of great fame.
>
> This princeling's name was Siegfried · a noble, gallant knight;
> in many lands he tested · his mettle and his might.
> His strength and courage took him · through many a far countree;
> hey, afterwards what valiant knights · he found in Burgundee!
>
> Whenever he went riding · an escort fine he had,
> and Siegmund and Sieglind made sure · that he was finely clad;
> wise men, well-versed in honour · took him into their care,
> so that he won to love him · the people everywhere.

As a 'gallant knight', Siegfried is naturally expert at jousting, and the court of his still-living parents is of a resplendence matched only by the court of Gunther at Worms. In both cases, great emphasis is laid on magnificent clothes and jewels, and a reckless generosity with money and gifts. As said in the first part of this chapter, Siegfried falls in love with Kriemhild in the manner of a knight-errant, being smitten by the mere fame of her beauty before he even sets eyes on her; moreover, his wooing of Brünn-hilde for Gunther, so as to win Kriemhild for himself, is performed as an act of knightly service. Finally, there is the incongruous Christian background: the quarrel between Brünnhilde and

Kriemhild approaches its climax through a dispute as to which of them shall take precedence in entering Worms Cathedral for Vespers; and Siegfried's dead body is taken there for a Requiem Mass to be sung.

Even more valueless to Wagner was the curious treatment of Brünnhilde: the poet, faced with the task of presenting this primitive character to a courtly audience, took refuge in making her a figure of farce. She appears as an amazonian Queen of Iceland, a formidable female athlete, whom Siegfried 'woos' for Gunther by sailing to her country and defeating her in a gruelling triathlon of throwing the javelin, putting the shot, and long-jump. Apart from the incongruity, even Wagner could never have contemplated staging this event, in which Gunther goes through the motions while Siegfried, in a 'cloak of invisibility', does the deeds. The two contestants throw the javelin (spear) *at each other*: Brünnhilde's (which three male warriors can only just lift) penetrates Siegfried's shield and brings blood gushing from his mouth; he, chivalrously intent on not hurting a lady, throws his spear butt-first, but even so, it penetrates her shield, hits her coat of mail, and knocks her flying. The putting of the shot is followed *immediately* by the long-jump: the 'shot' (a huge boulder which it takes twelve warriors to carry) is hurled twenty-four yards by Brünnhilde, and she follows through with a standing long-jump which clears it easily. This distance is not recorded, nor is either of Siegfried's, but since he beat her, he must have set up an all-time world record – especially as in the long-jump he was of course carrying Gunther with him.

Again, back at Gunther's court, Brünnhilde's refusal to accept Gunther as her husband takes an entirely ribald form: on the bridal night, she binds him hand and foot, and hangs him on a large nail in the wall till dawn; so Siegfried's help has to be enlisted again. The following night, after Gunther has been thrown out of bed and wedged between a heavy chest and the wall, Siegfried substitutes for him in the darkness, overpowers Brünnhilde in a mighty wrestling match (not before being thrown out of bed himself), and then leaves Gunther to exact his marital rights from his exhausted bride. Moreover, Siegfried takes not only a ring from Brünnhilde, but her girdle as well, and later gives both to Kriemhild.

None of this, clearly, could serve Wagner's lofty purpose. But in any case it was useless for *The Ring*, since the *Nibelungenlied* follows the German tradition in which the Brünnhilde Siegfried wins for

Gunther is a woman he has never met before; and she does not join him in death, but fades from the scene, leaving Kriemhild as the great tragic heroine, who takes her revenge in the post-Siegfried part of the story.[8] As regards Siegfried's origins, on the other hand, the poem actually diverges from the original German tradition, which here Wagner needed to follow – that of Siegfried the orphan, brought up by a foster-father. As we have seen, Siegmund and Sieglinde are still living, as a rich king and queen, when Siegfried goes to Gunther's court – and Siegmund even lives on to lament Siegfried's death. Clearly, in drawing up the text of *The Ring*, Wagner could only follow other sources on these and similar points.

This does not mean, of course, that in every case, or even in the majority of cases, he was necessarily going back to an earlier, more authentic tradition. He himself, having first encountered the character of Siegfried in the *Nibelungenlied*, and having only discovered the other sources afterwards, definitely believed this to be the case (as the German scholars of his own time also believed). He said, in *A Communication to my Friends* (1851):

> My studies drew me on, through the poems of the middle ages, right back to the foundations of the ancient German mythology; I was able to strip away one distorting veil after another which later poetry had thrown over it, and so set eyes on it at last in all its chaste beauty . . . Although the splendid figure of Siegfried had long attracted me, he only fully enthralled me for the first time when I had succeeded in freeing him from all his later trappings, and saw him before me in his purest human form. It was then for the first time, too, that I recognized the possibility of making him the hero of a drama, which had never occurred to me while I knew him only from the medieval *Nibelungenlied*.

Wagner was certainly right on the last point: if the *Nibelungenlied* had been the only extant source, we should not have had even a single music-drama about Siegfried from him, let alone *The Ring*. And his statement about stripping away distorting veils is also true as regards the general atmosphere: the Scandinavian sources retain something of the primitive pagan character of the myth, as against the medievalizing of it in the *Nibelungenlied*; moreover, they preserve Siegfried's status as a (semi-)orphan brought up by a foster-father. Otherwise, the problem of the reliability of the

[8] It should be said here that Wagner went against all the sources in making Gunther's sister a minor character – as he had to do to leave the field clear for his tremendous 'true-wife' figure of Brünnhilde. In every source, she is at least equal in stature with Brünnhilde.

various sources is exceedingly complex; but modern scholarship tends to the view that several of the features in the Scandinavian sources were local accretions on the original German myth – notably the Valkyrie status of Brynhild (Brünnhilde) and her punishment by Odin (Wotan), Sigurd's (Siegfried's) passing through a wall of fire to meet her, his forgetting her through the agency of a potion, and her joining him in death. It seems that Wagner, believing that he had dug down to the foundations of the ancient German Siegfried-myth, had actually uncovered, to a considerable extent, the Scandinavian superstructure.

However, we may well ask ourselves what such a consideration implies. It suggests that there was once an original German story of Siegfried and Brünnhilde which was *authentic* – which must presumably mean *true*. But if such a thing existed, it was a mere fragment of history, and not a myth at all. Who the historical individuals were who gave rise to the myth, or if there ever were any, is completely unknown; and even if they could be identified – as Gunther has been convincingly identified with the fifth-century Burgundian king Gunthaharius – the only truth that would matter about them, as in Gunther's case, would still be the myth. Fragments of ancient history deal with shadowy real-life individuals, myth with vivid larger-than-life figures which sum up a whole people's way of viewing the world; and myth is a living and growing thing, which can sometimes increase in depth and significance as it develops. If Wagner was deluded in his quest, he was nevertheless acting with the sleep-walking certainty of genius in taking all that was most significant from the whole surviving corpus of Teutonic mythology – even if certain features were later than others – and in adapting it to create his own dramatic synthesis of that mythology.

The above may have given the impression that Wagner took hardly anything from the *Nibelungenlied*, but this is not so. The poem's detailed narrative, stripped of its medieval trappings, and sometimes considerably transformed, gave him several important features of the action of *The Twilight of the Gods*, notably as regards Siegfried's arrival at Gunther's court, the double marriage, the betrayal of Siegfried's vulnerable spot, and the last hours of his life. It also offered him a clear basis for the weak, vacillating, gloomy character of Gunther; and above all, it supplied the definitive German form of Siegfried's death, with the magnificently saturnine and implacable Hagen lusting after his treasure and murdering him during a hunt. In the three pure Scandinavian sources, Hagen (called there Hogni) is a much less commanding figure, the murder is done by someone else, and Siegfried (Sigurd) is killed in bed.

Another striking feature which Wagner took over from the poem was the ferocious figure of Alberich, with his status as a dwarf connected with the 'Nibelung hoard' and with the 'cloak of invisibility' which Siegfried won; but since he plays a quite different role there from the one Wagner gave him in *The Ring*, it will be best to leave this feature until we come to consider the later and lesser German sources, with which it is closely connected. The *Nibelungenlied* itself provided Wagner with nothing usable about Siegfried's earlier life, beyond the unanimously attested feature that he had killed a dragon; and so we will turn to the second surviving German source, which gave him a foundation for the first two acts of *Siegfried*.

The second 'German' source, *Thidriks saga af Bern* (The Saga of Dietrich von Bern) is actually in old Norse, but it is largely based on the German tradition, with only one important case of Scandinavian influence. It was compiled around 1260–70 in the Norwegian city of Bergen, from material believed to have been taken there by merchants from Northern Germany. Only the language is Scandinavian: the characters are heroes of German myth, more or less as they figure in the German sources. The chief one, who gave the saga its name, is another legendary transformation of a real-life Teutonic king: Thidrik of Bern, or Dietrich von Bern as he was called in German,[9] is Theodoric the Ostrogoth, who conquered Italy in 493 and ruled it almost until his death in 526. But Thidrik is only one of many heroes in the saga; it has a secondary title – *Vilkina- oc Niflunga-saga* – since it also deals at length with a mythical King Wilkinus and (what is important to us here) weaves in the whole material covered by the *Nibelungenlied*, plus a clear account of the earlier life of Siegfried.

We have seen how three early Germanic lays were the distant origin of the comprehensive epic of the *Nibelungenlied*. These lays dealt with self-contained episodes, unconnected with each other: they might be called 'How Siegfried killed the Dragon and won the Treasure', 'How Siegfried wooed Brünnhilde and met his Death',

---

[9] 'Bern', here, is not the name of the Swiss city, but a medieval Germanization of 'Verona'.

and 'The Fall of the Burgundians'. The *Nibelungenlied*, on the other hand, is more like a long verse novel, weaving all three separate episodes into a continuous, coherent whole. And this is what happened to the early Teutonic lays in general: connections were established between them, and they were eventually developed into long 'biographical' works. Sometimes, the resultant 'novel' – like *Thidriks saga*, which is a picaresque one – was written, not in poetry, but in prose. It seems likely that the material the North German merchants took to Bergen was itself already prose; but in any case, it had descended from the same early German lays that had led to the *Nibelungenlied* – though they had undergone a quite different kind of evolution.

In this case, the primitive heroic character of the lays had become transformed, not in the comparatively sophisticated romance fashion seen in the *Nibelungenlied*, but in a more naïve, still partly pagan way. It had been debased by developing through a Low German tradition, which was that of a people impressed less by character than by accounts of impossible feats of physical strength, and by the fantastic marvels of fairy-tales. Considered as a work of art, *Thidriks saga* is immeasurably inferior to the Austrian epic, and indeed, practically non-existent: it has no depth of characterization; it continually summarizes important events, sometimes with a startling baldness; and its narrative style is normally no more than merely adequate. Yet its pagan simplicity has its own kind of impressiveness, producing some remarkably vivid passages here and there. One such is the description of the crude, larger-than-life, even monstrous Siegfried,[10] taking a nine-days supply of food with him to make charcoal in the forest for Mime, and then killing the dragon. This may not be great art, but its bare fairy-tale primitivity is a refreshing change from the 'gallant knight' conception of Siegfried in the *Nibelungenlied*:

Now Siegfried went into the forest and got himself ready: he went about and hewed down strong trees, and made a great fire, and brought to it another strong trunk which he had just cut down. And then it was meal-time; and he set to, and ate for so long that all the food gave out, and he left not a drink of the wine that Mime had thought would last him for nine days. And now he said to himself: 'It would be hard for me to find a man with whom I could not fight, if the mood was on me, and I fancy no

[10] In *Thidriks saga* the characters are given Norse names – Sigurd, Gunnar, and so on; but since it is basically a German source, I shall use the German nomenclature, and, as with the *Nibelungenlied*, give the Wagnerian names wherever possible.

man's hand could overcome me!' And while he was saying this, there came a great dragon towards him. Then he spoke further: 'Now it can happen – I can put to the test exactly what I was just wishing'; and he sprang to the fire and grasped the largest tree which was blazing in the fire, and ran with it to the dragon and hit it on the head; and with one blow he struck the dragon down; and again he hit the dragon on the head, and the dragon fell to the earth; and now he struck again and again, until the dragon was dead. With that, he took his axe and hewed off the dragon's head. And now he sat down, and he was quite weary. It was now fully midday . . .[11]

Not all the striking episodes of the saga are concerned with crude and fantastic action, however. Some have a strong sense of passionate emotion, such as the passage corresponding to the moment in *The Twilight of the Gods* when Brünnhilde, confronted with the ring that Siegfried has taken from her, realizes how shamefully she has been abused:

And when Brünnhilde saw this ring, she recognized that it had once belonged to her, and it became clear in her heart how things had come to pass; and now it grieved her greatly that she had argued so much over the whole matter, and that so many people had heard, and that this story had come out in front of so many people, which before but few had known. And this made Brünnhilde so angry that her whole body turned as red as freshly-spilt blood . . .

Thidriks saga does in fact have one great advantage over the *Nibelungenlied*, considered as a source-book of Teutonic mythology: although written down some sixty years later, and mainly in the fairy-tale genre, it largely preserves a more primitive version of the material. In the first place, it retains far more faithfully the pagan atmosphere of the myth, with scarcely any infiltration of medieval chivalry, comedy, or Christianity. Although the characters are mostly kings, and the children of kings, there are no resplendent courts; no sumptuous clothes, jewels, or lavish gifts; no knights-errant, joustings, or scenes of courtly love; no comic athletic contests; and no cathedral services. The mythic figures move in a timeless world, and in this sense are quite free from 'later trappings'. Also certain events of the story are presented in their more primitive form – though this is partly counter-balanced by the case of Scandinavian influence mentioned above.

The story of Siegfried's later life (together with the second part of

[11] In quoting passages from the two Norse-language sagas, I have given my own English version of the German translation Wagner used; in this case, *Wilkina- und Niflunga-saga, oder Dietrich von Bern und die Nibelungen*, translated by Freidrich Heinrich von der Hagen, Breslau, 1814.

the material, following his death) presents to a large extent the same German version as the *Nibelungenlied*, and it had little to offer Wagner that he could not find in that far more richly-textured work. Moreover, it is here that the Scandinavian influence occurs, and instead of clarifying things, it throws one whole aspect of the story into confusion. This is the feature of a previous meeting between Siegfried and Brünnhilde, which, as we have seen, is absent from the *Nibelungenlied* and every other pure German source; it is woven in here from the Scandinavian tradition, but awkwardly, and without being given its true Scandinavian form. Brünnhilde, though mercifully not a comic Queen of Iceland, is not a Valkyrie either, but simply 'a woman', living in a castle; and at Siegfried's first encounter with her, there is no wall of fire, but only a body of castle guards, through whom he fights his way with a sword to reach her. Nor is there any love-scene, nor even, as the story is told at this point, any plighting of troth, but only a practical matter of his getting a horse. After spending a night in the castle, 'in great comfort', he rides away, 'thanking Brünnhilde for her great hospitality'. Later he goes to 'Nibelungenland' and marries King Gunther's sister, Grimhild;[12] no potion is necessary to make him forget Brünnhilde, since there is no special attachment between them.

Siegfried then tells Gunther about her, and presses him to marry her, as being 'before all women in the world in beauty and every virtue, and moreover surpassing all other women in wisdom and every kind of cleverness, manliness[!], and high gifts'; and he merely takes Gunther to her castle to arrange the marriage – no trial of strength or courage is involved. But bewilderingly, she now receives Siegfried 'very ill' – because, the first time they had come together (the story-teller suddenly informs us at this last moment), 'he had sworn to her with oaths that he would take no other woman but her, and she likewise that she would marry no other man'. Siegfried offers the excuse that he preferred to marry Gunther's sister because he and Gunther had sworn to be brothers; and Brünnhilde lets herself be talked into marrying Gunther.

After this incoherent interweaving of the Scandinavian tradition,

[12] 'Grimhild' is the Norse equivalent of the German 'Kriemhild', which is confusing for the Wagnerian, since Grimhild is Gunther's dead *mother* in *The Twilight of the Gods*. Wagner took the names from the pure Scandinavian sources, in which the mother is Grimhild, the daughter Gutrune (Gudrun).

the story continues with what is possibly the 'authentic' German version of Siegfried's 'wooing' of Brünnhilde for Gunther – the primitive bedroom-scene, which may have been bowdlerized in the *Nibelungenlied*, and was certainly made farcical there. As mentioned above, *Thidriks saga* introduces no trial of strength when Siegfried takes Gunther to Brünnhilde to arrange the marriage; this is left for the bridal night, which although exaggerated into four nights, is less ribald than barbaric. Brünnhilde, repulsing Gunther, reveals for the first time a tremendous strength, binding him and hanging him on the wall three consecutive nights. Siegfried, consulted by Gunther, declares that her strength resides in her virginity; and on the fourth night, at Gunther's request, he deflowers her by force – after which she is no stronger than any other woman. As in the *Nibelungenlied*, he takes a ring from her and later gives it to Grimhild, thereby causing all the trouble; but in this case he is guilty, not only of impersonation, assault, robbery, and betrayal, but of rape as well.

Neither this possibly 'authentic' German version of Siegfried's 'wooing' of Brünnhilde for Gunther, nor the confusion of German and Scandinavian traditions in the account of the Siegfried-Brünnhilde relationship, could help Wagner to put together a stageable drama out of the whole source-material. Nor could the subsequent treatment of Brünnhilde, since it corresponds with that in the *Nibelungenlied*: after Siegfried's death she fades from the story, leaving Grimhild as the great tragic heroine in the second part. Those events in *The Twilight of the Gods* which do coincide with events in the saga – such as the hunting-scene and Hagen's killing of Siegfried – are really taken from the much fuller version in the *Nibelungenlied*; and nearly all the events in both *Siegfried* and *The Twilight of the Gods* concerning the Siegfried-Brünnhilde relationship come not from the saga but from the three pure Scandinavian sources.

Apart from a few striking details, and an occasional feature which Wagner completely transformed to suit his own purpose, the saga provided only one important element for *The Twilight of the Gods*: Hagen's supernatural parentage, establishing his half-brother relationship to Gunther. In the other sources this character is a normal human being: in the *Nibelungenlied* Hagen is Gunther's liegeman and distant relative; in the three pure Scandinavian sources Hogni is Gunnar's full brother, who advises against killing Sigurd, and leaves it to another character who does have the half-brother relationship to Gunnar. But the Hagen of *Thidriks saga* not only figures as Siegfried's murderer, but is the son of Gunther's mother by an elf (a species of creature sometimes confused with dwarfs in Teutonic mythology). Whether this is an early German or later Scandinavian feature of the myth, scholars cannot agree; but it enabled Wagner to make his Hagen the son of his Alberich. Moreover, the saga offers a vivid description of Hagen's terrifying appearance which must have impressed Wagner; and his Hagen has always appeared like that on the stage.

The greatest value of the saga to Wagner, however, was its account of Sigurd's early life. In the *Nibelungenlied*, as we have seen, Siegfried's parents, Siegmund and Sieglinde, are still alive when he goes to Gunther's court; moreover, the only information about his previous life comes from Hagen – rather as in *The Twilight of the Gods*, but the information is largely different. He has killed a dragon, certainly, and won the 'Nibelung hoard'; but the hoard did not come from the dragon – it came from two brothers, 'mighty princes', whom he had killed, and whose army of seven hundred men he had overcome. *Thidriks saga*, though knowing nothing about the 'Nibelung hoard', tells another, fuller story, including certain features which are believed to preserve the original German myth. Siegfried's mother, although wrongly named Sisibe, dies almost immediately after giving birth to him in a forest; his father, Siegmund, is still living, but he promptly vanishes from the story, leaving Siegfried effectually an orphan who does not know who his parents are. He is brought up in the forest by a smith called Mime, and becomes so strong and unmanageable that Mime sends him to make charcoal near the lair of a dragon, hoping it will kill him.[13] But instead, Siegfried kills the dragon – and cooks it; and when he tastes the broth, he immediately understands the speech of two woodbirds, one of whom advises him to kill Mime. Having done this, he goes to Brünnhilde's castle; and although, as we have seen, the story becomes confused from here on, Brünnhilde does give him a horse called Grane (a feature contained in no other source).

Certain important elements differ from the version presented in the first two acts of *Siegfried*. Mime is a man, not a dwarf; there are

[13] The dragon is called Regin here; Wagner took the name Fafnir from the pure Scandinavian sources, and Germanized it as Fafner. Also the dragon is the brother of Siegfried's foster-father (as in the pure Scandinavian sources) – a point which Wagner altered.

no fragments of Siegmund's sword to be re-forged; Siegfried, as we have seen, kills the dragon with a blazing tree-trunk; and only after this is he given his first sword – by Mime. Also it is Mime, not the woodbird, who sends him to Brünnhilde, and for the sole purpose of getting Grane; most important of all, there is no treasure.[14] On all these points, Wagner followed the contrary account in the pure Scandinavian sources, which, as regards the existence of a treasure, are backed by the *Nibelungenlied* and the lesser German sources. Nevertheless, the main outline of the first two acts of *Siegfried*, as well as the name Mime and the whole mysterious atmosphere – the lonely forge in the forest – he took from *Thidriks saga*.

Further back than Siegfried's birth the saga does not go – except for an attempt to provide a history for his parents which is obviously mere idle romancing; and so, leaving the (equally Siegfried-bound) lesser German sources till later, we will pass straight on to the pure Scandinavian sources, which provided Wagner with the main basis of *The Valkyrie* and *The Rhinegold*.

The Scandinavians, like their fellow-Teutons the Germans, originally preserved their mythology in comparatively short lays, relating self-contained episodes unconnected with one another beyond dealing with the same mythic world and the same group of mythic characters. And some of their poems, unlike those of the Germans, have actually survived – in a collection compiled in Iceland some time between 1150 and 1250, which is known as the *Poetic Edda* (or *Verse Edda*, or *Elder Edda*).[15] As has been said, it was owing to the much later and smoother conversion to Christianity in Iceland (in 1000) that such a collection could be made at such a late date; and for the same reason, some of the poems (14 of them) are about the gods, in addition to those others (21 in all) which are about the heroes.

The first important contribution which this collection had to make to the text of *The Ring* was a fundamental stylistic one, since it alone preserved the original form of Teutonic poetry. It was here that Wagner found the successions of unrhymed lines with three or four stresses, hammering their points home by means of the

[14] Not in the story as told, that is. Later, we hear of 'the treasure that Siegfried won from the dragon' – another incoherent interweaving of the Scandinavian tradition.
[15] The title 'Edda' will be explained when we come to the *Prose Edda*, or *Younger Edda*, since the title of the present book derived its title from that one.

type of alliteration known in German as *Stabreim*, which suited his purpose perfectly. Furthermore, the poems present the characters speaking mythic poetic language, which offered him a far more stimulating model than the banal prose conversation of the sagas, or even the verse utterances of the figures in the *Nibelungenlied*. An example has already been given (p. 75), quoting the ecstatic words of the awakening Valkyrie in the *Ballad of Sigrdrifa*, which are on an incomparably higher level than her matter-of-fact greeting to Sigurd[16] in *Volsunga saga* (see p. 112).

Nevertheless, the *Poetic Edda* can hardly be regarded as a pure and undefiled well-spring of Scandinavian mythic poetry. In the first place, it seems that its Christian compiler did not properly understand the poems, since he indulged in a good deal of patchwork and interpolation. But in any case, although they show little or no sign of Christian influence, they do not date very far back, in the forms in which they are set down: only a few are believed to be as old as the ninth century, and a fair number of them – the best-preserved, of course – are thought to be little earlier than the time of the collection itself. They represent, almost certainly, the kind of poetry that came between the old short self-contained lays and the later epics and sagas that arose from combining and expanding them. In fact, we can actually see the combining tendency at work in this collection, since it contains some prose introduction, links and epilogues which supply missing information, and thus tie the separate poems, as far as possible, into larger wholes. Indeed, the next Scandinavian source we shall come to – the 'novel-type' *Volsunga saga* – is partly an expanded prose redaction of the relevant poems and prose-links in the *Poetic Edda*, with some of the actual verses quoted from them.

It should not be assumed that the poems do not contain materials which are ancient in themselves – though this is more likely to be true of those about the gods than of those about the heroes. The latter are mainly concerned with Siegfried's life and death, and with the subsequent fall of the Burgundians; and these stories, as we have seen, crystallized in Frankish and Burgundian lays as late as the fifth century. Exactly when these German lays (or

[16] In dealing with the pure Scandinavian sources I shall use the Norse names, which are not all that different from Wagner's German ones, with one exception. Siegfried becomes Sigurd; Siegmund, Sigmund; Brünnhilde, Brynhild; Gunther, Gunnar; Hagen, Hogni. Kriemhild, or Grimhild, becomes, fortunately, Gudrun; Mime, unfortunately, Regin.

poems descended from them) made their way to Scandinavia is unknown; but it must have been fairly soon, since the tradition presented in the Scandinavian sources shows a marked divergence from the German one preserved in *Thidriks saga* and the *Nibelungenlied*, which must have taken a long time to evolve. Which version is more faithful to the original lays? The question cannot be answered with certainty, of course; but scholars are generally agreed that while the Scandinavian one keeps here and there to the older tradition (it preserves, for example, the original motivations of Kriemhild and Etzel in the story of the fall of the Burgundians), the majority of its features, especially those concerning Brünnhilde and the part played by the gods in the story, are later accretions.[17]

The poems about the heroes in the *Poetic Edda* have no names, but the titles given them by scholars over the years indicate their nature. Some of them are the *Ballad of Regin* (i.e. of Mime), the *Ballad of Fafnir*, the *Ballad of Sigrdrifa* (i.e. of the 'Victory-Bringer', or the Valkyrie, or Brynhild), *Fragment of a Lay of Sigurd*, the *Short Lay of Sigurd*, three *Lays of Gudrun*, the *Lay of Attila*, and the *Ballad of Attila*: these, together with their prose-links, cover· the same ground as *Thidriks saga* and the *Nibelungenlied*. The part of them that was quite useless to Wagner was that concerned with Sigurd's betrayal and death: in this, Gunnar is the instigator, his brother Hogni (Hagen) is against it, and Sigurd is killed in bed by their half-brother Guttorm. The compiler of the *Poetic Edda* has an amusingly conscientious note about Sigurd in one of his prose-epilogues – 'But German men say that they killed him out of doors, in the forest'; and Wagner himself preferred the German tradition. Not simply because he was a 'German man', however: as regards the whole account of the Siegfried-Brünnhilde relationship, he rejected the confused German version entirely, and followed the Scandinavian one. This offered him the intelligible story he needed: how the Valkyrie Brynhild was punished by Odin (Wotan) for taking the wrong side in a warrior's combat, and doomed to sleep, encircled by fire, until awakened by a man who knew no fear; how Sigurd passed through the fire, awakened her, plighted troth with her, and gave her the ring he had won from the dragon; how he went to Gunnar's court, and was tricked by a magic potion into forgetting her and falling in love with Gunnar's sister, Gudrun; how he won Brynhild for Gunnar, passing through the

[17] See R. G. Finch, op. cit., Introduction, pp. xxi–xxx, which have been drawn on here.

fire again in Gunnar's shape, taking back the ring, and laying his sword between himself and her that night; and how she eventually immolated herself on his funeral pyre. Much of this is in the *Poetic Edda*, though the features of the ring and the potion are in *Volsunga saga*.

As regards Siegfried's earlier life, Wagner followed neither the German nor the Scandinavian tradition exclusively, but fused the two. As said earlier, he followed *Thidriks saga* for the whole atmosphere – the lonely forge in the forest – for the name of Mime, and for Siegfried's status as a rough, primitive, orphan-and-foundling hero. The Sigurd of Scandinavian tradition is no foundling, and no more than a semi-orphan: he is a royal prince, and his father King Sigmund having been killed, his mother (Hjordis) has married another king, and given Sigurd over to a chosen foster-father[18] at her new husband's court. On the other hand, this foster-father is still a smith, and – in the *Poetic Edda* and *Norna-Gests thattr* – he is a dwarf; indeed, the *Ballad of Regin* and the *Ballad of Fafnir* provided several features which Wagner needed to clothe the bare bones of the saga's account and knit them together. Here is the foster-father's lust for the dragon Fafnir's treasure; his concern that Sigurd shall get that treasure for him; the killing of Fafnir with a sword; the dialogue between the dying Fafnir and Sigurd; and all three of the woodbird instructions to Sigurd – not only to kill his treacherous foster-father, but to take Fafnir's treasure, and to go and awaken the sleeping Valkyrie.

Moving back beyond Siegfried's birth, Wagner was obliged to follow the Scandinavian tradition entirely, since it alone could tell him the history of Sigurd's parents and of the ring. As regards the former, however, the *Poetic Edda* contains very little information about Sigmund. There are no actual poems about him, but only one or two prose-links (which nevertheless establish the name of his mortal enemy as Hunding, and tell of his death – in battle with the sons of Hunding); as we shall see, it was in *Volsunga saga* that Wagner found a full history of Sigurd's parents. But the *Poetic Edda* does, in one of the prose-links in the *Ballad of Regin*, explain the origin of the ring. The story, narrated to Sigurd by his foster-father

---

[18] Called Regin in all the pure Scandinavian sources – the name of the dragon in *Thidriks saga*, where the foster-father is called Mime; a particularly awkward example of the confusing change of nomenclature from one source to another. But again the foster-father is the dragon's brother, as in all the Scandinavian sources – a point which Wagner altered.

to arouse his interest in the dragon's treasure, tells how Loki (Loge), wandering one day with Odin (Wotan) and another god, killed an otter, which unfortunately turned out to be a man in animal form. The man's family demanded blood-money, in gold, and Loki obtained it by robbing a dwarf called Andvari, who lived beneath a waterfall; the dwarf tried to keep back a certain ring and, on having it taken from him, said that to possess it would bring death. Odin and Loki paid the otter-man's family with the gold and the ring; one of them, Fafnir, promptly murdered another, to have the treasure all to himself, and later turned into a dragon to guard it. This myth is common to all three of the Scandinavian sources: it gave Wagner a part-basis for *The Rhinegold*, which he was able to build on, as we shall see, by using two further stories from one of them.

The gods have now entered the story, and indeed they figure almost exclusively in the fourteen poems of the first part of the *Poetic Edda*. As said earlier, these poems, in the forms in which they are preserved, include only a few which are thought to be even as old as the ninth century; even so, this means that these particular ones antedate the conversion to Christianity by some hundred-odd years, and in any case, all of them must contain material going back into the unknown past of the Teutonic peoples. To read them is to find oneself confronted by an entirely primitive mythic cosmogony, with its own version of the beginning and end of all things, and its own gods and goddesses. Here Wagner found much that he was looking for: not any actual stories of the gods that he could use (the one about the ring, summarized above, is of course from the second part of the collection), but the gods' characters, and their way of speaking and acting, which enabled him to put them on the stage as living figures. In *Loki's Wrangling*, for example, we find Loki taunting each of the other gods in turn, as Loge does in Scene 2 of *The Rhinegold*; the *Ballad of Vafthruthnir* shows Frigg at first intent on keeping Odin at home, and then fearful for his safe return, as with Fricka and Wotan in the same scene; and in the prose introduction to the *Ballad of Grimnir*, Frigg and Odin argue over the rights and wrongs of two warrior-rivals, as Fricka and Wotan argue about Siegmund and Hunding in Act 2 of *The Valkyrie*.

More than this, it was here that Wagner found the inspiration for the great mythic dialogues in *The Ring* – those between Wotan and Erda, Wotan and Mime, Wotan and Alberich, and Wotan and

Siegfried. Again, there were no actual poems that he could use as they stood, but he took some of them as models: the famous *Voluspo* (the Wise-Woman's Prophecy), in which Odin raises a prophetess from the dead, to learn of the end in store for the gods; the *Ballad of Vafthruthnir* and the *Ballad of Alvis*, in which Odin outwits a giant, and Thor (Donner) a dwarf, in a question-contest; and the *Ballad of Svipdag*, in which a Siegfried-like figure argues his way past a giant warder to reach a maiden in a flame-surrounded castle. The value of such poems can be judged from two verses of *Baldr's Dreams*, in which Odin rides to the world of the dead to summon a wise-woman from her grave, and question her about the fate of his favourite son, the god Baldr. This is the origin of the tremendous opening of Act 3 of *Siegfried*:

> Then Odin rode · to the eastern gate,
> where he knew well · was the wise-woman's grave.
> Charms he uttered · enchantments strong,
> till spell-bound she rose · and spoke from death:
>
> 'Who is the man · to me unknown,
> that disturbs my sleep · and destroys my peace?
> I was snowed on by snow · sodden with rain,
> and drenched with dew · I was dead for long.'[19]

What the *Poetic Edda* could not give Wagner was a fully coherent tying-together of the whole main story; but this could be found in our next source.

The famous *Volsunga saga* (Saga of the Volsungs) was compiled in Iceland some time between 1200 and 1270. Like *Thidriks saga*, it is

[19] All quotations from the *Poetic Edda* are my own versions, based on the various German translations which were available to Wagner. These are, in order of publication, Friedrich Heinrich von der Hagen: *Die Edda-Lieder von den Nibelungen*, Breslau, 1814; Jacob and Wilhelm Grimm: *Lieder der alten Edda*, Berlin, 1815; Friedrich Majer: *Mythologische Dichtungen und Lieder der Skandinavier*, Leipzig, 1818; Gustav Thormod Legis: *Edda: Die Stammmutter der Poesie und der Weisheit des Nordens*, Leipzig, 1829; J. L. Studach: *Sämund's Edda des Weisen*, Nuremberg, 1829; Ludwig Ettmüller: *Die Lieder der Edda von den Nibelungen*, Zurich, 1837; Karl Simrock: *Die Edda die ältere und jüngere*, Stuttgart, 1851. It is not certain how many of the German versions Wagner read: those by the Grimm brothers and Majer formed part of his Dresden library, but he could have studied any of the others in libraries, as with *Volsunga saga* – except Simrock (1851), of which he could have had a copy sent to him in Zurich. Moreover, when he was in Zurich he saw a great deal of Ettmüller, who could supply all his needs in this respect. Since not all the poems are in all the versions, I have used Simrock's complete translation as a main basis. In any case, all the German versions agree with one another in all important essentials, and with the two best English versions (Henry Adams Bellows: *The Poetic Edda*, New York, 1923; Paul B. Taylor and W. H. Auden: *The Elder Edda*, a selection, London, 1969).

an anonymous prose narrative; but it is quite independent of that work, apart from sharing with it a single chapter, which is a mere description of Sigurd's appearance and character, probably stemming from a common source which has not survived. As mentioned above, part of it is a prose conflation of some of the poems in the *Poetic Edda*, together with their prose-links: this part consists of twenty-eight chapters which recount the life and death of Sigurd and the fall of the 'Niflungs' (otherwise 'Nibelungs', i.e. Burgundians). These are followed by four chapters telling of further events which are of no interest to us here, and preceded by twelve chapters which give a full history of Sigurd's parents, beginning with the origins of the Volsung dynasty.

The saga's narrative style is no more polished than that of *Thidriks saga*, but the work is much more impressive, owing to its greater breadth and clarity, and its more detailed account of events. It shares the other saga's merit of preserving the primitive character of the myths, without any medievalization; in fact it is even more pagan, in that it shows the gods still walking the earth. Yet the whole atmosphere is different: whereas the German-based saga has all the mysterious timelessness of a collection of fairy tales, this pure Scandinavian one is more like an ancient realistic novel, told with a blunt matter-of-factness. As said earlier, we have only to compare the ecstatic words given to the awakening Valkyrie in the *Ballad of Sigrdrifa* in the *Poetic Edda* (quoted on page 75) with Brynhild's down-to-earth greeting to Sigurd in the saga:

> She asked: 'What was strong enough to cut through my coat of mail and thus disturb my sleep? Or is it Sigurd, the son of Sigmund, who has come here, bearing Fafnir's helmet in his hand, and Fafnir's bane?'[20]

Indeed, apart from one or two fantastic features in the Sigmund part of the story, the characters are largely presented as primitive royal warriors, and their women, going about their everyday lives. Even when the gods appear, it is usually to offer immediate practical advice – a naïve attitude towards the supernatural which is itself, of course, entirely primitive. A characteristic example is an episode in which Odin helps Sigurd to choose a horse:

[20] As with *Thidriks saga*, the extracts quoted are my own translations of Wagner's German source: *Volsunga saga oder Sigurd der Fafnirstodter und die Niflungen*, translated by Friedrich Heinrich von der Hagen, Breslau, 1815. 'Fafnir's helmet': Hildegrim (Helm of Terror), wherewith Fafnir terrified would-be assailants. 'Fafnir's bane': a poetical periphrasis for Sigurd's sword, which was the death of Fafnir.

   The next day Sigurd went into the forest, and met an old man he didn't know. He asked where Sigurd was going. 'We're going to cnoose a horse', he answered; 'come and help me'. The other said 'Let's go and drive the horses into the river they call Busiltjorn'. They drove the horses into the deep river, but none of them swam across to the shore, except one stallion: that was the one that Sigurd took. It was grey in colour, young in years, large of stature, and strong: no man had ever been on its back. The man with the beard said 'This stallion was sired by Sleipnir [Odin's own steed], and it must be carefully reared, for it's the best of horses'. With that the man vanished. Sigurd called the stallion Grani, and it was the best horse ever – given to him by Odin.

   As we have seen, Wagner preferred to follow *Thidriks saga* on this point, letting Siegfried be given Grane by Brünnhilde; nevertheless the episode, together with another of the same kind, gave him the idea of bringing Wotan continually into the action of *Siegfried*, disguised as the Wanderer. Moreover, *Volsunga saga* provided further details for the part of the plot we have been concerned with so far: it alone introduces the fragments of Sigmund's sword, preserved by his wife for her as-yet-unborn son; the foster-father's inability to forge a normal sword suitable for Sigurd's strength; the reforging of Sigmund's sword, and the killing of Fafnir with that sword; Sigurd's giving Brynhild the ring that came from the dwarf Andvari through the gods, and his taking it back from her; the magic potion whereby he forgets her and falls in love with Gudrun. The saga superimposes all these features on the account given in the *Poetic Edda* – from what source is not known, though one or two of the features are obviously taken from the pages of the *Fragment of a Lay of Sigurd* which are missing from the only surviving copy of the *Edda*.
   More than this, *Volsunga saga* was really Wagner's main source, in the sense that it alone offered him a continuous and coherent tying-together of most of the main episodes he used for the plot of *The Ring*. It not only covers the whole of Sigurd's life, in considerable detail, including the complete Sigurd-Brynhild relationship and the account of the origin of the ring, but it gives a full history of Sigurd's parents, and thus offered Wagner a basis for the first two acts of *The Valkyrie*. What materials the saga-writer had at his disposal, as a basis for these first twelve chapters, is completely unknown; but although obviously very ancient, they cannot have been German lays – or Scandinavian lays either, since this is clearly not a conflation of separate self-contained episodes, but a discursive, 'biographical' narrative. It is so discursive, in fact, that

Wagner was obliged to compress it drastically for dramatic purposes. There are generations between Odin (Wotan) and Sigmund's father Volsung (Wälse); Sigmund is one of Volsung's
eleven children, and has himself four children by three different
wives; and he engages in many battles before he dies, usually at
the head of an army. Yet the main events set forth in *The Valkyrie*
are all to be found in the saga, even if Wagner completely
transformed them. Taken in isolation, they are as follows: Sigmund has a twin sister, who is married to a chieftain against her
will; Odin appears at the wedding, disguised as an old man, and
drives a sword into the house-tree, as a gift for any man with the
strength to remove it; Sigmund draws the sword out; he mates
with his twin sister, who conceives a child by him; Odin shatters
Sigmund's sword with his spear, and Sigmund is killed; Sigmund's wife preserves the fragments of his sword for her as-yet-
unborn son, who is Sigurd.

It is some measure of Wagner's dramatic genius that, to anyone
who knows *The Valkyrie* but not *Volsunga saga*, the isolated events
set out above can only cohere into one clear and obvious pattern.
But to read *Volsunga saga* is to realize what a tremendous feat of
imagination was needed to single out these events only from a
plethora of material, and to compress them into that pattern.
Detailed examination of this feat of Wagner's must wait until later:
it is enough to say here that the crucial creative act was the fusion
of two of Sigmund's three wives – the first, his twin sister Signy,
who bears him a son called Sinfjotli, with the third, Hjordis, not a
relative, who bears Sigurd and preserves the sword-fragments for
him – and then to call this character by the name given to
Siegfried's mother-without-a-history in all the pure German
sources, that of Sieglinde. And one further Wagnerian feat of
compression should be mentioned before we leave *Volsunga saga*:
the fusion of one Agnar – the practically anonymous warrior whom
Brynhild supports against Odin's orders – with Siegmund, so as to
bind the myth of the Volsungs as tightly as possible to that of the
gods.

It will now be clear that *Volsunga saga*, supported by parts of the
Poetic Edda, *Thidriks saga*, and the *Nibelungenlied*, provided Wagner
with the whole material for the main plot of *The Ring*, except for a
significant form of the original trouble the gods brought upon
themselves. This he found in our next source, the *Prose Edda*,

which gave him a firm foundation for the action of *The Rhinegold*.

The *Prose Edda* is the only ancient source which is not anonymous, being the work of a prominent and well-documented Icelandic notability of the thirteenth century. This was Snorri Sturluson, who was born in 1178 of the turbulent family of the Sturlungs, and lived a full and adventurous life as landowner, chieftain, warrior, politician, judge, scholar, historian and poet, before he was assassinated by one of his sons-in-law in 1241. The title, 'Edda', is obscure, but is believed to be the old genitive form of the place-name Oddi – the great Icelandic centre of learning where Snorri studied in his youth – and thus to signify 'The Book of Oddi'; its date is not known for certain, but is thought to be around 1223. When the (actually nameless) *Poetic Edda* was eventually rediscovered, and was found to deal with the same material as Snorri's work, it was promptly given the same name (and misattributed to the famous Saemund, who had founded a school at Oddi); and it was called the *Poetic Edda*, or *Verse Edda*, or *Elder Edda*, while Snorri's work was called the *Prose Edda*, or *Younger Edda*.

It is generally agreed that by Snorri's time – some two centuries after the conversion of Iceland to Christianity – the old mythology was in danger of being forgotten, and that this is why he set down in his book as complete a compendium as possible of the myths of the Scandinavian gods. But the *Prose Edda* is anything but a piece of dry antiquarianism: Snorri was a literary artist, writing for the instruction of poets, so that they could continue to draw on the materials of the old myths (as the medieval Romance poets continued using the materials of the defunct Greek and Roman mythology). His work is in fact the only one of the ancient sources which is the product of a sophisticated mind and a conscious stylist (apart from the *Nibelungenlied*, in its rather more awkward way). This can be seen by comparing its account of Loki's robbing of the dwarf Andvari's treasure with that in *Volsunga saga*. The saga deals with the matter quite bluntly:

> Loki saw now all the gold that Andvari had. And when the latter had brought forth the gold, he kept back a ring; but Loki took even that from him. The dwarf went back into the rock and said that to possess it, or any of the gold, would bring death. The gods handed over the gold [to the father of the otter-man] . . .

This is simply a factual précis of a prose-link and a single verse of the *Ballad of Regin* in the *Poetic Edda*. Whether this was also Snorri's source is not known, but his account of the incident has far more style and significant detail, and was therefore much more useful to Wagner:

Loki . . . demanded from him, as ransom, all the gold that he had in his rock; and when they went into the rock, the dwarf produced all the gold he had, and it was very much wealth. Then the dwarf hid under his hand a little gold ring; Loki saw this, and ordered him to hand the ring over. The dwarf begged him not to take the ring from him, since with that ring, if he kept it, he could increase his gold. But Loki said that he should not have a penny left; he took the ring from him and went out. Then the dwarf said that the ring should cost anyone who possessed it his life. Loki answered that he accepted this and it should be as he prophesied: he himself would make it known to the future possessors of the ring. Then he went back . . . and showed Odin the gold; and when Odin saw the ring, it seemed beautiful to him, and he took it from the treasure . . .[21]

This account occurs in the second part of Snorri's book, a technical section for contemporary 'skalds', or bards, dealing with their 'kennings', or poetic periphrases for simple objects. The point here is to explain why a common 'kenning' for 'gold' is 'Otter's Blood-Money' (rather as one would have to recount a famous Greek myth to explain why a man's fatal weakness can be called his 'Achilles heel'). Snorri goes on from here to tell the whole story of Sigurd and the fall of the 'Niflungs', so as to explain what happened to the gold and the ring, and how they did in fact become the ruin of everyone who possessed them. But his account is uncharacteristically cursory: it offered Wagner little or nothing he could not find in other sources, nor is there anything about Sigurd's parents. The truth is that Snorri was less interested in the myths of the heroes than in those of the gods, which he dealt with fully in the first part of his book (and further in the second as well).

---

[21] As with the *Poetic Edda*, all quotations from the *Prose Edda* are my own versions, based on the German translations available to Wagner. These are, in order of publication: Christian Friedrich Rühs: *Die Edda, nebst einer Einleitung über nordische Poesie und Mythologie*, Berlin, 1812; Friedrich Majer: *Mythologische Dichtungen und Lieder der Skandinavier*, Leipzig, 1818; Karl Simrock: *Die Edda die ältere und jüngere*, Stuttgart, 1851. Again, it is not certain how many of the German versions Wagner read: those by Rühs and Majer formed part of his Dresden library, but he could have had a copy of Simrock (1851) sent to him in Zurich. So again, I have used Simrock as a main basis, since it is the fullest and the most accurate. There is one exception – the myth of the loss of the golden apples, which, surprisingly, he omitted: here I have used the version of Rühs, which is fuller than that of Majer (see pp. 189–93). Otherwise, the German versions again agree with one another in all important essentials, and with the two best English versions (Arthur Gilchrist Brodeur: *The Prose Edda*, New York and London, 1916; Jean Isobel Young: *The Prose Edda of Snorri Sturluson*, Cambridge, 1954).

This first part is in fact the only coherent and comprehensive account of the Scandinavian gods in existence. It sets out in schematic form the whole world which is presented more episodically and allusively in the *Poetic Edda*; if it had not survived, our knowledge of this world would have been tantalizingly fragmentary. Here, plain and clear, is the one-eyed Odin (Wotan) with his spear and his fortress Valholl (Valhalla) – ruler of all things, god of battle and victory, wanderer over the earth. Here too are his wife, Frigg (Fricka), goddess of marriage; Freyja (Freia), goddess of love; and her brother Frey (Froh), the bright shining god; Thor (Donner), the thunder-god and scourge of giants, with his mighty hammer; Loki (Loge), the cunning trickster, perpetually getting the gods into trouble and out of it again; and several other gods as well. Here also are the Nornir (Norns) who determine the fates of men at the well of wisdom by the world-ash-tree; the Valkyrjar (Valkyries) who fight alongside heroes and choose the slain for Valholl; the Jotnar (giants) who continually strive to bring the gods down; the Dvergar (dwarfs) who fashion magic rings, caps, armour and weapons; and the myth of Ragnarok – the end of the gods foredoomed by fate. It was due to Snorri's book (taken in conjunction with Jacob Grimm's partial reconstruction of the German forms and names of the various mythical figures in his *Deutsche Mythologie*) that Wagner was able to build up convincingly the whole coherent cosmos of *The Ring*.

And it was indispensable to him on another count. If he could never have created *The Valkyrie* without *Volsunga saga*, he would have been at a complete loss over *The Rhinegold* without the *Prose Edda*. The incident of the killing of the otter-man, in all three Scandinavian sources, was clearly useless to him as it stood, since, considered as the initial crime of the gods from which everything else followed, it was both insignificant (being a mistake and not a crime) and unstageworthy. But the *Prose Edda*, and that work alone, contained two other myths which could provide a profoundly significant and eminently stageworthy form of the gods' primal fault. These were the promise to give Freyja as a wage for the building of a fortress, and the loss of the golden apples of immortality. By fusing the two, and dovetailing the result on to the incident of the robbing of the dwarf Andvari's treasure to pay a ransom, the whole main plot of *The Ring* was made complete.

The *Prose Edda* was not Snorri's only book. Among the others is one (confidently attributed to him) called *Heimskringla*, an exhaustive history of the kings of Norway. Wagner actually listed this among his sources; but all it offers, from the mythological point of view, is a little information about Odin and Frey, and this adds nothing to what can be found in the *Prose Edda*. However, it gives a hint as to the way that Wagner approached the whole material, since these gods figure here in a *historical and social* context, being introduced at the beginning as the first kings of Norway i.e., as *rulers of a whole people*.

The above statement that the two myths in the *Prose Edda* made the main plot of *The Ring* complete is not quite true, since, as will have been noticed, we have not yet accounted for Alberich. There is in the Scandinavian sources, of course, the dwarf from whom the ring and the gold were stolen by Loki; but his name is always given as Andvari, and he plays no further part in the story. There is also the elf in *Thidriks saga* who is the father of Hagen, but he has no name at all, unless we accept the view of scholars that it should be Aldrian (the name of Hagen's normal human father in the *Nibelungenlied*, which the saga, obviously in error, gives as the name of the father of Gunther). Again, this elf plays no other part in the story; and nowhere, in fact, in the whole material, does an Alberich appear doing any of the actual things he does in *The Ring*. Here we have to turn to the lesser German sources, postponed from earlier, since it was by sifting and interpreting the tangled mass of material they offered that Wagner was able to create the character he needed.

First, however, we must return to the *Nibelungenlied*, which is the only source to contain a character called Alberich as part of the story of Siegfried. As said earlier, the only information that work gives about Siegfried's earlier life is put into the mouth of Hagen, on his arrival at Gunther's court; and according to this, the treasure he won came not from the dragon, but from two brothers, 'mighty princes'. The story, vague and confused, is as follows. Siegfried once came to a mountain in 'Nibelungland', and found a whole army of men surrounding a great treasure, including much gold, which had belonged to a certain King Nibelung, and which they had brought out of a cave. They were sharing it out amongst themselves, and in charge of the operation were the two sons of King Nibelung, one likewise called Nibelung, the other Schilbung; finding some difficulty in dividing it fairly, they appealed to Siegfried, whom they recognized, offering him King Nibelung's sword, Balmung, in payment. He tried to help them, but tempers became frayed, and a fight began; eventually it ended with Siegfried killing the two princes with the sword, together with twelve giant retainers, and subduing their large army. The only real trouble he had was with the princes' ferocious steward, Alberich, who tried to avenge his masters; but Siegfried overcame him, won from him a 'cloak of invisibility' and took possession of the whole Nibelung treasure (*Hort der Niblunge*). He had it carried back into the cave, putting Alberich in charge of it; and the whole Nibelung host agreed to serve Siegfried as a private army.

We actually see this at work later in the poem: when Siegfried and Gunther go to Iceland to woo Brünnhilde, they take only Hagen and a few men; but fearing treachery, Siegfried goes and collects his Nibelung army, having to fight Alberich again before he can do so. Again, when Gunther and Hagen appropriate the Nibelung treasure after Siegfried's death, they have to send eight thousand men to make sure that Alberich and the Nibelung army hand it over. All this, no doubt, helps to explain the confusing fact that in the German sources the Burgundians themselves eventually became known as 'the Nibelungs' – because they came into possession of the Nibelung treasure; but the point that matters here is that the name goes back to the original owners of that treasure, King Nibelung and his two sons. Who were they really supposed to be? It is here that the lesser German sources offer a powerful clue.

Following the *Nibelungenlied*, a number of shorter German epics were written – naïve phantasmagoric affairs, with scarcely any literary merit at all, but containing, nevertheless, certain features which are believed to be more faithful to the original material. The last to appear, and the crudest, was *Das Lied vom hürnen Seyfrid* (The Song of the Horny Siegfried): it was printed as late as the sixteenth century, but is clearly a clumsy patchwork put together from earlier poems, which have not survived, and whose dates of origin are unspecifiable. Some idea of its character can be gained from the verse describing Siegfried's goings-on in the forge (the Mime-figure here is not a foster-father, but simply a master-smith, and is given no name). This Siegfried, incidentally, is the same larger-than-life and even monstrous character as the one in *Thidriks saga* (see p. 101):

> Das eysen schlůg er entzwey
> Den Amposs in die erdt
> Wenn man jn darumb straffet
> So nam er auff keyn leer
> Er schlůg den knecht und meyster
> Und trib sie wider und fůr
> Nun dacht der meyster offte
> Wie er seyn ledig wur.

Or, in a comparably crude English rendering:[22]

> He smashed the iron in pieces,
> The anvil through the floor;
> And when they blamed him for it,
> He didn't give a straw.
> He chased them, man and master,
> And smote them head and limb;
> The master fell to thinking
> How to be rid of him.

The work is confused in the extreme, since the poems it drew on told conflicting stories. For example, although it confirms the names of Siegfried's parents as Siegmund and Sieglinde, it first of all presents Siegmund as the still-living King of the Netherlands, as in the *Nibelungenlied*, from whose court Siegfried sets out in search of adventure; but later it reintroduces Siegfried as an orphan who does not know who his parents are. Again, it confirms that Siegfried was trained by a smith, killed a dragon, and made himself nearly invulnerable with its horn; but later it has him kill another dragon, and a giant as well, to rescue a maiden who is none other than Kriemhild, the sister of Gunther.

Yet in spite of its confusions and contradictions, it throws a clear light on the identity of the Nibelungs. It tells how Siegfried comes to a mountain in which three brothers have hidden their treasure: they are dwarf-kings, sons of the dead King Nibelung, and the only one who is named (Eugel) is said to be far richer than any human king. He is coerced by Siegfried into helping him, which he does by covering him with a 'cloak of invisibility' when he is in danger of being killed by the giant; and the giant, after being overcome by Siegfried, shows him a sword which is the only one that can kill the dragon.

There are obvious points of resemblance between this account and the one in the *Nibelungenlied*, and the latter work provides another, not yet mentioned: Alberich is described there as *das starke*

22 My own.

getwerc and *ein wildes getwerc* – that is, 'a strong and savage dwarf'. It seems most likely that, in the original material from which both accounts ultimately derive, King Nibelung and his sons were dwarfs; and that this feature was retained in the crude *Lied vom hürnen Seyfrid*, but refined in the courtly *Nibelungenlied*, by making the father simply a 'king', two of his sons 'mighty princes', and the third son a dwarf steward. This would mean that Alberich was at least a Nibelung dwarf-prince, with some claim to the Nibelung treasure; so we can see that Wagner was by no means unjustified, as some have accused him of being, in equating the 'Nibelungs' with dwarfs, and making Alberich the original owner of the 'Nibelung hoard'.

As regards this last point, he found some confirmation in another lesser German epic – one preserved in the *Heldenbuch* (the *Book of Heroes*), which, although printed in the fifteenth century, is partly thirteenth-century, and is anyway based on materials of unascertainable origin. The epics in this collection are mainly concerned with Dietrich von Bern and kindred figures; but the one in question – *König Otnit* (King Otnit) – is of Frankish origin, and seems to contain a disguised scrap of early Nibelung lore. Although it has nothing to do with Siegfried, Alberich appears in it (as Elberich), and calls himself *ein wilder Zwerg* (a savage dwarf); he also claims to be 'lord of many a valley and mountain', and he has a ring which makes him invisible. Moreover, in a prose introduction to the poem, printed as an appendix to one edition of the *Heldenbuch*, this character is described as *Küng Elberich der Zwerg* (King Alberich the dwarf), and is said to be the true father of King Otnit, whose mother he overcame by force while made invisible by the ring, which is itself defined as a *nebelkap* (a cloak of invisibility). Now since, in the *Nibelungenlied*, Alberich is a far more impressive character than the practically anonymous princes Nibelung and Schilbung, it would seem that he might well have been the original Nibelung dwarf-king of the mythology, possessed of the Nibelung hoard and a ring – a means of making himself invisible. It was this possibility that led Wagner to make him the dwarf-king in *The Ring*, with a ring and a Tarnhelm, and with a dwarf-brother who disputes possession of the treasure with him; and the account of the fathering of Otnit also helped to make possible the identification of Alberich with Aldrian, the elf-father of Hagen in *Thidriks saga*.[23]

---

[23] The name Aldrian is actually used as that of Gunther's father, but, it is believed, wrongly: see p. 124.

One further point may be mentioned, arising out of the complex of treasure, dwarf-prince, quarrelling brothers, giant, and dragon. All five elements are present in the *Nibelungenlied*: Siegfried wins the treasure by killing two quarrelling brother-princes and twelve giants, and by overcoming a dwarf; also, at some (other?) time, he kills a dragon. So likewise in the *Lied vom hürnen Seyfrid*, except that there is no quarrel: Siegfried wins a treasure belonging to three dwarf brother-princes, after killing a giant and a dragon. And the same elements are present, in a different way, in the Scandinavian tradition, except that the 'prince' element is lacking: Sigurd's foster-father is identified in the *Poetic Edda* and *Norna-Gests thattr* as a dwarf; in all the Scandinavian sources, as we have seen, the dragon Fafnir is his brother, and they have quarrelled over the treasure, Fafnir having taken possession of it; Fafnir, although not actually a giant, is described in *Volsunga saga* as 'the biggest and fiercest' of the two brothers; finally, Sigurd wins the treasure by killing the dragon (giant?), and afterwards kills his (dwarf) foster-father. Exactly what original single story these various versions stem from, it is impossible to say, but in Act 2 of *Siegfried* Wagner ingeniously reconciles all five elements in his own individual way: Siegfried wins the treasure by killing the dragon, who is also a giant, while the two dwarfs, Alberich the Lord of the Nibelungs and his brother Mime, quarrel as to which of them shall eventually reclaim it.

In achieving this reconciliation, Wagner was clearly indebted both to the *Lied vom hürnen Seyfrid*, which indicated that the original owners of the treasure were Nibelung dwarfs, and to *König Otnit*, which identified Alberich as a dwarf-king. But threading his way through the contradictions of the German sources must have been a perplexing business, and he was greatly helped in this by our next source – a nineteenth-century one; this was *Die deutsche Heldensage* (The German Hero-Saga) by Wilhelm Grimm.

The Grimm brothers were outstanding among that group of German scholars who, during the first half of the nineteenth century, devoted their energies to recovering the pagan past of the German and other Teutonic peoples. This quest, which had received its impetus from the Romantic movement, got under way with a number of publications by Friedrich Heinrich von der Hagen: an edition of the relevant lays of the heroes from the *Poetic Edda* (in the original Icelandic) in 1812; a German translation of some of these and of *Thidriks saga*, plus Icelandic texts of the story of the origin of the ring from the *Prose Edda* and the whole of *Volsunga saga*, all in 1814; a translation of the latter in 1815; editions of the original texts of the *Nibelungenlied* (1816) and the *Heldenbuch* (1820), the latter including *König Otnit* and the *Lied vom hürnen Seyfrid*. 1815 had brought another translation of the hero-lays from the *Poetic Edda*, by the brothers Grimm; and the following year Karl Lachmann produced an important essay on the *Nibelungenlied*, which he followed with the first critical edition in 1826 and a textual commentary on it ten years later. In 1827 Carl Simrock published a modern German 'translation' of the work, and during the eighteen-forties issued a similar edition of the *Heldenbuch*, including *König Otnit* and the *Lied vom hürnen Seyfrid*. It was in 1829 that Wilhelm Grimm brought out his book on the German cycle of hero-legends, *Die deutsche Heldensage*; in 1835, Jacob Grimm's *Deutsche Mythologie* appeared; and a year later, Franz Josef Mone, who had published a critical edition of *König Otnit* in 1821, produced an analysis of the historical foundations of the legends, *Untersuchungen zur Geschichte der deutschen Heldensage*. Finally, in 1851, Simrock issued translations of both *Eddas*, parts of which works, in various translations, had appeared from 1812 onwards.

This was a formidable array of material, but Wagner read and absorbed all (or practically all) of it, before and during his period of work on the basic text of *The Ring*, which lasted from 1848 to 1853. And the work which helped him most to sort out the contradictions of the German sources, as said above, was Wilhelm Grimm's *Die deutsche Heldensage*.[24] This book was the first comprehensive attempt in a field of research which has since expanded to enormous proportions, and naturally many of its findings have been developed further, or thrown into doubt and discredit; but it was of great assistance to Wagner, whose artistic use of it is of course not invalidated by more recent scholarship. Its chief value was that it collated with the utmost thoroughness every known German and Scandinavian source, including several which were so little connected with the story of Siegfried that Wagner himself might probably not have bothered with them.

To take a minor point first, it established that the name of Siegfried's mother-without-a-history is given as Sieglinde, not only in the *Nibelungenlied* and the *Lied vom hürnen Seyfrid*, but also

---

[24] Göttingen, 1829; there is no English translation.

in the only two other German epics that mention her – *Dietrichs Flucht* and *Biterolf und Dietlieb*, both of which only touch on Siegfried in passing. Wagner may well have received encouragement from this to use the name, as against that of Sisibe in *Thidriks saga*, or those of Sigmund's two wives-*with*-a-history in *Volsunga saga* whom he actually fused to create Siegfried's mother in *The Ring* – Signy and Hjordis. From a more comprehensive point of view Grimm indicated the similarity between the complexes of treasure, dwarf-prince, quarrelling brothers, giant, and dragon, in the *Nibelungenlied*, the *Lied vom hürnen Seyfrid*, and the Scandinavian sources; and he also compared accounts in the other sources. He drew attention to a brief one in *Biterolf und Dietlieb*; to a longer one in *Thidriks saga* (which Wagner might have missed, since the complex is attached there, not to Siegfried, but to Dietrich von Bern); and to a similar one in another epic, *Ecken Ausfahrt*, where Dietrich receives a different kind of help from another dwarf, called Aldrian.

Concerning this last name, Grimm comments as follows:

> I have no doubt that the familiar Alberich should be understood here, who gives assistance to Dietrich, as to Otnit, and who, in this late and probably summarized account, has merely been introduced in the wrong context.

It was this kind of thinking, as much as any of Grimm's actual conclusions, that may have led Wagner to make his own more far-reaching fusions of diverse but rather similar characters. Since Grimm was prepared to equate Alberich with a dwarf named Aldrian in *Ecken Ausfahrt*, it was possible for Wagner to identify Alberich with the elf-father of Hagen in *Thidriks saga:* as we have seen, the name Aldrian is floating around in the saga, attached in error to the father of Gunther, since it is the name of Hagen's (normal human) father in the *Nibelungenlied*. And as we have also seen, in *König Otnit* Alberich does appear as an elf-father (of the title-character).

Moreover, it may have been Grimm's method that led Wagner to make his rash but artistically crucial identification of Alberich with that totally unconnected Scandinavian dwarf Andvari, who had his gold and his ring stolen from him by the gods – an identification which would hardly have been approved by the cautious Grimm, and would not be accepted by any modern scholar either. But in fact, this identification was made before Wagner by two less cautious scholars than Grimm, and Wagner could have taken the idea from either of them. Karl Lachmann,[25] the great editor of ancient classical and Middle High German texts, had made his own bold attempt to reconstruct the original 'authentic' form of the Siegfried myth, by collating the *Nibelungenlied* with the Scandinavian sources only, ignoring *Thidriks saga* and the *Lied vom hürnen Seyfrid*. Apart from his own individual identification of Alberich with Siegfried's foster-father (called Regin in the Scandinavian sources, it will be remembered), the beginning of Lachmann's reconstruction reads very much like the kind of preliminary process of fusion that must have gone on in Wagner's mind before he broached the text of *The Ring*:

> Siegfried, Siegmund's son, a Volsung with bright eyes and incredible strength, is brought up by a wise and cunning elf [*Alb*][1], called Regin (that is, Counsellor),[2] who has a human form, but that of a dwarf. He gives him a horse and forges him a sword, with which Siegfried splits an iron anvil:[3] he urges him to seek the Nibelung hoard and immeasurable gold. In the first place this gold had been stolen[4] by three gods, and brought up from the depths of the waters. Even to them its mysterious destructive power would certainly have brought death, had they not given it as blood-money for the murdered otter-man – and not only the gold . . . but also the ring that they at first wanted to keep . . .

> [1] Who therefore becomes king of the elves [*Alben*]: Alberich.
> [2] Regin is not a real name, but a purely allegorical one.
> [3] According to the German saga, the sword . . . belongs to the Nibelung hoard.
> [4] From the Nibelungs, I believe: the name of its keeper is purely allegorical, Andvari, *sedulitas* [carefulness].

The footnotes are Lachmann's own, and Nos. 1, 2, and 4 are of particular interest. They show that he dismissed the names of the dwarfs in the Scandinavian sources as being merely allegorical, and as confusing what seemed to him the true identity of Alberich with Siegfried's foster-father, and of the dwarf whom the gods robbed with a Nibelung – which on one interpretation would mean with Alberich again. Lachmann's is only one of many possible reconstructions of the fragmented material, and Wagner made a different one; but he could well have drawn the identification of Alberich with Andvari from Lachmann (not to mention the transformation of Andvari's waterfall into 'the depths of the waters' and the emphasis on the gods' wishing to keep the ring).

[25] *Kritik der Sage von den Nibelungen*, written in 1829, and published as an appendix to Lachmann's textual commentary on his edition of the *Nibelungenlied: Zu den Nibelungen und zur Klage: Anmerkungen*, Berlin, 1836. There is no English translation.

Yet the crucial Alberich-Andvari identification had been made more decisively, before Lachmann, by Friedrich Heinrich von der Hagen. In the introduction to his first edition of the original Icelandic text of the hero-lays in the *Poetic Edda*,[26] he had already made his own analysis of the complexes of treasure, dwarf-prince, quarrelling brothers, giant, and dragon, in all the sources, and had tried to reconstruct the original form of the myth. And in reference to this part of the material he said:

> The dwarfs are lacking at this stage [i.e. the stage where Siegfried kills the dragon] in the Nordic myth . . . they appear earlier, however, since Loki fetches the gold from the black dwarves and Andvari (Alberich, Eugel), so that here, as in the *Lied* [*vom hürnen Seyfrid*], they are the original possessors of the gold . . .

Was it here that Wagner found the idea of identifying Andvari with Alberich? Or in Lachmann? Or was he led to it independently by the method of Grimm? It is impossible to say now, as we do not know the order in which he read the various sources. But what is certain is that his wholesale manipulation of all the sources, whereby he created the dramatically coherent text of *The Ring*, was a supreme artistic feat beyond the powers of any of the scholars he studied. Even so, their writings must have been invaluable to him in clearing his mind and stimulating his imagination, and this is especially true of our final source – the even more far-reaching work on the German gods by Wilhelm Grimm's greater brother Jacob. What this book had to offer, Wagner could not find anywhere else, not even in his own fertile imagination.

Notwithstanding the extraordinary learning of Wilhelm Grimm, it would be hard to find a man of more enormous erudition than his brother Jacob, with his encyclopaedic knowledge of ancient European history, myth, legend, and folk-lore, of European languages old and new, of European religion and literature. The aim of his monumental *Deutsche Mythologie* (German Mythology)[27]

[26] *Lieder der älteren oder Sämundischen Edda*, herausgegeben zum erstenmal durch F. H. von der Hagen, Berlin, 1812.

[27] Göttingen, 1835; enlarged second edition, 1844. The only English translation is that by J. S. Stallybrass: *Teutonic Mythology*, London, 1883–8. Stallybrass used the word 'Teutonic' because the book, although primarily about German mythology, does cover the whole field. His translation has been re-issued as a Dover Edition paperback, New York, 1966; the last of the four volumes is made up of notes by Grimm which were not published until after his death (he died in 1863), and which were thus not available to Wagner.

was, in the words of his own introduction, 'to collect and set forth all that can now be known of German heathenism, and that exclusive of the complete system of Norse mythology'. To this end he tracked down every surviving trace of it he could find in old documents, historical, ecclesiastical, or legal; in old poems and sagas; in words of the various German dialects, old and new; in place-names, names of stars, plants, and days of the week; in Christian demonology; in curious superstitions and religious customs; in fairy-tales, proverbs, curses, riddles, games, and everyday idiomatic phrases.

By saying that his aim was 'exclusive of the complete system of Norse mythology', Grimm meant that he would take that system for granted, without trying to extend our knowledge of it any further; but he used it as a foundation on which to erect his reconstruction of the cognate German mythology – which in his own time was widely reckoned never to have existed. An idea of his method can be given by a brief abstraction of elements from his densely-packed chapter, 'Wuotan, Wôdan, Oðinn'. He establishes the German name itself, as found in little-known old writings, and gives various forms of it – Old High German *Wuotan*, Saxon *Wuodan* or *Wôdan*, Anglo-Saxon *Wôden*, plus several others. And these are then equated with the old Norse Oðinn – by the linguistic rule known as Grimm's Law, i.e. the law he himself had established, governing changes in vowels and consonants from one language to another. The German name he derives from the Old High German verb *watan* (to move, to go across, to be swept along), and he connects it with the old German noun *wuot* (modern German *Wut*), meaning fury; likewise, the name Oðinn he connects with the old Norse word öðr, which had, however, only the connotation of movement. Certain linguistic survivals of Wuotan's name are also adduced, such as the Upper German dialect word *Vut*, meaning an idol, or a false god (a submerged memory of the execration of Wuotan after the conversion to Christianity), and the Bavarian dialect verb *wueteln,* meaning to bestir oneself, to swarm, to grow luxuriantly, to thrive.

This connection of the god with restlessness and wildness is then confirmed by a hostile Christian reference, from the *History of the Church of Hamburg* by Adam of Bremen (c. 1075): 'Wôdan, id est furor' (Wôdan, that is to say frenzy). On the other hand, an ancient legend is quoted, again in Latin, from another Christian source – the *History of the Lombards* (c. 787) by Paulus Diaconus – which gives a clearer view of the god's nature. This 'ridiculous fable', as Paulus understandably calls it, tells how Wôdan was tricked by his wife Frea[28] into granting victory to a tribe called the Winniles, although he himself favoured the Vandals. She told the Winniles to come to Wôdan at sunrise, bringing their women, with their long hair hanging down in front of their faces; and she turned Wôdan's bed to face the east – the direction from which they would be coming. When he woke up, he looked down through a window, and seeing them some way off, asked 'Who are these long-beards?' – and by an old custom, having thus given them a name, he had to grant them victory.

Grimm was less interested in the fanciful derivation of the name 'Lombard' from 'Long-beard' (Longo bardo) than in two features which connected Wôdan with the Scandinavian god Oðinn. In the first place he is represented as the dispenser of victory, just as Oðinn is called *Sigföðr* (German *Siegvater*, i.e. father of victory). Secondly, he is pictured sitting on high, looking down on the world, as Oðinn was said to sit in the sky, on his famous throne Hliðskialf, and hear all that went on among men. Grimm then adduces similar ideas from other mythologies: he quotes an old French saying about the Lord 'qui haut siet et de loing mire' (who sits on high and looks afar), refers to the ancient Greek Zeus enthroned on Mount Ida, and even brings in a widely-known German fairy-tale about the peasant who was let into heaven by Saint Peter, climbed into the Lord's chair, looked down, saw a thief at work, and hurled the Lord's footstool down at him.

There is a vast amount more about Wuotan-Wôdan-Wôden in this chapter, of course – he is even pursued through Woodnes-borough in Kent and Wednesbury in Staffordshire amongst other places; but this brief abstract will be sufficient to indicate the scope and thoroughness of Grimm's method, which he applied to all the other gods – and to giants, dwarfs, norns and valkyries as well, not to mention innumerable other supernatural figures of myth, legend and folk-lore. His insistence on leaving no stone unturned, together with his habit of quoting at length in Latin or old Norse without translating, leads him into tedium at times and endearing comicality at others; but this is, after all, a specialist work – indeed, the great foundation of all subsequent research in the field. It is nevertheless fascinating for the interested layman to skip through; and it must have been a godsend to Wagner.

[28] This is Fricka, not Freia: the two names became linguistically confused.

In working through the ancient sources, he had traced the perplexing way back from the German heroes of the *Nibelungenlied* to the Scandinavian gods of the two *Eddas* and *Volsunga saga*. It was clearly impossible for a stage-work to move from one world to another – from Odin to Siegfried, from Loki to Gunther and Hagen; but if the gods had once existed in Germany, all trace of them had apparently vanished. Luckily, Jacob Grimm stepped in and largely proved otherwise, thus enabling Wagner to make *The Ring* a homogeneous German whole. As can be seen, the points summarized above established the identity of a very real German equivalent of the Odin of the *Eddas*. Furthermore, one of them indicated contention between this god and his wife as to the granting of victory, comparable with the similar scene[29] between Odin and Frigg in the prose introduction to the *Ballad of Grimnir* in the *Poetic Edda* (a connection Grimm did not fail to point out), and thus provided a firm basis for the scene between Wotan and Fricka in Act 2 of *The Valkyrie*.

However, Grimm by no means provided everything that Wagner needed. He could find no evidence, for example, that Wuotan-Wôdan-Wôden possessed the striking personal characteristics of the Scandinavian Odin – his spear, his lack of an eye, his ravens, and his habit of wandering the earth disguised as a graybeard, in a hat and cloak. And as regards the other gods – except for the case of Wôdan's wife mentioned above – he could do little more than show that some of them had existed in Germany, and to establish, or sometimes conjecture, their names. Of Loki he could find no trace at all in Germany, and the name 'Erda' is simply the Old High German feminine noun for 'earth' (modern German, *Erde*). Here Grimm postulated an earth-goddess not known to have existed in Germany, except for a tantalizing reference in the *Germania* of Tacitus to the worship by certain first-century Teutonic tribes of 'Nerthus' or 'terra mater' (Mother Earth) – a name relatable to that of the Scandinavian earth-goddess, Jord, which is also the word for 'earth'.

But as with Wilhelm Grimm's book, it was not only the author's findings that influenced Wagner, but his method and his mass of suggestive detail. In all cases, Wagner boldly assumed total equivalence of the German gods with the Scandinavian ones (and even postulated an equivalent of Loki which Grimm had not

[29] See p. 150.

proven). In certain cases – notably that of the characteristics of Odin given above – later research, following Grimm, has justified Wagner's temerity;[30] but more often, such posthumous support has not been forthcoming. *The Rhinegold* – and *The Valkyrie* too, for that matter – remains a dramatization of Scandinavian myths, with the figures given German names, and, in the cases of Wotan and Fricka only, a certain German actuality. Yet there is still the influence of Grimm's suggestive detail, which confers an unmistakably German atmosphere on the whole. The equating of Freia at one point with the firmly-established German goddess Holda ('Freia, die Holde, Holda, die Freie'); the 'wish-maidens' (Wunschmädchen) mentioned by Brünnhilde as serving the heroes in Valhalla; the 'furious host' ('das wütende Heer' – i.e. 'Wuotans Heer') that Siegmund says has been hunting him; – evocative mythic elements like these are essentially German, and they were inspired by Grimm's book.

One final point, before we leave *Deutsche Mythologie*. Wagner did not take over the German names of the gods slavishly from Grimm – as will have been noticed in the case of Wotan. Here he clung for a long time to the old Saxon name established by Grimm – 'Wodan' – which appears in all his sketches; only very late did he decide on the more incisive form 'Wotan', which is not given by Grimm at all, being simply a modernization of the Old High German form, 'Wuotan'. Likewise, Fricka, Donner, and Froh are modernizations of Grimm's Frikka, Donar, and Frô; and whereas Grimm postulated 'Frouwa' for the Scandinavian 'Freyja', for reasons to do with the origins of the German word *Frau*, Wagner (perhaps not caring to see the love-goddess in the light of a *Frau*) preferred to take over the Scandinavian name itself, and simplify it as 'Freia'.[31] For Loki, Wagner took the Scandinavian name of what Grimm believed to be Loki's elemental counterpart – the primeval fire-god Logi – and Germanized it as Loge, ignoring Grimm's postulated 'Locho' and 'Loho'; on the other hand, he found Grimm's postulation of 'Erda' for the German earth-goddess entirely to his satisfaction. Let us say at least that, however freely he drew on Grimm's nomenclature, he could not, without him, have even drawn up the *dramatis personae* of *The Ring*.

---

[30] See Brian Branston, op. cit., on the Anglo-Saxon Wôden; also H. R. Ellis Davidson, *Gods and Myths of Northern Europe* (Penguin Books, 1964), on the ancient German Wotan.

[31] The 'j' in the Norse name 'Freyja' is pronounced as an 'i'.

This brings us to the end of Wagner's sources. He himself also listed Franz Josef Mone's writings on the historical basis of the German hero-sagas, but these can have been no more than 'required background reading', since they contributed nothing concrete to the text of *The Ring* – even if, as with Snorri's *Heimskringla*, they indicate that Wagner's approach to the material was fundamentally from a historical and social point of view. Ernest Newman[32] tracked down three other, very minor sources – a *conte* by Alexandre Dumas *père* based on the Siegfried myth, the well-known fairy-story about the boy who could not learn what fear was, and a popular Faust play: these will be referred to later, at the appropriate points. One other 'source' suggested by Newman[33] cannot really be called a source at all – an essay *Vorschlag zu einer Oper* (Suggestion for an Opera) by Friedrich Theodor Vischer, published in the second volume of his *Kritische Gänge* (Tübingen, 1844). Although it seems certain that Wagner read it, and was stimulated by its suggestion that the Nibelung myth should be made the basis of a German opera, just as the Greek myths had been made the basis of Greek tragedies, it offered him no assistance at all in drawing up the text of *The Ring*. The scenario with which Vischer ended his essay was for a five-act grand opera based exclusively on the *Nibelungenlied*, to be given on two consecutive evenings – the first presenting the life and death of Siegfried, beginning from his arrival at Gunther's court, the second dealing with Kriemhild's vengeance on her brothers. As Newman himself said, it bears little relation to *The Ring*, or even to *The Twilight of the Gods*, and as we have seen, Wagner himself said that it had never occurred to him to make an opera out of the Siegfried myth while he still only knew it from the *Nibelungenlied*.

To make a symbolic music-drama with universal meaning, he had to fuse all the available versions of the myth. And now that we have a general idea of what each of his sources provided, we can begin our detailed examination of the way in which he adapted, manipulated, and transformed them, which will give us a clear understanding of the overt meaning he deliberately forced them to bear.

---

[32] *The Life of Richard Wagner*, Vol. II, 1937, pp. 32–3, 313ff, and 335.
[33] Op. cit., p. 30.

The Rhinegold

In assessing the various sources' contributions to the text of *The Ring*, we have largely moved backwards, from Siegfried's betrayal and death to the building of the gods' fortress. This was, for reasons which will have become obvious, the easiest way of treating the matter; but it is an old joke that Wagner himself wrote his text backwards, and then set it to music forwards.

It is, of course, essentially true. He began, in 1848-9, with the text of a single music-drama, *Siegfried's Death* (which eventually became *The Twilight of the Gods*). Then, finding this too overloaded with back-narration of earlier events, he decided to precede it with another music-drama, and in 1851 wrote the text of *The Young Siegfried* (which eventually became just *Siegfried*). Finding these two dramas still too overloaded with back-narration, he decided to precede them with yet another, and to add a further one as a prelude; and so he wrote the texts of *The Valkyrie* and *The Rhinegold*, completing both in 1852. Later that year, he revised *The Young Siegfried* and *Siegfried's Death*; and in 1853 he began composing the music. He completed *The Rhinegold* in 1854; *The Valkyrie* in 1856; Acts 1 and 2 of *Siegfried* in 1857; Act 3 (*Tristan* and *The Mastersingers* having intervened) in 1869; and *The Twilight of the Gods* in 1874.

However, this bald summary of the work's evolution overlooks one crucial fact. In building his text backwards from *Siegfried's Death*, Wagner was simply extrapolating a sequence of dramatic events which he had conceived from the start, and had set down succinctly before beginning the actual work. On 4 October 1848, four days before starting the text of *Siegfried's Death*, he wrote a prose résumé of the whole material, which he called *The Nibelung Myth as a Sketch for a Drama*, and it begins:

From the womb of night and death, a race was begotten that lives in Nibelheim (Nebelheim), i.e. in gloomy subterranean clefts and caves; they are called *Nibelungs;* with restless agility they burrow through the bowels of the earth, like worms in a dead body; they heat, smelt, and forge hard metals. The pure and noble Rhinegold was seized by Alberich, abducted from the water's depths, and forged with the most cunning art into a ring, which gave him absolute power over his whole race, the Nibelungs; so he became their lord, forced them to work from then on for him alone, and amassed the immeasurable Nibelung hoard, whose most important treasure was the Tarnhelm, conferring the power to take on any shape – a work that Alberich forced his own brother, Regin (Mime – Eugel) to forge. Thus equipped, Alberich strove for mastery of the world, and everything in it.

If this beginning lacks the Rhinemaidens, Alberich's unsuccessful wooing of them, and his renunciation of love, it nevertheless prefigures Scene 1 and part of Scene 3 of *The Rhinegold*; and prefigurations of the remaining scenes and acts of the whole tetralogy follow (all with similar deficiencies), culminating in a much more detailed scenario for *Siegfried's Death*. So the whole main plot was there from the start; but Wagner, working on the hitherto immutable principle of a single opera, mistakenly imagined he could plunge *in medias res* as late as Siegfried's arrival at Gunther's court – a procedure which actually involved an intolerable amount of back-narration, as he soon realized.

In view of this, our investigation of the way Wagner adapted his sources to produce his text will proceed forwards. Moreover, it will deal with the text as it stands, only touching on the stages it went through when this is necessary to clarify some particular point.[1]

---

[1] The fascinating story of the stage-by-stage evolution of the text of *The Ring* has already been told in *Richard Wagner: Skizzen und Entwürfe zur Ring-Dichtung*, edited by Otto Strobel, Munich, 1930. This contains all Wagner's prose-sketches, as well as the text of *The Young Siegfried*; the text of *Siegfried's Death* is in Wagner's *Gesammelte Schriften und Dichtungen*, Vol. 2. Strobel's book has not yet been translated into English, but there are summaries of the whole process, together with commentary and criticism, in two books by Ernest Newman: *The Life of Richard Wagner*, Vol. II, London, 1937; and *Wagner Nights*, London, 1949.

Scene 1

Turning to Scene 1 of *The Rhinegold*, our procedure will be (as throughout the whole tetralogy), first, to establish what elements Wagner drew from his sources, and then to examine how he manipulated these elements, and added to them, to confer on them an overt meaning of his own. In this first scene the task is easy enough, since it contains only eight elements: the Rhine; the Rhinemaidens; Alberich; his unsuccessful wooing of the maidens; the Rhinegold; its potentiality for being made into a ring conferring absolute world-power; the condition that this potentiality can be realized only by one who renounces love; and Alberich's theft of the gold. We have first to ask the mythology where Wagner found these elements.

And the mythology's answer, amazingly, is a dead silence. Nowhere, in any of the sources, does a dwarf, or any other creature, go into the Rhine, or any other river, and meet three water-nixies and woo them, with or without success, or discover gold that can be stolen and made into a ring conferring absolute world-power, by renouncing love, or by any other means, and then perform that feat. The Alberich of *The Rhinegold* is of course the dwarf Andvari of the Scandinavian sources, whose treasure is taken from him by the gods – but this does not happen until Scene 4; the gold is, in a sense, Andvari's treasure – but again, this treasure is not amassed until Scene 3. We face the extraordinary fact that this opening scene of the tetralogy, despite its profoundly mythic character, is Wagner's own invention.

The reason is that the story had to be provided with a beginning, which it lacks in all the sources. Naturally, in providing this beginning, Wagner made it as consonant as possible with the sources, by utilizing every hint they contained; and it is best to begin with the gold – or rather, with the Nibelung treasure, the central feature of the German mythology. The famous 'Nibelung hoard', mentioned so persistently in the German sources, must originally have had some tremendous significance for the heathen Franks; but by the time that the *Nibelungenlied* came to be written, its mythical origins had been completely forgotten. As we have seen (p. 93), according to a reasonable interpretation of the German sources, Siegfried won the treasure from some brothers, Nibelung dwarf-princes, who were quarrelling over it; or possibly from the Nibelung dwarf-king, Alberich. But where did they or he get it from? Wagner, finding no answer in the German sources, turned to the Scandinavian ones, with their different account of the treasure's origin. According to them, Sigurd won it from the dragon Fafnir, who had quarrelled with his brother after it had come into their hands from the gods, who had taken it by force from the dwarf Andvari – whom Wagner therefore boldly equated with Alberich. But where did *he* get it from? With no answer forthcoming anywhere, Wagner provided his own: Alberich amassed it himself, being enabled to do so by stealing pure natural gold from the Rhine.

Several factors determined Wagner's choice of the Rhine as the gold's original home. To begin with, when the gold first appears in the Scandinavian sources, in the possession of Andvari, this character is living under a waterfall in a river, in the form of a fish, with his gold nearby, in a cave. Moreover, in the *Ballad of Regin* in the *Poetic Edda*, Loki, when asking Andvari to surrender his gold, refers to it by the familiar 'kenning' (poetic periphrasis) of 'the water's flame' – derived from the myth that the sea-god, Aegir, illuminated his halls with the glitter of all the gold he possessed. So here, already, we have an intermediate watery origin for the gold, plus the idea that gold is indigenous to water. Andvari's (unnamed) river must of course have been a Scandinavian one; but since Wagner transferred Loki and the other Scandinavian gods to Germany, and equated the Scandinavian dwarf Andvari with the German dwarf-king Alberich, the obvious equivalent of that Scandinavian river was the German Rhine – especially since the whole story of Siegfried centres on the Rhine, in both the German and the Scandinavian sources.

Furthermore, in all the sources except *Thidriks saga*, the Rhine is the treasure's ultimate destination. In the *Poetic Edda*, the *Prose Edda*, *Volsunga saga*, and the *Nibelungenlied*, Gunther and Hagen, having appropriated Siegfried's treasure after his death, hide it in the depths of the Rhine before setting out for Etzel's kingdom; and in the *Lied vom hürnen Seyfrid*, Siegfried, immediately after winning the treasure, throws it into the Rhine himself, (having been forewarned by the dwarf Eugel that he will not live long to enjoy it), before going to Gunther's court. And since Wagner also, in his

quite different way, made the Rhine the gold's ultimate destination, it was only artistic logic to make it the gold's original home, so
that *The Ring* could move round in a perfect circle.

Jessie L. Weston[2] maintained that Wagner was mistaken – that
the treasure's original home was almost certainly not water, but
the earth: in the German sources, which after all claim priority as
regards the Nibelung hoard, it first appears when it emerges from
the Nibelung dwarfs' cave in a mountain. But in fact Wagner, as so
often, was clever enough to have it both ways: if he made water the
original home of the *gold*, adopting Scandinavian tradition, he
made the earth the original home of the *treasure*, following the
German one – since in Scene 3 of *The Rhinegold*, the treasure which
the Nibelungs make for Alberich is fashioned from gold found in
the earth.[3]

So two of the eight elements in Scene 1 of *The Rhinegold* – the
Rhine, as the original home of the gold, and the gold, as a natural
element from which the Nibelung treasure eventually results –
were created by Wagner out of only the faintest of hints in the
mythology. What of Alberich, and his theft of the gold? In an
episode in *Thidriks saga* having nothing to do with the plot of *The
Ring*, where Alberich[4] helps Dietrich von Bern to win a treasure, he
is described as 'the great thief', and again as 'the most notorious
thief and the most cunning of all the dwarfs': this no doubt
suggested to Wagner the idea of making him steal the Rhinegold.
Also, in a further episode, another character is seen, some distance
away, half-submerged in a stream, and is immediately (if mistakenly) identified by one of Dietrich's men as 'dwarf Alberich':
this indicates that Alberich was commonly thought of as being at
home in water. If Alberich, then, in Scenes 3 and 4 of *The
Rhinegold*, is the dwarf-king of German myth, acting out a Wagnerian pre-history partly based on what is related of the Scandinavian dwarf Andvari, his activities in Scene 1 are an extra bit of
pre-history invented by Wagner himself, building on the hint of
Alberich's (and Andvari's) connection with water, and on his
reputation as a notorious thief.

[2] Op. cit.

[3] See p. 207.

[4] In the original Icelandic, the name is given as 'Alpris' in one of the manuscript
sources, and in the other as 'Alfrigg'; the latter is an Icelandic form of 'Alberich' (*Albe*
being the German for 'elf', which in Norse is *alf*). Wagner had no need to work this
out, since in his German source – the translation of the saga by Friedrich Heinrich
von der Hagen – the name is rendered 'Albrich'.

The question might be raised here whether Wagner's Alberich is in fact a thief – whether he really does *steal* the Rhinegold. Wagner certainly saw it this way: in his prose sketches and letters, he used the word 'steal' (*rauben*); he introduced it frequently into the text; and indeed, one of his ideas for a title for *The Rhinegold* was *The Theft of the Rhinegold (Der Raub des Rheingoldes)*. Yet the condition is clearly stated, in Scene 1, that anyone who renounces love can take the gold and make from it a ring of absolute world-power; so Alberich, by renouncing love, would seem to be entitled to abduct the gold. This, however, is to take Wagner's symbolism too literally: what it signifies, surely, is that the gold can, like anything else, be stolen, but it would normally never occur to anyone to steal it; the only kind of individual who might do so would be one who (almost unthinkably) could dispense with love; unfortunately, there *was* such an individual – Alberich – and he stole the gold.

The whole importance of the gold in Wagner's work, of course, is its potentiality for being made into a ring conferring absolute world-power; and again, this element is absent from the mythology. In the Scandinavian sources, Andvari's treasure certainly includes a ring, and an aura of mysterious potency surrounds it in the *Prose Edda* (see quotation on p. 116). But its potency is clearly defined there, when Andvari tries to retain it in the first place: 'with that ring he could increase his gold'. Wagner actually took over this property of the ring: already in Scene 3 of *The Rhinegold*, Alberich begins increasing his gold with it. Moreover, he makes clear there that the whole essence of his bid for world-mastery will be his use of this wealth to corrupt the world's existing masters, the gods: 'You gods', he says vehemently to Wotan, 'lured by gold, shall hanker only for gold'. Thus the power of Wagner's ring is ultimately the power of the ring of the Scandinavian sources to multiply wealth; but in making this power an absolute dominion over the world, he added a crucial element of his own, which these sources do not contain.

Nor do the German sources contain it: any ring of this kind is entirely absent from the Nibelung hoard. A ring does appear in the *Nibelungenlied*, and in *Thidriks saga*, but it is a perfectly normal one belonging to Brünnhilde, which Siegfried takes from her after overpowering her in bed for Gunther, and later gives to his wife; once it has played its part in creating the scandal, it vanishes from the story. There is, however, in the *Nibelungenlied*, a different talisman of absolute world-power amongst the Nibelung hoard:

> The hoard's treasure lay there · a little rod of gold.
> He who knew its secret · the mastery would hold
> over all men living · in the whole wide world . . .

– but it is no mere quibble over shape to say that this rod is not Wagner's ring. It is mentioned once only – after Siegfried's death, when Gunther and Hagen fetch his treasure from 'Nibelung-Land' – and this mention is a mysterious aside of the poet's: not a single character in the poem knows of the rod's existence. No doubt it gave Wagner the idea of a talisman of absolute world-power; but in attaching this concept to the ring of the Scandinavian sources, he created a symbol entirely his own.

We have now established that Wagner invented five of the eight elements out of no more than the slightest of suggestions in the mythology: the Rhine, Alberich, the Rhinegold, Alberich's theft of the Rhinegold, and the ring. These are, in fact, the only five present in his original prose résumé of the whole material (see quotation on p. 132); and it is obvious that, in themselves, they could not provide sufficient dramatic content for this first scene of the tetralogy. To have made Alberich simply abduct the gold from an untenanted Rhine would have been a poor piece of drama; and so, from a purely practical point of view, something more was needed. What Wagner added, when he came to sketch the action of the scene, was three guardians of the gold (The Rhinemaidens), a condition on which the gold could be stolen (the renunciation of love), and a conflict between Alberich and the maidens (his unsuccessful wooing of them) resulting in his readiness to fulfil that condition. Being Wagner, he thus solved the practical problem by creating a central symbolic complex of the tetralogy; but where did he find this complex in the sources?

As regards the guardians of the gold, the presence of water-nixies in the Rhine seems so natural that it comes as even more of a surprise to realize that the mythology does not contain any Rhinemaidens at all. There is, of course, the famous Lorelei of German legend, but she stands alone, and is something quite different: she was supposed to have been a human girl who threw herself in the river out of disappointed love; she became a siren, luring fishermen to their death by so fascinating them with her singing that they forgot to steer their boats and ran on the rocks. We can only accept the conclusion of Jacob Grimm, who must have been disappointed to admit that 'a daemon of the Rhine is nowhere named in our native traditions'.

Yet Wagner was able to adapt an episode from one of the sources for his purpose: it appears in that part of the *Nibelungenlied* which has no connection with the story of *The Ring* – the second part, concerned with the events after Siegfried's death. Gunther and Hagen, on their way to Etzel's kingdom, reach the Danube; Hagen, searching for a ferryman, encounters some mermaids, who warn him that neither he nor Gunther, nor any of their warriors, will return from Etzel's land, but will meet their death there. The exact number of these mermaids is not clear in the poem: Hagen is first addressed by one called Hadburg, by another called Sieglinde(!) and finally by 'a mermaid', who could be one of the first two, or possibly a third. The latter seems most likely, since Hagen calls her 'the wisest of women'; but in any case, Wagner no doubt accepted Jacob Grimm's assumption that the mermaids were three in number.

It will be remembered that Wagner's first text was *Siegfried's Death*, which later became *The Twilight of the Gods;* and it was here that he first introduced these mermaids – into the opening scene of Act 3. He boldly transported them from the Danube to the Rhine, and brought them back in time to just *before* Siegfried's death. Giving them no individual names, but describing them collectively as 'Die drei Wasserjungfrauen' (the three Watermaids), he made them give their warning to Siegfried instead – that *he* would meet his death, through the curse on the ring (almost exactly as in the present *Twilight of the Gods*). Even here, however, with *The Rhinegold* not yet in existence, he made them lament the loss of the gold; and so, when he came to sketch the *Rhinegold* text, he projected the watermaids back into its first scene, as the gold's actual guardians. Now they became 'Die Rheintöchter' (the Rhinedaughters – Wagner's final name for them, which is, curiously, always rendered into English as 'the Rhinemaidens'); and they also acquired their individual names. Wagner rejected those in the *Nibelungenlied* (Hadburg probably as too unpoetic, Sieglinde for obvious reasons), and taking the basic feminine suffixes *linde, gunde,* and *hilde,* he invented names of his own: Woglinde (from *Woge*, billow) and Wellgunde (from *Welle,* wave) for the first two, and Flosshilde (from *Flosse,* fin) for the third (the 'wisest of women' – which is a possible description of Flosshilde, since she is at least the one most concerned to guard the gold carefully).

So this element too, though based on a suggestion in the mythology, is really Wagner's creation, since he gave the maidens the guardianship of the gold, which is their basic function in the tetralogy. It could be that the ultimate source of this idea lay outside Teutonic mythology altogether – in those three land-maidens of Greek myth, the Hesperides, who guarded the golden apples growing on a tree in an Arcadian garden. But this again would have been the merest hint, since the theft of the apples has no consequences comparable with those which follow that of the Rhinegold, and indeed, no clear consequence at all.

When we turn to the last two elements – Alberich's unsuccessful wooing of the Rhinemaidens, and his renunciation of love – we find that they are absolutely pure Wagner, with nothing even faintly suggestive of them in the mythology. It might perhaps be thought that somewhere – in some obscure piece of folk-lore that even Jacob Grimm had overlooked – there could be some hint which Wagner built on; but in fact we have evidence that this was not so. Obviously, he must have had difficulty in finding the symbolic foundation he needed for this opening scene; and two letters, written shortly after he had set down his first brief sketch of it, reveal that he had hit on the idea of the renunciation of love of his own accord, and regarded it as a major inspiration. In the first, to his friend Theodor Uhlig, dated 12 November 1851, he wrote:

> It begins with Alberich, who pursues the three water-women of the Rhine with his lust for love; is rejected by one after the other (laughing and fooling); and in his fury, eventually steals the Rhinegold from them. This gold is in itself only a glittering ornament of the water's depths . . . but another power resides in it, which can be drawn from it, however, only by *him who renounces love.*

Wagner's italics (or rather, his written underlining) tell their own story, and the same applies to the letter he wrote to Liszt eight days later:

> Alberich comes up out of the depths of the earth to the three daughters of the Rhine; he pursues them with his repugnant wooing . . . laughing and teasing, they all scorn the gnome. Then the Rhinegold begins to glitter; it fascinates Alberich; he asks what use it is. The maidens inform him that it serves them for pleasure and games . . . yet many marvels might be achieved with it – power and might, riches and domination – by him who knew how to force it into a ring; but only *he who renounces love* could understand how to do that!

Again the underlining, plus an exclamation mark this time. Wagner, evidently, was delighted at having created at last the ultimate symbolic foundation of his Nibelung tetralogy.

This is, of course, only the element of the renunciation of love; the other element – Alberich's unsuccessful wooing – is not emphasized at all. But it obviously follows from the other. For Alberich to have made a purely *formal* renunciation to the maidens would again have been poor drama: only after his wooing is rejected by all of them is he ready to take this terrible step – in order to make 'the revenging ring', as he himself says. The two elements are inseparable, and both were Wagner's own invention.

And here, issue must be taken with Robert Donington's treatment of the scene. As mentioned in Chapter 1, he says, referring to Alberich's renunciation of love:

> What Wagner, according to his published account of the matter, supposed Alberich to be renouncing by the act of forswearing love was that very principle of sympathy and compassion by which Wagner, by no means mistakenly, believed the world to be knit together.

No doubt the word 'supposed' here is meant in a psychological sense: although Wagner's conscious mind assumed Alberich's action to be simply a renunciation of that love which knits the world together, his unconscious was expressing something deeper as well – that something deeper being (according to Donington) that Alberich was renouncing 'escapist infantile fantasies' and in particular 'the fantasy of being mothered through life by one woman after another'. Even so, Donington does tend to interpret the original mythology rather than Wagner's re-creation of it; and the word 'supposed' carries the implication that Alberich's renunciation has an existence quite separate from Wagner and *The Ring*, as an autonomous symbol of myth or legend. But as we have seen, this is not so. Alberich's renunciation of love was Wagner's own deliberate artistic creation, and so it is hard to see how he can have 'supposed' anything about it at all. It was he who made it mean what it says it means; and he confirmed this meaning by making Alberich, throughout the rest of *The Ring*, a figure devoid of sympathy and compassion, motivated only by hatred and a consuming desire for revenge.

And it is the same with the ring. Donington asks us to take into account, as well as Wagner's clear presentation of it as a talisman of absolute world-power made out of revenge, the beneficent psychological connotations of the Jungian 'libido' (life-energy) and 'spread of consciousness' which are inseparable from gold; but we may wonder how this is possible, since that talisman is again

Wagner's own deliberate artistic creation. The ring of Andvari, in the Scandinavian mythology, has no coherent symbolic meaning at all; Wagner could have given it any meaning he pleased; but he actually chose to transfer to it the symbolism of absolute world-power attached to the obscure golden rod of the *Nibelungenlied*. The difficulty of accepting Donington's interpretation is perhaps best indicated by a question: if gold must always symbolize life-energy and the spread of consciousness, how can any artist ever make a golden object bear a quite contrary symbolism? It would be more logical of Donington to say that Wagner, in trying to make a golden ring symbolize world-power, was going against the inherent psychological function of the symbol established by Jung. As it is, it seems more realistic to interpret Wagner's symbols according to the unequivocal meanings he himself gave to them.

Summing up this first scene, it is clear that Wagner virtually created it out of his own imagination, and with it, the overt meaning it so manifestly bears. It says that absolute world-power can be achieved by ravishing and exploiting the raw material of nature, but such an action is possible only for one who has expelled love from his being; and in the present case, this drastic step is taken only as a means of revenge by one whose own search for love has been totally frustrated. This is the overt meaning which Wagner deliberately put into Scene 1 of *The Rhinegold*, and it has to be accepted as the inalienable basis of any interpretation which is aimed at elucidating the full symbolic significance of *The Ring*.

Scene 2: The Gods

Throughout the rest of the tetralogy, we shall have much better luck in tracing the various elements back to the sources. We shall still find Wagner adding features of his own; but more often we shall find him taking over elements from the mythology, either unchanged, or compressed through certain omissions, or fused with one another, or altered in some way. Nevertheless, the compressions, fusions, and alterations will themselves betray the overt meaning which he intended the material to bear.

In dealing with Scene 2 of *The Rhinegold*, it will be most convenient to consider the gods and goddesses themselves before turning to the action. They are quite simply most of the main gods and goddesses of Scandinavian mythology, each given a German habitation and a name (the latter usually adapted from Jacob Grimm):

Scandinavian	*Grimm*	*Wagner*
Odin	{ Wuotan Wôdan	Wotan
Frigg	Frikka	Fricka
Freyja	Frouwa	Freia
Frey	Frô	Froh
Thor	{ Donar Thunar	Donner
Loki and Logi	{ Loho Locho	Loge

Turning first to Wotan, his seven chief properties, in *The Ring*, are his status as chief of the gods, his knowing wife Fricka, his function as god of battle, his fortress Valhalla, his lack of an eye, his ravens, and his spear. Of these, six are taken over practically unchanged from the Scandinavian Odin, the first three being summed up in a brief passage in the *Prose Edda:*

Odin is the foremost and oldest of the Aesir [gods]. He rules over everything, and although the other gods are also mighty, they all serve him as children serve a father. His wife is Frigg; she knows all the fates of men . . . Odin is called Allfather, because he is the father of all the gods, and Father of the Slain, because all those who fall on the battlefield are his chosen sons . . .

(Wagner, as we shall see, dropped the idea of Wotan-Odin being the father of the gods – which in any case is not actually true in the mythology itself.)

Another passage speaks of Valhalla and its attendant Valkyries:

Valholl was roofed with shields . . . a hall so high that one could hardly see the top of it . . . All the men who have fallen in battle from the beginning of the world have come to Odin in Valholl . . . There are also maidens who serve in Valholl, who bring drink, and look after the table-service and the ale-vessels . . . they are called Valkyries. Odin sends them to every battle. They choose who shall be slain, and dispense victory . . .

(Wagner made Wotan rather more discriminating in his choice of the slain for Valhalla, since Hunding is not wanted there.)

Wagner's account of how Wotan lost an eye (told by the First Norn in *The Twilight of the Gods*) is based on a further passage:

The ash is the greatest and the best of all trees: its branches spread out over the whole world, and reach up to heaven . . . By that root that turns towards the Frost-Giants is the Well of Mimir, in which wisdom and understanding are hidden . . . Allfather came there once, and craved a drink from the well, but he did not get it until he gave his eye as a forfeit . . .

Here Wagner dropped the name Mimir (probably to avoid confusion with Mime) and identified the well as the one by which the three Norns dwelt, as pictured in the *Wise-Woman's Prophecy* in the *Poetic Edda:*

> I know an ash · called Yggdrasil,
> a great tree washed · with water white;
> down from it falls · the dew on the dales;
> by Urd's Well · it is ever green.
>
> Thence come the women · wisest of all,
> three from the hall · by the high-spreading tree:
> one is Urd · and one Verdandi,
> (they scored the bark) · Skuld is the third.
> By laws they determined · the length of lives,
> and set the fates · of the sons of men.

Wotan's two ravens – which he mentions to Siegfried in Act 3 of *Siegfried*, and which in Act 3 of *The Twilight of the Gods* fly off to tell him of Siegfried's death – are also properties of Odin, as recounted in the *Prose Edda:*

> Two ravens sit on his shoulders and tell in his ear all the tidings they hear and see; they are called Hugin [Thought] and Munin [Memory]. He sends them in the morning to fly through all the worlds, and they return at midday-meal, and so he is aware of many tidings. Men call him therefore the Raven-God . . .

So these first six properties of Wagner's Wotan are taken over practically unchanged from the Scandinavian Odin. But with the seventh and last, the famous spear, the situation changes. Odin certainly possessed a mighty spear, but the only time he is mentioned as using it (in another verse of the *Wise-Woman's Prophecy*) it features simply as a weapon of war – and indeed, as the weapon through which war first came into existence (between the Aesir – the race of gods headed by Wotan – and the Vanir, usually called in English the Vanes):

> At the host Odin   ·   hurled his spear,
> and the first war   ·   in the world broke out;
> the gods' bastions   ·   were beaten down,
> as the warlike Vanes   ·   invaded the field.

Historically speaking, Odin-Wotan was originally the battle-god of the ancient Teutons, Wodenaz, with all the gruesome characteristics which that implies; and his spear was his all-important property. The verse quoted above refers to the custom of the Norsemen whereby, at the beginning of a battle, the leader of the army would hurl a spear over the heads of the opposing host to 'dedicate them to Odin' – i.e. to death, Odin being the God of the Slain.

As regards the actual origin of Odin's spear, the only account is given in the *Prose Edda:*

> Thereupon Loki went to those dwarfs which are called the sons of Ivaldi. They made . . . Odin's spear, which is called Gungnir . . . Loki gave the spear Gungnir to Odin . . . and explained the property of this weapon, that it would never fail in its aim . . .

So again the spear features simply as a weapon.

Now Wagner changed all this, giving Wotan's spear an origin and function of his own invention. The origin is recounted by the First Norn in *The Twilight of the Gods:*

> *A bold god* [Wotan]
> *came for a drink from the spring;*
>   *one of his eyes*
> *he gave in perpetual payment.*
>   *From the World Ash-Tree*
> *Wotan then broke off a branch;*
>   *the shaft of a spear*
> *the strong one cut from the trunk.*

The spear's function is explained by the Second Norn:

> *Truly sworn*
> *treaty-runes*
> *Wotan cut*
> *in the spear's shaft;*
> *he held it as control of the world.*

Wotan himself confirms all this in his dialogue with Mime in Act 1 of *Siegfried* (speaking of himself in the third person):

> *From the World Ash-Tree's*
>   *holiest branch*
> *he cut himself a shaft . . .*
>   *With its point*
> *Wotan controls the world.*
>   *Holy treaties'*
>   *faithful runes*
> *he cut in the shaft.*
>   *Control of the world*
>   *holds in his hand*
>   *he who wields the spear*
> *that Wotan's fist grasps.*
>   *Before him bowed*
>   *the Nibelung army;*
>   *the race of giants*
>   *his counsel tamed.*
> *For ever they all obey*
> *the mighty Lord of the Spear.*

Thus Wagner altered the mythology drastically at this crucial point, to give the character of Wotan a quite different main motivation. He remains the god of battle, certainly, and he dominates the world with his spear; but the spear is not a mere invincible battle-weapon made by dwarfs. He made it himself from a branch of the Tree of Life, as a direct consequence of his drink from the Well of Wisdom, granted in exchange for one of his eyes; and he dominates the world with it, not as a weapon of war, but as *an instrument of law* (treaties, contracts), whereby he attempts to build up and control an ordered civilization of an authoritarian kind.

As so often, there are faint hints that Wagner made use of. In two dark verses of the *Ballad of the High One*, in the *Poetic Edda*, Odin himself describes a very different visit to the World Ash-Tree:

> Once I hung · on the wind-swept tree,
>   nine unending nights:
> gored with the spear · given to Odin,
>   myself offered to myself.
>
> No one brought me · bread or mead;
>   at last I looked below:
> I took up the runes · took them shrieking;
>   and from the tree I fell.

Behind these verses lies another grisly ritual belonging to the cult of the ancient Teutonic war-god: those captured in battle were 'offered to Odin' by being hanged from trees and pierced through with a spear. Odin was, amongst so many other things, God of the Hanged; but here, uniquely, he appears as the Self-Hanged, whose sacrifice won the runes – the characters of the first primitive Scandinavian writing, which were magic signs as well as the letters of an alphabet. Although Wagner preferred his 'bold god' simply to cut his spear from the tree, he drew from this myth Wotan's discovery of the runes as a result of his primal visit, even if he interpreted these runes as symbols of law, not of magic, and made Wotan actually engrave them on the spear.

As regards this last point, he was giving more concrete and intellectual form to the ancient Teutons' custom of swearing their oaths on weapons; and Wotan's building up of an ordered civilization has perhaps some slight connection with a myth in which Odin and his two brothers, Vili and Ve, actually created the world from the carcass of a giant they had killed, making from it the earth, the sea, the sky, the stars, the sun and moon. Yet the law-enforcing, civilizing aspect of Wotan remains Wagner's own creation. Perhaps this may seem a curious description of Wagner's brutal and hypocritical world-ruler, but we should remember that Wotan's first use of the spear is to enforce the latest contract engraved on it, and prevent the murder of the giants by Donner – which, after all, would have solved all his problems about Freia and Valhalla. His attempt to evade his own laws will not be overlooked, and neither will one other essential point: that the spear itself represents first and foremost Wotan's sheer will to dominate – the laws engraved on it are *his* laws, and everyone, including himself, obeys them only because he wills it so. Nevertheless, the prime motive behind all this is the building up of an ordered civilization.

One further Wagnerian manipulation of the mythology remains to be considered – the one whereby Wotan's cutting of the spear causes the Well of Wisdom to dry up and the Tree of Life to wither. The former feature is entirely Wagner's own invention, and the latter has only a slight basis in the mythology. The World Ash-Tree, in the two *Eddas*, is certainly in a state of decay – innumerable serpents are gnawing at its roots, and its trunk is rotting; but this has nothing to do with Odin. In *The Twilight of the Gods*, however, the First Norn, after describing how Wotan cut his spear from the Tree of Life, goes on to say:

> *In the long course of time*
> *the wound ate away the wood;*
> *the sear leaves fell;*
> *the dry tree withered;*
> *sadly dried up*
> *the draught of the well.*

The implication, surely, is that Wotan's primal act has resulted in an impoverishment of nature – an idea which must wait until later for clarification.

If we now consider the overt meaning of the history of Wotan, which Wagner conferred on the mythological original, we find immediately a startling central resemblance to the overt meaning he gave to the history he actually created for Alberich. Absolute world-power can be achieved by ravishing the raw material of nature (the Rhinegold, the World Ash-Tree) and exploiting it (making and using the ring, the spear). And this resemblance is enhanced by having the raw material presided over, in each case, by three wise-women (the Rhinemaidens created by Wagner, the Norns which he took over from the mythology).

There are, of course, crucial differences – which nevertheless run parallel. Alberich sought love, Wotan knowledge; Alberich's search was frustrated, Wotan's satisfied. Where Alberich had to give up love to obtain power, Wotan had to give up half his vision; and whereas Alberich's bid for power, born of the renunciation of love, is revengeful and unscrupulous, Wotan's, born of the acquisition of knowledge, is creative and subject to law, which is binding even on himself. Only one feature of Wotan's case seems to lack an equivalent in Alberich's, and to be curious in itself: the withering of the Tree of Life and the drying up of the Well of Wisdom, caused by the cutting of the spear. But if, as suggested, this must imply an impoverishment of nature, it does have an equivalent in Alberich's case: partly that all the gold is ravished, as opposed to only a branch of the tree; but more important (a point not yet mentioned), that the abduction of the gold plunges the Rhine into permanent darkness, as Alberich is grimly delighted to tell the Rhinemaidens ('Your light I put out'), and as they themselves are still lamenting in Act 3 of *The Twilight of the Gods* ('Night lies in the depths').

The really puzzling difference is that Alberich's renunciation of love is paralleled by Wotan's loss of half his vision, since the implications of the latter deprivation are as yet unclear. But this difference is only apparent: we shall find later that Wotan's impaired vision has led him to reject love as decisively, if not as irrevocably, as Alberich.

Fricka, like her husband, is a largely faithful replica of her Scandinavian original with a main motivation provided by Wagner. As said above, Frigg 'knows all the fates of men'; so does Fricka, as she shows in Act 2 of *The Valkyrie*, when she tracks Wotan down and reveals that she knows the whole truth about Siegmund, Sieglinde, and Hunding, which he has been trying to keep from her. Frigg also, as Jacob Grimm says, 'presides over marriages'; and Fricka is likewise goddess of marriage, as becomes clear in that same scene, when she supports Hunding's claims as a husband, describing herself as *der Ehe Hüterin* (the guardian of wedlock). And of the four wifely characteristics she reveals immediately in Scene 2 of *The Rhinegold* – her possessive desire to keep Wotan at home, her fear for his safety when he leaves for Nibelheim, her contentious opposition to his dubious projects, and her jealousy with regard to his infidelities – three are taken over from the Frigg of the *Poetic Edda*.

The first two come from the *Ballad of Vafthruthnir*. When Odin leaves for a question-contest with a giant, Frigg says first:

> At home, I warn you · Warfather, stay:
> in the midst of the gods remain . . .

and then:

> Safe may you go   ·   and safe return,
> and safely wend your way . . .

And Frigg's contentious opposition to Odin is revealed in the prose introduction to the *Ballad of Grimnir*, in which they argue over the merits of two brothers:

> Odin and Frigg sat in Hlidskjalf and looked out over all the worlds. Then Odin said: 'Do you see your fosterling Agnar, how he begets children with a giantess in a cave? But Geirröd, my fosterling, is a king, and rules over his own land'. Frigg said: 'He is such a niggard that he tortures his guests, for fear too many should come'.

She turns out to be right, and causes her husband to destroy his own favourite, like Fricka in *The Valkyrie*. (See also p. 128 for similar marital strife between the German counterparts, again followed by the wife's triumph.)

As regards Fricka's jealousy, however, thi, emotion is not attributed to Frigg anywhere in the mythology. Yet she has good cause to be jealous: not only does Odin beget the Volsungs by a mortal woman, but he has children by two goddesses and two giantesses. Frigg's difficulties as a wife are crystallized in a quaint bit of phraseology in the *Prose Edda*:

> How is Frigg to be periphrased? In this way: call her Daughter of Fjorgyn, wife of Odin . . . Co-Wife of Jord and Rind [goddesses] and Gunnlod and Grid [giantesses] . . .

'Co-wife' of four others! No wonder Fricka says to Wotan in Scene 2 of *The Rhinegold*:

> *Anxious over my husband's fidelity,*
> *I must sadly ponder*
> *how to bind him to me*
> *when he is lured far away.*

Actually, in the mythology, Frigg is herself unfaithful; but Wagner preferred to keep Fricka's morals irreproachable. And by so doing, and by making her jealous, he superimposed a motivation of his own on the traits he took over unchanged from Frigg. Fricka, with her righteous concern for the sanctity of marriages (including her own), with her wifely possessiveness, contentiousness, and jealousy, enshrines *her husband's conservative conscience*, his rigid super-ego ideals, from which he is trying to break free – first, criminally, to increase his power, and later, idealistically, to discover a higher morality. Wotan's whole aim has been to establish an ordered civilization through the immutable laws engraved on his spear: Fricka attacks him in *The Rhinegold* for seeking to evade those laws in drawing up the fraudulent contract which is to increase his power; and again in *The Valkyrie* for trying to create a 'free hero' who will be exempt from those laws in a quest for true justice. When Wotan begets the Valkyries on Erda and the Volsungs on a mortal woman, Fricka, like many a deserted wife, sees her husband as abandoning her, not only for other women, but also for other ideals, which cannot be justified by his conservative conscience enshrined in her. And it is in so far as that conscience still remains enshrined in himself that she is able to keep him temporarily tied to it – when she forces him to abandon the new ideals embodied in Siegmund and Sieglinde, which postulate the *non*-sanctity of any marriage-bond as coercive and as loveless as that between Sieglinde and Hunding. In the Wotan-Fricka relationship, Wagner, as so often, uses sexual situations to symbolize ideals and moral principles.

This central motivation which Wagner conferred on Fricka lies behind his other two additions to the mythology in respect of Frigg. First, in Scene 2 of *The Rhinegold*, Wotan reminds Fricka of the sacrifice he made to marry her:

> *to win you as my wife,*
> *one of my eyes*
> *I gave as a wooing-pledge.*

This idea has no basis whatsoever in the mythology,[1] and moreover it seems to flagrantly contradict the First Norn's statement that it was for a drink from the Well of Wisdom that Wotan sacrificed his eye. But there is really no contradiction at all, if we assume that Wotan is thinking of cause and effect: his drink from the well, enabling him to cut from the tree the spear of world-domination-through-law, inevitably brought him a wife like Fricka, enshrining the ideal of the spear. She is even more devoted to domination and law than Wotan is, since she wants both to remain fixed immutably. She 'begged' Wotan to have Valhalla built – as a permanent home to keep him in; but she is appalled at his disregard for law in striking the fraudulent contract with the giants. He, on the other hand, regards Valhalla as a base for further activity, and is ready to evade his 'immutable' laws in the process,

---

[1] Ernest Newman, in *Wagner Nights*, says that Wagner was 'following two different legends' in his two different accounts of Wotan's loss of his eye; but in fact the mythology nowhere says that Odin gave up an eye to win Frigg as his wife.

if necessary. The ruler who lives by the ideal of world-domination-through-law is, as it were, wedded to it: he finds difficulty in breaking free from it, to increase his power illegally (or, later, to further the higher ideals of true justice and love for mankind). As can be seen, Wagner's representation of the ruler's wife as the keeper of his conservative conscience is a concrete symbol, since the situation is familiar in life itself.[2]

Wagner's other alteration of the mythology in respect of Fricka was a drastic one: he made her barren. In the *Eddas*, Odin and Frigg do have a single child – the radiant god Baldr; but Wagner made the marriage between Wotan and Fricka childless – and with Fricka as the infertile partner, since Wotan later proves his fertility by begetting the Valkyries and Volsungs on other women. So again a sexual situation is used to symbolize ideals and moral principles. The ideal of immutable law to which Wotan is wedded, as a principle of world-domination, is unproductive of any more fruitful developments; and so his wife, who enshrines that ideal, is made symbolically barren. And his later fostering of the principles of true justice and love for humanity is only achieved by employing his own fertility to beget children by other women enshrining more productive ideals: the mother of the Volsung twins (humanity) and Erda (the sense of destiny that will lead to his rediscovery of love).

Three of the other gods – Freia, Froh, and Donner – are relatives of Fricka and Wotan; and once more we encounter a Wagnerian alteration of the mythology. In the *Eddas*, Frey and Freyja (Froh and Freia) are not related to Odin and Frigg, being children of an earth- or sea-god, Njord, who came to the Aesir (the race of gods headed by Odin) from another race, the Vanir. Thor (Donner), on the other hand, is Odin's son – one of his by-blows, by the earth-goddess Jord. But Wagner, who knew all this well, changed it completely. In Scene 2 of *The Rhinegold*, when Fricka attacks Wotan for promising Freia as a wage to the giants, she refers to her

---

[2] His final prose-sketch for *The Rhinegold* was more explicit on this point: to win Fricka, Wotan 'willingly pledged one of his own eyes to her obstinate kindred'. At this time, the Norns' scene in *Siegfried's Death* did not contain the account of Wotan's sacrifice of an eye for a drink from the well, which is in the present *Twilight of the Gods*, and so there was no 'contradiction': this came later, when he revised *Siegfried's Death* and added the passage in the Norns' scene. But Wagner's total absorption in his whole text makes it impossible to suppose that he overlooked this 'contradiction': in fact, the removal from the final *Rhinegold* text of the actual details of Wotan's sacrifice of an eye to win Fricka left no contradiction at all, as we have seen.

as 'mein holdes Geschwister' (my beloved sister).[3] And Freia herself confirms this, when she runs to Fricka and Wotan, pursued by the giants, crying:

> *Help me, sister!*
> *Protect me, brother-in-law!*[4]

And finally, a little later, Freia cries:

> *Where are my brothers,*
> *who should come to my rescue,*
> *since my brother-in-law is giving me, the weak one, away?*
> *Help, Donner!*
> *Hither, hither!*
> *Save Freia, my Froh!*

Contrary to one widely-accepted opinion, Wagner's whole text is meticulously organized, not only from a dramatic point of view, but also to give maximum information in a minimum of space; and his deft pin-pointing of the gods' relationships, as early as possible, is to be taken seriously. Whereas, in the mythology, Odin is 'Allfather' and 'father of the gods', in a real or general sense in different cases, Wagner made Freia, Froh, and Donner the sister and brothers of Wotan's wife Fricka. So the gods belong to one generation, even if Wotan is their leader; and Wotan's father-figure status is reserved exclusively for his relationship with the Valkyries and the Volsungs. The overt meaning of this alteration of the mythology must be left until later; in the meantime, we may register the fact that Wotan's sacrifice of an eye for a drink from the Well of Wisdom, enabling him to cut from the Tree of Life the spear of world-domination-through-law, has brought him, not only a wife like Fricka, but companions like her sister and her two brothers.[5]

Of these three, Freia is the most important, being the impossible wage Wotan has promised the giants for building Valhalla. And the mythology does offer a slight basis for Wagner's decision to make her Fricka's sister – not in any actual statement to that effect, but rather in its tendency to confuse the two figures. For example,

[3] 'Geschwister' actually means 'sibling' – brother *or* sister.

[4] The term 'brother-in-law' – Wagner's archaic *Schwäher*, modern equivalent *Schwager* – is as natural a form of address in German as it is unnatural in English.

[5] Those who derive amusement from making fun of *The Ring* will be delighted to realize that one of Wotan's problems is 'in-law trouble'.

the *Prose Edda* says that, of those slain each day in battle, half go to Odin, half to Freyja: this would be more naturally the province of Frigg, as Odin's wife. Elsewhere we find Frigg named once as the possessor of Freyja's famous necklace, Brisingamen, and again of her hawk-plumage; and similar stories are told of both goddesses' infidelities. As Jacob Grimm says, opening his section on the Scandinavian goddesses:

> Foremost of these are *Frigg* the wife of Oðinn, and *Freyja* the sister of Freyr, a pair easy to confound and often confounded, because of their similar names. I mean to try if a stricter etymology can part them and keep them asunder.

Grimm traced the confusion to the original Teutonic name for Frigg, which was Frija (with the 'j' pronounced as 'i', as in 'Freyja'); hence the two goddesses' names became mixed up.[6] It could be that the two separate figures were divergent offshoots of some original fertility- or mother-goddess; but separate they are, in the mythology, Frigg being concerned with marriage, Freyja with love. Grimm, after admitting that 'the forms and even the meanings of the two names border closely on each other', came to his final conclusion:

> In so far as such comparisons are permissible, *Frigg* would stand on a line with Hera [wife of the Greek Zeus] or Juno [wife of the Roman Jupiter] . . . and *Freyja* with Venus . . .

Grimm's statement would itself account for Wagner's interpretation of the slightly ambiguous Freyja as simply the goddess of love. But the mythology provides enough support to make it difficult to understand why some modern scholars consider Grimm's conclusion a dubious one. The *Prose Edda* says of Freyja:

> She is fond of love-songs, and it is good to call on her in matters of love.

And later, it shows that her function in the Scandinavian thearchy was acknowledged in a common periphrasis:

> How is Freyja to be periphrased? In this way: call her Daughter of Njord, Sister of Frey . . . Goddess of the Vanir, Goddess Beautiful in Tears, Goddess of Love.

Nor is there any lack of those scurrilous stories that accumulate around love-goddesses (cf. Venus). H. R. Ellis Davidson summarizes them conveniently in *Gods and Myths of Northern Europe:*

[6] We have seen (p. 128) that the eighth-century German historian Paulus Diaconus gives to Wôdan's wife the name of 'Frea'.

One of Loki's scandalous assertions was that she had love-dealings with her brother Frey . . . Loki accused her of taking all the gods and elves for lovers, while the giantess Hyndla taunted her with roaming out at night like a she-goat among the bucks . . . However, no [actual] stories of unseemly behaviour by Freia have survived, with the exception of a late account in *Flateyarbók* of how she won her necklace by sleeping one night in turn with each of the four dwarfs who forged it. There are several cases of giants who wanted to carry her off, but she does not seem to have given them any encouragement. However, the jokes made in *þrymskviða* [in which Thor comically masquerades as Freyja, in bridal dress, to outwit and kill a love-sick giant], about Freyja's eagerness for the bridal night, which, according to Loki, had given her an amazing appetite and burning eyes, fit in with the general picture, and confirm the idea that ritual marriage formed some part of the rites of her cult.

And perhaps it is not without significance that Freyja's chariot is drawn, not by goats, rams or bulls, but by cats.

Wagner's Freia, then, is what Freyja was – the goddess of love.[7] He nowhere states this explicitly; but when Loge, in Scene 2 of *The Rhinegold*, explains that he could find no substitute for Freia, as the giants' wage, except Alberich's gold, he says:

> *What indeed, to a man,*
> *could seem mightier*
> *than the delight and the worth of Woman? . . .*
> *No man will go without*
> *Love and woman.*
> *Only one did I see*
> *who renounced Love:*
> *for red gold*
> *he gave up the favour of Woman.*

Freia stands out so unequivocally here as the goddess of love that it is hard to understand why so many commentators have burked the issue and called her the goddess of youth, or beauty, or charm, and so on – especially since mythologies do not normally have such goddesses, though each does have a goddess of love.

Freia has only one personal property – the golden apples[8] which

---

[7] He even made this clear by Germanizing the name as 'Freia', as against Grimm's 'Frouwa', since whereas 'Frouwa' is connected with 'Frau', 'Freia' is connected with the verb 'freien' (to woo, or to make love to).

[8] The apples are not golden in the mythology, but apples which can be eaten in the normal way; nor are they said to be golden by any of the German scholars Wagner relied on, though they are sometimes referred to as golden in modern English books about Teutonic mythology. There seems to have been some influence of the idea of the golden apples of the Hesperides in Greek mythology – and there may have been in Wagner's case. It is really an unimportant point: in *The Ring*, the 'gold' of the apples can obviously have no symbolic connection with the gold of the ring, or that of the Nibelung treasure.

keep the gods young; and again Wagner manipulated the mythology. In the *Prose Edda*, these apples are the property of the obscure goddess Idun, about whom little else is known. In transferring them to Freia, Wagner simply equipped the love-goddess with the natural symbol of her complementary function as fertility-goddess, the apple being a common fertility-symbol (a childless marriage in *Volsunga saga* is made fruitful by the gift of an apple from Odin). Fertility, love, and enduring youth belong together, of course – a point that will be considered further in dealing with the actual action of Scene 2 of *The Rhinegold*.

Yet, it may be asked, if Freia is supposed to be the goddess of love, why does she not function as such more decisively? Why, compared with Wotan and Fricka, is she such a pale reflection of her vivid Scandinavian original, to the extent of being practically characterless? The goddess of love should surely cut a more impressive figure then Freia does.

But this, surely, is the very point that Wagner intended to.make. The love-goddess should certainly cut a far more impressive figure – but how can she when, as she herself says, Wotan is bartering her, 'the weak one' (*die Schwache*), away? Represented by this single myth, Freia stands as the goddess of love in a world which has rejected love: in Scene 1, Alberich has renounced love altogether, in return for world-domination; and in Scene 2, Wotan's own appetite for world-domination has led him to seek it at the possible price of the love-goddess. In the world of *The Rhinegold*, ruled over by Wotan, love does not exist – or rather, it has shrunk into the weak, helpless, hunted figure of Freia.

If this crucial symbol in *The Rhinegold* has hitherto failed to register altogether, it is due to the weakness inherent in Wagner's use of Teutonic mythology as the basis of his great artistic diagnosis of the loveless, power-ridden, political world in which we live. As said in Chapter 1, in modelling himself on the ancient Greek dramatists, whose inherited mythology he described as 'the poem of a life-view held in common', he was idealizing his own situation: the Teutonic gods had long been forgotten. Who was Freia? Wagner, absorbed in Teutonic mythology, knew that she was the great love-goddess: he expected his audiences to start with that knowledge, and to be amazed at the treatment meted out to her by the chief of the gods, Wotan. But his audiences lacked (and still lack) that knowledge. We can understand his intention clearly if we imagine a drama based on the still well-remembered Roman mythology, with Jupiter bartering the Roman love-goddess in return for an increase in his power: when that goddess appeared, with the familiar name of Venus, she would not need to do anything to establish her identity as goddess of love – the whole monstrous situation would be immediately clear.

Even had Wagner thought it necessary, he could hardly have elaborated Freia's identity as the goddess of love within the tight dramatic framework of *The Rhinegold*. Yet he did provide two clear indications. One is Loge's panegyric on Woman and Love, partly quoted above, which of course refers to Freia; the other is that Freia is the only character in *The Rhinegold* to whom love and affection are shown – by Fricka and Froh, above all by the amorous Fasolt, and even, in the end, slightly, by Wotan himself. Perhaps Freia's identity could be projected more decisively in performance by the right kind of production: if the soprano taking the role could be made to realize that she is supposed to be impersonating the great love-goddess, we might be given something more numinous than the pretty young woman in distress we invariably encounter – something more indicative of divinity despised.

Once we realize that Freia is the goddess of love, it becomes clear what Wagner meant by making her Fricka's sister. As said above, Wotan's drink from the Well of Wisdom, enabling him to cut from the Tree of Life the spear of world-domination-through-law, inevitably brought him a wife like Fricka, enshrining the ideal of the spear. But it must also have brought him love: Wotan originally *loved* Fricka, as is evident from her attempts to recall him to that love. Indeed, Fricka is herself a love-goddess, being goddess of marriage – but here, as sometimes in real life, marriage and love are two different things. Since world-domination-through-law and the capacity for love are mutually exclusive, Wotan's marriage has become a loveless one: the barren Fricka no longer enshrines his capacity for love, since she enshrines his ideal of world-domination-through-law. And so beside Fricka stands her *alter ego* – the figure sometimes indistinguishable from her in the mythology, and hence made by Wagner into her sister: the goddess of love-itself, Freia, who does enshrine Wotan's capacity for love – what little is left of it.

The symbolism is complex, but it has a concrete reality, owing to the sister-relationship invented by Wagner. Fricka is as incensed by Wotan's indifference to Freia as by his indifference to herself: the two sisters are inseparable – the goddess of love, abandoned by

Wotan, and the goddess of married love, here a particular case of that abandonment. Fricka really speaks for both of them when she attacks Wotan for offering Freia as a wage to the giants (and incidentally gives another clue to Freia's identity as goddess of love):

> *Are you gambling away, in criminal mockery,*
> *Love and the worth of Woman?*

And yet the two figures are also separate, in a way which becomes decisive later. Fricka, no longer enshrining Wotan's capacity for love, remains the barren goddess of marriage-without-love, upholding the loveless and childless marriage of Sieglinde and Hunding. Freia, who does enshrine Wotan's (much diminished) capacity for love, remains the goddess of love-itself; and she (in the form of her musical theme, Ex. 28, p. 49) blesses the love-relationships he furthers between his offspring (Exs. 30, 31, 33–40, pp. 50–3).

The overt meaning of the Wotan-Fricka-Freia relationship is clear enough: Wotan, in pursuing power, has lost his love for his wife, and is in danger of losing his very capacity for love, in the person of Freia. And this leads us back to the parallelism between his history and that of Alberich, which is now complete. The one puzzling feature was the equivalence of Alberich's renunciation of love and Wotan's loss of half his vision – but this now makes perfect sense.

Wagner's symbols being always concrete, Wotan's lack of an eye should mean that, in the drama, he is blind to one half of existence – and he is. What is his remaining eye fixed on? Obviously, the world, as something to dominate. What is he blind to? Obviously, the claims of love, urged by his wife Fricka, and embodied in the love-goddess Freia. This completes the parallelism between his case and Alberich's, which can best be shown schematically:

Alberich	Wotan
	went to
the Rhine,	*the Well of Wisdom,*
	with its three guardian spirits
the Rhinemaidens.	*the Norns.*
	His desire for
love	*knowledge*
	being
frustrated,	*satisfied,*
	he made from
the Rhinegold	*the Tree of Life*
	a talisman of
unconditional power,	*power conditioned by law,*
	which was
the Ring;	*the Spear;*
	but first he had to
renounce love,	*lose an eye and thus become blind to the claims of love,*
	and the result impoverished nature through
the disappearance of the Gold and the consequent darkening of the Rhine.	*the drying up of the Well and the withering of the Tree.*

One difference still remaining is that Wotan, unlike Alberich, hopes to have it both ways – attain to world-domination (possess Valhalla) and yet not have to do without love (lose Freia). But he cannot have it both ways: just as Alberich has to renounce love altogether, to pursue power single-mindedly, so Wotan will have to abandon his power more and more, to further the claims of love through his offspring.

Clearly, Wagner made Alberich and Wotan opposite sides of the same coin, representing two complementary images of man-in-pursuit-of-power – a huge composite symbol later ratified, in

Siegfried, when Wotan refers to himself as 'Licht-Alberich' (Light-Alberich) and to Alberich as 'Schwarz-Alberich' (Black-Alberich).[9]

If Freia is necessarily a pale reflection of her vivid Scandinavian original, the same is even more true of her brother and male counterpart, Froh. Historically speaking, Frey was a very powerful deity, worshipped as widely as Odin, and even rivalling him in certain areas – notably among the Swedes. In the *Eddas,* little is related of him, but he is nevertheless represented as a figure of prime importance in the *Prose Edda* – as a beneficient fertility-god:

> Frey is the most splendid of the gods. He rules over the rain and the sunshine, and over the fruits of the earth, and it is on him that one should call for fertility and peace. He also has power over the wealth of men . . .

And later:

> How is Frey to be periphrased? In this way: call him Son of Njord, Brother of Freyja, and also God of the Vanir . . . and God of the Seasons, and God of Wealth . . .

Wagner's Froh hardly lives up to this reputation. Admittedly, in the original myths which Wagner used for *The Rhinegold,* Frey plays no part. But the same is true of Frigg; and whereas Wagner presented Fricka in the round, and gave her an indispensable part in the action, it almost seems as if he included Froh simply to make up the number, or perhaps because he could not imagine the great love-goddess Freia at all without her famous brother. Or it could be that, with the domineering Wotan, the contentious Fricka, the aggressive Donner, and the sarcastic Loge, plus the entirely passive role given to Freia herself, he felt a need to provide a touch of that brightness which might be expected to emanate from a company of gods – and yet realized that such brightness could be of little account in a story as dark as that unfolded by *The Rhinegold.* For certainly, Froh is the most minor of minor characters. Even his music betrays the fact that Wagner could take little interest in him, being far below the lofty level of the rest of *The Ring:* the theme to which he enters (Ex. 60) is no more than a hopeful attempt at a more masculine version of the lovely theme of Freia's apples (Ex.

---

[9] *Albe* is German for 'elf', in the general sense of 'spirit'; and *Albe-rich* means *'elf the mighty',* or 'elf-ruler'. Scandinavian mythology distinguished between 'light elves' (liosâlfar) and 'black elves' (svartâlfar), which in German translations (including Jacob Grimm's) became *Lichtalben* and *Schwarzalben;* hence Wagner's *Licht-Alberich* and *Schwarz-Alberich* (Light-Spirit Ruler and Black-Spirit Ruler).

61), and is scarcely heard again, while the rest of his material – of the once-only variety – scarcely bears examination.

Ex. 60

Ex. 61

Yet Froh does fulfil a useful function, which – to indulge a little special pleading – the emptiness of his music actually enhances. If Freia is in one sense the *alter ego* of Fricka, Froh is, in another, the *alter ego* of Freia, as was again the case in the mythology, at least according to Jacob Grimm:

> Freyr and his sister Freyja are made alike in their attributes, and each can stand for the other . . .

And since, in *The Ring*, these inseparable figures came to Wotan together, as adjuncts of their sister Fricka, Froh also embodies one of the qualities of Wotan originating with his youthful love. Not, certainly, Wotan's actual capacity for love, which is entirely embodied in Freia; but rather the naïve self-confidence brought by early love, which led him to embark so rashly on his quest for world-power, even at the expense of love, and which still survives in his readiness to imperil Freia's status as love-goddess, together with his unrealistic hope to have it both ways.[10] The accusation Fricka hurls at Wotan in Scene 2 of *The Rhinegold* is a just one:

[10] This might seem to support Robert Donington's identification of Freia as the goddess, not of love itself, but of 'youth and youthful love' – but only if musical considerations are ignored. Froh has no theme of his own, and what music he does have is subsidiary and unproductive, not reaching out beyond *The Rhinegold*. Freia, on the other hand, has a momentous theme, the second half of which (Ex. 28B) becomes central to the score of the whole tetralogy. Freia is the goddess of love – which in *The Rhinegold* is despised, but is later to burgeon; Froh merely embodies the easy optimism which accompanies youthful love, but soon vanishes under the pressure of hard reality.

> *O laughing criminal levity!*
> *Loveless cheerfulness!*

Froh is in fact a foolish optimist[11] (how Loge rounds on him when he suggests it will be easy to get the ring from Alberich!); and Wotan, who has been one himself, has surely had some time to spare for his sanguine brother-in-law, as he once had love to spare for his wife Fricka and her *alter ego* Freia. But now he ignores Froh completely, beginning to be disillusioned, through his troubles over Valhalla, with the easy optimism which Froh embodies. In this he is certainly much wiser than in his ignoring of love, in the person of Freia: the dark cross-roads he has reached is no place for easy optimism, whereas the recovery of love, leading to the abandonment of the power-lust which has caused it to be so very nearly lost, is the only right road to follow.

Again, the mythology offers a slight basis for Wagner's treatment of the character, since the one striking story about Frey, in the *Eddas*, presents him as a curiously feckless god. When he sent his servant Skirnir to woo the giantess Gerd for him, he gave him, as an inducement, his own horse and his own sword (the famous sword which fought by itself, not needing a hand to guide it); this piece of folly left him weaponless at the great battle with the powers of evil on the last day of the world – and it is one we can easily imagine Wagner's Froh being guilty of. It may indeed have been this myth which gave Wagner the idea of representing Froh as such an ineffectual exponent of bright hopes – an interpretation which he effectively crystallized in the single property he conferred on him at the end of *The Rhinegold*. There, Froh does finally 'rule over the rain and the sunshine': not however, to bring 'fertility and peace', but to conjure up the comforting rainbow-bridge of illusion leading to the glittering fortress that has at last been paid for – 'with bad money', as the by-now-realistic Wotan admits. In the *Prose Edda*, the rainbow-bridge – called Bifrost – has nothing to do with Frey (or with Valholl either, for that matter): it was 'made by the gods', at some time unspecified, as 'a bridge from earth to heaven'. But in letting Froh be its tutelary deity, and in making it

[11] It is significant that Wagner Germanized the name Frey as Froh – which means 'happy, glad'. The Scandinavian name meant 'Lord': Jacob Grimm established the ancient German equivalent as Frô, which had the same meaning, and regarded the adjective *froh* as being no more than a derivative of this. Incidentally, the word translated above as 'cheerfulness' is *'Frohsinn'* (literally 'happymindedness') which also links up with the present interpretation.

an illusory pathway to an illusory stronghold,[12] Wagner summed up what little of character he put into this god. And he confirmed it in the music, whether consciously or unconsciously, by the empty glitter of Froh's huge arching Rainbow-Bridge theme (Ex. 9, p. 41). After it has been blared out, blatantly and repetitively, to celebrate the hollow triumph of 'The Entry of the Gods into Valhalla', it promptly vanishes from the tetralogy – in which it could certainly have had no fruitful part to play.

Donner is also a minor character; and if he is a rather more impressive one than Froh, this is not so much because he is a slightly clearer reflection of his Scandinavian original, as because that original, Thor,[13] is himself a much more dynamic figure than Froh's original, Frey. As a matter of historical fact, Frey, Thor, and Odin were the great three among the Scandinavian gods, and received more or less equal worship, each having his own areas of influence; but in the *Eddas*, Thor has much more space devoted to him than Frey, and even more than to Odin himself. In the *Prose Edda*, several extended episodes are devoted to his journeys to Jotunheim (Giant-Land), often in the company of Loki, and to his grimly comic encounters there, which usually result in the death of one or more giants (though once in his – and Loki's – total discomfiture, of a kind endured by Gulliver among the Brobding-nagians).

Visually, too, Thor presents a most striking picture. In several of the sagas he appears as a huge figure with a red beard, which bristles when, as so often, he gets angry; and the *Prose Edda* introduces him as follows:

Thor has two he-goats, which are called Tanngnjostr [Tooth-Gnasher] and Tanngrisnir [Tooth-Gritter], and these draw the chariot in which he drives . . . He has also three great treasures: the first is the hammer Mjollnir, which the Frost-Giants and the Hill-Giants know all about, when it is swung; and this is not to be wondered at, since it has cracked many a skull of their fathers and their kinsmen. A second treasure is the girdle of

[12] By now Valhalla is a totally useless protection against Alberich, if he should ever regain the ring, as Wotan admits to Brünnhilde in Act 2 of *The Valkyrie*.

[13] The name is the same. Jacob Grimm established the ancient German name of this god as Donar, which meant 'thunder' (Wagner preferred to use the modern German word for thunder, *Donner*); and by Grimm's linguistic law, the Norse equivalent of the German 'D' is 'Th' (or rather þ), and the 'n' tends to drop out before 'r'. The latter change happened between Anglo-Saxon and English: the original Anglo-Saxon name for the god was Thunor, and his day of the week was Thunores daeg, which became, in English, Thursday.

strength, called Megingjard: when he fastens it on, his godlike strength is increased by half. Yet a third thing he has, of great value: his iron gloves, which he cannot do without when he grasps the haft of the hammer.

The hammer, we are told, was made for Thor by the same dwarfs who made the spear for Odin, and it was likewise delivered to him by Loki:

> Then Loki gave the hammer to Thor, and said that he might strike with it anything he encountered, as hard as he liked, and the hammer would take no harm; and however far he hurled it, he would never lose it – it would never fly so far as not to return to his hand . . .

Within the scope of *The Rhinegold*, the above main features of this tremendous god could be retained in only a restricted way. Thor was essentially the storm-god – Jacob Grimm equated his bristling red beard with the lightning, his rumbling chariot-wheels with the thunder, and his hurled hammer with the thunderbolt; but Wagner had to make Donner's (unthrown) hammer do duty for all three, letting him swing it round his head to summon up the storm. Thor's other two properties – his girdle of might and his iron gloves – may sometimes be suggested in the opera-house, in Donner's costume, together with the red beard, but they play no symbolic part there, not being part of Wagner's text.

The really significant characteristic of Thor retained in Donner is the hammer's function as an aggressive weapon against giants. As we shall see, Wagner minimized the part played by the hammer in the myth of the building of the fortress; but the impulse behind it – the god's inflammable anger – is Donner's essential function. And again we encounter an *alter ego* relationship – this time with Wotan. As Jacob Grimm wrote:

> . . . thunder is especially ascribed to an angry and avenging god; and in this attribute of *anger* and *punishment* . . . Donar resembles Wuotan . . .

As Grimm also indicated, the office of thunder-god is in other mythologies held by the chief god (cf. Jupiter *tonans*). And in fact Donner embodies the aggressive anger of Wotan in his role as dictatorial ruler – a characteristic which will have stood Wotan in good stead in his quest for world domination, and which manifests itself quintessentially when he tears the ring from Alberich's finger, fully deserving the dwarf's condemnation 'herrischer Gott!' (high-handed god). For his irascible brother-in-law, Wotan must have had plenty of time to spare.

This particular *alter ego* interpretation may seem at odds with the fact that Donner, like Freia and Froh, came to Wotan as an adjunct of his sister Fricka: she may have brought a capacity for love, in the person of Freia, together with the unreflecting optimism of youthful love, in the person of Froh, but did she bring the aggressive anger embodied in Donner? From this point of view, it might be tempting to suggest that Wagner, if he was determined to represent the gods as belonging to a single generation, should have made Donner Wotan's actual brother, rather than his brother-in-law. But he surely wanted Wotan to stand alone, and the symbolism still holds: in that Fricka has enshrined Wotan's ideal of world-domination-through-law, she has also embodied the aggressive anger which has forwarded that domination. This becomes evident in *The Valkyrie*, when she turns that anger on himself, and forces him to destroy his 'free human hero', Siegmund, for the purpose of preserving the total hegemony of the gods:

> Laughed at by men,
> divested of power,
> we gods would be ruined,
> if today my rights were not
> sacredly and proudly avenged
> by the bold maiden [Brünnhilde].
> The Volsung shall fall to satisfy my honour . . .

Fricka embodies all Wotan's original qualities, which are also embodied separately, in her sister and her two brothers, for the sake of dramatic force and clarity. Wotan would certainly like to kill the giants, if it were not for the contract, and so would Fricka; but any statement to this effect, by either of them, would have had far less impact than the physical enactment of their wish by Fricka's choleric brother, raising his hammer, followed by Wotan's immediate interposition of the spear, to enforce the contract.

But in fact, since Wotan's quest for world-domination is controlled in this manner by his own laws, it is obvious that he cannot afford to let his murderous brother-in-law have his way; and the time is indeed coming when he will have as little time for the unreflecting aggression of Donner as he has already for the unreflecting optimism of Froh. At the end of *The Rhinegold*, after the murder of Fasolt by Fafner, he lets the angry Donner clear the troubled air by calling up a storm, just as he lets the optimistic Froh conjure up the illusory rainbow-bridge to Valhalla; but Donner's music, magnificent though it is, will disappear from the tetralogy almost as quickly as the empty music of Froh. Not quite, however, since Wotan is by nature more interested in storms than in rainbows, and he still has a use for anger. Donner's theme (Ex. 62) soon sweeps into the storm that opens *The Valkyrie* – a storm which marks the culmination of the persecution of Siegmund deliberately engineered by Wotan to harden him and stir him up against the laws of the gods, as well as the beginning of a drama in which Wotan figures as god of anger and punishment *par excellence*. But even before the end of this second drama, any further need for Donner's theme disappears: Wotan's anger is mollified by Brünn-hilde, and from then on he figures as a detached and benevolent observer of events, except for one last flare of temper when he is treated so disrespectfully by Siegfried.

Ex. 62

At this point we may sum up by saying that Wotan has practically lost interest in all the qualities which have made him what he is, and which are embodied in his wife and her relatives. In fact, Fricka reproaches him for just this, in Act 2 of *The Valkyrie*:

> *Is it all over then*
> *with the eternal gods . . . ?*
> *You set no store by*
> *your holy, divine relatives!*
> *You are throwing away*
> *everything you used to value . . .*

Fricka, of course, blind with jealousy, cannot be expected to see that Wotan's new plans are actually resulting in the reinstatement of the hegemony of the one divine figure that really matters, the goddess of love, Freia. The love that is emerging between Sieg-mund and Sieglinde is the outcome of his liaison with another woman, a mortal; and this only emphasizes his loss of love for Fricka herself, as wife and goddess of marriage. His observation to her in Scene 2 of *The Rhinegold*, if unkind, is entirely accurate:

> *I honour women*
> *even more than it pleases you . . .*

– that is, women enshrining new ideals, and especially that of love. All the rest – world-domination-through-law, and the unreflecting optimism and aggression that have been part of this, will eventually go by the board. Later on, if Wotan still tries to dominate, or gets optimistic or aggressive, it will not be in the ways embodied in Fricka, Froh, or Donner – though when he furthers the claims of love, it will certainly be in the way potentially embodied in Freia.

If we ask why Wotan should so have lost interest in his wife and her relatives, part of the answer, surely, is the increasing interest he has been taking in the last god to appear in Scene 2 of *The Rhinegold*, the one on whom he has begun to set all his hopes: Loge.

This enigmatic figure, as vivid a Wagnerian counterpart of his Scandinavian original as Wotan and Fricka are of theirs, has six rather contradictory functions. He is a free agent, unrelated to the other gods; a mischief-maker who gets the other gods into trouble and out of it again; an uncompromising teller of unpalatable truths; a mocker of the other gods; an old friend and favourite of Wotan, distrusted as such by the other gods; and the god of fire. The first two of these functions are taken straight over from the Scandinavian Loki, whom the *Prose Edda* introduces as follows:

> They also number among the Aesir one whom some call the mischief-maker among the gods, the contriver of all fraud, and the shame of gods and men. His name is Loki or Lopt; his father is the giant Farbauti, his mother is called Laufey . . . Loki is handsome and attractive in appearance, but evil in spirit and very fickle. He surpasses all others in slyness and every kind of trickery. He brought the Aesir into many a plight, but he often got them out again through his cleverness . . .

Loge's third function – as a teller of unpalatable truths – might seem to be Wagner's own invention, conflicting with the above statements that Loki was 'the contriver of all fraud', 'the shame of gods and men', and 'evil in spirit'. But there is some basis for this apparent contradiction, in the source from which Wagner drew Loge's fourth function – that of a mocker of the other gods. This is one of the most entertaining of the ballads in the *Poetic Edda*, called *Lokasenna* (Loki's Wrangling): it tells how, at a great feast held by the sea-god, Aegir, Loki makes scandalous accusations against each of the gods in turn – and in practically every case it seems that he is telling the truth. To Odin he says:

> Silence, Odin · you settle unjustly
>> the strife between mortal men;
> often favouring him · who no favour deserves,
>> letting the lesser man win.

Odin, in fact, eventually came to be regarded by the Norsemen as a treacherous god, who would abandon his human followers in their hour of need – a reputation which even has a repercussion in *The Ring*, when Wotan abandons his own son, Siegmund, and gives the victory to Hunding.

As mentioned earlier, the mythology represents Frigg as having been unfaithful to Odin, and Loki is right again, in saying that it was with Odin's two brothers, Vili and Ve:

> Silence, Frigg · Fjorgyn's daughter,
>> too often you license your lust:
> though Vidrir's wife[14] · both Vili and Ve
>> you allowed to lie with you.

Loki's accusation against Freyja, that she had love-dealings with her brother Frey, and with all the gods and elves, is not confirmed in the mythology; but he is entirely accurate in saying that Frey foolishly lost his sword through his love for a giantess, as mentioned earlier. Thor he taunts – quite unjustly – with cowardice during that unfortunate visit to the land of the giants, but then, himself afraid of Thor's anger and tremendous strength, he finally takes his leave:

> I have said to the gods · and the sons of the gods
>> what matters I had on my mind;
> to you alone · do I yield, and depart,
>> for I know with what strength you strike.

It was no doubt this ballad which gave Wagner the idea of making Loge, not only a mocker of the other gods, but also a teller of unpalatable truths – as when he keeps on reminding Wotan that the gold really belongs to the Rhinemaidens, and should be restored to them. And it also contains the basis of Loge's fifth function – that of being an old friend of Wotan, distrusted by the other gods. On Loki's arrival at the banquet, a prose-link tells us that 'they who were there, when they saw who had entered, were all silent'. And the god of song, Bragi, said to him:

[14] 'Vidrir' is one of the many names of Odin.

> At the table the gods · will give you no place,
>   now, nor nevermore;
> for well they know whom they want to invite
>   as a fellow of their feasts.

Whereupon Loki appealed to Odin:

> Remember, Odin · in olden times,
>   as brothers we mingled our blood;
> You told me then · you would take no drink
>   unless it were brought for us both.

And Odin gave Loki a place at the feast – only to regret it later, as indicated above.

These first five characteristics of Loge, then, are taken over, more or less unchanged, from the Loki of the *Eddas*; and so far, the overt meaning of the Wagnerian character would seem to be practically the same as that of the mythological figure. If we ask what human faculty is independent of ideals, instincts, and emotions; is at times a mischief-making contriver of awkward problems for the sake of solving them, a purveyor of unwelcome truths, and a mocker of hypocrisy; is a faculty needed by man, but mistrusted by his ideals, instincts, and emotions; – there is only one answer – the intellect. If Donner, or Thor, is obviously the 'strong man' amongst the gods, then Loge, or Loki, is no less obviously the 'brains' of the company.

In Scene 2 of *The Rhinegold*, however, we find a sudden change in the way the character-symbolism functions. Loge is the only god who is not related to Wotan; and this suggests that what he embodies is not simply Wotan's own intellectual faculty, but rather the elemental power of thought, which, though available to all, will serve only the individual with the determination to harness and use it – as Wotan has harnessed and is using Loge. And the way Wagner handles the character and behaviour of Loge under-lines this feature of the symbolism. A man's ideals, instincts, and emotions are inherent in his nature, inseparable from him, or at instant beck and call: when we first encounter Wotan, Fricka is at his side, Freia soon comes running up in distress, Froh and Donner quickly appear when she calls for help. But thought is independent of these elements, and less ready to respond at a moment's notice: not always easy to summon, it is difficult to control, often at odds with a man's ideals, instincts, and emotions, and impossible to coerce into producing the answers they demand – like Loge in *The*

Rhinegold. He arrives late, is infuriatingly slow to come to the point, mocks the gods he is supposed to be serving, and reaches one unexpected and unpalatable conclusion; and at the end of *The Rhinegold* he vanishes, to 'turn himself back into flickering flame'. Moreover, he does not serve only the gods: in Scene 3, it appears that he has aided the Nibelungs by providing them with the fire that makes their work possible; in Scene 4, he gives a little elementary advice to Fasolt, telling him to secure the ring, whatever happens to the treasure. This would certainly suggest that he embodies the elemental power of thought, which Wotan has been able to harness and use only to a very limited extent, as intellect.

But does his disappearance mean that Wotan loses interest in him, as in Froh and Donner – i.e., that Wotan has no more use for thought? Hardly, since Loge continues to play his part through his music: whereas the material of Froh and Donner disappears, Loge's music, like Freia's theme, remains central to the score of the tetralogy. At the end of *The Rhinegold*, Loge is telling the truth again – he does 'turn himself back into flickering flame'; and Wotan continues to call on his services as a pure fire-spirit – to encircle the sleeping Brünnhilde in Act 3 of *The Valkyrie*, and to consume Valhalla at the end of *The Twilight of the Gods*. But what has this to do with thought? Here we reach the most elusive aspect of Loge's symbolism – his final function as god of fire.

This function has only a dubious basis in the mythology, resting on two conjectural deductions from mysterious features in the sources. The first occurs during the aforementioned visit of Thor and Loki to the land of the giants, which leads to their total discomfiture. This is one of several episodes revealing a conception peculiar to Scandinavian mythology: the idea that the gods themselves are helpless in the face of elemental forces far more powerful. Arriving at a great castle, Thor and Loki are welcomed derisively by the giant-king, and challenged to demonstrate their godlike powers in a series of insultingly simple tests. Thor, invited to drain a drinking-horn at one draught, manages to lower the level only by a fraction after three; asked to lift the king's cat from the floor, he can shift only one of its feet, and that by a tremendous effort; in a wrestling-match with an aged crone, he is forced to submit after a hard struggle. Afterwards, the king explains that Thor did pretty well: the drinking-horn was attached to the sea, and he did cause an ebb-tide; the cat was really the great serpent encircling the earth under the sea, and everyone was alarmed when he dislodged it a little; the crone was none other than Elli (Old Age), whom no one can overcome.

The name of the giant-king is Utgardar-Loki, meaning 'Loki of Utgard', otherwise 'Loki of the Outer Regions' – which seems curiously suggestive when we remember that Loki himself is the son of a giant. And this suggestion becomes more concrete in the account of the single test which Loki undergoes – an eating-contest with a giant. Each starts from one end of a long trough, filled with meat: Loki eats the flesh off the bones as fast as he can, but when he reaches the middle he finds that the giant has not only got there first, but has eaten flesh, bones, and trough as well. This time, Utgardar-Loki explains that the giant was Logi – otherwise 'Fire', which has no rival in eating things up as quickly and thoroughly as possible. The implication would seem to be that, just as elemental strength overcomes the strong god, Thor, so elemental fire overcomes the fire-god, Loki; but modern scholars, in the absence of any clearer evidence of Loki's function as the fire-god, tend to regard this episode as no more than a play upon words between his name and the name of fire.

The second deduction from the mythology, supposed to support the first, is even more tenuous. When Odin and Loki go off on various journeys together (like the one which results in their robbing Andvari of his treasure – see p. 179), they are accompanied by another god – a totally obscure figure, Hoenir. But in a passage in the *Wise-Woman's Prophecy*, a slightly different trio appears, to create man and woman, and breathe life into them:

> Soul they lacked · sense they lacked,
>   blood, motion, and bloom of life;
> soul gave Odin · sense gave Hoenir,
>   blood gave Lodur, and bloom of life.

The mythology says nothing else about this Lodur, and it can be argued that, to make up the usual trio, he must be Loki under another name; as we have seen earlier, Loki was also known as Lopt, so why not as Lodur? If this argument could be accepted, the fact that 'lodur' means 'blaze' or 'glow', plus the fact that 'Lodur gave blood' (and thereby heat) to the human body, could be set alongside Loki's eating-contest with the fire-giant Logi, and offer plausible grounds for regarding Loki as god of fire. But again modern scholarship, finding no evidence to support the identification of Loki with Lodur, rejects the argument.

Wagner, on the other hand, accepted the argument implicitly, as presented by Jacob Grimm:

> Loki's former fellowship with Oðinn is clearly seen, both from [Lokasenna] and from the juxtaposition of three creative deities on their travels, *Oðinn, Hoenir, Loður* . . . instead of which we also have *Oðinn, Hoenir, Loki* . . . or in a different order, *Oðinn, Loki, Hoenir* . . . From the creating Oðinn proceed breath and spirit . . . as from *Loður* (blaze, glow) came blood and colour . . .

And concerning the eating-contest:

> . . . a striking narrative . . . places *Logi* by the side of *Loki:* a being from the giant province beside a kinsman[15] and companion of the gods. This is no mere play upon words; the two really signify the same thing from different points of view, *Logi* the natural force of fire, and *Loki* – with a shifting of the sound, a shifting of the sense: of the burly giant has been made a sly, seducing villain.

It was on this basis that Wagner made his Loge not only the god of thought but also the god of fire.[16] The conception was no doubt a godsend to a composer of such vivid pictorial powers; but Wagner was never concerned with pictorialism for its own sake. He always used pictorial elements in the interests of symbolism, and so we still have to ask what the connection is between fire and thought. There is a very striking *metaphorical* connection between them in Wagner's music, of course: he uses the same musical ideas to represent Loge's cunning and his 'magic fire', portraying both as elusive, fitful, and brilliant – as indeed, both cunning and fire are. But this leaves the actual symbolism unexplained. What identity or continuity of symbolic meaning is there between Loge's 'crafty counsel' in *The Rhinegold* and the conflagrations he produces in *The Valkyrie* and *The Twilight of the Gods?*

The answer can be found only if we take a deeper and more comprehensive view of the nature of thought. The general tendency is to regard this element in the human make-up as the one that is uniquely under control – employed for cool abstract reason-

[15] One of Grimm's very rare slips: he reveals elsewhere his awareness that Loki is not a relative of the gods, being the son of a giant.

[16] Indeed, for the actual name, after taking that of the god Loki and Germanizing it as Loke in his sketches, he eventually preferred to take the name of the fire-giant Logi and Germanize that as Loge. (In doing so, he went against Grimm's conjectured Locho or Loho, but he did introduce into his text the modern equivalent of those two Old High German formations – *Lohe*, meaning 'flame' or 'blaze': Donner, Wotan, and Loge himself all use the word in close conjunction with Loge's name, as a play upon words.)

ing – while the instincts and emotions are seen as demonic, functioning spontaneously from their roots in the unconscious. But this is true only in so far as thought is equated with the reasoning faculty. Thought is really *mind*, and once we remember that the major function of the mind is to produce creative ideas, and that ideas are things which suddenly 'come to us' from nowhere, as 'inspirations', we realize that, in its essence, the mind is just as demonic and spontaneous as the instincts and emotions.[17]

Loge, then, really functions as this elemental power of mind, which Wotan has been able to harness and use to only a very limited degree, as intellect. It is to a small extent that, acting under Wotan's coercion, he figures in its controlled aspect – as the rational faculty – by using logic to find a way out of the dilemma with regard to Valhalla and Freia: his basic function is as a symbol of mind in its demonic aspect – as a source of ideas and inspirations. In the first place, the 'great inspiration' that 'came to' Wotan – that of consummating his power through the building of Valhalla, even though it meant risking the loss of his capacity for love once and for all, in the person of Freia – came to him from Loge, as he tells Fricka in Scene 2 of *The Rhinegold:*

> *He who advised me to the contract*
> *promised me to redeem Freia.*

Again, if the idea of entering on the contract was one inspiration, the actual redeeming of Freia necessitates another, and this also comes from Loge – only he is late to arrive: ideas of this order are not always at hand when needed. And even when he does arrive, he is recalcitrant, taking his time to produce the solution: ideas are often slow to take rational shape. Furthermore, in the process of finding the solution, he also taunts Wotan with the unacceptable truth – that the gold should be restored to its rightful owners, the Rhinemaidens – and he keeps harping on it: the truth will often break through into a man's mind, and keep nagging at him, however unpalatable it may be to his ideals, instincts, and emotions, and to his own will and ambition.

And this function of Loge as a demonic source of mental inspiration continues beyond *The Rhinegold* – negatively for a time. After he has vanished, Wotan is left barren of true inspiration: his immediate plan concerning the Volsungs, conceived and carried

[17] I am drawing here on a remembered idea of Goethe, the actual source of which I have been unable to trace.

out in Loge's absence, ends in utter disaster with the destruction of
Siegmund. Indeed, communing with Brünnhilde after his humiliation by Fricka, Wotan laments both Loge's disappearance and his
own folly. Of his quest for world-domination, he says:

> *When youthful love's*
> *delights grew pale,*
> *my spirit longed for power . . .*
> *Loge cunningly led me on,*
> *who has now wandered away and vanished.*

And of his shattered plan concerning the Volsungs:

> *Why be so clever*
> *at defrauding myself?*
> *How easily Fricka*
> *unravelled my deceit!*

At this point, it becomes obvious that Loge cannot simply
embody the purely intellectual aspect of the mind. Wotan himself
has been perfectly capable of reasoning – even of being 'clever'; but
his reasoning and cleverness have led him completely astray in the
absence of the kind of demonic inspiration provided by Loge. And
it is here at last that we find the identity and continuity between
Loge's activities as the god of intellect in *The Rhinegold* and as the
god of fire in the rest of the tetralogy. For when Loge does
eventually reappear, on two separate occasions – being called on
by name and responding as the god of fire in the shape of his music
– his reappearances take the form of two great conflagrations
which coincide, significantly, with the two decisive mental inspirations that eventually come to Wotan: the one at the end of *The
Valkyrie,* of bringing Siegfried and Brünnhilde together by encircling her with flames which only one who knows no fear can
penetrate;[18] and the one in *The Twilight of the Gods,* of annihilating
Valhalla by having it consumed by fire. What these two ideas
signify in themselves must be left until later; but in the meantime,
it is clear that Wagner used Loge's function as the god of fire to
symbolize mind in its most creative form, that of a demonic
(Promethean) source of inspiration.

We can now sum up the overt meaning of the relationship
between Wotan and Loge, which Wagner imposed on the

---

[18] These flames are actually Brünnhilde's idea, but this is another *alter ego* situation,
the clearest in *The Ring*; as she says to Wotan, in Act 2 of *The Valkyrie*, 'What am I, if I
am not your will?'

mythological material by his insistence on making the latter the god of fire as well as the god of intellect. Loge, in his essential role of fire-spirit, embodies the elemental force of mental inspiration, which Wotan, in *The Rhinegold*, has partly harnessed, but only in the service of his limited, blinkered aim of world-domination: the 'great inspiration' it produces for him is the fraudulent contract with the giants, consummating his power through the building of Valhalla; after which it acts under Wotan's coercion, partly as the 'controlled' rational intellect, cleverness and cunning – to find a way out of the dilemma created by the contract. In consequence, it is recalcitrant, insisting on the truth he does not want to accept, and under these circumstances its fire burns low; being thus misused, it deserts him entirely for the first two acts of *The Valkyrie*, during which time, although he tries to impose the principle of true justice on his power-ridden world, he does so entirely by an arbitrary exercise of his own power, thereby committing the folly of contending against himself. But at the end of Act 3 of *The Valkyrie*, when he has been won over by Brünnhilde (his love-child) to abandon his ideal of absolute power and to further the claims of love, mental inspiration comes to him in its fullness, as a great conflagration – as it does again at the very end of the whole tetralogy, when he accepts Loge's 'unacceptable' truth, and the ring is returned to the Rhinemaidens. We may say that Wotan was wise to make a friend of Loge, in spite of the mistrust of the other gods, and to set his hopes on him, even if at first he did not understand his true worth.

Scene 2: The Action

Having established the overt meaning which Wagner conferred on the characters of Wotan and the other gods, and on the relationships existing between them, we are now in a position to examine the construction of the actual action of Scene 2 of *The Rhinegold*.

For its absolute basis, he was dependent on a single source: the *Prose Edda* alone contains the myth of the building of the gods' fortress. Two immediate surprises for the Wagnerian are that the fortress in the myth is not Valhalla, and that there is one giant only; and there are bigger shocks to follow. The story begins:

> Soon after the gods had settled here, when they had created Midgard [the earth] and built Valholl, a master-workman came and offered to build a fortress in three seasons, which would be shield and protection for the gods against the Hill-Giants and the Frost-Giants ... But as wages he stipulated Freyja, and moreover the sun and the moon. Then the Aesir assembled and took counsel, and they struck a bargain with the workman that he should have what he had asked for, if he completed the fortress in a single winter; but if any part of it was not ready by the first day of summer, he should lose his wages, and further, he should receive no help from anyone with the work. When they told him these conditions, he asked them to allow him the help of his stallion Svadilfari, and on Loki's advice this was granted. He began building the fortress on the first day of winter, and he hauled stones each night with the stallion's aid. It seemed a great marvel to the Aesir what huge rocks the stallion pulled ... but the bargain had been strongly ratified with many witnesses and powerful oaths, since without such a truce the giant did not feel safe among the Aesir, if Thor should come home ...
>
> When the winter approached its end, the building of the fortress had gone very quickly ... and when there were only three days to summer, it had already reached the gate of the fortress. Then the gods sat themselves in their judgment-seats and took counsel, and they asked one another who had advised giving Freyja into Jotunheim [Giant-Land] and ruining the air and the heaven by taking away the sun and the moon and giving them to the giants. Then they all agreed that the one who had given this advice must be he who counselled all evil things, Loki, the son of Laufey; and they said that he should die an evil death if he did not find a way of denying the workman his wages. And when they set upon Loki, he was frightened of them, and he swore oaths that he would so manage things that, whatever it might cost him, the workman should lose his wages.

Up to this point, as can be seen, the myth offered Wagner a

solid basis for the action of Scene 2 of *The Rhinegold*, despite certain features which needed changing: put as simply as possible, Loki advised the gods to trade Freyja to the giants in return for the building of an impregnable fortress, and undertook to see that the wage would not have to be paid. But since the solution provided by Loki is not only sordid, farcical, and unstageable, but also final (i.e. allowing for no further continuation into a larger story), it was quite useless to Wagner. Nevertheless, as will be noticed, this part of the myth contained two vivid elements – the giant's fury and the arrival of Thor with his hammer – which he was able to transfer to the useful first part:

That same evening, when the workman went out after stones with the stallion Svadilfari, a mare ran out of a wood and whinnied to him. And when the stallion realized what kind of a horse this was, he went wild, burst the reins, and ran after the mare, and the mare ran in front to the wood, and the workman after the stallion to catch him. These horses ran around the whole night, and that night the labour was held up; and when day came the work had not been carried out as before. And when the workman saw that the work could not be completed, he fell into a giant's fury. But the Aesir, now that they knew for certain that he was a Hill-Giant, honoured their oaths no longer, but called on Thor. He came immediately, and straightway lifted his hammer Mjollnir, and therewith paid the workman's wages – and not with the sun and the moon: he even prevented him from building any more in Jotunheim, for with the first blow he smashed his skull into little pieces and sent him down to Niflhel [the land of the dead]. But Loki, having served Svadilfari as a mare, gave birth some time later to a foal, which was gray and had eight feet; and this is the best horse among gods and men.

So the story ends by explaining the curious origin of Odin's famous grey eight-legged steed Sleipnir – on which pretext, indeed, the myth is introduced into the *Prose Edda*.

Wagner's manipulations of this material fall under four overlapping headings: tidying up the plot; deliberately altering certain elements; shaping the story for dovetailing into the myth of Andvari which he used for the later part of *The Rhinegold*; and strengthening the characterization and the symbolism. Tidying-up involved, first of all, the rejection of two quite inessential features: the giant's attempt to play a trick on the gods, by pretending to be a mere harmless 'workman'; and the inclusion of the sun and moon in the stipulated wage (though this latter omission also served to strengthen the symbolism, by concentrating the whole interest on the goddess of love). The removal of the stallion also comes partly under this heading, but it was much more a matter of dovetailing: Wagner needed to replace the beast with a brother-giant, to link on to the Andvari myth, in which the gods' enemies, as we shall see, are two brothers.

The removal of the stallion, as is obvious, was also part of the larger process of dovetailing – the rejection of the time-limit set by the gods, together with the second part of the story, concerned with Loki's solution, which is dependent on both the time-limit and the stallion. And with the time-limit, inevitably, went the non-completion of the fortress; so that, in *The Rhinegold,* Wagner presents us with a quite altered situation. Instead of Loki's tricking of the giant into just failing to fulfil the contract – which gave the gods a technical victory, and thereby a technical justification for having him killed by Thor when he 'fell into a giant's fury' – the contract is actually fulfilled, and it is the giants' fury which is entirely justified, when Wotan simply refuses to pay them the stipulated wage, and waits for Loge to arrive with his idea for a substitute payment. This alteration is, of course, a major strengthening of the symbolism, since the primitive cunning of Loki in the myth is replaced by a flagrant act of bad faith on the part of Wotan.

But it is also the basic piece of dovetailing. When the giants' fury and Freia's cry for help bring Donner on to the scene, the hammer is raised aloft – but it does not fall: Wotan interposes his spear, and the giants are not killed. If this is a still further strengthening of the symbolism – reinforcing the purely Wagnerian significance of Wotan's spear as an instrument of law – it also provides the absolutely fundamental link with the myth of Andvari. For now, an entirely different solution is needed from the one in the fortress myth; and that solution can only be a ransom for Freia; and a ransom is exactly what the gods have to find in the Andvari myth, to extricate themselves from their (different) predicament. It may also be pointed out here that this is the really crucial bit of dovetailing in *The Ring*, since the Andvari myth, in the sources, leads straight on to the more or less cohesive remainder of the story.

The Andvari myth appears, not only in the *Prose Edda*, but also in the *Poetic Edda* and *Volsunga saga;* they all tell virtually the same story, however, and the fuller version in the *Prose Edda* is the best basis to work from. The general pattern is similar to that of the fortress myth: Loki gets the gods into trouble (innocently this time), and gets them out again. But in this case it was the first part of the story which Wagner rejected, since it was as useless to him as Loki's dealings with Svadilfari:

It is told that three of the Aesir went out to explore the earth: Odin, Loki, and Hoenir. They came to a river, and went along it until they came to a waterfall; and by the waterfall was an otter, which had caught a salmon and was eating it, blinking its eyes. Then Loki picked up a stone, and threw it at the otter, and hit it on the head. And Loki praised his own hunting, saying that he had bagged otter and salmon with one throw; then they took the salmon and the otter with them. They came to some farm-buildings and went in; and the farmer who lived there was called Hreidmar, a powerful man and well-versed in magic. The Aesir asked for a night's lodging, and said they had food with them, and showed the farmer their catch. But when Hreidmar saw the otter, he called his two sons, Fafnir and Regin, and told them that their brother Otter was killed, and who had done this.

[*Volsunga saga* is more explicit at this point, making clear that this brother was a man who took animal form; it calls him Otr, and says that 'he was a great fisherman, far excelling others, and in the daytime took the form of an otter, and was always in the river, bringing up fish in his mouth'.]

Then the father, with his sons, set on the Aesir, seized them, and bound them, and told them that the otter was Hreidmar's son. The Aesir offered a ransom, as much as Hreidmar wished; and this was agreed between them and confirmed with oaths.

And so we arrive at the second part of the story, with the need of a ransom, and Loki's solution of the problem, which Wagner dovetailed into the first part of the fortress myth. It begins:

Then the otter was skinned, and Hreidmar took the skin and said they must fill it with red gold and also cover it with gold, and therewith they could buy their freedom. Then Odin sent Loki to Svartâlfaheim [the Land of the Black Elves], and he came to the dwarf who is called Andvari . . .

At this point, we really reach the end of the part connected with the action of Scene 2 of *The Rhinegold*, but it will be convenient to continue to the end of the story, which covers much of Scenes 3 and 4, and looks beyond them:

. . . and he came to the dwarf who is called Andvari, who was as a fish in the water. Loki caught him in his hands and demanded from him, as ransom for his life, all the gold that he had in his rock; and when they went into the rock, the dwarf produced all the gold he had, and it was very much wealth. Then the dwarf hid under his hand a little gold ring: Loki saw this, and ordered him to hand over the ring. The dwarf begged him not to take the ring from him, since with that ring he could increase his gold. But Loki said he should not have a penny left; he took the ring from him and went out. Then the dwarf said that the ring should cost everyone who possessed it his life. Loki answered that he accepted this, and it should be as he prophesied; he himself would make it known to the future possessor of the ring. Then he went back to Hreidmar's house and showed Odin the gold; and when Odin saw the ring, it seemed beautiful to him, and he took it from the treasure and gave the rest of the gold to Hreidmar. Then Hreidmar packed the otter-skin with gold as tightly as he could, and stood it up when it was full. Then Odin went up to it, and had to cover it with gold. When he had done that, he asked Hreidmar to look, and see if the skin was completely covered. Hreidmar went up to it, and looked carefully and saw a single whisker, and ordered that this too should be covered, otherwise the contract was broken. Then Odin brought out the ring and covered the whisker, saying that he had now paid their debt concerning the otter. And when Odin had taken his spear, and Loki his shoes, so that they had nothing more to fear, Loki said that what Andvari had said should come true, that the gold and the ring should cost anyone who possessed them his life; and so it happened afterwards . . .

When Hreidmar had received the gold as his son's blood-money, Fafnir and Regin craved their share of it as brothers' blood-money; but Hreidmar gave them not a penny of it. Then the two brothers agreed to kill their father for the gold. When that had taken place, Regin asked Fafnir to share the gold with him, half each: Fafnir replied that there was little likelihood of his sharing the gold with his brother, after he had killed his father for it, and he ordered Regin to be on his way, otherwise what had happened to Hreidmar would happen to him . . . So Regin fled away; but Fafnir went up to Gnita-Heath, made himself a lair there, took the form of a serpent, and laid himself down on the gold.

By rejecting the first part of this myth entirely, Wagner was able to dovetail its second part into the first part of the fortress myth by means of three main manipulations. The blood-money for the otter became the ransom for Freia – even down to the method of measuring the ransom: the otter-skin was replaced by her body, and the still visible whisker by her hair and eyes (two elements instead of one, because Wagner added the Tarnhelm to the ring). Odin was transferred to the fortress myth which so surprisingly lacks him, and given, as chief of the gods, his natural status as controller of events. And Hreidmar's two sons were also transferred, replacing the giant and his stallion, to become two brother-giants who build the fortress: Fafnir and Regin are not actually said to be giants in the Andvari myth, but it seems difficult to imagine they are not, since mere men would hardly be represented as treating Odin and Loki in the way that they do.

One bit of obvious tidying-up was the omission of the obscure god Hoenir – who in any case, as will have been noticed, is no longer there in the second part of the myth. The most striking manipulation of all – the omission of Hreidmar, and the replacement of his murder at the hands of his two sons with the murder of one of them by the other – might also seem to come under this heading; but in fact it is another piece of dovetailing – a forward one this time. For in the mythology, when Fafnir and Regin have murdered their father and quarrelled over the gold, Regin 'flees away' – and he eventually becomes the foster-father of Sigurd, whom he incites to get back the gold for him by killing Fafnir; in other words, he goes on to occupy the place taken in *Siegfried* by Mime. But this was quite impossible in *The Ring*: Wagner had made Fafnir and his brother into giants, and he wanted to make Siegfried's foster-father a dwarf (following the *Poetic Edda* and *Norna-Gests thattr*), giving him the name Mime (following *Thidriks saga*), and making him a Nibelung-brother of Alberich (in defiance of the whole mythology). He solved this awkward problem brilliantly, by altering the Hreidmar-Fafnir-Regin complex in such a way as to kill two birds with one stone: he dispensed with Hreidmar altogether, thereby tidying up the plot; and he replaced the sons' killing of their father with Fafnir's killing of his brother, thereby terminating that brother's part in the story, and so leaving himself free to make Sigurd's foster-father the dwarf Mime, Nibelung brother of Alberich. In doing so, of course, he had to find a new name for Fafnir's brother, since the name Regin was well-known to connoisseurs of Scandinavian mythology as that of Sigurd's foster-father; and he chose the name of a German wind-giant which Jacob Grimm had disinterred from various obscure sources – Fasolt – primarily, no doubt, because of the alliteration (common between brothers in the mythology) with Fafnir – or, in Wagner's Germanization, Fafner.

We have been looking forward again – necessarily, in order to understand Wagner's masterly manipulation of the various elements of the mythology – but we must now examine Scene 2 of *The Rhinegold* under the most important heading: that of the strengthening of the characterization and the symbolism. To begin with, the fortress myth speaks only of 'the gods', without even mentioning Odin; but as said above, Wagner transferred him back from the Andvari myth, giving him full control of the whole course of events. And as Wotan, he provided him with a character in depth, based partly on the Odin of the mythology as a whole, but much more on his own personal interpretation of the spear as an instrument of world-domination-through-law.

In the myth, the suggestion for the fortress comes from the giant, but in *The Rhinegold* Wotan *compels* the giants to build it: 'By a contract I tamed their defiant race', he says, 'so that they should build me the noble hall'. This contradicts the whole general situation in the mythology, where the giants remain a perpetual danger (even if they are usually outwitted or killed), until some of them take part in the battle against the gods on the last day of the world, in which every single combatant except one is annihilated. Nevertheless, the gods actually created the world out of the carcass of a primeval giant whom they slew; and Wagner may have been following Grimm again, who describes the giants as

. . . specimens of a falling or fallen race, which with the strength combines the innocence and wisdom of the old world, an intelligence more objective, and imparted at creation, than self-acquired.

Certainly, the giants in *The Rhinegold* feature as underprivileged members of the world ruled over by Wotan. The 'bargain' of the myth, and the 'oaths' demanded by the giant, become the 'contract' engraved on the spear – which is *imposed* by Wotan. First and foremost stands his own stipulation – that the fortress shall be built; only secondly – and not seriously – the giants' stipulation that the wage shall be Freia. Furthermore, the unnamed fortress[1] itself becomes Valhalla, despite the myth's statement that Valholl was already in existence when the fortress was built; this strengthened the symbolism greatly, owing to the echoes awakened by the name, as the seat of military power of the chief of the Teutonic gods, and as the 'paradise' of the Teutonic heroes.

Wagner's other reinforcements of the characterization and symbolism were largely achieved through his convincing dramatization of the material. Along with Wotan he introduced immediately his wife Fricka – although she plays no part in the myths used for *The Rhinegold* – and gave her also a character in depth, based partly on the equivalent figure in the mythology, but more on his own interpretation of her as the upright, jealous, barren wife, and

[1] H. R. Ellis Davidson has pointed out to me, in a private letter, that the 'fortress' (*biorg* in the original Norse, *Burg* in the German translations available to Wagner and hence in *The Ring*) would have been thought of by the ancient Scandinavians as a great wall encircling all the halls already built by the gods, including Valholl.

goddess of marriage. And by weaving in the recurrent (German and Scandinavian) motif of an altercation between the two, he succeeded in fulfilling a threefold dramatic purpose: to expose the immediate dramatic situation – the pledging of Freia as the giants' wage for building the fortress; to present Wotan's ambivalent attitude to his ideal of world-domination-through-law, imposed by his spear but enshrined in a wife he no longer loves; and to establish his indifference to the claims of love, as represented by women -- not only in his readiness to put Freia in pledge, but also in the fact that he has entered on the contract in consultation with the other gods, but not with the goddesses.

Next, Wagner brought Freia right into the foreground. Whereas in the fortress myth she is no more than a name, he made her a central figure of the action through a striking piece of dramatization, emphasizing her plight as the abused goddess of love by having her run on in terror, pursued by the giants. For her character as love-goddess he relied mainly, as we have seen, on her actual identity as such in the mythology, supporting this by establishing her *alter-ego* sister-relationship with Fricka, by making her the starting-point of a panegyric on love by Loge, and by letting her be the only character in *The Rhinegold* to whom love and affection are shown. And he also added further support: he represented Fasolt as being *in* love with Freia, and made him re-buke Wotan for prizing her so little as to put her in pledge in the interests of increasing his power.

This brings us to the giants, whose character and symbolism Wagner clarified in one case and created in the other. The character of Fafner is a fusion of two elements in the mythology: the desire of the giant in the fortress myth to ruin the gods by depriving them of Freia, the sun, and the moon; and a statement in *Volsunga saga* that, of the sons of Hreidmar in the Andvari myth, Fafnir 'was the biggest and fiercest, and wanted everything for himself'. From these two elements Wagner created his brutal, greedy, cynically realistic Fafner, for whom the securing of Freia is no more than a means of bringing the gods down, and for whom the possession of the treasure is an even more desirable end; and he took straight over from the mythology, of course, Fafnir's brutish violence in murdering a kinsman for the hoard, as well as his brutish stupidity in merely storing the hoard away and turning himself into a dragon to guard it.

The character of Fasolt, on the other hand, was entirely created by Wagner, as a complete foil to Fafner. There is in fact a foil-relationship between the two brothers in the Andvari myth: whereas *Volsunga saga* describes Fafnir as 'the biggest and fiercest' of Hreidmar's sons, it describes Regin as 'the least gifted and made least of' – which ties up suggestively with the fact that, in his capacity as Sigurd's foster-father, the *Poetic Edda* and *Norna-Gests thattr* represent him as a dwarf. But since Wagner separated off this foster-father figure altogether from the Regin of the Andvari myth, making him a Nibelung dwarf-brother of Alberich with the *Thidriks saga* name of Mime, he was free to give Regin an entirely new character, just as he gave him the new name of Fasolt and the new destiny of being killed by his brother Fafner. And whereas he had to make Fafner a giant, Fasolt was one anyway; but he made him less brutal and greedy, and not a cynical realist at all – on the contrary, a moral idealist, with a primitive intuition of love. Again, the hint may have come from Grimm – in taking the name Fasolt from him, Wagner may have been influenced by the following reference:

> . . . [the giants] sometimes leave on us the impression of older nature-gods, who had to give way to a younger and superior race; it is only natural, therefore, that in certain giants, like Ecke and Fasolt, we should recognize a precipitate of deity.

Nevertheless, Wagner's Fasolt is entirely his own creation. Whereas, for Fafner, the securing of Freia is purely a means of ruining the gods, Fasolt's whole interest centres on Freia herself, as an object of love. His chief aim, he says, is

> *to win a woman*
> *who, lovely and gentle,*
> *shall dwell with us poor creatures.*

Indeed, when Freia first appears, she names Fasolt as her actual pursuer; when the giants decide to accept the hoard and the ring as a substitute for her, Fafner takes the decision, while Fasolt is only with reluctance persuaded to agree, being still desirous of Freia; and when the giants take her away as a hostage, it is Fasolt who actually lays hold of her. Again, in Scene 4, Fafner's insistence that he can still see her hair through a gap in the pile of gold is a mere pretext for having the Tarnhelm added to the hoard; but Fasolt's subsequent glimpse of her eyes, through a last chink (even though it serves Fafner as a pretext for securing the ring), moves him to declare that he cannot give her up – and he seizes her eagerly when Wotan refuses to stop this chink with the ring. Finally, the whole characterization is clinched by Fafner when, having murdered Fasolt to get the ring, he mocks his body with the words:

> *Now dazzle yourself with Freia's glance!*
> *You'll never touch the ring again!*

Wagner's creation of Fasolt, as a complete foil to the existing character of Fafner, is by no means the least important of the manipulations and additions whereby he constructed *The Rhinegold*. For it ratifies the overt meaning which we have seen him conferring on his whole material so far, through a reinforcement of the power-versus-love symbolism on yet another plane. If Alberich has renounced love in order to pursue power, and Wotan has pursued power to the point of practically losing his capacity for love, the two principles of power and love are embodied separately in the two giants, and brought into conflict. Fafner stands as the pure seeker for power – first through his intention of ruining the gods by taking Freia from them, and then by his determination to secure the treasure and the ring; Fasolt stands, uniquely, as a seeker for love, in the person of Freia; and again, power has the upper hand. Fafner attains the power he is seeking, by cunning, brute force, and lovelessness: first he seduces his brother into giving up his quest for love in exchange for the hope of power; then he makes sure that he loses that, by murdering him.

Nor is this the only function of Fasolt: the other side of his character – his moral idealism – enhances the symbolism of Wotan's spear as an instrument of world-domination-through-law. Like the giant in the fortress myth, Fasolt falls into a 'giant's fury' when he realizes he has been hoodwinked; but whereas the mythological figure is merely furious that the gods have tricked him into failing to fulfil his contract, the moral Fasolt, having actually fulfilled his contract, is full of righteous anger when Wotan simply refuses to pay the stipulated wage. Indeed, he rebukes him for breaking the laws engraved on the spear, whereby he rules the world:

> *What you are,*
> *you are through contracts only;*
> *conditioned and*
> *well thought out is your power . . .*
> *I curse all your knowledge . . .*

> *if you do not know how, frankly,*
> *honourably and freely,*
> *to keep faith with contracts!*
> *A stupid giant*
> *tells you that:*
> *you wise one, learn wisdom from him!*

And here again, the double-symbolism of the two brothers is immediately in evidence: the cynically realistic Fafner, having expected chicanery from the start, tells his moral idealist of a brother to 'stop his idle chatter'.

This reinforcement of the symbolism of the spear, through the characterization of Fasolt, is further enhanced when Donner arrives to quell the 'giant's fury': he lifts his hammer murderously, like Thor in the myth – only to be restrained by Wagner's Wotan through the interposition of the law-enforcing spear. Donner's aggression is futile: there is no intention of breaking the contract, but only the problem of finding a substitute for Freia. Also the easy optimism of the supernumerary god Froh, who arrives at the same time, is equally useless, since that problem looks fairly insoluble. And so the stage is set for the long-awaited arrrival of the 'brains' of the company of gods, Loge.

The part played by this figure in the fortress myth was also changed and amplified to great advantage. Instead of the mere malicious mischief-maker who advises the unthinking gods to enter into an impossible contract, and then has to be frightened into getting them out of it, we are mainly confronted with the cool, capable, resourceful figure in the Andvari myth – Odin's old friend and trusted ally, who knows exactly what to do, and can be relied on to do it. And he is also provided with a character in depth, based on his equivalent in the mythology as a whole, plus an extra identity as god of fire, drawn from the speculations of Jacob Grimm. But Wagner did retain from the fortress myth Loki's indifference to the problem he has created, and the need for him to be at least browbeaten into taking it seriously. As a result of this, Loge emerges decisively as the god of demonic mental inspiration, disdainful of having to act in his purely intellectual, rational capacity to further Wotan's petty aim of world-domination.

Moreover, the combination of mockery and truth with which he propounds his solution further reinforces the power-versus-love symbolism. First, he praises the fortress, Wotan's great power-symbol – but sarcastically,[2] implying its worthlessness – a fact which Wotan will only come to realize in *The Twilight of the Gods*, when he decides that it shall be consumed in Loge's fire. Then he says that, although he promised to find a substitute for Freia, he could hardly find something that did not exist, thereby accusing Wotan of trying to have it both ways – dominate the world and yet retain his capacity for love – a fact which Wotan will only appreciate in Act 2 of *The Valkyrie*, when he acknowledges it to Brünnhilde. Next he delivers a panegyric on love (referring to Freia) as the one thing no one wants to lose, because it is the creative force of life – a truth which Wotan will only accept in Act 3 of *Siegfried*, when he tells Erda he is bequeathing the world to Siegfried and Brünnhilde. He then goes on to disclose the existence of Alberich's ring, and points out that its absolute power is dependent on the renunciation of love – a condition which repels Wotan, even though he is himself near to fulfilling it in his own pursuit of world-domination. And finally, he insists that the only thing to do with this ring of loveless power is to return it to its owners, the Rhinemaidens – another truth which Wotan has to wait until *The Twilight of the Gods* to appreciate, when he decides to act on it. It would perhaps not be going too far to describe Loge as the god of truth.

Once he discloses the existence of Alberich's ring, the reactions of the other characters immediately reinforce its symbolism. They are all, except one, greedy for it, and all for the same reason – the power it will give them over others. Wotan (who significantly has heard rumours about it) sees in it a further extension of his own world-domination; Fricka sees in it the wealth it will confer, which (Loge assures her) will enable her to so beautify herself as to be irresistible to Wotan, and thereby keep him uxoriously at home in the fortress once and for all. Donner wants it taken from Alberich to prevent him from having the upper hand of the gods, and Froh adds to this his fatuous comment that it will be easy to get it now without renouncing love. Fafner's motivation is similar to Donner's – the need to prevent Alberich from becoming master of them all; and by assuring Fasolt that the ring will be a much more valuable acquisition than Freia, he carries his reluctant, love-smitten brother with him.

The only character who expresses no desire for the ring at all is

[2] Not perhaps in the text alone, but certainly in the music – a brisk, flippant version of the solemn Valhalla theme.

Freia, and this further underlines the basic power-versus-love symbolism: she above all might be expected to insist that Wotan gets the ring from Alberich, since it is her only chance of being ransomed – but as goddess of love, how can she even consider having anything to do with a talisman dependent on the renunciation of love? Loge, of course, is not greedy for the ring either. As one concerned for the truth, he has already had his say – it belongs to the Rhinemaidens, and should be given back to them; even so, he says it again, twice. What he does not say is that it can be used as a substitute wage for Freia, which is clearly the one possible solution to the contract problem. The god of mind can only indicate the truth, and hint at possible alternatives: the moral decision and action, like all others, must be taken by the will of the chief god, Wotan.

But of the three possible decisions – to restore the ring to its rightful owners, to use it to ransom Freia, and to possess it himself – Wotan is at present inclining towards the last and worst. His three comments on the ring have been as follows:

> *(reflectively)*
>   *Of the Rhinegold*
>   *I have heard tell:*
>   *runes of wealth*
> *are hidden in its red glow;*
>   *power and riches*
> *immeasurable could be achieved by a ring.*

And later:

> *(as if in a state of increasing fascination)*
>   *To take control of this ring*
> *is a good idea, it seems to me.*

And then, simply:

> *I must have the ring!*

Finally, when the suggestion is at last made – by Fafner – that the ring can replace Freia as the wage for building the fortress, Wotan's reaction shows that this is the last thing he is thinking of:

> *Are you out of your minds?*
> *What does not belong to me,*
> *shall I make a present of to you shameless ones? . . .*
> *Am I to exert myself*
> *against the dwarf for you?*

Here the power-versus-love symbolism is brought to a head for the first time in the scene. If Wotan has shown himself blind to the claims of love, in pledging Freia for an increase in his power in the first place, he at least wanted to have it both ways, in that he did not seriously intend to part with her; but now the chance has come to ransom her with the ring, he sees that talisman entirely as a means of attaining absolute world-domination, not as a ransom for Freia at all. His lust for power is driving love from his being entirely: his situation is becoming perilously close to that of Alberich.

But one aspect of the symbolism still remains unclarified. If power is so infinitely desirable, where would be the harm in settling for it and letting love go hang? After all, what difference would it make to Wotan if he actually abandoned Freia to the giants? What would the loss of her matter? Wagner wanted to raise and answer these questions in dramatic form, so as to clinch the symbolism; and to do so, he crammed into the scene one final element from his sources – the myth of the loss of the apples of immortality.

The story, which is contained in the *Prose Edda* only,[3] follows the same pattern as those of the fortress and Andvari myths; Loki gets the gods into trouble (this time under severe coercion from outside), and gets them out again. In this case, it was the beginning and end that were of no use to Wagner, and the middle that he needed. The story begins, like the Andvari myth, with one of those ill-fated foraging expeditions by the three inseparables:

Three of the Aesir, Odin, Loki and Hoenir, set out from home and journeyed over mountains and through wastes, where there was often no means of life. They came at last to a valley, where they saw a herd of oxen; they took one of them, and prepared and cooked it. When they thought it was cooked sufficiently, they took it from the fire, but found it was not so. Somewhat later, they took it again, but it was still not cooked. Then they heard something in the oak-tree they were under, and looking up, they saw a great eagle, who said that it was he who had prevented the ox from cooking; if they would give him his share, he added, it would be cooked soon enough. When they agreed, he flew down from the tree and started cooking; and he took both the shoulders of the ox for himself. At this, Loki became angry, took a great pole, lifted it with all his strength, and struck at the eagle. The eagle avoided the blow, and flew up in such a way that one end of the pole was in Loki's hands, and the other attached to the eagle's back. The eagle flew at such a height that Loki's feet stumbled against

---

[3] In this case, the German version I have translated from is the condensed one by C. F. Rühs (op. cit.); Simrock does not include the myth.

tree-stumps and rocks, and he thought his arms would be torn out. He shouted to the eagle, begging him urgently to let him go . . .

And so we come to the middle part of the story, which Wagner was able to weave in between the first part of the fortress myth and the second part of the Andvari myth:

> . . . but the eagle said that Loki should never go free unless he undertook by oath to bring Idun out of Asgard [the home of the gods] with her apples. And when Loki agreed, he set him free . . . At the appointed time, Loki enticed Idun to leave Asgard and to go with him to a certain wood, on the pretext that he had found some apples there that would seem good to her; and at the same time he asked her to take her own apples with her, so that she could compare them with those in the wood. Then the giant Thjazi came in his eagle-plumage, took Idun, and flew away with her to his home in Thrymheim.
> The Aesir suffered greatly through the abduction of Idun: they became grey-haired and old . . .

So, as in the fortress myth, a giant in disguise plays a trick on the gods, through Loki's agency, to try and bring them down; and this enabled Wagner to tie to his adaptation of the fortress myth this other myth's basic idea of a giant abducting the goddess with the apples. Freia took over the apples from Idun; Fafner took over from Thjazi the aim of bringing the gods down by depriving them of the apples; and the attempted once-for-all abduction of Idun became the mere temporary removal of Freia, as a hostage. The apples themselves – which Idun kept in a chest – would have been an awkward stage-property, so Wagner left them growing in 'Freia's garden', and made the mere removal of her influence on them cause the gods to start ageing.

The Idun myth concludes very much like the fortress myth, with the terrorizing of Loki, his assumption of animal (bird) form to outwit the giant, and the final (more justified) killing of the giant:

> The Aesir held council and asked who had last heard anything of Idun; and the last trace they could find of her was that she had left Asgard with Loki.` He was now brought before the assembly, and threatened with a shameful death; he became frightened, and promised to go and seek Idun in Jotunheim, if Freyja would lend him her hawk-plumage. When he had received this, he flew northwards to Jotunheim, and came to the home of the giant Thjazi: he had just rowed out to sea, and Idun was at home alone. Loki changed her into a nut,[4] took her in his claws, and flew away with her swiftly. When Thjazi came home and found that Idun was gone, he flew

[4] This word is mistranslated in Wagner's source, the German translation by C. F. Rühs, as 'swallow'.

after Loki, and caught up with him, so swiftly he flew. But when the Aesir saw the hawk flying with the nut, and the eagle after it, they went to the walls of Asgard, and took with them a load of wood-shavings. As the hawk reached the citadel, it dived down by the walls; whereupon the Aesir set light to the shavings, and since the eagle could not stop its flight quickly enough, the flames burnt its wings, so that it could fly no longer. The Aesir were ready, and killed the eagle; and so the giant Thjazi paid with his life by the walls of Asgard, an event which is exceeding famous.

This final part of the story, like that of the fortress myth, was of course replaced by the latter part of the Andvari myth – yet Wagner still managed to have it three ways: Loge, in securing the ransom, also rescues Freia, and at the same time regains the apples.

All that is known about Idun, apart from this myth, is told in one other brief passage in the *Prose Edda*. She is the wife of the god of song, Bragi, and

> . . . she keeps in a chest the apples which the gods have to eat when they grow old; and then they all become young again; and this shall continue until Ragnarok [the end of the gods].

She is certainly a quite separate figure from Freyja, as is clear from the above myth, in which Freyja and her famous hawk-plumage play their own roles: she was no doubt a goddess of fertility, since both apples and nuts were common fertility symbols. But Wagner, in transferring her apples to Freia, was not going against natural symbolism: he was simply endowing her with a symbol appropriate to her status. As love-goddess, Freia was also, inevitably, a goddess of fertility; and if the fortress myth had represented her as being actually carrried off by the giant, her abduction would surely have been viewed as a catastrophe equal to the abduction of Idun.

It was this way of thinking, in fact, that led Wagner to incorporate the myth of the apples. His first brief prose-sketch for *The Rhinegold* does not contain them, nor even any abduction of Freia; in some supplementary sketches, made soon afterwards, they are still not mentioned, though Freia is abducted, and her mere absence causes the gods to 'break out into lamentation', and Valhalla to 'darken'. Even in the final, detailed, definitive prose-sketch, the apples are still not there, though the gods now do begin to feel old when Freia is taken away – because, Loge reminds them, she possesses 'the magic of youth'. Only when Wagner came to write the actual text of *The Rhinegold* did he give concrete form to this part of the symbolism, by endowing Freia with Idun's apples of immortality. And in doing so, he crowned the love-symbolism with an overt meaning which is unmistakable: love is no mere component of life, among other components, but its very foundation. It is what gives fertility and enduring youth, and to lose it is to become sterile and prematurely old.

As in the final prose-sketch, it is Loge who reminds the gods of this unwelcome fact, as befits his status as god of mind; and his reminder links back to his panegyric on love, in which he stressed the function of love as the creative force which constantly renews nature. At the same time he emphasizes that he alone amongst the gods is not affected by the loss of the apples: the free spirit of thought is not dependent on fertility and enduring youth, as instincts, ideals, and emotions are. The symbolism of the loss of the apples, of course, like all Wagner's sexual symbols, reaches out beyond sexuality to imply a social meaning: there could be no productive future for Wotan and the civilization he has built up, if it finally shut out love and compassion. It would become a stagnant, brutal dictatorship, of the kind that Alberich hopes to establish with the ring of loveless power – a further piece of parallelism between the god and the dwarf.[5]

Thus the introduction of the apples also helped to reinforce the power-symbolism, and it did so in two other ways as well. In the first place, it further strengthened the foil-relationship between the two brother-giants. The love-seeking Fasolt is interested only in Freia herself, as an object of love, without a thought of any benefit the apples might bring; the power-seeking Fafner, on the other hand, is concerned entirely with the apples *as a means to power*. At first, he sees them as a means of bringing the gods down, since if Wotan honours the contract and hands Freia over, the gods will be ruined through the loss of her apples; later, when it becomes a question of accepting a substitute for Freia, he realizes that the indispensability of the apples to the gods enables him to demand what he considers an even greater prize – the ring of absolute power.

But more important is the further reinforcement of the power-symbolism in relation to Wotan. Now that it has been borne in on

[5] If the love-renouncing Alberich does not become prematurely old, he certainly shows no signs of enduring youth; and if he is not sexually sterile, the child he begets (Hagen – the product of a commercial, not an amorous union) describes himself as 'frühalt' (prematurely old) and says that his blood 'stagnates, sluggish and cold' – at which point, significantly, a sad minor version of the theme of Freia's apples (Ex. 61) enters on the orchestra.

him what a catastrophe it would be for the gods to lose Freia, he has no option but to meet Fafner's demand and get the ring to ransom her; but even so, he is still not concerned with Freia herself, any more than Fafner is. Like Fafner, he is now concerned with the apples only, *as a means to power* – as a means of preserving the power he has, since without the apples he will be nothing. When he makes his decision to rob Alberich of the ring, he says nothing about Freia at all, but only:

> *For our lost youth*
> *I'll track down redeeming gold.*

And so the inclusion of the myth of the apples helped to further the plot as well, by making it essential for Wotan to gain possession of the ring. At last, the fortress myth, strengthened by the Idun myth, dovetails into the myth of Andvari, and the affairs of Wotan in *The Rhinegold* begin to be involved with the affairs of Alberich. We have reached the point of transfer to the Andvari myth:

Then Odin sent Loki to the Land of the Black Elves, and he came to the dwarf who is called Andvari . . .

Wagner's Wotan, of course, continues to act in his capacity as chief of the gods, controlling the course of events: he goes with Loge himself.

Scene 3

From the complexity of Scene 2 we return to a simplicity comparable with that of Scene 1, since in the third scene there are only nine main elements: Nibelheim; the Nibelungs; Alberich in his new role as Lord of the Nibelungs; his brother Mime; the quarrel between them; the Tarnhelm; the Nibelung treasure; the confrontation between Alberich and Wotan; and the trapping of Alberich by Loge. And we also return to a comparable independence of the sources, since only the last of these elements has a simple basis in the mythology. The reason for this, as in Scene 1, is that Wagner was obliged to invent certain essential origins which are lacking in the sources: how the treasure came into being, and how Alberich became Lord of the Nibelungs. Again, in providing these origins, he made them as consonant as possible with the sources, by utilizing every hint they contained; and here it is best to begin with Nibelheim and the Nibelungs.

In the *Prose Edda*, Loki, to find the dwarf Andvari, goes to Svartâlfaheim (the Land of the Black Elves); but in *The Rhinegold*, Loge and Wotan, to find the dwarf Alberich, go to Nibelheim, the Land of the Nibelungs. As with Wagner's identification of Andvari's river with the Rhine, this is his transference of the scene from Scandinavia to Germany; but it raises certain questions. Jessie L. Weston[1] objected:

> Alberich, or Elberich, is, as his name implies, an elf, or *elbe* . . . certainly he is not a *Schwarzalbe* [black elf] in the sense that Wagner gives us to understand . . .

To this it may be answered that Alberich is described in the German sources as a *dwarf* – as 'a strong and savage dwarf' in the *Nibelungenlied*, and as 'King Alberich the dwarf' in the appendix to the *Heldenbuch* – and that dwarfs and black elves were often confused with one another in the mythology. But in any case, Wagner was relying on Jacob Grimm again. Grimm, after mentioning that the *Poetic Edda* distinguishes sharply between dwarfs and elves, quotes the *Prose Edda* as distinguishing between two different *kinds* of elves:

[1] Op. cit.

In Alfheim dwells the nation of the *liosâlfar* (light elves), down in the earth dwell the *döckâlfar* (dark elves), the two unlike one another in their looks and their powers, *liosâlfar* brighter than the sun, *döckâlfar* blacker than pitch . . .

But then he goes on to say:

. . . Another name which . . . at first sight seems synonymous with *döckâlfar* is *svartâlfar* (black elves); and these the *Prose Edda* takes to be the same as *dvergar* [dwarves], since the *dvergar* dwell in Svartâlfaheim. This is . . . at variance with the separation of *âlfar* and *dvergar* in the *Poetic Edda*, and more particularly with the difference implied between *döckâlfar* and *dvergar* . . . But ought we not rather to assume three kinds of Norse genii, *liosâlfar, döckâlfar, svartâlfar*? No doubt I am thereby pronouncing the [*Prose Edda*] statement fallacious: 'the *döckâlfar* are blacker than pitch'. *Döckr* seems to me not so much downright black, as dim, dingy . . . In that case, the identity of dwarfs and *black* elves would hold good, and at the same time the old Eddic distinction between dwarfs and *dark* elves would be justified.

And later he adds, conclusively:

One thing we must not let go: the identity of *svartâlfar* and *dvergar.*

So it can be seen that Wagner, from the point of view of the scholarship of his own time, was quite justified in equating the Scandinavian 'land of the black elves' with the German land of the dwarfs, and in describing Alberich as a 'black elf'.

The name he gave to the German dwarfs themselves – 'the Nibelungs' – he of course took from the *Nibelungenlied*, where it is applied to the only sizeable body of 'dwarfs' which appears in any of the German sources: the armed host controlled by the 'strong and savage dwarf' Alberich for Siegfried. These 'Nibelungs' are not, of course, *said* to be dwarfs by the poet; on the contrary, they seem to be human warriors, at first serving King Nibelung's two sons, who are also presented as human princes. But as we have seen (p. 121), the *Lied vom hürnen Seyfrid* strongly suggests that, in the original mythology, King Nibelung and his sons were dwarfs, so his 'Nibelung' warriors would have been dwarfs too.[2]

[2] The nature of the Nibelungs in *The Ring* is obscured, in performance, by the unfortunate necessity of having them played by children on their only two appearances, in *The Rhinegold*, in order to give them their appropriate smallness of stature; the childish screams that result, when they are terrorized by Alberich's ring in Scene 3, are especially misleading. Since they are of the same race as Alberich himself, they must have a comparable fierceness and strength (except perhaps for some who are as cowardly and weak as Mime), and are only reduced to terror by the absolute power of the ring. If it were not so, Alberich could hardly refer to them, when he threatens Wotan, as *das nächtliche Heer* (the *army* of night).

Wagner's representation of the dwarfs as smiths and artificers, who work in a land beneath the earth, is based on the mythology in general. This aspect of it is conveniently summed up by Grimm:

> . . . all or most of the dvergar in the Edda are cunning smiths . . . Their forges are placed in caves and mountains . . . And our German folk-tales everywhere speak of the dwarfs as *forging* in the mountains . . . Slipping into cracks and crevices in the hills, they seem to vanish suddenly . . . and as suddenly they come up from the ground . . . So the *ludki* in Lausitz make their appearance out of underground passages like mouseholes . . . In such caves they pursue their occupations, collecting treasures, forging weapons curiously wrought; their kings fashion for themselves magnificent chambers underground; Elberich, Laurín dwell in these wonderful mountains, men and heroes are tempted down, loaded with gifts, or held fast . . .

So Alberich comes up from under the earth into the Rhine in Scene 1 of *The Rhinegold*, and later forges a ring; his brother Mime fashions a magic helmet, and later, swords; and his race, the Nibelungs, amass a vast treasure for him. So Wotan and Loge go down to Nibelheim through a 'sulphurous crevice' in the mountain top in Scene 2.

The word 'Nibelheim' itself, however, though it would seem a natural name for the home of the Nibelungs, raises difficulties. It is actually Wagner's Germanization of the old Norse 'Niflheim'[3] – but this word meant 'land of mist', and the place itself was the underground home, not of the dwarfs (who lived in Svartâlfaheim, as we have seen), but of the spirits of the dead: the Scandinavian sources know nothing of the German *Nibelung* dwarfs. Yet in spite of this, they do use the word 'Niflungar' for the German word 'Nibelungen', *as mistakenly applied to the Burgundians, or Gibichungs, in the post-Siegfried part of the myth* (see p. 93). There is inextricable confusion here, but as Grimm pointed out, both 'Nifl' and 'Nibel' (Nebel) mean 'mist', and the etymological connection between the Norse *Niflheim* and the German *Nibelung* is a real one. The probable truth of the matter is as follows. The immemorial German word 'Nibelung' descended from a primitive Teutonic word which was based on the root-syllable meaning 'mist', and was used to denote a 'denizen of the mist', otherwise one of the spirits of the dead. As the German mythology developed, however, these 'spirits of the dead' developed into the more sophisticiated forms of elves and

[3] An archaic Germanization, in fact; the modern German would be 'Nebelheim', as Wagner himself indicated in his original prose summary of the whole myth (see p. 132).

dwarfs[4] – hence the Nibelung dwarfs of the German sources (though the Scandinavians still retained the idea of 'Niflheim' as the home of departed spirits). Later still, when the mythology was practically forgotten in Germany, the word 'Nibelungen' came to be applied, through some confusion, to the Burgundians, or Gibichungs, on their last journey to King Etzel's land; and when this part of the German mythology penetrated into Scandinavia, the word was automatically naturalized as 'Niflungar', without any notion of its connection with German dwarfs, or even with the ancient indigenous word 'Niflheim'. Wagner's Germanization of the latter as 'Nibelheim' seems such an obvious gift of a name for the land of the Nibelungs that he might be imagined as having adopted it without further thought, even though it was really the name of the land of the dead; but it seems certain that he was basing himself on the above theory, an adumbration of which he would have found in Lachmann.[5]

It was out of all these hints and suggestions in the mythology that he established his convincing conception of a race of Nibelung dwarfs, living and working in their subterranean land of Nibelheim. And he made them too, even more than the giants, underprivileged members of the world ruled over by Wotan – an idea which has a firmer basis in the mythology. Again there is a suggestive remark in Grimm, who describes the dwarfs as 'giving the impression of a downtrodden, afflicted race'; but this time, it is borne out more unequivocally by the sources. In the *Wise-Woman's Prophecy* in the *Poetic Edda*, we are told that the gods actually created the dwarfs – out of the carcass of the same primeval giant from which they created the whole world – and the *Prose Edda* is more explicit, describing how

. . . the dwarfs came into being in the flesh of Ymir [the giant in question], and were maggots there. But now, by a decree of the gods, they received human intelligence and human shape, though they dwelt in the earth and in rocks.

Wagner certainly had this subhuman conception in mind, as he shows at the beginning of his original prose summary of the source-material (see p. 132). And indeed, the dwarfs, unlike the giants, remain totally subservient to the gods throughout the Scandinavian mythology: they have to provide whatever the gods

[4] See R. G. Finch, op. cit., p. 91: Glossary of technical terms, *Alfar* and *Dvergar*.
[5] Op. cit.

need, at Loki's bidding (for instance, Odin's spear and Thor's hammer, as we have seen); another example is the ruthless robbing of Andvari's treasure, of course. And in the German sources, in which there are no gods, the dwarfs are equally subservient to the heroes; so are the 'Nibelungs' of the *Nibelungenlied*, under Alberich, to Siegfried.

But the really important thing, once more, is the overt meaning which Wagner deliberately superimposed on the whole conception. Although, in the German mythology, the dwarfs are often represented as having a king of their own, possessed of an enormous wealth which they have presumably amassed for him, there is nowhere the slightest suggestion that they are absolutely enslaved to him, toiling away ceaselessly for his benefit only, without rest and without any life and possessions of their own. But the Nibelungs in Scene 3 of *The Rhinegold* are presented by Wagner as abject slaves, forced against their will to serve the ambition of a lord who is a ruthless tyrant, without hope of the slightest reward.

The tyrant is, of course, Alberich, who is the third element of the scene. In Scene 1 he has acted out a piece of pre-history invented for him by Wagner, on the basis of only four hints in the mythology: the general idea of gold lying in the Rhine; the indication that the German dwarf Alberich and the Scandinavian dwarf Andvari were creatures at home in water; the reputation of Alberich as a 'notorious thief'; and the conception of a talisman of absolute power. But at the beginning of Scene 3, Alberich becomes more recognizably the dwarf-king of German mythology (before acting out Andvari's unhappy fate of having his treasure and his ring stolen from him by the gods). As a figure, he is now clearly referable to 'King Elberich the dwarf' in the appendix to the *Heldenbuch*, 'lord of many a valley and mountain', and even more to the 'wild and savage dwarf' Alberich in the *Nibelungenlied* – who, although demoted there to the position of a princes' steward, features as the effective and repressive controller of an army of 'Nibelungs'.[6]

However, even here, Wagner is providing Alberich with a piece

---

[6] At this point we may simply dismiss Jessie L. Weston's criticism that 'the character of Alberich as represented in *The Ring* does a grave injustice to a very graceful and charming figure of German legend'. However graceful and charming he may be in minor and later sources, such as *König Otnit*, his attitude in the *Nibelungenlied*, from which Wagner took his character, is tough, fierce, and hostile.

of pre-history absent from the sources – showing how he actually became Lord of the Nibelungs. And the important point is that the two parts of his invented pre-history – in Scene 1 and Scene 3 – are inseparably linked, being twin aspects of the basic power-versus-love symbolism of *The Rhinegold*. In Scene 1, Wagner made Alberich renounce love in order to forge from the Rhinegold the 'revenging ring' of absolute power; and at the beginning of Scene 3 he created a concrete dramatic demonstration of what that apparently abstract decision of Alberich's really amounted to. Before Alberich returned from the Rhine (as Mime is shortly to inform us, in his encounter with Wotan and Loge), the Nibelungs were contented with their humble lot, happy at their work of smithying. But since then, Alberich has forged the ring; and when we see him using it, to terrorize and slave-drive Mime and the other Nibelungs, we witness the use of absolute power in all its naked obscenity, unredeemed by the slightest trace of consideration, let alone sympathy, let alone compassion, let alone love. Wagner's power-versus-love symbolism, entirely abstract in Scene 1, concrete but equivocal in Scene 2, has suddenly swung right over to power-without-love at the start of Scene 3. Wherever Wotan stands, it is clear that Alberich has not the slightest love for anybody, not even for his fellow-Nibelungs.

And not even, we must add, for his own brother Mime, for whom he might surely be expected to feel at least some slight consideration, perhaps even a little sympathy: Wagner brings home even more conclusively Alberich's general lovelessness, revealed in his later terrorization of the mass of his fellow-Nibelungs, by giving it particularized form in the shape of his vicious treatment of this timid brother of his. No doubt there was a practical need to introduce Mime as the fourth element in this scene, to give sufficient dramatic content to the action, and to establish him as a character before he appears in *Siegfried*. But Wagner, once having decided to do so, made him a pitiful victim of Alberich's brutality, for the express symbolic purpose of pinpointing Alberich's lovelessness. And again, he deliberately created this situation: there is no basis for it in the mythology.

Indeed, there is no basis even for Mime's identity as Alberich's brother: his presence in this scene, and the part he plays in it, are the products of one of Wagner's most subtle and complex manipulations of his source-materials. It is most convenient to approach this character through his main role as the foster-father of Siegfried, in which, in all the pure Scandinavian sources, he figures as Regin, the brother of the dragon Fafnir, with whom he has quarrelled over the gold that came to them from the gods, and from whom he hopes to regain it through Siegfried's (Sigurd's) agency. But as we have seen in analysing Scene 2 (p. 181), Wagner made Fafnir and Regin into the giants who built the fortress for Wotan, gave Regin the new name of Fasolt, and had him killed by Fafner, before the latter made off with the gold and turned himself into a dragon to guard it. And by thus disposing of Regin, so that there was no longer any brother to dispute possession of the gold with the dragon Fafner, he left himself free to give Siegfried's foster-father a completely different identity.

What he did was to retain the basic Scandinavian conception of this figure as one who came off worst in quarrelling with his fiercer brother over the gold, but to transfer the motif of the quarrelling brothers to its German context. As pointed out in the previous chapter (p. 122), this motif runs through the whole mythology, in two different forms: in the pure Scandinavian sources, Fafnir and Regin quarrel over the gold at the beginning of the story; in the *Nibelungenlied*, Siegfried encounters two 'mighty princes', who appear from nowhere, quarrelling over their treasure outside a mountain cave, and it is by killing them, and not the dragon, that he wins the treasure. These two 'mighty princes', who are called Nibelung and Schilbung, are the sons of King Nibelung, and they have for steward the 'wild and savage dwarf' Alberich. But since they bring their treasure out of a *mountain cave*, and since the *Lied vom hürnen Seyfrid* represents the *dead* King Nibelung and his *three* sons as dwarfs who keep their treasure in a mountain, it seems evident that all three characters in the *Nibelungenlied* – Nibelung, Schilbung, and Alberich – were in the original mythology Nibelung dwarf-princes; that two of them quarrelled over the treasure they inherited from their father; and that one of these might well have been Alberich, the ubiquitous dwarf-king of German mythology.

It was to this German context that Wagner transferred the Scandinavian motif of the two brothers quarrelling over the treasure they were to lose to Siegfried: although he preferred to let Siegfried win the treasure from the dragon, he introduced the two quarrelling Nibelung brothers as well at this point (*Siegfried*, Act 2, Scene 3), and he also gave their quarrel its necessary pre-history as the fifth element of Scene 3 of *The Rhinegold*. In doing so, he tidied up the plot by dispensing with the dead King Nibelung and his inheritance, and by reducing the three Nibelung dwarf-brothers to the quarrelling two only; he also strengthened the symbolism by getting rid of the completely anonymous Nibelung and Schilbung; he replaced one of them by the real dwarf-king Alberich, and made him the actual amasser of the treasure; and finally, he dovetailed the Nibelung myth more closely into the Siegfried myth by making the other quarrelling brother the character who eventually becomes Siegfried's foster-father.

Put like this, the last step may seem entirely arbitrary, but it was based on certain elements in the mythology. In the *Poetic Edda* and *Norna-Gests thattr*, Siegfried's foster-father Regin, although he is the brother of Fafnir, is described as 'having the stature of a dwarf';[7] and in the *Lied vom hürnen Seyfrid*, although Siegfried has no foster-father at all, but simply goes to work with a master-smith, there is a later scene in which one of the dwarf-sons of King Nibelung (called Eugel) takes a great interest in him, tells him who his parents are, and helps him during his fight with a giant by covering him with a cloak of invisibility. It was on these suggestive hints that Wagner based his conception of Siegfried's foster-father as a Nibelung dwarf, brother of the Nibelung dwarf-king Alberich, and maker of the Tarnhelm. For the name, he rejected the 'Regin' of the pure Scandinavian sources, which was too well-known as that of the brother of Fafnir, and the 'Eugel' of the *Lied vom hürnen Seyfrid*, probably because he thought it apocryphal – though he considered both in his original prose summary of the whole myth (see p. 133). He eventually decided on the 'Mimir' of *Thidriks saga* (which gave him such a firm basis for Act 1 of *Siegfried*), and Germanized it as Mime.

Once again, then, Wagner had it both ways: the quarrelling brothers of the Scandinavian sources are present in *The Ring*, in the shape of Fafner and Fasolt; and so are the quarrelling Nibelung brothers of German mythology, in the shape of Alberich and Mime. And as with Fafner and Fasolt, Wagner created a foil-relationship between the two brothers – but a different one this time. As said above, the power-versus-love symbolism has sud-

[7] It will be remembered that it was Wagner who made Fafner and his brother into giants: in the Scandinavian sources they are represented as men, even if their treatment of Odin and Loki is suspiciously giant-like.

denly swung over to power-without-love: whereas, in Scene 2, Fafner stands as the pure seeker for power, and Fasolt as the almost pure seeker for love, here, in Scene 3, Alberich and Mime both stand as pure seekers for power – loveless, cunning, malevolent, ruthless – and the differentiation between them begins from this point. In them, Wagner embodied the two contrasted main types of criminal power-maniac: the tough, direct, fearless, ferocious one in Alberich; the soft, lying, cowardly, ingratiating one in Mime.

The mythology does offer some basis for both these characterizations. The only portrayal of Alberich in the material used for *The Ring* is the one in the *Nibelungenlied*, which presents him in his capacity as dwarf-steward to the two Nibelung 'princes', and later to Siegfried; he is described there as 'küene, dar zuo stark genuoc' (bold, and very strong into the bargain), and on the two occasions when Siegfried has to subdue him – to win the Nibelung hoard and to claim the Nibelung army – he has a tough fight on his hands. As regards Mime, the conflicting accounts of Siegfried's foster-father, in the different sources, present a more complex case, which will be examined in detail when we come to consider the part he plays in *Siegfried*: it is enough to say here that, as Regin in *Volsunga saga* (Wagner's main source), he is portrayed as thoroughly treacherous, and as a coward who keeps well out of the way while Sigurd fights the dragon. Nevertheless, Wagner's bringing together of the two figures as brothers, at daggers drawn, representing the two opposite types of the loveless seeker for absolute power, was an extreme manipulation of the source-material, whereby he forced it to bear a meaning all his own.

And once again, the interpretation of Robert Donington has to be challenged. He admits that Alberich is 'an evil character' and 'the chief villain', and that Mime 'really is a rather nasty piece of work' who, while 'hardly strong enough to be a villain', is 'certainly not amiable enough to be anything much else'. But he insists that 'we must be able to feel the positive elements in these harsher characters after their own fashion', because 'the *Ring* is not a crude melodrama'. Seeing both figures as Jungian archetypes, he makes much of the fact that dwarfs are 'phallic symbols', standing for 'male sexuality' and for 'Logos, the typically male principle of discriminating intelligence'; that smithying is a creative occupation; and that Mime 'will have the enterprise to bring up the infant Siegfried to manhood'. But Wagner has made it impossible to have it both ways in the Jungian manner. Whether or not such Jungian concepts can be validly applied to the figures of the mythology, the interpreter of *The Ring* should concern himself entirely with the characters that Wagner created from them; and it is clear that he deliberately represented the sexuality of Alberich (his begetting of Hagen), the intelligence and smithying of both brothers, and Mime's bringing up of Siegfried, as serving, not positive and creative ends but, on the contrary, negative and destructive ones.[8] And even so, this does not in the least make *The Ring* a 'crude melodrama'. The work presents, in symbolic terms, an entirely realistic diagnosis of the power-ridden world in which we live; and just as this world tends to be governed by ruthless rulers of the Wotan type, so do we find plenty of out-and-out criminals of the Alberich and Mime types – who usually content themselves with ruling the underworld, but occasionally aspire to take over from the Wotans the government of the upper world.

At the beginning of Scene 3, Wagner shows his usual mastery of dramatic compression by starting immediately with the strife between the two brothers, and using it to fulfil a fourfold dramatic purpose: to introduce the new character of Mime; to demonstrate Alberich's lovelessness through his vicious treatment of his brother; to present the contrast between the aggressive and cowardly types of power-seeker; and to bring in the Tarnhelm straightaway by making it the subject of the quarrel. And the moment this brief encounter ends, with Alberich making himself invisible by means of the Tarnhelm he has forced Mime to make for him and thrashing Mime for trying to keep it for himself, his particular lovelessness towards his brother is shown in general terms, as he goes away, still invisible, and begins slave-driving the mass of the Nibelungs.

The Tarnhelm is the sixth element we have to consider in this scene, and, like the previous ones, it is being provided here with an invented pre-history: the object, which is found in the German mythology only, appears exclusively in connection with the dwarfs' dealings with the heroes. To quote Jacob Grimm:

---

[8] The solitary redeeming feature is that touching glimpse of genuine fatherliness in Mime's character – his having used his skill as a smith to make toys for Siegfried, and also his horn (purely Wagnerian inventions which Donington, strangely enough, makes no mention of).

These light airy sprites [the elves] have an advantage over slow unwieldy man in their godlike power of *vanishing* or making themselves *invisible* . . . With the light elves it is a matter of course but neither have the black ones forfeited the privilege. The invisibility of dwarfs is usually lodged in a particular part of their dress, a *hat* or a *cloak*, and when that is accidentally dropped or cast aside, they suddenly become visible.

In the sources for *The Ring*, such a garment occurs twice in relation to Siegfried. In the *Lied vom hürnen Seyfrid*, when Siegfried is in danger of being killed by a giant, the Nibelung dwarf-prince Eugel protects him with a cloak of invisibility; and more basic to Wagner's purpose, in the *Nibelungenlied* Siegfried himself secures such a cloak, along with the Nibelung treasure, from the dwarf steward Alberich, and later uses it to help Gunther win the amazonian Icelandic queen Brünnhilde in that gruelling athletic contest (see p. 97).

Wagner dispensed with the garment's original name and shape, however, and gave it a name and shape of his own. The garment in the *Lied vom hürnen Seyfrid* is called a *nebelkap* (mist-cap), and the one in the *Nibelungenlied* a *Tarnkappe* (concealing cap). It was not because the idea of a 'cap' was too trivial that Wagner rejected this part of the word, but because the Middle High German word 'Kap' or 'Kappe', in this context, actually meant a cloak, and such a garment would obviously have been too unwieldy for stage-business. Since in fact the German mythology did contain the idea of a piece of pure headgear used for this purpose (as indicated in the last quotation from Grimm), Wagner chose the syllable 'Helm' (helmet) and attached to it the syllable 'Tarn' (concealing) from the *Nibelungenlied*, on the analogy of the Old High German word *helothelm* mentioned by Grimm (*helot* also having the significance of 'concealment', as indeed has 'helm').[9]

Finally, Wagner altered the actual properties of the garment in certain respects. Its primary function in the German mythology, outlined in the last quotation from Grimm, is to make its wearer invisible, but it has three others which Grimm mentions as well. At one point he says:

Besides invisibility, this cloak imparts superior strength, and likewise control over the dwarf nation and their hoard.

[9] Wagner did, however, retain the *idea* of the *nebelkap* (mist-cap), in addition to retaining the syllable 'Tarn' from *Tarnkappe*. When Alberich uses the Tarnhelm to make himself invisible, the stage-direction reads: 'His form disappears; in its place can be perceived a column of mist' (eine Nebelsäule).

And later he refers to

> . . . the Tarnkappe, which one only has to put on, to be in a twinkling at some distant place.

Neither the function of 'imparting superior strength', nor that of giving 'control over the dwarf nation and their hoard', can be found in the actual sources Wagner used for *The Ring*, except in so far as invisibility itself inevitably gives greater power and control – as it does to Alberich in Scene 3 of *The Rhinegold*. The other two properties feature more decisively in Wagner's sources: that of conferring invisibility appears in both the *Nibelungenlied* and the *Lied vom hürnen Seyfrid*, as indicated above, while that of instantaneous transportation occurs in the *Nibelungenlied* alone, when Siegfried transports himself in a flash into Gunther's bedroom, for the purpose of subduing Brünnhilde. And Wagner retained both these properties: in Scene 3 of *The Rhinegold*, the Tarnhelm makes Alberich invisible, and in Act 2 of *The Twilight of the Gods* it transports Siegfried back instantaneously from Brünnhilde's rock to the hall of the Gibichungs.

To these, however, he added a further function which is to be found in neither the sources for *The Ring* nor the mythology as a whole: he made the Tarnhelm confer on its wearer the power to transform himself into an animal (Alberich turns himself into a serpent and a toad) and, more important, into another person (Siegfried takes on the shape of Gunther). His reason for this addition has to do entirely with the last case. In the *Nibelungenlied*, when Siegfried wins Brünnhilde for Gunther by defeating her in the athletic contest, he does not take Gunther's shape: he makes himself invisible by donning the Tarnkappe, and does the deeds unseen, while Gunther goes through the motions. But Wagner, as we have seen, followed the Scandinavian sources, in which Sigurd takes on Gunnar's actual shape, and passes through the fire that Gunnar is unable to cross. The Scandinavian sources, however, know nothing at all of the German *Tarnkappe:* the transformation is effected by the older magic of 'exchanging shapes' by means of a spell. So Wagner simply Germanized this feature by conferring on the Tarnhelm the property of enabling its wearer to take on the shape of another person; and he prepared this idea in Scene 3 of *The Rhinegold* by making Alberich, after he has demonstrated the garment's true function of conferring invisibility, use it to turn himself into a serpent and a toad.

The Tarnhelm as such, then, is based firmly on material in the sources. But its appearance in Scene 3 of *The Rhinegold* is still a piece of pre-history invented for it by Wagner – and by means of this invented piece of pre-history he killed six birds with one stone. He gave it an origin, as a direct product of Alberich's loveless pursuit of power; he used it to establish the crafty cleverness of Mime (by making him the actual fashioner of it) and the characters of the two contrasted brothers-in-lovelessness (by making it the subject of their initial quarrel); he also used it to establish the total lovelessness of Alberich (by making him avail himself of its cover to give his brother a sound thrashing); he thus gave it a meaning of his own, making its power of conferring invisibility a symbol of that evil guile which offers its victim no chance; and later he gave it another personal meaning; adding to it the power of transforming its wearer into an animal, and using that as a symbol of the repellent images that the loveless power-seeker can present (the monstrous serpent, the contemptible toad).

The Tarnhelm, of course, like the ring, is part of the Nibelung treasure, which is the seventh element of the scene. Wagner was basing himself firmly on the mythology here, since in the *Nibelungenlied* the *Tarnkappe* goes with the Nibelung treasure, and so does that obscure golden rod of world-domination on which he based his conception of the ring. The remainder of the treasure there consists of 'precious stones and gold', as much as 'twelve waggons could hardly carry away from the mountain in four days and nights, making three journeys a day' – otherwise 144 waggon-loads. In *The Rhinegold* there would seem to be rather less since, when heaped up, it just hides Freia from view (but how large is a goddess?) and Fafner finally carries it all away in 'an enormous sack' (but how much can a giant carry?).

The important point, however, is the actual nature of the treasure, as given its pre-history by Wagner, and its relationship to the Rhinegold and the ring. There has been some confusion about this, but a close reading of Wagner's text shows that his intentions are perfectly clear (as indeed they already were when he drew up his original prose-summary of the mythology – see p. 133). The gold which Alberich steals from the Rhine is merely a large lump, as is clear from the fact that he, although only a dwarf, 'tears it from the rock and rushes swiftly with it into the depths'. And it was the *whole* of this that he made into the ring: Woglinde tells Alberich that anyone who renounces love will attain the magic 'to force the gold into a circle' (*zum Reif zu zwingen das Gold*); and again, in Scene 2, Loge tells Wotan that a magic rune 'forces the gold into a circle' (*zwingt das Gold zum Reif*). The verb *zwingen* has the sense of 'compel with great force', and in the present context indicates, not only the difficulty of making this particular ring, but also the idea of magically compressing a large lump of gold into a ring small enough to be worn on the finger. And this sense of compression is confirmed by Brünnhilde in the final scene of the tetralogy, when she addresses the Rhinemaidens, to whom the ring is about to return. She says: 'In the flood loosen it (*löset ihn auf*), and keep pure the clear gold that was stolen from you to your bane'. The verb *auflösen* can also signify 'dissolve', but this is clearly not its meaning here: even if a golden ring could be dissolved in water, its gold would be dispersed for ever. *Den Ring auflösen* stands as the opposite of *das Gold zwingen*, signifying the release of the gold from the state of compression that made it a ring, and its restoration to its original form of a lump of pure natural gold.

So the objection sometimes offered, that the whole Rhinegold is not restored to the Rhine, but only the ring and not the treasure, is the result of a misunderstanding. Brünnhilde restores the Rhinegold to the Rhinemaidens in the form of the ring; the treasure is something else. What it is we learn from Mime, in his encounter with Wotan and Loge in Scene 3, when he describes how Alberich is amassing it:

> *By virtue of the ring's gold*
> *his greed divines*
> *where new gleams*
> *are hidden in the shafts:*
> *we have to peer for them,*
> *track them down and dig them out,*
> *smelt what we find,*
> *forge the cast,*
> *and without rest or respite*
> *heap up the treasure for our lord.*

The treasure, then, is gold mined from the earth by the Nibelungs, after Alberich has 'divined' it there, using the ring for this purpose like the forked twig of present-day 'water-diviners' – or, more to the point, like the original forked twig of the fifteenth-century German prospectors who 'divined' mineral deposits in the Harz mountains. The basis of Wagner's idea is of course the remark of Andvari in the *Prose Edda*, when he begs Loki not to take the ring from him: 'with that ring he could increase his gold' (see p. 180).

We find here one more example of Wagner's having it both ways, as said in the section on Scene 1. There, he followed the Scandinavian mythology in making the gold (and therefore the ring) come from the water; here, he followed the German mythology in making the Nibelung treasure come from the earth. And he even followed the German mythology further, by making the treasure, not merely gold, but minerals in general: the Nibelungs heap up 'gold- and silver-work' for Alberich, and the Tarnhelm is described as 'a metal tissue' (bringing to mind the mailed helmets of the old Teutonic warriors). But there is no need to make much of this aspect of Wagner's symbolism. Both the gold and the treasure symbolize in general the raw material of nature, but the result of exploiting that material is wealth, and the natural symbol of wealth is gold: the treasure, in fact, is referred to as gold throughout *The Ring*.

What really matters is the actual meaning which Wagner conferred on the treasure. In all the main sources, it stands merely as a vast personal fortune, which gives its possessor greater status than his fellows (Siegfried, primarily, greater status than Gunther); but in *The Rhinegold*, where it is the direct product of the forging of the ring from the gold, it stands as the actual means whereby alone the maker of the ring can realize that instrument's power of making him master of the world. There has been further confusion here, of a more serious nature; but again Wagner's intentions are absolutely clear, in both *The Rhinegold* and his original prose summary (see p. 133). It is often asked why, if the ring confers absolute world-power on its master, Alberich should be unable to prevent Wotan from wresting it from him in Scene 4. But to ask such a question is to assume that the ring is intended to function as an instrument of *instantaneous* world-power, and no such idea can be found in Wagner's text: if it could, there would be nothing to stop Alberich from taking over control of the world from Wotan the very moment he has made the ring.

The way the symbolism functions is as follows. We have established, as part of the overt meaning of Scene 1, that absolute world-power can be achieved by ravishing and exploiting the raw material of nature, but such an action is possible only for one who has expelled love from his being. And this somewhat general and sweeping statement is given a more precise significance by the overt meaning of the beginning of Scene 3: the reason why complete lovelessness is essential for this purpose is that to ravish and exploit the raw material of nature, sufficiently to achieve world power, needs continuous slave-labour on a vast scale; and only one completely devoid of love can dominate his fellows so ruthlessly as to force them to provide such slave-labour. The bald statement in the text that the ring can confer absolute world-power on its maker is a condensed summary of the following process: the ring itself merely symbolizes Alberich's utter ruthlessness, made possible by his rejection of love; but this ruthlessness enables him to concentrate single-mindedly on discovering fresh raw materials to exploit ('divining where new gleams are hidden in the shafts') and – together with the evil guile symbolized by the Tarnhelm – to terrorize his fellow-Nibelungs into working like slaves on those materials, in order to amass a great fortune for him; finally, this fortune, he hopes, will eventually make him master of the world. The ring itself gives him no immediate power over anyone but his fellow-Nibelungs.

All this is confirmed during the confrontation between Alberich and Wotan; but first we must briefly consider the conversation between Mime and Loge when the two gods enter and find Mime whimpering after his thrashing. This is mainly expository: Mime's complaints serve to inform us that Alberich has made the ring and enslaved the formerly happy Nibelungs, and to inform Loge and Wotan of the existence of the Tarnhelm – which, as Loge says, will not make their task easy. But at the same time they further establish the rather pathetic side of Mime's character (in his self-pitying monologue about how happy he and the other Nibelungs once were, making trinkets for their womenfolk); and they demonstrate his slyness as a power-seeker and the ineffectualness of his attempts to be cunning (in his confession to Loge that he got his thrashing for trying to keep the Tarnhelm for himself – his intention having been to use it against Alberich and snatch the ring from him, but he could not work the magic). Immediately after this conversation, Alberich returns, visible again, driving with a whip a gang of Nibelungs carrying loads of gold- and silver-work; he recognizes Wotan and Loge, and it is at this point that we witness the demonstration of the dreadful power of the ring, deliberately staged by Alberich to impress the two gods. Holding it out menacingly, he orders the Nibelungs to get straight back to work – and they and Mime rush away into the mine-shafts with shrieks of terror.

Wotan and Loge remain impassive, and wait. Alberich mistrusts them, but Loge draws him into conversation: he reminds him that it was he, Loge, who provided light for the dark world of Nibelheim, and the fire for the forges[10] (thereby reminding us of his independence as the free spirit of mind, formerly helping the dwarfs with their technical labour, at present serving the gods in the more ambitious business of ruling the world, and in the future, perhaps, undertaking more elevated tasks). The ice once broken, Alberich begins boasting of his treasure; Wotan asks him what use it is to him, 'in joyless Nibelheim, where riches cannot buy anything'; and so begins the confrontation between the two which is the eighth main element of Scene 3. And this has less basis in the mythology than any preceding event in the scene – none at all, in fact, since in the Scandinavian sources, it will be remembered, Odin and the dwarf Andvari never meet: the confrontation is entirely between Andvari, who has no ambition to gain mastery of the world, and Loki, who traps him immediately, before he can say a word (see p. 179).

But in *The Rhinegold*, the confrontation is between the two absolute lords of their respective domains, each in pursuit of world-domination: Wotan, the chief of the gods and the actual ruler of the world, and Alberich, the lord of the underprivileged Nibelungs, who aims to take over Wotan's rulership from him. The confrontation is brief, with Alberich having practically all the dialogue, but it is crucial, since what he has to say is revealing – and appalling. To Wotan's question, he replies:

> *To make riches*
> *and hide riches,*
> *the night of Nibelheim serves me;*
> *but with the treasure*
> *heaped up in the cave*
> *I intend then to work miracles:*
> *the whole world*
> *I shall win therewith for my own.*

And in answer to Wotan's contemptuous question 'How, worthy soul, will you set about that?', he makes a direct avowal of his destructive intentions:

---

[10] This is Wagner's manipulation of the *Prose Edda's* account of Loki's familiarity with the dwarfs – his getting of the sons of the dwarf Ivaldi to make, amongst other things, Odin's spear and Thor's hammer (see pp. 145 and 164).

Wafted by soft breezes,
  you live up there,
  laughing and loving:
  my golden fist
shall capture you all, you gods!
As I forswore love,
  everything that lives
  shall forswear it:
  lured by gold,
you shall hanker only for gold.
  On wondrous heights,
  in blissful vibration,
  you lull yourselves.
  The Black Elf
you despise, immortal revellers:—
  Beware!
  Beware! —
  For once you men
  are under my power,
  your lovely women,
  who despise my wooing,
the dwarf will subject to his pleasure,
though love smiles not on him. —
  Ha ha ha ha!
  Did you hear?
  Beware!
Beware of the army of night,
when the Nibelung treasure rises
from the silent depths to the daylight!

Wotan's outraged reply – which promptly ends the confrontation, since Loge immediately warns him to control himself and changes the subject – is 'Perish, criminal idiot!'; and since Alberich's intentions are patently those of a sadistic power-maniac, we naturally identify ourselves with Wotan's sense of disgust. Yet we have to remember that Wotan too is a power-seeker – the opposite side of the coin from Alberich, perhaps, but that side has been looking more and more like Alberich's all the time. Whereas Alberich is lawless, Wotan has established the control of law – but in his dealings with the giants he has sought to evade the law; and in his pursuit of power he has put one of the goddesses – Alberich's sexual intentions towards whom he finds so monstrous – in danger of becoming a chattel of two giants. And now he is here in Nibelheim to capture Alberich by guile and force, with a view to robbing him of his ring – which might be all very well if he were intent on restoring it to its rightful owners, or even, perhaps, if he meant to use it to ransom Freia for her own sake. But in fact, he wants it merely to ransom her for the sake of her apples of immortality – which his folly has brought him so near to losing – in order to ensure the continuing existence of the gods and, more particularly, of his own power. Even more damning, as we have seen, is the strong probability, in view of his reflections about the ring towards the end of Scene 2, that he wants it for the worst of all possible reasons: to keep it himself, and with it wield over the world that utterly ruthless power which depends on casting out love altogether, and which knows no other law than that of 'Might is Right'. If this were to happen, he would finally sink to the level of Alberich.

Since this is as yet only a probability, however, we still side with Wotan, partly because we feel it would be better for anyone to possess the ring than Alberich, and partly because we hope that Wotan's better judgement will eventually prevail. In the meantime, two other interesting points emerge from Alberich's outburst, the first being a clear confirmation that the treasure is the actual and sole means whereby he can realize the ring's potentiality for bringing him world-domination. He intends, evidently, to use his wealth to buy the gods out – to 'take over' Valhalla and run it as a private pleasure-palace, with the gods as his slaves and the goddesses as his harem – and in this, one wonders whether he is being realistic: the pride and self-esteem of Wagner's gods – or at least those of Wotan, as their chief – are surely greater than their cupidity. Fortunately, the fact that the eventuality never arises makes this an idle speculation.

The second point arising from Alberich's outburst is of crucial importance, since it concerns the relationship between love and sex with regard to his character. So far we have passed this over; but it now has to be made clear (by looking back to Scene 1), if we are to get a precise understanding of the whole symbolism of the tetralogy. Once more, there has been confusion on this issue; and once more Wagner's intentions are perfectly clear. It is sometimes asked how Alberich can really be said to have renounced love, if he later envisages satisfying his sexual desires with the goddesses and, later still, actually begets Hagen. But this is simply to equate love, in Scene 1 of *The Rhinegold*, with physical sex – a misunderstanding which is caused, in some cases, by a confused pseudo-

Freudian notion that Alberich's renunciation of love, following the rejection of his wooing by the Rhinemaidens, symbolizes a sudden affliction with impotence, or even, in some sense, actual castration.

It might perhaps seem that Alberich's approach to the Rhinemaidens is no more than a desire for physical sex, but the text does not justify such an interpretation. There is certainly a large physical component – which, since a sexual encounter between a dwarf and three water-nixies is a rather quaint bit of fairy-tale *grotesquerie*, Wagner presents in comical terms. Alberich woos Wellgunde as follows:

> *Wind around me*
> *your slender arms,*
> *that I may tease*
> *the nape of your neck,*
> *and with wheedling passion*
> *snuggle to your swelling bosom.*

But there is also a strong component of 'being in love', in the adolescent sense of idealizing the object of desire; and the expression of this is not comical at all. Alberich's reaction to his first sight of the Rhinemaidens is an immediate infatuation with their beauty:

> *How graceful you are,*
> *you enviable creatures!* . . .
> *How bright and fair*
> *in the shimmering light!*

The adolescent type of idealization[11] is of course a component of 'romantic love'; and it is entirely in the familiar manner of the romantic lover (even if Wagner returns to his comical vein) that Alberich conducts his longest and most passionate piece of wooing – that of Flosshilde:

> F.   *Sing on and on,*
>   *so sweet and fine;*
>   *how sublimely it enchants my ear!*

---

[11] It will be noticed that we come within hailing distance of Robert Donington's interpretation here, since he regards the Rhinemaidens as embodying Alberich's (and Wagner's) 'escapist infantile fantasies' – which is one way, perhaps, of describing the sexual idealization of adolescence. Donington, however, regards the 'fantasies' as harmful, and sees Alberich (and Wagner) fruitfully renouncing *them*, not love. I believe the sexual idealizations of adolescence to be fruitful, provided they develop into a main component of mature romantic love; and I am certain that Wagner's text presents Alberich as unfortunate in that, being given no chance to develop them, he (most harmfully) renounces love itself.

> A. *My trembling, quivering*
> *heart is consumed*
> *when such exquisite praise smiles on me* . . .
>
> F. *Most blessed of men!*
>
> A. *Sweetest of maids!*
>
> F. *Could I hope that you loved me!*
>
> A. *Could I clasp you for ever!*

Mature romantic love superimposes, of course, on the enduring adolescent elements of sexual infatuation and idealization, an adult love for, and identification with, the beloved as a person – which is naturally not the case with Alberich. The 'underprivileged' Nibelung, suddenly confronted with the radiant beauty of the Rhinemaidens, is immediately smitten with an idealizing sexual infatuation, and this, together with the comical dwarfish grotesqueness of his attempts to woo them, makes him a rather pitiable figure: Wagner himself said that he felt sorry for Alberich in Scene 1 of *The Rhinegold*, however much he came to hate him later. Nevertheless, there is this undeniable extra component of idealization in Alberich's 'love' for the Rhinemaidens, over and above his desire for physical sex – and they reject this 'love' in such a humiliating way as to embitter him completely. The idealization vanishes, leaving only his inflamed desire for physical sex, now turned sadistic, as he vainly chases them with the aim of raping them; and this is why he is able, soon afterwards, to take the terrible step of renouncing love altogether, in return for the ring of absolute power.

That it is love which he renounces, and not physical sex, is clear from two passages of the text. The first is Woglinde's original statement of the condition: he who wants to attain the magic to force the gold into a circle can do so only by forswearing *der Minne Macht* and driving out *der Liebe Lust*. In English, *der Minne Macht* has to be rendered 'the power of love', though '*Minne*' is a more precise word than 'love': it is used exclusively for the love of lovers, with its elements of sexual infatuation and idealization. '*Liebe*', though as comprehensive as the English 'love', appears here in parallel with '*Minne*', and it consequently takes on the connotation of that word; '*Lust*' is not equivalent to the English word 'lust', but signifies 'pleasure'; and so *der Liebe Lust* means 'the pleasure of love'. What Alberich does, then, is to forswear the power, and drive out the pleasure, of the kind of love that exists between lovers – the kind of love, in fact, that he has himself been groping towards in his wooing of the Rhinemaidens.

The symbolism is perfectly clear if we remember that, for Wagner, love was indivisible – as he declared in the passage in *Art and Climate* already quoted in Chapter 1, referring to

> that *love* which proceeds from the power of true and undistorted human nature; which in its origin is nothing else but the most active expression of this nature, that proclaims itself in pure delight in sensuous existence, and, starting from sexual love, strides forward through love of children, brothers and friends, to *universal love of humanity*.

Alberich, clearly, does not remain undistorted, and so is unable to follow this process. Finding his advances rejected at the stage of sexual love, on the level of idealized sexual infatuation, he expels love from his being altogether, and seeks revenge through absolute power – a psychological transformation which is familiar enough in real life.

But to give up sexual love is not necessarily to give up physical sex, of course; and that this is true of Alberich is indicated by the second of the texts' two clarifying passages. It consists of a single sentence, uttered by Alberich himself as he contemplates taking his crucial decision: 'If I could not extort love (*Liebe*), could I not cunningly extort pleasure (*Lust*)?' For him, in his altered state of mind, it has become entirely a matter of 'extortion' (*erwingen*); and although, as said above, '*Lust*' is not equivalent to the English word 'lust', in this particular context it approaches very near to it. For '*Lust*' is offered here as a direct alternative to '*Liebe*'; the implication is that, although he could not extort sexual *love* from the Rhinemaidens, he might at least, if he forges the ring, be clever enough to use its power to extort *pleasure* from women, in the form of a satisfaction of his desire for *physical sex*, without love at all. And this is exactly what he is envisaging, with regard to the goddesses, in his outburst to Wotan in Scene 3: 'Your lovely women, who despise my wooing, the dwarf will subject to his pleasure' (*Sie zwingt zur Lust sich der Zwerg*).[12]

Alberich then, in his outburst, stands revealed as the worst (psychotic) type of power-seeker: one who, to avenge himself on

---

[12] Alberich's later begetting of Hagen is, of course, a different case: a single, loveless, physical coupling, attained by money, for the sole purpose of producing a son who will avenge him by getting back the ring for him. This will be dealt with when the time comes; here it is enough to say that it demonstrates that Alberich did not renounce physical sex.

the world for his own sense of inferiority as one of the underprivileged, which has been given dynamic force by the frustration
of his attempts to find love, is determined to love no one and to
prevent everyone else from loving, as far as he can – to make all
men the slaves of his will, and such women as attract him the
slaves of his lust. This is the ultimate reason why we hope that
Wotan, however dubious his own motives may seem, will get the
ring from Alberich. And so we arrive at the final element of the
scene – the trapping of Alberich by Loge.

The whole action of the scene, up to here, was created by
Wagner to provide a full dramatic and symbolic context for this
final element, the only one which has a simple basis in the
mythology: Alberich now begins to act out the fate of Andvari in
the Scandinavian sources. But in fact the basis was too simple
altogether for Wagner's purpose, as it stood. All that the *Prose Edda*
says is:

> Loki . . . came to the dwarf who is called Andvari, who was as a fish in
> the water. Loki caught him in his hands . . .

For Wagner to have simply translated Loki's handy bit of trout-
tickling into the terms of *The Ring* – to have made Wotan and Loge
merely pounce on Alberich and pinion him – would have resulted
in a feeble piece of dramatic business, lacking any real dramatic
tension or symbolic content, or even plausibility: Alberich, unlike
Andvari, has his Tarnhelm, and would surely, at the first sign of
violence, clap it on his head and vanish. For these reasons, Wagner
provided dramatic tension and symbolic content by making Loge
inveigle Alberich into trapping himself, through his pride in the
Tarnhelm's powers.

After warning Wotan to control himself, Loge changes the
subject by pretending to be lost in admiration of Alberich's treasure
– but how, he asks, can he be sure that thieves will not steal it?
Alberich is thus led on to boast of the Tarnhelm's powers of
making him invisible, and of changing his shape: Loge professes
incredulity, and Alberich makes good his boast by turning himself
into a monstrous serpent. Loge, after a suitable display of terror
(Wotan merely laughs), says that Alberich's best defence would be
to make himself small, but that would surely be too difficult.
Alberich's answer is to turn himself into a toad – and the moment
has arrived: Wotan puts his foot on it; Loge pulls the Tarnhelm off;

and Alberich, restored to his own shape, is bound fast.

There is only a very slight basis for this business in the sources – the fact that Loki encounters Andvari in the form of a fish, and is clever enough to catch it. But the vivid scene that Wagner built on this was not his own invention: we find here one of the rare cases of his drawing on material outside Teutonic mythology altogether. For it seems certain, as was suggested by Ernst Koch in Wagner's lifetime,[13] that the whole idea was taken straight from what would seem to be the unlikeliest of sources: Perrault's famous fairy-tale *Puss-in-Boots* (*Le chat botté*).[14] In the story, this remarkable cat is the servant of a poor miller's son, and by his subtle tricks he wins great riches for his master from unsuspecting victims (as the subtle Loge wins great riches for Wotan from the unsuspecting Alberich). In the episode in question, the victim is an ogre, not a dwarf, and he meets his death; also, the booty is not only a treasure, but a castle too. The method, however, is exactly the same – the flattery, the large transformation, the display of terror, the pretended incredulity, the small transformation, and the capture:

Puss-in-Boots came at last to a fine Castle, the Master of which was an Ogre, the richest that was ever seen . . . The Ogre received him as civilly as an Ogre can, and invited him to rest himself. 'I have been assured', said the Cat, 'that you have the gift of changing yourself into all kinds of Animals, that you can turn yourself into a Lion, for example, or an Elephant?' – 'That's true', replied the Ogre brusquely, 'and to show you, you're going to see me become a Lion'. The Cat was so frightened to see a Lion in front of him that he immediately got out on to the gutter, not without difficulty and danger, on account of his boots, which were no good for walking on the tiles. Some time after, the Cat, seeing that the Ogre had thrown off this first shape, came down, and confessed that he had been really frightened. 'I have also been assured', said the Cat, 'but I can't believe it, that you have the power to take on the forms of the smallest animals, to change yourself into a Rat, for example, and a Mouse; I confess that I regard that as quite impossible'. – 'Impossible?' replied the Ogre, 'you're going to see', and at the same time he changed himself into a Mouse, which began to run across the floor. The Cat no sooner saw it than he pounced on it and ate it.

By turning Loge into Puss-in-Boots for a few minutes, Wagner was able, not only to give dramatic tension to the business of trapping Alberich, but also to introduce his own idea of adding to

[13] Ernst Koch: *Richard Wagners Bühnenfestspiel Der Ring des Nibelungen in seinem Verhältnis zur alten Sage, wie zur modernen Nibelungendichtung betrachtet*, Leipzig, 1876.
[14] Wagner, an omnivorous reader of folklore of all kinds, would undoubtedly have known Perrault's (folk-inspired) fairy-tales, which had been issued in several German translations. I have translated from the original French of 1697.

the Tarnhelm's powers that of changing the wearer's shape, thereby preparing Siegfried's use of it, in *The Twilight of the Gods*, to assume the shape of Gunther. And at the same time he was able to enlarge the Tarnhelm's symbolism: the evil guile it represents, demonstrated openly by its possessor, is seen to be monstrous and terrifying (the serpent) and yet contemptible and weak (the toad) – this latter aspect providing not only the opportunity to stamp it out, but the impulse as well.

In the Scandinavian sources, when Loki catches in his hands the fish that is Andvari, in the land of the black elves, he despoils him of his gold and his ring there and then; but Wagner preferred to make Loge and Wotan, when they have trapped the toad that is Alberich, in Nibelheim, bind him and drag him away into the upper world, to despoil him there. The reasons for this we shall consider in turning to the final scene.

Scene 4

The main action of the scene is Wagner's completion of his dramatization of the Andvari myth; and in the first part of it, Alberich continues to act out the fate of Andvari himself to the bitter end (see p. 116). He is despoiled of his treasure and his ring, and after putting his curse on the ring, he withdraws from the action.

Wagner could have let all this happen in Nibelheim, in Scene 3, just as it happens in the land of the black elves in the *Prose Edda*; but he preferred to transfer it to the upper world of Scene 4, for three reasons. The first was purely practical: in Scene 3, it would have involved Wotan and Loge in packing up the large treasure (presumably in a sack) and carrying it back themselves to the upper world – not a very likely activity for gods! (How Loki carried Andvari's treasure back, in the myth, the *Prose Edda* neatly refrains from telling us.) But more important was his dramatic reason: to have begun Scene 4 with the toilsome business of the paying of the ransom for Freia would have been to lower the tension considerably; it was much more striking to begin it with a larger and more crucial confrontation between Alberich and Wotan.

Most important of all was Wagner's symbolic reason. He had made Wotan accompany Loge on the expedition to trap the dwarf, in spite of the mythology, in order to keep him in the forefront of the action, as the chief of the gods, controlling the course of events; also, although he allowed Loge to carry out the actual trickery, as befitted his status as god of intellect, he made Wotan perform the decisive act of capture – that of putting his foot on the toad; and he also decided to make Wotan carry out the despoliation of Alberich, instead of Loge. But to have let this take place in Nibelheim would have left Alberich merely a mysterious and ultimately ineffectual creature of the underworld. It was necessary to set him firmly on a par with Wotan, as Wotan's opposite number and formidable rival; so Wagner brought him to the surface, and used the despoliation as the basis of the larger and more crucial confrontation between the two, in the upper world.

To begin with, instead of a mere handing over of the treasure in subterranean darkness, we have that tremendous moment when Alberich, at Wotan's command, brandishes the ring to summon the Nibelungs, and the Nibelungs bring the treasure up from under the earth. This serves to demonstrate, in the most concrete way, the very real danger to the gods of Alberich's thwarted bid for power, since it actually enacts his threat to Wotan in Scene 3 – 'Beware the army of night, when the Nibelung treasure rises from the silent depths to the daylight': the effect is of some monstrous evil emerging from underground to engulf the world. As things now stand, of course, its emergence is neutralized, since it represents Alberich's defeat instead of his triumph: the treasure, which was to have bought out the gods and achieved the takeover of Valhalla, simply passes into Wotan's possession. And yet there is dramatic irony here. Wotan should still beware, because, notwithstanding Alberich's personal downfall, the treasure has in fact risen to the daylight; and it (and particularly the ring), still represents an evil that threatens to engulf the world, beginning with Wotan himself.

Alberich is unsubdued in defeat: he faces defiantly the appalling humiliation of being forced to use the ring for the purpose of his own despoliation (all the worse for being witnessed by his Nibelung slaves), just as he has been tricked into using the Tarnhelm for the purpose of his own capture. And when the Nibelungs have gone, and the Tarnhelm has been tossed on to the pile by Loge, he consoles himself, in his rage, with the reflection that he can get himself a new treasure and another Tarnhelm, as long as he still has the ring. He asks to be set free, and Loge, in character as ever, asks Wotan if he is satisfied, leaving the moral decision to him. But it is the ring, of course, that Wotan wants most of all: he asks Alberich to hand it over, and when Alberich refuses, he is as ruthless with him as Loki is with Andvari in the original myth. To quote the *Prose Edda* again:

> The dwarf begged him not to take the ring from him, since with that ring he could increase his gold. But Loki said he should not have a penny left; he took the ring from him . . .

Wagner's Alberich, naturally, keeps his thoughts about 'increasing his gold' to himself. Trembling with emotion, he replies to Wotan's request: 'My life, but not the ring'. Wotan's brutal answer is 'I want the ring – do with your life what you want'; and he takes it by force.

But this is Wotan and Alberich, not Loki and Andvari; and before the act of robbery takes place, Wagner interpolated the second, climactic confrontation between the two power-seeking rulers – a moral one this time. Alberich claims that the ring is as much his own as his head, hands, eyes, and ears are, and when Wotan points out that its gold was stolen from the Rhinemaidens, he replies that Wotan is only too glad that the theft has happened: he can now take the ring that Alberich has created for himself through the terrible sacrifice of renouncing love, and use it as a toy for his amusement. And Alberich ends with a desperate moral warning:

> Look to yourself,
> high-handed god!
> What crime I committed,
> I committed against myself;
> but against all that was,
> is, and shall be,
> your crime, Immortal, will stand,
> if you shamelessly seize my ring!

To which Wotan merely replies that such twaddle cannot justify Alberich's claim on the ring, and tears it from his finger.

It seems easy to side with Alberich here. He is right, in a sense, in saying that the ring is his own talisman and no one else's, made by him at the terrible cost of renouncing love. And he speaks no more than the truth when he says that if Wotan takes it, he will be committing a crime far worse than his own – a crime against all creation. His own crime – of stealing the Rhinegold and making from it the ring of absolute power by renouncing love – was certainly 'committed against himself', being that of a solitary, one of the underprivileged, undergoing a psychosis, as we have seen; but Wotan's crime – of stealing the ring with the intention, not of restoring it to its rightful owners, but of using it himself – is that of a world-ruler, one of the privileged, who is responsible for his own actions. Moreover, Wotan stands in the worst possible light here: a compound of hypocrisy (in pointing out that the ring belongs to the Rhinemaidens without any intention of restoring it to them), arrogance (in his whole high-handed attitude), and brutality (in robbing Alberich by force).

Yet it is not as simple as this: Alberich's denunciation of Wotan is impressive in its sense of outrage, but it lacks the moral weight of Fasolt's, since he matches Wotan in hypocrisy. Notwithstanding the hypocrisy of Wotan himself, we have to admit that nothing Alberich can say justifies his claim to the ring: if it is his, in the sense that he, and he alone, made it, at the cost of renouncing love, it is certainly not his, in the fundamental sense that he made it from gold which he stole from the Rhinemaidens, and which really belongs to them. Furthermore, if his original crime was merely committed 'against himself', in that it reduced him to the psychotic state of lovelessness, he has since committed a crime against all his fellow-beings, by enslaving the Nibelungs, and has also intended to commit a crime against all creation – that of enslaving the gods, debauching the goddesses, and ruling the world with loveless ruthlessness, to gratify his personal lust for revenge.

Not that this in any way exonerates Wotan, who in robbing Alberich of his ring has practically sunk to Alberich's level. If he intends to keep it – and it seems that he does – then he will be committing exactly the same crimes as Alberich: theft of the gold (in the form of the ring), renunciation of love (for he will have to lose Freia to the giants), enslavement of his fellow-beings (since he will be wedded to the principle of 'Might is Right'), and domination of the world with loveless ruthlessness. Moreover, in committing the crime 'against himself' of renouncing love, he will become a psychotic like Alberich; and (Alberich's one bit of truth, even if stated hypocritically) this crime will be far worse, in that creation's hopes of justice and love have been centred on Wotan, as the actual ruler of the world. It is significant that the one crucial charge that Wotan could have brought against Alberich – loveless exploitation of his fellow-beings – he does not bring at all: loveless exploitation is so much part of his own way of life that he does not even think of finding it reprehensible. And if now, having disarmed Alberich, he does not rise above him, but sinks to his level, finally and irrevocably, there is no hope for the world.[1]

The truth is that, in this confrontation, it is impossible to side

[1] It might be objected, by those who find it easy to side with Wotan, that the power conferred by the ring would enable him to keep Freia. This is, of course, illegitimate conjecture outside the text of the drama, which carries Wagner's symbolism beyond its terms of reference, and involves it in contradiction. Even so, the symbolism is so consistent that an answer may be offered: the retention of the fertility-goddess by means of the ring, whose use involves the renunciation of love, would reduce her from her status as the great love-goddess to a mere embodiment of physical-sex-without-love, which would again mean that Wotan had sunk to Alberich's level. The whole implication of Wagner's symbolism is that a Wotan who kept and used the ring would become even worse than the Wotan of *The Rhinegold*, and immeasurably worse than the Wotan of the rest of the tetralogy.

with either party. If we side with Alberich, it is only because he is
the underdog, treated by Wotan with the utmost brutality; if we
side with Wotan, it is only because, being familiar with the
tetralogy as a whole, we know that he is eventually going to part
with the ring, take back Freia, and grope his way towards a
recognition of the claims of justice and love. Taking the confrontation by itself with all its mutual hypocrisy, and not sentimentaliz-
ing Alberich's plight, we find ourselves faced with Wagner's two
great complementary images of man-in-pursuit-of-power, brought
together decisively for the first time, as opposite sides of the same
coin, with one side (Wotan's) now almost identical with the other.
The ruthless but ultimately civilizing ruler, whose quest for
world-domination-through-law has led him to ignore the claims of
love, has defeated and disarmed the revengeful psychotic, who
has expelled love from his being altogether in order to pursue a
criminal totalitarianism unhampered; but in doing so, he has
become practically indistinguishable from his rival. Power breeds
power, and, in Lord Acton's too familiar phrase: 'All power tends
to corrupt and absolute power corrupts absolutely'. Wotan was
only corrupted; now he is near to becoming as absolutely corrupt
as Alberich. His very first utterance as the possessor of the ring, in
fact, confirms this: it is a self-regarding echo of Alberich's very first
self-pitying utterance as the non-possessor of the ring, belonging
to the same power-ridden circle of ideas. Alberich's words are:

> *Ah! ruined! broken!*
> *The sorriest of sorry slaves!*

And Wotan, contemplating the ring, now on his finger, echoes:

> *Now I possess what exalts me to*
> *the mightiest of mighty lords!*

Evidently, we conclude, he intends to keep it.

Faced with total ruin – loss of love, loss of wealth, loss of power –
Alberich completes his enactment of the fate of Andvari by putting
a curse on the ring. In the *Prose Edda*, where the ring is not a
talisman of world-domination, the curse is short but basic: 'Then
the dwarf said that the ring should cost everyone who possessed it
his life'. Wagner, in putting this curse into Alberich's mouth,
expanded it: not only shall the ring bring death to anyone who
possesses it, but it shall bring unhappiness to everyone connected
with it; those who do not possess it shall be consumed with

envious longing for it; he who does possess it shall be so consumed with care, through fear of being killed for it, that he shall long for the death that he knows awaits him; 'the ring's master shall be the ring's slave' – until it returns to the hand of its maker.

A curse was always an excellent piece of stock-in-trade for a romantic musical dramatist, but Wagner did not take over the one in the mythology purely for this reason: as expanded by him, it further reinforces the power-symbolism. Wielders of tyrannical power have always been quite liable to come to a sticky end; and it is a truism that tyrannical power brings no joy to its possessor, because he must constantly guard against being eliminated by one of the envious who covet it – and they are no more happy than he is. Alberich does not really need to put the curse on the ring, we might say, since it is already there in the nature of things. Indeed, it was already there from the moment the ring was made, since Alberich was hardly happy in possessing it, Mime was already consumed with envious longing for it, and Alberich was soon despoiled of it (if not actually killed) by the covetous Wotan; moreover the curse still applies to Alberich as to everyone else, since he will spend the rest of the tetralogy as one of the non-possessors of the ring who are consumed with longing for it. Nevertheless, his savage delivery of the curse – and not in the obscurity of Nibelheim, but in the broad daylight above, where Wotan holds sway – serves to remind us, and Wotan too, that the tyrannical power which lies latent in the ring is a terrible evil threatening the whole world.

But Wotan does not get the message. In the *Prose Edda*, Loki takes Andvari's curse coolly: knowing that the ring will soon pass out of his (and Odin's) hands, he delightedly undertakes to inform the future possessors of its about the curse himself (see p. 116). But in Scene 4 of *The Rhinegold*, when Alberich has disappeared down a cleft in the mountain, Loge, who is entirely subordinate to Wotan, asks him quizzically if he listened to Alberich's 'fond farewell'; and Wotan merely answers 'Let him vent his rage!' He is too absorbed in gazing at the ring on his finger to consider the implications of what Alberich has said.

When Fasolt and Fafner return, bringing Freia with them, and the other gods reappear, the scene continues its dramatization of the Andvari myth with the paying of the ransom. In the *Prose Edda* (see p. 115), the ransom is blood-money for the dead otter-man, and Andvari's gold is measured out by means of the otter-skin: the skin has to be filled with gold, then stood up, and entirely covered with gold; when the gold gives out, a single whisker remains visible, and Odin has to cover it with Andvari's ring, which he took from the gold earlier, with the intention of keeping it himself. Wagner translated this whole episode almost literally into the terms of *The Rhinegold*: the otter-skin becomes Freia's body; Andvari's gold becomes Alberich's Nibelung treasure; the whisker becomes both Freia's hair, which has to be concealed by the Tarnhelm, and Freia's eyes, which have to be concealed by Alberich's ring – which Wotan wants so much to keep.

The paying-out of the treasure itself was used by Wagner to reinforce the characters of all concerned. Whereas in the myth the otter-skin is no more than the befitting measure, in *The Rhinegold* the amorous Fasolt says that he will only be able to forget Freia if the treasure is heaped up so as to hide her from view; and he and Fafner set their staves on either side of her, for the treasure to be piled between them. The greedy Fafner, however, is not interested in Freia, but only, while the treasure is heaped up, in seeing that it is packed as tight as possible. When Loge starts the work, Froh helps him, 'in a hurry to put an end to Freia's shame'; but Donner gets murderously angry, and again has to be restrained by Wotan. Fricka is deeply distressed at the degradation brought on Freia by the barter; and even Wotan regains a little of our sympathy by losing his arrogance for a moment and admitting that he is burning with shame at the whole sordid business.

When the treasure gives out, the demand for the two final pieces serves again to bring out the foil-relationship between the two brother-giants. First Fafner, to secure the Tarnhelm, finds he can still see Freia's hair glinting through a gap; and Loge throws the helmet on to the pile. Then Fasolt, unable to bear losing even the sight of Freia, finds he can still see her eyes shining on him through a last chink – but this, Fafner immediately points out, can be stopped by the ring he sees gleaming on Wotan's finger. Here is the culminating image of the power-versus-love symbolism: the shining eyes of the goddess of love against the gleaming gold of the 'accursed ring' of tyrannical world-domination.

Indeed, the symbolism has now reached its climax: Wotan cannot hope to have it both ways any more. It is love or power, Freia or the ring; and he confirms all our worst suspicions by clinging to the ring and deciding for power. This great Wagnerian moment is built on only the faintest of suggestions in the original myth. In the *Prose Edda*, on Loki's return with Andvari's gold and ring (which is not of course a ring of world-domination), we read that

> . . . when Odin saw the ring, it seemed beautiful to him, and he took it from the treasure . . .

But when it came to handing it over:

> Then Odin brought out the ring and covered the whisker, saying that he had now paid their debt concerning the otter.

Wotan, however, in spite of urgent appeals from Fricka, Froh, and Donner (not from Loge, who gives him a final malicious reminder about the Rhinemaidens), refuses, and is adamant:

> *For all the world*
> *I will not part with the ring!*

(But 'all the world' is what he believes the ring will bring him.) And again:

> *Leave me in peace!*
> *I will not give up the ring!*

(But peace is the last thing the ring would bring him.)

Fasolt seizes Freia, to drag her away: Wotan has finally sunk to Alberich's level – and irrevocably, unless someone can change his mind. Luckily, someone does: into the middle of the Andvari myth intrudes the last character to appear in *The Rhinegold* – Erda, the earth-goddess, who half-emerges from the earth to intervene.

Erda is Wagner's own creation, in one sense: there is no clearly identifiable earth-goddess in the mythology as it has come down to us. Both *Eddas* mention a certain 'Jord' (Earth), on whom Odin begot Thor; but they also give the name of Thor's mother as Fjorgynn, and since 'Jord' does simply mean 'earth', it would seem that Fjorgynn was the (or an) earth-goddess. But inextricable confusion surrounds the name (it appears in one context in a masculine form, 'Fjorgyn', as that of the father of Frigg); and in any case, both it and 'Jord' remain no more than names.

Wagner's name 'Erda' is simply the Old High German word for 'earth' (modern German *Erde*); he took it from Jacob Grimm, who postulated it as the name of the ancient German earth-goddess. Grimm supported his claim that such a goddess existed by quoting a passage from the *Germania* of the Roman historian Tacitus, which tells of certain first-century Teutonic tribes who 'worship in common Nerthus, or Mother Earth, and believe that she intervenes in the affairs of men'. Wagner's Erda certainly intervenes with decisive effect in the affairs of the *gods*,[2] in Scene 4 of *The Rhinegold*, but apart from this reference in Tacitus, he had nothing to go on. For the actual nature and function of Erda, he had to turn elsewhere.

He turned to two poems in the *Poetic Edda*, in which Odin calls up from the earth (or from the land of the dead underneath the earth) a 'volva', or wise-woman, or prophetess, to question her about the fate in store for the gods. As a matter of historical fact, such women were Scandinavian priestesses with medium-like powers, akin to the Greek sibyls with their oracles; but in relation to Odin, in the mythic poems, they feature as mysterious supernatural beings, spirits of the earth. In one of these poems – the most famous of all, the *Wise-Woman's Prophecy* (*Voluspo*, literally *The Soothsaying of the Volva*) – the *volva* gives a condensed history of creation, and then foretells the fate in store for the gods: a battle against the powers of evil on the last day of the world, in which every single combatant, save one, will be destroyed. This is the poem which Wagner took as a suggestion for the appearance of Erda to Wotan in Scene 4 of *The Rhinegold*, with her warning about the end of the gods; the other poem – *Baldr's Dreams*, in which Odin questions a *volva* about the fate of the god Baldr, his favourite son – provided a starting-point for the other scene in which Erda appears, at the beginning of Act 3 of *Siegfried* (see p. 111). Actually, in both poems, the *volva* is forced to appear against her will, by being called up by Odin, and gives her answers unwillingly, as with Erda in the *Siegfried* scene; but Wagner no doubt derived the idea of letting Erda appear unbidden, in *The Rhinegold*, from the 'Nerthus' of Tacitus, who 'intervenes in the affairs of men'.

The similarity between the idea of a female spirit who rises from the earth with a knowledge of fate, and the idea of an earth-goddess who interests herself in human destinies, is obvious and natural; and that Wagner simply identified the two kinds of being is evident from his text. Grimm postulated, as the Old High German equivalent of the Norse word *volva*, the formation *Walawa* or *Wala*; and Wagner's Erda, after saying that she has full know-

[2] Who are, of course, symbols of humanity.

ledge of past, present, and future, describes herself immediately as *der ew'gen Welt Urwala* – the everlasting world's primordial *Wala*, or *volva*. She is represented by Wagner, then, as the original mother of all supernatural wise-women; and this explains how he came to make her the actual mother of the Norns and the Valkyries, in defiance of the mythology, whose Norns and Valkyries have no parents at all.

The three Norns were the Norse fates, who wove the destinies of men: the eldest presided over the past, the second over the present, and the youngest over the future. They were sometimes represented as appearing to newly-born children, to decide their destinies; one such case, quoted by Grimm, occurs in *Norna-Gests thattr*, and here the words *norn* and *volva* are used as synonyms. If, then, the *nornir* were *volvar*, with knowledge of past, present and future, and if they intervened in the affairs of men, they were for Wagner the daughters of the primordial *volva*, Erda. The Valkyries, too, were wise-women, represented as having a knowledge of the future and intervening in the affairs of men, since they determined the fate of warriors in battle. Moreover, in the *Wise-Woman's Prophecy*, the *volva* raised by Odin gives one of the Valkyries' names as Skuld, which was also the name of the youngest Norn, who presided over the future; this, as Grimm again pointed out, indicates the affinity between the Norns and Valkyries as *volvar*, and it explains why Wagner made his Valkyries the daughters of Erda too. In all this, his instinct was sound, since if the mythology had actually contained an earth-goddess who gave birth to Norns and Valkyries, no one would have been in the least surprised. (His reason for making Wotan the *father* of the Valkyries will be discussed when we turn to *The Valkyrie*).

Erda, then, the earth-goddess, the primordial wise-woman, half-emerges from the earth, like a *volva*; but unlike a *volva*, who simply prophesies doom, she intervenes in the affairs of men, like Nerthus. She solemnly warns Wotan to give up the ring, and in the most cryptic terms, befitting her mysterious nature:

> *Give in, Wotan, give in!*
> *Flee the curse on the ring!*
>   *To irretrievable*
>   *dark perdition*
> *it will doom you, if you possess it . . .*
> *All that is must end;*
>   *a dark day*

> *dawns for the gods:*
> *I counsel you, shun the ring!*[3]

Erda's sudden appearance is the most unexpected of all the unexpected events in *The Ring*: it comes as a tremendous, breathtaking surprise, and has the effect of a visionary revelation. What in the scheme of human affairs does she represent, and what does her intervention imply? Far more even than Loge, she is clearly independent of Wotan and the other gods, and she gives the impression of being something greater than them, something more fundamental. Since she is female, comes out of the earth, and succeeds in dragging Wotan back from the brink of an irrevocable act of criminal folly, when nothing else could, she would seem to embody some mysterious fundamental wisdom emerging from the unconscious[4] – some basic intuition of what is ultimately right and fitting. And yet, if that is what Erda is, why does she not advise Wotan to return the ring to the Rhinemaidens?[5] It is evident that Wagner regarded this action as the only right one, since he made Loge urge it over and over again, and in *The Twilight of the Gods* he made Wotan, and eventually Brünnhilde, recognize it as the only solution of the world's troubles.

We can perhaps come a little nearer to understanding the symbolic function of Erda, if we remember that her knowledge is

[3] In some of Wagner's prose-sketches, and even in the first version of the actual text (the one printed in 1853), there is a suggestion on Erda's part that the gods will perish, or at least perish sooner than they normally would, *unless* Wotan gives up the ring – the implication being that if he *does* give up the ring, this fate will be avoided; and many people have been puzzled by the fact that, in *The Ring* as we know it, the gods perish *although* Wotan gives up the ring. But in fact, the final text, as quoted above, puts no condition into Erda's mouth at all: she simply advises Wotan to give up the ring because its possession will doom him to 'irretrievable dark perdition' – which is something other than just perishing – and she reminds him that the gods are not immortal. And Wotan, by giving up the ring, does avoid 'irretrievable dark perdition', even though, in the end, the gods perish. It is on the implications of the final text that the following interpretation is based.

[4] I use the word 'unconscious' circumspectly here, well aware that, in Donington's interpretation, practically everybody and everything in *The Ring* represents something unconscious. But it does seem to me that, whereas everything up to this point needs no more for its immediate interpretation than the terms of everyday conscious existence, there is here a sudden breakthrough of something which is not to be understood in those terms – something of which Wotan himself is *literally* unconscious, until it suddenly manifests itself to him: *he does not know Erda, but has to ask her who she is.*

[5] There was, of course, the purely practical necessity of not ending *The Ring* with Scene 4 of The Rhinegold; but Wagner – as we have seen with Donner's being prevented from killing the giants – made a symbolic virtue out of necessity.

essentially a knowledge of fate. Wagner made her the mother of the Norns, who in the mythology and in *The Ring* have between them the knowledge of past, present, and future; moreover, he made her claim a *complete* knowledge of all three:

> *How all things were, I know;*
> *how all things are,*
> *how all things will be,*
> *I also see . . .*

And he also made her say (in complete defiance of the mythology) that what she sees is told to Wotan every night by the Norns – but now the greatest danger brings her to him herself. What the Norns tell him must of course be things about the past, present, and future – obscure intimations of the necessary coherence of the developing process of life, which do indeed come to men from unconscious sources, and particularly in the silence of the night. But what is it that Erda can tell him that the Norns do not know? She warns him that 'all that is must end' – a truth which he knows as a fact, of course, but which, owing to his enduring youth (symbolized by Freia's apples), he had not taken into serious account.

In other words, she knows what Wotan's fate is – and the world's too: to pass away. She confronts him with the reality of death, for himself and for everything, and it is for this reason that he must give up the ring. He does not have eternity at his disposal, as it has seemed to him; and in the little time he has, he must not come to 'irretrievable dark perdition'. It is not his destiny to damn himself by exercising a loveless, tyrannical power over the world, which will fill his life with care and fear, and hasten his end; nor is it the world's destiny to be damned through being ruled by such power. A sense of destiny is essentially a profound intuitive awareness of what it is one's nature to do with one's life before it ends; and Erda embodies this sense of destiny, which does on occasion reveal itself, at moments of crisis, to certain people.

It might seem that we are diminishing the significance of the mysterious figure of Erda by interpreting her as no more than humanity's sense of its destiny, which comes to Wotan at the turning-point of his career. But in fact, Wagner did not intend to represent her as ultimate wisdom. She may impress on Wotan that he and the world must come to an end, and that it is not his and the world's destiny to rule and be ruled by the ring, but she does not know how the end will come, or what the actual destiny of

Wotan and the world is. It could be thought that she knows, but will not tell; but that this is not so is evident from the fact that, when Wotan calls her up in Act 3 of *Siegfried* to acquaint her with his plans concerning Siegfried and Brünnhilde, she is bewildered, and does not understand what he is trying to do. Even if this means that he is even now going against his and the world's true destiny, Erda still cannot tell him what that destiny is. Wotan himself does not know in *Siegfried* – but he does by the beginning of *The Twilight of the Gods*: the ring is to be returned to the Rhinemaidens, the Tree of Life to be cut down to make a bonfire, and Valhalla and the gods to go up in flames.

To understand this supersession of Erda by Wotan, we have to remember that Wagner, from his revolutionary standpoint, did not regard the wisdom bound up with a knowledge of human fate as absolute and insurmountable. Fate is to be overcome; and so Wotan's final knowledge is a great and final step forward on Erda's. In the Prelude to *The Twilight of the Gods*, while her daughters the Norns are weaving the apparently endless thread of fate they have been weaving since the beginning of all things, that thread snaps, once and for all. As Wotan has said to Erda in *Siegfried*, the Norns 'weave in thrall to the world' – they are bound by their knowledge of the limits of human fate, which is all they understand; and their weaving eventually ends when the youngest Norn can no longer see the future – because the destiny of Wotan and the world is in process of passing beyond the limits of fate altogether. The meaning of this, which is closely connected with the philosophy of Schopenhauer, will be considered when we come to *The Twilight of the Gods*; in the meantime it should be clear that Erda embodies no more (and no less) than humanity's profound but obscure sense of destiny – which suddenly reveals itself to Wotan, confronts him with the reality of death, and saves him from taking an irrevocable step which would have led to degradation for himself and for the world.

But Erda vanishes as suddenly as she materialized. Wotan vainly tries to hold her back by force, but she has no more to tell him – and she leaves him to 'meditate' (her words as she descends into the earth again) 'in care and fear'. And these are the very two emotions that Alberich's curse would condemn him to, if he kept the ring! But there is a vast difference: as ruler of the world, with a new-found sense of destiny, he will indeed know care and fear only too well, but they will not afflict him in the destructive way they would have done if he had refused to part with the ring. They will be the care and fear that beset a ruler with a sense of responsibility; and they will cause him suffering that will lead him to understand what his true destiny is. Already, in what is left of *The Rhinegold*, we shall find him beginning to change: his old unreflecting optimism and lordly arrogance will begin to be undermined by a sense of guilt for the shameful predicament he has brought upon himself, and tempered by a resolution to use his power to make the world a better place. This will not be easy, because his sense of domination will remain, and in trying to exercise his power to carry out his resolution, in *The Valkyrie*, he will find it taking on an even greater brutality, and leading him into an even worse predicament. But in finding his way out of this with the help of Brünnhilde (his love-child by Erda), he will begin to move towards his true destiny at last.

At the moment, however, he is still only intent on power. As he throws the ring on to the pile of treasure, he is glad to have Freia back, but basically so that he can regain the apples of immortality:

> *To me, Freia!*
> *You are set free;*
> *brought back again,*
> *our youth shall return to us!*

With the rescue of Freia and her apples, we reach the end of the part played by the fortress and Idun myths; and the two giants now act out the end of the Andvari myth – as manipulated by Wagner. In the *Prose Edda*, the brothers Fafnir and Regin kill their father Hreidmar because he will not share the treasure with them, and then quarrel over it themselves; and all this happens in the seclusion of their own home, after Odin and Loki have left (see p. 180). But in *The Rhinegold*, Hreidmar having been omitted, the two brothers Fafner and Fasolt quarrel immediately over the treasure – or rather, over the all-important ring of absolute power; Fafner kills Fasolt to gain possession of it; and this happens in the world of the gods, in front of their eyes. As a result, the power-versus-love symbolism is given one final spotlit emphasis: Fasolt, the former seeker for love in the person of Freia, having given up that love in return for the ring of absolute power, has sunk to Fafner's level, wrangling with him over the ring; and Fafner, to gain possession of the ring, finally demonstrates his total lovelessness by murdering his own brother for it.

And here we reach the juncture where the Andvari myth ends and points forward to the Siegfried myth – though the myth's two pointers are reduced to one. Since Fafner's brother, instead of simply going away in fear, is killed, it will be another character, Alberich's brother Mime, who will bring up Siegfried and incite him to kill Fafner for the treasure and the ring; Fafner himself, on the other hand, like his counterpart in the myth, carries off the treasure and the ring, and (as we shall learn from back-narration in *The Valkyrie*) makes himself a lair, turns himself into a dragon,[6] and lies down on the gold. The symbolic addition, with Wagner, is that the ring is a talisman of absolute power, which Fafner has neither the intelligence nor the energy to make use of.

From the moment when Fafner clubs Fasolt to death, Wagner builds the action of *The Rhinegold* freely, with only an occasional suggestion from the mythology. First, we begin to encounter that change in Wotan mentioned above: for the first time he is shaken – appalled by the prompt fulfilment of Alberich's curse. And when Loge, sardonically logical as ever, congratulates him on the fact that his enemies are killing one another, he can only reply that 'care and fear' enchain his mind. These are the two emotions bequeathed to him by Erda; and indeed, he avows his intention of consulting her one day as to how to get rid of them – of finding out more from his mysterious new-found sense of destiny. And still, when Fricka tries to wheedle him into delighting in the beauty of the fortress that is now theirs, he can only reply, gloomily, that he has bought it with bad money. The ideal of law that Wagner superimposed on the Odin of the *Eddas* has now been joined by another added quality – a sense of guilt.

For the moment, however, Wotan can only fall back on his habitual attitudes. He lets Donner, in his capacity as the thunder-god, embody his anger again, 'clearing the air' by gathering together the murky mists that surround the whole scene into a brief storm. When this subsides, he lets Froh, as 'ruler over the rain and the sunshine', embody his unrealistic optimism once more, pointing the way across the 'terror-free' path of the rainbow bridge that leads to the now unveiled fortress. And finally, he himself

[6] By means of the Tarnhelm? Wagner does not say so – and indeed, in the Scandinavian sources, which alone contain the story, there is no Tarnhelm at all; presumably Fafnir, like his father Hreidmar, was 'well-versed in magic', and like his brother Otr, could change his shape.

begins to take a pride in his new power-symbol, admiring it with affection. Nevertheless, the change in his character remains unaffected: he still remembers that the fortress was 'won in trouble and anxiety, not in delight'. And then, suddenly, this chastened mood releases a completely new state of mind: a moral determination to build on what he has salvaged and set things right – which Wagner added to the ideal of law and the sense of guilt he had already superimposed on the Odin of the *Eddas*. 'With great resolution, as if struck by a grand idea' – the stage-direction reads – 'Wotan picks up a sword, belonging to the Nibelung treasure but left behind by Fafner, and raises it solemnly towards the fortress'. In doing so, he apostrophizes his power-symbol with the words:

> *Thus do I greet the fortress,*
> *safe from fear and dread!*

And in bidding Fricka accompany him into its shelter, he at last finds a name for it:

> *Follow me, wife:*
> *In Valhalla dwell with me!*[7]

In Wagner's score, and in the final text as published, there was no stage-direction about the sword to indicate the nature of the 'grand idea' that strikes Wotan: the whole burden of this crucial moment of the drama was to have been carried by Wotan's words and the music – the bold, majestic fanfare-phrase for solo trumpet (Ex. 63) which is in *The Valkyrie* to attach itself to the sword provided by Wotan for Siegmund. But during the rehearsals for the original Bayreuth production of *The Ring* in 1876, Wagner realized that Wotan's utterance by itself – even backed by the trumpet's fanfare-phrase – would create no decisive theatrical impression; wherefore he invented the stage-business of the sword, to indicate more forcefully that something momentous was

Ex. 63

Moderate tempo

[7] It has been necessary, occasionally, in this chapter, to call the fortress Valhalla, since the experienced Wagnerian knows it as such from the beginning of *The Ring*; but in fact it remains, up to this point, simply 'the fortress' (*die Burg*), and it is only now that Wotan baptizes it with the name of Valhalla (Walhall).

coming to birth in Wotan's mind – and this was eventually incorporated as a (footnote) stage-direction in the Breitkopf vocal score of 1910.[8]

There has been a good deal of argument over this point. In the first place, the business of the sword left behind by Fafner is very difficult to make plausible on the stage. The Nibelung treasure, having to be piled up vertically to cover Freia's erect form from sight, is inevitably, in production, reduced to a lot of cubic blocks of gold, to make such a piling-up possible: in consequence, the 'gold- and silver-work' amassed by the Nibelungs for Alberich in Scene 3 has to be ignored, so that there are no bits and pieces lying around – the sword lies there all on its own, and it seems unlikely that the greedy Fafner would overlook it when packing up the gold blocks.[9] But secondly, and more important, the objection has been raised that, if Fafner leaves a sword behind from the Nibelung treasure, and Wotan hails Valhalla with it to the sound of Ex. 63, the fact that Wagner later attaches Ex. 63 to the sword that Siegmund draws from Hunding's house-tree, in Act 1 of *The Valkyrie*, will imply that it is the actual sword from the Nibelung treasure that Wotan thrusts into Hunding's house-tree for Siegmund to claim; whereas Wagner's original intention was that Wotan should be merely 'struck by a grand idea', and that this idea should later materialize in the heroism of Siegmund, symbolized by the sword Wotan provides for him.

Yet it seems impossible not to respect Wagner's last-minute decision, based on his intimate understanding of theatrical effect. For even *with* the business of the sword, Wagner's original intention remains obscure: at the actual moment when Wotan hails Valhalla with the sword, to the sound of Ex. 63, it has no identity at all, but simply functions as a mysterious symbol, reinforcing the fact that Wotan has been 'struck with a grand idea', without defining what that idea is. Of course, it may be that a literal-

[8] The original Schott scores of *The Rhinegold* do not, of course, contain this stage-direction, as they were published before the first complete production of *The Ring* at Bayreuth (the vocal score in 1861, the full score in 1873).

[9] In a recent performance – by the Sadler's Wells (English National) Opera Company in 1972 – the producer was so baffled by the situation that he preferred to make Wotan take Froh's sword from him, and hail Valhalla with that. But this, apart from the fact that it hinders the impulsiveness of Wotan's gesture, is manifestly impossible: Froh, as we have seen, is a nonentity, ignored by Wotan, and he can have no connection with one of Wotan's great inspirations. In any case, he is the one god in the original mythology who has no sword at all, having fecklessly given it away in pursuit of love (see p. 162), so he should be the last character to hand a sword to Wotan.

minded spectator, finding Ex. 63 attached later to Siegmund's sword in *The Valkyrie*, will not only realize that this is Wotan's 'grand idea' come to particular fruition, but will also assume that this sword must be the one Wotan acquired in Scene 4 of *The Rhinegold*. If so, that is his own business: nowhere in Wagner's text are the two said to be identical.

But perhaps Wagner *was* prepared to let it be inferred that the sword Wotan provides for Siegmund is the one that he acquires from the Nibelung treasure? The Wagnerian will have a natural reluctance to believe this, since it entails the idea that Siegmund's sword was originally made by a dwarf. But in fact, this idea is perfectly consonant with the mythology, since there the swords of the heroes are almost invariably made by dwarf-smiths. The main exception, certainly, is the one in question. In *Volsunga saga* – the only source to contain the weapon – the sword that Sigmund draws from the tree is simply set there by Odin, and has no pre-history at all. But Wagner could have been relying on the mythology in general – and indeed in particular, following in essence those sources which give an origin for Siegfried's sword, knowing nothing of its having been made from the shattered sword of Siegmund. In the *Nibelungenlied*, Siegfried's sword was originally King Nibelung's, and thus part of the 'Nibelung hoard'; it is given him by the sons of King Nibelung, whom the *Lied vom hürnen Seyfrid* identifies as dwarfs. In *Thidriks saga*, Sigurd receives his sword from his smith of a foster-father, whose identity as a dwarf is made clear by the *Prose Edda* and *Norna-gests thattr*. Moreover, even in *Volsunga saga*, where alone Sigurd's sword is refashioned from the shattered sword of Sigmund, it is Sigurd's dwarf-smith foster-father who refashions it.[10] Assuming that Wagner *did* intend the swords in *The Rhinegold* and *The Valkyrie* to be identical, we could say that his idea was justified by all these examples – and that it enabled him to tie the story of the Volsungs even more closely to that of the gods, by weaving a stronger thread of purpose into the whole. In *Volsunga saga*, Odin's sword comes from nowhere, and its only function is to serve Sigmund, and later Sigurd, as a particularly powerful weapon; but in Wagner's tetralogy, on the above assumption, the sword Wotan acquires from the

[10] Wagner of course altered this, making Siegfried refashion his father's sword himself, but his alteration still links up with the ideas indicated above. For him, this was the single smithying task that could *not* be accomplished by a dwarf – an exception to the general rule, which he added to reinforce his symbolization of Siegfried as 'the man of the future'.

Nibelung treasure functions as a crucial instrument in his plan to regain the Nibelung's ring through the agency of Siegmund.

We must postpone examination of this aspect of the drama until we come to *The Valkyrie*; and indeed, Wagner himself, despite his last-minute invention of the stage-business of the sword, preferred to leave an aura of mystery around Wotan's momentous decision. For the symbol of the sword, decisively theatrical though it may be, remains for the time being inscrutable. What is its purpose? What is Wotan's intention? Only those who are familiar with *The Ring* know in advance that the idea stirring in his mind is to create a race of human heroes, the most valiant of whom shall be assembled in Valhalla, after their deaths, to defend it against any possible attack. Actually, Wagner's final definitive prose-sketch for *The Rhinegold* shows that he thought of providing a hint as to Wotan's intentions, since, when hailing the fortress there, Wotan says:

> In you, sacred dwelling, I will gather together noble companions, to win for me, gladly, the world . . . Thither I now summon a new race, and I baptize the fortress Valhalla.

And when Fricka asks what the name means, he replies:

> When they are born, whom I shall summon thither, then will the name be clear to you.[11]

But when Wagner came to draw up the actual text of *The Rhinegold*, he preferred to leave Wotan's intention embryonic, by putting into his mouth the enigmatic greeting to the fortress quoted earlier (p. 234), and by giving him an equally enigmatic reply to Fricka's question about the meaning of the name Valhalla:

> *That which, victorious over fear,*
> *my spirit conceived,*
> *if it survives triumphant,*
> *will make the meaning clear to you.*

And by being so enigmatic, Wagner was able to forge his strongest theatrical link between *The Rhinegold* and *The Valkyrie*. He who, as the creator of *The Ring*, has been accused of dotting every 'i' and crossing every 't' with such 'Teutonic thoroughness' as to leave nothing to the spectators' imaginations, leaves his audience completely in the dark here. What is Wotan up to? To judge by the symbol of the sword, and the power of the completely new musical idea introduced by the trumpet (Ex. 63), something tremendous;

[11] The German 'Wal-hall' means 'Hall of those slain in battle'.

but the only way to find out the actual nature of that something is to attend *The Valkyrie*. *The Ring* is, after all, a four-part 'serial'; and each of the first three parts ends with a decided sense of 'to be continued in our next instalment'.

The packed and complex action of *The Rhinegold* now at last moves to its positive conclusion – the triumphant 'entry of the gods into Valhalla'. But lest we should forget that this 'triumphant' ending is a temporary and hollow one, Wagner interpolated before it two remarkable and unexpected elements which leave the issue completely open: a contemptuous soliloquy from Loge, and a final accusatory song from the distant Rhinemaidens.[12]

As the gods move towards the bridge, Loge remains behind, looking after them, and in an enigmatic self-communing expresses his half-formed intention of parting company with them:

> They hasten towards their end,
> so sure of their power to endure.
>   I am almost ashamed
>   to work with them;
>   to turn myself back
>   into flickering flame
> I sense a gnawing desire.
>   To burn them up
>   who once did tame me,
>   instead of perishing
>   feebly with the blind
> – were they the godliest of gods –
> seems to me far from stupid.
>   I'll think it over:
>   who knows what I'll do?

For the time being, he puts on a nonchalant manner and follows the gods; only some time later, between *The Rhinegold* and *The Valkyrie*, does he take his decision, and 'turn himself back into flickering flame'.

In making Loge disappear from the company of the gods some time before their eclipse, and eventually play a decisive part in that eclipse by consuming them in his fire, Wagner drew on one of the most vivid strands in the mythology – but his manipulation of it was extreme. In the *Prose Edda*, Loki does leave the gods – but not as an independent spirit, out of his own high-mindedness: he leaves them as 'the contriver of all fraud, and the shame of gods and men' (see p. 167), out of fear of retribution for his treacherous

[12] The music helps, anyway, by making the 'triumph' a palpably unreal one.

destruction of Baldr, the brightest god in the Norse thearchy. The story is too long to quote entire, but the gist of it is as follows.

Baldr the Beautiful, the only son of Odin and Frigg,[13] began to have ominous dreams prefiguring his death. Whereupon Frigg demanded of all things on earth, animate and inanimate, that they should never do him any harm – and they consented; only the mistletoe was left out of account by Frigg, because it was 'too young'. After this, the gods made a sport of throwing all kinds of weapons at Baldr, to marvel at his immunity from injury; the only one who could not join in was Baldr's brother Hodr, because he was blind. But Loki, by guile, found out from Frigg about the mistletoe, cut a shaft of it, took it to Hodr, and invited him to take part in the sport – he would direct his aim. Hodr threw the shaft; it pierced Baldr and killed him; and so Baldr went the eventual way of all living things – to Hel, the land of the dead.[14] The gods were overcome with grief; and at Frigg's request, the god Hermodr took Odin's eight-legged steed Sleipnir, and galloped the nine nights' journey along the dark and icy road to Hel, to offer the goddess of death (also named Hel) a ransom for the release of Baldr. But when Hermodr told her how all the gods were weeping, Hel said that Baldr should be released only if all things on earth, animate and inanimate, would weep for him. Hermodr returned with the message; and at the gods' request, all things on earth did weep for Baldr – except only a certain giantess named Thokk, who said she hated him. So Baldr remained in Hel – and it was generally believed that Thokk was Loki in one of his many disguises.

Loki sought to escape retribution by hiding away in a river, in the form of a salmon, but the gods finally tracked him down and caught him in a net: they took him into a cave, bound him down immovably to a rock with his own son's entrails, and fastened a venomous snake above his head, so that the venom continually dripped on to his face. Luckily for him, his wife Sigyn stayed with him faithfully, and held a bowl to catch the venom. 'And when the basin is full' – the myth ends – 'she goes and pours the venom away; but meanwhile the venom drips on to his face, wherefore he writhes so powerfully that the whole earth trembles, and it is this that men call earthquakes. There he lies in bonds, even to Ragnarok' [the end of the gods].

[13] His brother Hodr is said to have been 'the son of Odin', but the name of his mother is not given.

[14] Hel is not like the Christian Hell, but more like the ancient Greek Hades – a realm of the 'shades' of the dead, guilty or innocent.

As indicated earlier, Ragnarok, prophesied throughout the Scandinavian mythology, is nothing like Wagner's 'Götterdämmerung';[15] it is pictured as a battle between the gods and the powers of evil, on the last day of the world, in which every single combatant on both sides, save one, is to be annihilated. Among these powers of evil are two monsters which Loki begot on a giantess: the enormous wolf Fenrir, which was fettered and bound to a great rock by the war-god Tyr, at the expense of his hand; and the vast serpent Jormungandr, which Odin thrust into the depths of the sea, where it encircles the earth, with its tail in its mouth. When the last day comes, according to the prophecy, these monsters will burst their bonds, and so will Loki himself – to steer the ship Naglfar, made of dead men's nails, with a crew of giants, to do battle with the gods. But when the battle is over, it will not be Loki who will destroy the world with fire, since he will be killed by, and will kill, the god Heimdall (in any case, as we have seen, his claim to be the god of fire is a very tenuous one). The all-consuming fire will be let loose by the single surviving combatant, Surtr – the primordial 'giant with the sword of flame', leader of the giants from the southern realm of elemental fire, Muspell,[16] – who was present when the cosmos came into being through the conjunction of fire and ice. The single similarity between Ragnarok and Wagner's 'Götterdämmerung' – a fundamental one, however – is that fire and water finally destroy the world, and fire reaches up to heaven, as is graphically described in a verse of the *Wise-Woman's Prophecy* in the *Poetic Edda*:

> The sun grows dark · earth sinks in the deep;
> the bright stars vanish · from the vault of heaven;
> fire and steam · rage fiercely together;
> flame leaps high · about heaven itself.

Here, as sometimes elsewhere, what Wagner omitted from the mythology is as indicative of his symbolic intentions as what he altered or added. In this case, as can be seen, he simply dispensed with the evil side of Loki's activities outlined above. One reason for this was, of course, purely practical: there was no room for the

---

[15] 'Götterdämmerung', incidentally, is simply a German translation of 'Ragnarok', as Wagner found it in the various German versions of the *Prose Edda*.

[16] This ancient word, incidentally, was one of Jacob Grimm's trump cards in his bid to prove the existence of a heathen German mythology equivalent to the Scandinavian one. It is to be found surviving in manuscripts of Saxon and Bavarian poems of the eighth and ninth centuries – Christian poems in which, as *mudspelli*, *mutspelli*, and *muspilli*, it functions as a word for 'hell-fire'.

business of Baldr's death in *The Ring* – and especially since the mythic motif it represents was already present there in the business of Siegfried's death. Siegfried is just such a bright 'sun-god' type of figure, who is treacherously murdered by his dark counterpart, through the discovery of the single chink in his supposed invulnerability from the protector who has sought to make him invulnerable.[17]

Much more important, however, was Wagner's symbolic reason for dispensing with the evil side of Loki's activities. The Loki who destroys Baldr, disguises himself as a giantess, causes earthquakes by his struggles against the punishment inflicted on him by the gods, leads a shipload of giants against the gods at Ragnarok, and fights on the side of monsters he himself has begotten – *this* Loki is clearly an evil giant, 'whose father is the giant Farbauti' (see p. 167); and Wagner had no use for this aspect of him at all. Norse mythology tends to be ambiguous at all times, and it seems that Loki, for the Old Norsemen, represented their suspicion of the two-faced nature of 'cleverness': useful and helpful – if still dangerous – when harnessed to practical ends (Loki the servant of the gods), but quite monstrous and destructive when out of control (Loki the giant). For Wagner however, as nineteenth-century artist, mind was essentially a source of demonic inspiration, which might perhaps be harnessed to menial tasks (the solution of Wotan's problems over Valhalla), but which, in its elemental form, acted as a champion of the truth, and as an inspiration in the solution of fundamental problems (the intermediate establishment of the reign of love, through the bringing together of Siegfried and Brünnhilde, and the ultimate rejection of the material world, through the destruction of Valhalla). For this reason Wagner rejected the 'evil giant' aspect of Loki, and represented him entirely in his capacity as an (equivocal) ally of the gods. All he retained from the other side of Loki was two things: his disappearance from the company of the gods (changing the motive from fear

[17] Wagner was in fact loath to forego all mention of Baldr. In the final definitive prose-sketch for *The Young Siegfried* (the first version of the text of *Siegfried*) he made Wotan tell Erda, in Act 3 Scene 1, that 'the gods have been anxious about their end, ever since Baldur, the most gracious god, went under'. In the actual text of *The Young Siegfried* he removed the name Baldur, and replaced it with 'the gladdening one', but now linked the god with Siegfried by adding the words 'der im *Frieden Siege* schuf' (who achieved victory through peace). But in the final text for *Siegfried* itself, he removed the reference to the god altogether, having realized that the figure of Siegfried had absorbed him, as it were, and made him redundant.

of retribution for evil-doing to an intellectual disdain for the gods' self-destructive power-mania), and his final part in the destruction of the gods (changing the motive from revenge for punishment to a collaboration with Wotan in that destruction, and transferring to him the function of Surtr as the incendiary who consumes the world in fire).

Wagner's Loge, for the time being, follows the gods as they walk to the rainbow bridge that will lead them over to Valhalla. But just as Wotan is about to set foot on it, the voices of the Rhinemaidens are heard from the valley below, lamenting their loss of the gold, and pleading for its return. This is, of course, one of Wagner's pure inventions, without basis in the mythology (since the Rhinemaidens themselves and their guardianship of the gold were, as we have seen, created by him out of his own imagination); and it is one of his finest strokes of genius.

Robert Donington shows himself aware of both these facts, in the telling phrase with which he describes this moment:

> As the gods line up for their ceremonial entry into Valhall, there breaks into the confident Valhalla music, *of all poignant inspirations*, the song of the Rhinemaidens, out of sight down there in the river below. [My italics].

And yet Donington's interpretation must once again be challenged. His phrase 'of all poignant inspirations' does not cover the full meaning of the song, and neither does his haunting description of it:

> Up float their voices in three-part harmony, creamy as ever, piercing our hearts with sudden longing, melting our bones with nostalgic desire, unreal, sweeter-seeming than any reality, making the grandeur of the gods momentarily of no consequence and the perilous bliss of their own siren seduction the one attraction. 'Rhinegold, Rhinegold, give us back our Rhinegold!'

Nor, we must add, does his interpretation of the song's effect on Loge, or his final summing up:

> Only Loge, who knows too much about unreality from the inside, remains unshaken; but no one has any intention of giving them back their gold, even if it were now possible. Their cry goes unheeded – but not unheard. We are none of us too mature to be enchanted by the sirens' song . . . Whatever is human has an element of compromise. If we reject the part of the compromise which keeps us in touch with nature, we are completely lost. But we are just as lost if we try to evade our commitment to conscious civilisation. Just because the Rhinemaidens' cry makes Valhalla look

shabby, we cannot give up all that Valhalla stands for and go back to the state of nature with which *Rhinegold* began. Shabby Valhalla may partly be, but it stands here for our average human condition, and we need its uncertain shelter and its overrated justice, culture and amenity. It is a stage to be passed through, and there is no avoiding it. On the other hand, it is not the end of the journey. Wotan's intuition of both these aspects seems sound enough.

I have quoted Donington's interpretation at length because it surely goes against everything that Wagner was trying to say. And it does so, first of all, because of its Jungian side-slipping of the moral issue altogether – its concentration on the first verse of the Rhinemaidens' song only, and its avoidance of the moral implications of even that. After all, if the Rhinemaidens are crying for their gold to be returned to them, it is because – as Wagner's overt meaning indicates all along – *it is theirs by right, it has been stolen from them and turned into a talisman of loveless power by a psychotic criminal, and it has not been returned to them by the ruler of the world because he, in taking it by force from that criminal, has evaded his own aspirations towards law and justice in his own loveless quest for power.* And this is further confirmed by the fact that, in *The Twilight of the Gods,* the return of the gold to the Rhinemaidens is represented by Wagner as a consummation devoutly to be wished, and as the only means whereby the wrongs of the world can at last be set right (through the desire of the repentant Wotan in the first place, and through the action of the enlightened Brünnhilde in the end).

Secondly, if Loge is the only one who 'remains unshaken' by the Rhinemaidens' song, this is not for Donington's curious reason that 'he knows too much about unreality from the inside', but for the straightforward reason that he is, as we have seen, the single character who has persistently urged the truth that the gold actually belongs to the Rhinemaidens and should be restored to them. When Wotan, halfway through the first verse of their song, asks 'What complaint is that I hear?' (*Welch Klagen klingt zu mir her?*), he is not really seeking information, but striking an aggressively defensive attitude: he knows all about the gold and the Rhinemaidens, and so he must also know what the 'complaint' is. And Loge's answer is not a supplying of information, but a reiteration of the truth he has been trying to hammer home all the time: 'The children of the Rhine are lamenting the theft of the gold' (*des Goldes Raub*). Loge's harping, throughout *The Rhinegold*, on the words '*Raub*' (robbery), '*rauben*' (to rob), '*Räuber*' (robber), and

'*Dieb*' (thief), makes it impossible for us to take an easy Jungian attitude to Alberich's (and Wotan's) action in depriving the Rhinemaidens of the gold. The whole text insists that this action is no less than a crime.

This might be less easy to substantiate if the Rhinemaidens' song itself was, as Donington's description suggests, a mere lamentation for the loss of the gold, 'piercing our ears with sudden longing, melting our bones with nostalgic desire'. By concentrating on the first verse only – 'Rhinegold, Rhinegold, give us back our Rhinegold!' – it is easy to dismiss the Rhinemaidens' complaint as 'unreal'; but if we take into account the second and final verse, a very different view is necessary. Following Wotan's guilty question during the first verse, and Loge's factual answer to it, Wotan reverts to his old unreflecting arrogance, saying to Loge 'Damned nixies! stop their teasing'; whereupon Loge, sarcastically obedient as ever, tells the Rhinemaidens that if the gold no longer gleams on them, they can bask in the gods' new-found radiance. And it is this cheap insult which motivates the angry second verse of the Rhinemaidens' song, where their complaint (*Klagen*, as Wotan calls it) becomes an actual *accusation* (the basic legal meaning of the verbal noun *Klagen*):

> *Rhinegold! Rhinegold!*
> *Purest gold!*
> *If only your bright*
> *Gleam in the depths still shone!*
> *Trust and truth*
> *are in the depths only:*
> *false and cowardly*
> *are those who rejoice up there!*

The gods calmly ignore this indictment, and pass across the rainbow bridge to Valhalla in a blaze of orchestral triumph.[18] But these are *the last words in the drama*; and they hang on the air, after the curtain has fallen, like an unanswerable denunciation.[19] The whole transaction whereby Wotan has paid for Valhalla has indeed

[18] One final Wagnerian adaptation of a general element in the mythology – the statement in the *Prose Edda* that each day the gods ride over the bridge to hold their tribunal (not in Valholl, however, but in an unnamed hall near the well of Urd by the World Ash-Tree).

[19] Helped to do so, musically, by the two high *forte* double-subdominant minor chords (C flat minor!) to which are sung the forceful monosyllables 'falsch' (false) and 'feig' (cowardly): the Rhinemaidens' voices, here, merit anything but Donington's adjectives 'creamy', 'melting', and 'sweet'.

been a false one: and Wotan, in justifying his theft of the ring from Alberich by saying that it belongs to the Rhinemaidens, without the slightest intention of returning it to them, does stand convicted of hypocrisy and moral cowardice. Wagner's whole point, in introducing the Rhinemaidens' song, was surely to remind us that Wotan is wrong and they are right – as is confirmed by Wotan's repentance in *The Twilight of the Gods*, and by the restoration of the ring to them. Certainly we have 'a commitment to conscious civilization', but we still have to measure the good against the bad.

This is merely the *overt* meaning of the drama, of course; but as such, it has to be taken as the inescapable basis of any interpretation which seriously aims at bringing out Wagner's symbolic intentions.[20] We must agree with Donington, certainly, that the Rhinemaidens symbolize nature, that we cannot go back to the state of nature with which *The Rhinegold* began, and that this is a stage to be passed through, which cannot be avoided. But it seems impossible to accept his assumption that Wagner represented nature as 'unreal' (and therefore of no account), human development as something far more important, and the whole state of affairs as basically satisfactory. Clearly, it is nature that is 'real', since the Rhinemaidens will be there when every other character has perished; and it is humanity's achievement at nature's expense, if anything, that is 'unreal', since Valhalla will go up in flames when the ring has been restored to the Rhine. Wagner – rightly or wrongly – saw nature as the ultimate reality, and human development as a power-struggle based on a crime against nature; he believed the restoration of the ring to the Rhinemaidens to be the only right course of action at any stage of that development; and if this restoration is not made at any particular stage, it is not because that is the basically satisfactory way that human development has to take place, but because that is the unfortunate way that things actually happen – humanity takes the wrong course, and has to learn the hard way, by passing through catastrophe, before it is ready to make the restoration. What the restoration itself signifies must be left until we come to examine *The Twilight of the Gods*; it is enough to say here that the whole remainder of *The Ring*, after *The Rhinegold*, is just that story of humanity learning the hard way, before it adopts the one right solution of the world's problems.

[20] Donington, of course, is not so much concerned with Wagner's own intentions as with the meanings that emerge from *The Ring* for the Jungian, *in spite of* Wagner's intentions. We have to remember his phrase 'What Wagner . . . supposed Alberich to be renouncing . . .' (see p. 141).

First summing-up

Before passing on to *The Valkyrie*, it seems most convenient to take stock of the whole overt meaning of *The Rhinegold*, since once its power-versus-love symbolism is fully understood, the symbolism of the rest of *The Ring* falls more easily into place. We must decide on what levels, and with what conceptual terms, the symbolism of this first part of the tetralogy may best be interpreted – which is no very difficult task, since the levels and the terms impose themselves, indeed have already imposed themselves in the foregoing. The central reality the drama is concerned with, obviously, is the social and political history of mankind.

This might seem to contradict what Wagner himself said in his famous letter to Röckel of 23 August 1856 concerning his change of intention: how his first conceptual idea had been the 'hellenistic-optimistic one of showing the original injustice from which a whole world of injustice arose and therefore fell to ruins, so as to teach us a lesson how to recognize injustice, tear it out by the roots, and establish a just world in its place'; and how, nevertheless, he had been 'unconsciously following a quite different, much deeper intuition', and therefore, 'instead of conceiving a phase in the development of the world', he had 'conceived the essence of the world itself and recognized its nothingness'.[1]

But in fact, nothing in this letter conflicts with the natural view of *The Rhinegold* itself as a social-political parable, since Wagner was writing about *The Ring* as a whole, and about the change in its *ultimate* meaning. In his revolutionary period, just prior to the Dresden uprising of 1849, he had drawn up his first prose-sketch of the whole material, as well as the text of the single music-drama he then intended to create – *Siegfried's Death*; and both were indeed conceived from a 'hellenistic-optimistic' point of view. The former began with 'the original injustice from which a whole world of injustice arose' (the main events of *The Rhinegold*), and both ended in such a way as to 'establish a just world in its place' (the ascent of Siegfried and Brünnhilde, after their deaths, to join Wotan in Valhalla in triumph, and bring in a new social order). But by 1856,

[1] The complete passage is quoted on p. 21.

when Wagner wrote this letter to Röckel, he had worked out the whole text of *The Ring* (as well as the music of *The Rhinegold* and *The Valkyrie*), and he had altered the end of the tetralogy to its present form – the destruction of Valhalla, the gods, and the world, by fire. This is what he was referring to when he said that he had been 'unconsciously following a quite different, much deeper intuition', and that 'instead of conceiving a phase in the development of the world', he had 'conceived the essence of the world itself and recognized its nothingness'. The 'phase' in question had been the envisaged revolutionary achievement of replacing an unjust world by a just one – but Wagner had come to believe that this would never happen, and that it was in any case irrelevant: what really mattered was to 'recognize the world's nothingness' (his own phrase for Schopenhauer's Buddhistic rejection of the material world as an evil illusion).

It would, however, be foolish to try and interpret *The Ring* on this level from the very beginning. In fact, the tetralogy cannot be consistently interpreted on a single level, since it develops, transforms, and deepens its meaning as it proceeds, until it arrives firmly on the ultimate metaphysical level at the end of *The Twilight of the Gods*. And the first drama, *The Rhinegold* – whatever happens later – begins the tetralogy unmistakably in the world of social and political actuality: Wagner's first conception of *The Rhinegold* – as 'showing the original injustice from which a whole world of injustice arose' – remains embedded in that work, and is its manifest overt meaning. Although he eventually came to change his ideas about the nature of the *sovereign remedy* for the world's ills, and represented it in *The Twilight of the Gods* as a metaphysical, not a political one, he nevertheless felt no need to go back and alter the basic content of *The Rhinegold*.

Realistic acceptance of these plain facts will allow us to take *The Rhinegold* as saying what it claims to say, and prevent us from trying to force on to it meanings which it shows not the slightest trace of bearing in itself. One can, of course, if one so desires, interpret it as symbolizing the early stages in the self-therapeutic development of Everyman's Jungian psyche, as Donington does; one can in fact interpret it as symbolizing practically anything one likes – the early growth of an artist's imagination, for example, or the basic principles of Freudian psychology. But the result of any such approach can only be the kind of monumental irrelevancy produced by the early Catholic theologians when they interpreted the patently erotic *Song of Songs* as an allegory of the 'marriage' between Christ and his 'bride' the Church. *The Rhinegold* was intended as, and stands as, an allegory of the social and political world we live in (with the moral and psychological considerations that go with this, of course); and it is nothing else.

If this still seems a somewhat categorical statement, let us recall just what *The Rhinegold* is about. The central character, plainly, is Wotan; and he seems to be intended, in some sense, as a symbol of Man. But in what sense? He can hardly be taken as a symbol of Everyman, since he is clearly a very particular kind of man. As we watch him on the stage, in fact, there is obviously only one kind of man that he is, and that is a *ruler*; so he can only symbolize Man in the sense of Man-in-power. But again, not in the sense of Man-in-power in general, because he exercises a very particular kind of power. Naturally, in so far as his actions are characteristic of any man in power, they can be interpreted in relation to the exercise of power on any level; but what Wotan rules is the *world*, and so he must symbolize Man in the sense of Man-in-supreme-power. He is, then, a symbol of the type of man who has governed humanity throughout its history – chieftain, king, emperor, dictator, president.

But in what sense is Wotan a symbol of this type? In the broadest sense, surely, since Wagner presents him, in the first place, as *primordial* man-in-supreme-power. The story told in *The Ring*, undeniably, is the history of a whole world, from its origins to its dissolution, since nothing is imagined as having happened before its first event, or as capable of happening after its last event.[2] And the first event, which happened long before the curtain rises on Scene 1 of *The Rhinegold*, was Wotan's drink from the Well of Wisdom, which enabled him to cut from the Tree of Life the spear with which he controls and rules the world. Before this event, there *were* no events, but only the unconscious world of nature, in which Erda slumbered, the Norns guarded the Well and the Tree, and the Rhinemaidens guarded the Gold; after that event, conscious life began. This is where the First Norn – the Norn with knowledge of the past – begins her history of the world at the opening of *The Twilight of the Gods*:

[2] As Wagner said, in a letter to Liszt dated 11 February 1853: 'Consider well my new poem [the newly published text of *The Ring*]: it contains the beginning and end of the world!'.

*Once I wove
by the World Ash-Tree . . .
In its cool shade
murmured a spring;
whispering of wisdom
its waters flowed;
I sang then of holy things.*

*A bold god
came for a drink from the spring;
one of his eyes
he gave in perpetual payment.
From the World Ash-Tree
Wotan then broke off a branch . . .*

Wherefore, Wotan's primal act of drinking from the Well of Wisdom stands as a symbol of man's first step on the road to power: his self-emancipation from nature by his acquisition of consciousness. Likewise, his subsequent cutting of the spear from the Tree of Life symbolizes the same step, but in its dynamic aspect: the evolution of Man's conscious *will*, with its drive towards *power* – first and foremost over nature itself. Finally, Wotan's carving of the runes on the spear, and his subsequent exploitation of it as a means of world-domination, stand as an allegory of the history of man's will gaining control over fellow-man, and creating an authoritarian society, based on law.

These might seem purely arbitrary interpretations of Wagner's intentions, were it not for the fact that such ideas about the origin and development of human consciousness and power were basic to his way of thinking during the early stages of the creation of *The Ring*, as is evident from the books he wrote at the time.

And at this point, we must be very careful what we are talking about. Wagner was not, as he believed himself to be, an original and profound philosopher, and the 'philosophical' ideas he put forward in his prose-writings have been first dismissed and then ignored – and very rightly so, from the purely philosophical point of view. What we are concerned with here, however, is not their value or lack of value as a contribution to the development of philosophy, but the light they throw on the view of life held by the artist who created *The Ring*. Every thinking man, without being a philosopher in the true sense of the word, has his own 'philosophy of life': normally, this has no value for anyone beyond the man himself and his immediate circle; but Wagner's 'philosophy of life', locked away in his unread books and pamphlets, is of crucial interest to us because it underlay and conditioned the music-dramas which are his real contribution to man's self-knowledge, and it can therefore help us to interpret their meaning more clearly.

In *The Art-Work of the Future*, written during October and November 1849 – only a year after the original prose-sketch of the whole material for *The Ring* and the text for *Siegfried's Death* – Wagner set out to show what was wrong with the dramatic art of his time, and how it could be remedied. But realizing that art is conditioned by life, he tried to show first what was wrong with the *life* of his time ('a whole world of injustice'), and how *that* could be remedied (by 'establishing a just world in its place'). And with his typically German cast of mind, he turned back to the very origins of humanity, so that we find in this book 'philosophical' passages which, whatever their intrinsic worth, enable us to understand the state of mind in which he conceived the symbolism of Wotan's primal acts in *The Ring*. The basic one is as follows:

> From the moment when man perceived the difference between himself and nature, and so began his own development as man by breaking loose from the unconsciousness of natural animal existence and passing over into conscious life – when he therefore set himself in opposition to nature, and, from the feeling of his dependence on her which then arose from that opposition, developed the faculty of thought – from that moment error began, as the first expression of consciousness. But error is the father of knowledge, and the history of the begetting of knowledge on error is the history of the human race, from the myths of the earliest times down to the present day.

Here we have the 'world-view' that motivated the image of Wotan's primal drink from the Well of Wisdom, as an artistic symbol of man's 'breaking loose from natural animal existence and passing over into conscious life'. What the 'error' was that Wagner postulated we will leave for the moment, and set beside this passage another one – this time from *Art and Climate*, written a year later – which reveals another facet of the same world of thought. To follow the drift of Wagner's argument here, we have to remember that he wrote the whole pamphlet in answer to a peculiar press-criticism of his own *Art and Revolution* of 1849. In that book he had envisaged the emergence of a new German form of musical stage-work, resuming and developing the humanistic aspirations of Greek tragedy; and the critic had objected that such a thing could never come to birth in a northerly climate (!). Wagner, replying in *Art and Climate*, again went back to human origins, stressing this time the *power over nature* brought to man by his acquisition of consciousness, and maintaining that only an inhospitable climate could create this power in man:

> Where nature's climate, through the all-pervading influence of her most luxuriant abundance, lulls man on her bosom, like a mother her child, – there, where we must recognize the birthplace of humanity, – there, as in the tropics, – man has indeed remained a child, with all a child's good and bad qualities. Only when she withdrew this all-conditioning, over-tender influence; where she left man – as a wise mother leaves her growing son – to himself and to his free self-determination; where, due to the waning warmth of nature's directly fostering climatic influence, man had to fend for himself; – only there do we see him ripen to the development of fullness of being. Only through the pressure of that need which surrounding nature did not, like an over-solicitous mother, know of and satisfy before it had scarcely arisen, but which he himself had to bestir himself to satisfy, did he become conscious of that need – and also, at the same time, of his *power*. This consciousness he attained through inner realization of *the distinction between himself and nature*; and so it was that she, who no longer *offered* him the satisfaction of his need, but from whom he had to *wrest* it, became the object of his observation, investigation, and dominion.

Wagner's italics are significant, in that they indicate the ideas which were clearly fundamental to his 'philosophy of life' at this time. Here again, in this intolerably verbose[3] pamphlet, we find him preoccupied with the origin and development of humanity; and this time he stresses, not only the evolution of consciousness through man's 'inner realization of the distinction between himself and nature', but also the 'power' which that consciousness gave him to 'wrest' the satisfaction of his needs from nature, and to make nature 'the object of his observation, investigation, and dominion'. And if, in *The Ring*, the first step (consciousness) is symbolized by Wotan's drink from the Well of Wisdom, the second (power over nature) is symbolized by his subsequent cutting of the spear from the Tree of Life, which he was enabled to do by having taken the drink. This interpretation is supported by the fact that the wound made by the cutting of the spear caused the Tree of Life to dry up and wither: the decay of the tree stands in one sense as a symbol of the gradual impoverishment of nature caused by man's ruthless exercise of his power over her (a point we are particularly well able to appreciate today). And incidentally, although the general theory in the above passage (that man's domination of

[3] Wagner's prose style became the more pretentious, involuted, and repetitious, the farther he moved away from what he was really expert in – music, literature, drama, and the theatre.

nature has been exclusively a product of colder climates) is really irrelevant to our purpose, it may be pointed out that, in Wagner's time and right up to our own, it has been mainly Europeans, or men of European origin, who have dominated and despoiled nature on a large scale; and in *The Rhinegold* Wagner was adapting North European myths to present an artistic diagnosis of the ills of *European* civilization.

As regards the third primal symbol in *The Ring* – Wotan's cutting of the runes on the spear, and his subsequent exploitation of it as an instrument of world-domination, to build up an authoritarian society based on law – it is not possible to confirm our interpretation of it by any immediate single quotation from Wagner's writings. Being a much more far-reaching symbol than the first two, it has numerous ideas connected with it, which are woven inextricably into Wagner's whole theory of the growth of civilization. It will therefore be necessary to summarize this theory, and introduce quotations on the subject from his writings as we go along. In doing so, we must keep in mind that it is not the value or lack of value of Wagner's philosophizing that matters, but the light it sheds on the artistic symbolism of *The Ring*.

Much of Wagner's thinking, during his revolutionary period, was inspired by the philosophy of Ludwig Feuerbach (1804–72), to whom he in fact dedicated *The Art-Work of the Future*. Feuerbach's iconoclastic theory, as set forth in his main work, *Das Wesen des Christenthums*,[4] was that all religions, including Christianity, are entirely anthropomorphic. God does not exist: his supposed attributes are in fact humanity's projections on to an imaginary being of its *own* attributes; and so the philosopher's task should be to investigate, not what has been supposed to transcend humanity, but humanity itself, and nature, in which humanity is rooted. It was not so much the theory itself that attracted Wagner (though he fully accepted it); what appealed to him was its social and political implications. Feuerbach himself ignored social and political questions, but Karl Marx hailed him as an unwitting prophet of the social revolution by pointing out the political implications of his theory. If religion was simply myth-making, then the supposed 'divine infallibility' of the existing church and state was pure illusion, and its tyrannical authority could no longer claim respect; it was ripe for destruction, and for replacement by a new social

[4] 1841; English translation by George Eliot, 1854, as *The Essence of Christianity*.

order based firmly on the principles of human justice. Wagner may have read some of Marx's writings, and been influenced by Marx's view of Feuerbach; his own individual theory, at any rate, is well in line with this view, in that it stresses, not only the illusory character of state and church authority, but also its inherent unnaturalness and inhumanity.

He begins by making a very sharp antithesis between nature and natural humanity, on the one hand, and the existing state and church, and state-and-church-conditioned humanity, on the other. Nature creates entirely according to her need, and therefore of necessity; and this same need, or necessity, in the form of the natural human instincts, is the creative force in humanity. At first, humanity followed its natural instincts, which were as follows: (a) a need to wrest from nature the means of existence; (b) a need for communication, which led to the evolution of language; (c) a need for mutual love and fellowship, which led to the establishing of the family, and eventually, of society; and (d) a need to explain to itself its relationship to nature, which led to the creation of myths, and thus to religion and art.

It is the third of these four instincts which mainly concerns us here – the need for mutual love and fellowship that led to the establishment of society. Or rather, to societies: Wagner postulates an initial number of racial communities, each consisting of separate families loosely bound together into a *free* society, with a council of elders and a chieftain. But at some prehistoric period, these gave way to authoritarian *states*, based on repressive laws, in which most of the people lived virtually as slaves. How did this happen? Wagner only once tried to offer an answer – in his first sketch for *The Art-Work of the Future*, a mass of jottings entitled *Das Künstlerthum der Zunkunft* (*The Artisthood of the Future*). This passage, which Wagner did not carry over into the finished work, reads as follows:

Beginning of history . . . The heroic period of the mass of the people, i.e. of th various racial communities . . . Subjugation of the land-tilling, farming peoples by warlike ones, for the most part mountain- and hunting-stock. Characteristics of the subjugated peoples: steadiness, sense of property, individual self-will (patriarchy). Weakness: eventually, as a result of the subjugation, loss and decline of nationality. Outcome: farmers – without property; labourers – without profit from their labour; slaves. Characteristics of the ruling stock: an enduring sense of racial community in language, religion, state . . .

Whether or not it happened like this is anybody's guess, of

course, but the authoritarian state did certainly arise – indeed, it has existed to the present day, in various forms, as the only way that human beings have found of living together. What has enabled it to persist for so long, if it is contrary to the natural instinctive human need for mutual love and fellowship? According to Wagner, that original 'error' of the mass of mankind postulated in the first passage quoted above from *The Art-Work of the Future* (p. 250). This error, he thought, was superstition – a trait common to all primitive peoples. The passage continues:

Man fell into error from the time when he set the causes of nature's effects outside nature itself, and attributed to her material phenomena an immaterial (i.e. an arbitrary, anthropomorphic) origin.

This 'error' on the part of primitive peoples – the creation of gods and of religion – was, Wagner maintained, a magnificent one, since it arose from that natural instinctive need of humanity to explain to itself its relationship to nature, and it led to the creation of the great myths, which were marvellous projections of humanity's own highest ideals and aspirations. And the factual error itself was eventually corrected by science, which discovered the causes of nature's effects entirely *inside* nature. But in the meantime, it had had consequences which had kept the mass of the people enslaved to their rulers:

The great instinctive errors of the people, as they manifested themselves from the beginning in their religious intuitions, and became the starting-point for arbitrary speculation and system-making in theology and philosophy, have been elevated in these sciences, particularly by means of their adopted sister statecraft, to powers which make no less a claim than to order and govern life and the world by virtue of their inherent divine infallibility.

Thus intellectuals (political philosophers and philosophizing theologians), following after the power-men, the conquerors, wove a web of perpetual tyranny. They transformed the free society born of the people's instinctive need into an authoritarian state based on a system of rigid laws; and the natural religion of myth, also born of the people's instinctive need, into a church theology based on an arbitrary system of rigid dogmas, *which supported the state*. Wagner inveighs against them with all the moral fervour of an Old Testament prophet:

Not you intellectuals are the inventors, but the people, since need drove them to invention: all great inventions are the deeds of the people, whereas the inventions of the intellect are only the exploitations, derivatives, yea, the splinterings and disfigurings of the great inventions of the people. Not you invented *language*, but the people; you have only spoiled its sensuous beauty, broken its strength, lost its depth of meaning . . . Not you are the inventors of *religion*, but the people; you have only mutilated its profound meaning, turned the heaven within it to hell, the truth manifest within it to lies. Not you are the inventors of the *state*, but the people; you have only turned it from a natural alliance of people whose needs were the same to an unnatural herding-together of people whose needs are not the same, from a beneficent defensive league of all to a maleficent bulwark for the privileged few . . .

The contrast between natural, instinctive man living in a free society, and unnatural, law-conditioned man living in an authoritarian state, is described in a passage in *Opera and Drama:*

An individual without society is to us completely unthinkable . . . for only through intercourse with other individuals do we find out how we differ from them, and are particularly ourselves . . . No one can portray an individual without the environment which conditions him as such; and if the environment were a natural one, providing air and space for the individual to develop in – and freely, instinctively, elastically shaping itself anew through contact with the individual – then this environment could be appropriately and accurately portrayed in the simplest of outlines . . . The state, however, is no such elastic and flexible environment, but a dogmatically rigid, fettering, domineering force, which decides in advance for the individual 'Thus shall you think and act!' The state has set itself up as the educator of the individual; it takes possession of him in his mother's womb, by predetermining him an unequal share in the means towards social self-sufficiency; it takes away from him, by forcing upon him its system of morals, his intuitive spontaneity; and to him, as its own property, it assigns the attitude that he shall take towards his environment. The state-citizen has the state to thank for his individuality; but that is nothing more than his foreordained attitude towards the state, in which his purely-human individuality is annihilated as regards his *actions*, and, at the most, is confined to what he quite silently *thinks* to himself.

The result is that civilization tends to stagnate; the laws which predetermine how the individual is to behave become fixed, and prevent anything new from emerging, as Wagner indicates in an earlier passage in *Opera and Drama:*

The life-impulse of the individual expresses itself *ever newly* and *immediately*, but the essence of society [sc. state-society] is *custom*, and its view a *mediated* one. The view of society therefore, so long as it does not fully grasp the essence of the individual, and its origin in this essence, is a limiting and hindering one . . .

And the effect of these hindering laws and customs is that man's natural instinctive need of mutual love and fellowship is left unsatisfied. This view is put forward in another passage in *Opera and Drama*, on the subject of age and youth:

> The true, reasonable love of age for youth establishes itself in this: that it does not make its own experiences the measure for the actions of youth, but directs youth towards experiencing things for itself . . . for the characteristic and convincing thing about an experience is its individuality, its particularity, its *intelligibility*, which it acquires from having been gained through the spontaneous act of this one particular individual in this one particular case . . .

> . . . the barrier which the egotistic vanity of experience, in the form of prejudice, has erected against the spontaneity of the individual's actions . . . at present takes the place that naturally belongs to *love*, and is, by its essence, *lovelessness* . . .

Wagner's whole argument can be summed up as follows. The first primitive societies arose naturally, out of humanity's need for mutual love and fellowship, as free communities which satisfied that instinctive need; but later, authoritarian states arose *un*naturally, out of *none* of humanity's instinctive needs, being *imposed* by the few on the many, as *despotic* communities which, sustained by a system of arbitrary, brain-spun *laws* and *dogmas*, do *not* satisfy humanity's instinctive need for mutual love and fellowship. In short, the authoritarian state is a crime against human nature, and therefore against nature itself.

As was said earlier, Wagner was not a philosopher in the strict sense of the word, and his theory is invalidated by the fact that one of his premises is a piece of dubious speculation, to say the least. We can certainly accept his ideas about man's self-emancipation from nature by his acquisition of consciousness, and the power over nature which this gave him: they are now truisms, though they were then in the forefront of the thinking of the time. Also, his analysis of the oppressive, stagnant, loveless character of the authoritative state – and even of the way it has been sustained by ideas of 'divine infallibility' representing a distortion of the true nature of religion by 'theology, philosophy, and statecraft' – was acceptable when it was written, from an extreme left-wing point of view, and is even acceptable from that point of view today, as far as it goes. We may even accept his notion of a natural instinctive need in primitive humanity for mutual love and fellowship, which found satisfaction in the family. But his postulation that it also soon found satisfaction in free and happy societies is a piece of pure conjecture, which even in his own time was beginning to be thought unlikely, and today is regarded as beneath consideration.

This whole aspect of Wagner's thinking is a blatant example of 'golden-age' romancing: it is based on an unthinking acceptance of the naïve eighteenth-century French conception of the 'noble savage', implying the original virtue of 'natural man', who had been corrupted by the evils of civilization. In Wagner's post-Feuerbachian (and even perhaps Marxian) thinking, there was an unconscious, outdated residue of the simplistic idea of Rousseau: 'Man was born free, and everywhere he is in chains'. What primitive humanity was like, and how it first grouped itself into societies, and what those societies were like – these are questions which still await a full answer, and it may never be forthcoming; but the research of modern archaeology and anthropology, as well as the investigations of psycho-analysis into the primitive strata of the human mind, suggest that if the full answer *is* ever found, it will be less simple and less beautiful than Wagner imagined. So this element in Wagner's theory can only be dismissed as so much wistful thinking.

However, if we dispense with this element, the theory does not collapse but, on the contrary, stands up more firmly. The natural instinctive need for mutual love and fellowship which Wagner postulated must have been there in humanity from the beginning, even if it was only latent, since it is undoubtedly a part of man's make-up, which has come more and more to demand satisfaction, and is more than ever demanding satisfaction today. But the truth is, most probably, that this instinct never *has* been satisfied by the establishment of a free and happy society. In a sense, the authoritarian state *is* unnatural, as Wagner claimed, because it has always denied this instinct satisfaction. But it has done so only because of the existence of something else in humanity, which is really just as natural – the aggressive instinct. There would seem to be, as Freud maintained in *Civilisation and its Discontents*, a perpetual battle between humanity's life- and love-instincts, on the one hand, and its instinct of aggression and self-destruction on the other.

Yet the highest ideals and aspirations of humanity have come to make the instinctive need for mutual love and fellowship seem what is natural and right, and the instinctive need for aggression seem what is unnatural and wrong. Dr. Philip Lee Ralph, writing of the evolutionary ascendancy of man over the animals, and especially over his cousins the other primates, has thrown out an interesting and plausible explanation of the extraordinary strength of the aggressive instinct in humanity, which has come to be seen as so disastrous:

> The successful species exhibits traits which are peculiarly useful in a particular environment; they may be a drawback in a different environment. We can never know, for example, how many agreeable or benevolent traits may have been squeezed out of man in his long struggle for survival, in which the race was often to the swift and the battle to the strong. We can only observe, gratefully, that enough altruism seems to be inherent in human nature to make us uncomfortable in many of the patterns of social behaviour to which human societies are addicted.[5]

Whatever the origin of the extremely powerful aggressive instinct in humanity, there is no doubt that this instinct has gradually come to be repudiated by the nobler types of humanity, and the instinct for mutual love and fellowship regarded as the really natural and human one. With this correction, Wagner's theory becomes valid: it may not be original, but it stands as a simple summing-up of humanity's greatest problem, and it finds the most original and profound artistic expression in *The Ring*.

   Returning to Wotan (from whom, it will have been noticed, we have never been far away), we find that Wagner the artist, with sure intuition, let drop the invalid part of the theory of Wagner the political thinker, and kept the remainder; also that this remainder supports our interpretation of the third primal symbol in *The Ring* – the carving of the runes on the spear by Wotan – as representing an allegory of the history of man's conscious will gaining control over fellow-man by building up an authoritarian state through a rigid system of laws. In the tetralogy, the questions of how this actually happened in pre-history, and of what primitive humanity and its first societies were like, are ignored as the irrelevancies they are. Wagner simply confronts us with Wotan and his rune-laden (law-laden) spear, as a pure symbol of the existing immemorial authoritarian state-ruler. And so, with this third primal symbol, Wotan becomes, as well as *primordial* man in power, *historical* and *contemporary* man-in-supreme power.

   For the absolute power of the rulers of Europe, during the years when Wagner did his political theorizing and drew up the first text

[5] *The Story of our Civilisation*, London 1955.

of *The Ring*, was basically no different from what it had been throughout history. It was still a matter of bogus 'divine infallibility' conferred by 'arbitrary system-making in theology, philosophy, and statecraft'. The authority of emperors and kings was still ratified by the church: even Napoleon had insisted on being crowned emperor by the Pope (though, characteristically, he took the crown from him and crowned himself). Also, the German philosopher Hegel could argue, as one of the conclusions of his political thinking, that the authoritarian state, and especially the (notoriously despotic) Prussian state, was the consummation of God's purpose for humanity, as revealed in the dialectical process of history. However, all this is not the really important point. Wagner, as political theorist, tended to hold forth, in a largely abstract way, against the state and the church; but as artist, in *The Ring*, he conceived concrete symbols to go right to the existential heart of the matter, thus making his tetralogy as relevant today (even when the 'divine' part of the 'infallibility' has practically disappeared) as his political theorizing is outdated. Although he certainly symbolized the 'arbitrary system-making in theology, philosophy, and statecraft' by the runes engraved by Wotan on the spear, and did give him a sense of his own 'divine infallibility', he laid by far the greater emphasis on the spear itself, as a symbol of the psychological motivation of the authoritarian state-ruler: the will to power.

After all, every authoritarian state, however complicated the machinery used to run it, does have one supreme ruler – a fact which Wagner just touched on in *Opera and Drama* when he wrote of 'the state, the substance of which Louis XIV correctly designated as *himself*'.[6] But if Wagner, as a writer of books on art with a political bias, in exile after the collapse of the 1848–9 German revolution, put forward his revolutionary ideas, in Paris and Zurich, largely in the form of abstractions, he had nevertheless, as a political pamphleteer in Dresden, on the eve of the uprising there, been far more forthright. Wagner was a much more effective pamphleteer than he was a theorist, owing to his superb command of a 'stream of lava' style of prose; and in his anonymous newspaper article *Revolution*, published as the leader of the *Volksblätter* (People's Paper) of 8 April 1849, he had addressed the supreme rulers of the German states in no uncertain terms. Into the mouth of 'The Revolution' (representing the masses) he put

[6] *'L'état, c'est moi.'*

these words:

> I will destroy the domination of one over others . . . I will break down
> the power of the mighty, of the law, and of property . . . Let the madness be
> destroyed which gives one man power over millions, and subjects millions
> to the power of one man . . .

This was only six months after he had drawn up his first prose-sketch of the whole source-material for *The Ring*, which he admitted, looking back seven years later, he had shaped with the intention of 'showing the original injustice from which a whole world of injustice arose, and therefore fell into ruins, so as to teach us a lesson how to recognize injustice, tear it out by the roots, and establish a just world in its place'. The origin of this 'world of injustice' lies just as much in Wotan's spear of lawful world-domination as in Alberich's ring of unlawful world-domination.

Wotan, then, stands as a symbol of primordial, historical, and contemporary man-in-supreme-power – man in possession of consciousness, using his conscious will to control and exploit nature, and that same conscious will to control and exploit his fellow-men, by establishing an authoritarian state sustained by a rigid system of arbitrary laws.

And here we should be very clear on one point over which there has been confusion hitherto. The rigid system of arbitrary laws whereby the ruler governs the state is symbolized, not by the spear, but by the *runes* on the spear: the spear itself symbolizes the ruler's conscious will to control and exploit his fellow men – in other words the lust for power arising from his aggressive instinct. Wagner himself made a clear distinction between the two symbols. In Scene 2 of *The Rhinegold*, Wotan tells Fricka how he gained control over the giants by one of the treaties (contracts, laws) engraved on his spear:

> *By a treaty I tamed*
> *their stubborn race,*
> *and made them build me*
> *the noble hall.*

But in Act 3 of *Siegfried*, Wotan, speaking of the spear, reminds Alberich:

> *The faithful runes of treaties*
> *bound you not,*
> *villain, to me:*
> *by its own strength it subdued you.*

What this difference signifies must be left until later, but it shows that the spear is the ruler's conscious will to power, while the runes are the laws through which he sustains that power.

Of course, the two symbols go hand in hand, because the laws are so arbitrary. They are the *ruler's* laws, which maintain his own supremacy. Whether controlled by the spear or by the runes on the spear – Wotan's will or Wotan's laws – the result is the same for the giants and the Nibelungs: they remain subject to Wotan. In fact everybody and everything is subject to Wotan, and this is the unnatural state of affairs that results from the exercise of the natural (if detestable) aggressive instinct: that in the authoritarian state, man's natural instinct for mutual love and fellowship is left totally unsatisfied, because of the all-pervading lovelessness of the ruler. The reason for this lovelessness, according to Wagner, is that the authoritarian ruler has wrongly adopted towards his fellow-men the same attitude that he adopted towards nature – one of control and exploitation – when he should have adopted an entirely opposite one. To quote from *The Art-Work of the Future* again:

> The terrible thing about the absolute egoist is that he sees in other human beings nothing but the natural means of his own existence, and – even if in a quite particular, barbaric-cultivated way – *consumes* them, like the fruits and animals of nature, and thus will not *give*, but only *take*.

And this brings us to the fourth primal symbol of *The Ring* – the fourth in order of consideration here, but in fact the first and most important: Wotan's sacrifice of an eye in return for a drink from the Well of Wisdom, which symbolizes just that lovelessness of the authoritarian state-ruler. It implies that, in gaining consciousness, the type of man who was destined to gain the knowledge necessary to become man-in-supreme-power lost half of his instinctual being – the half which is the instinct for mutual love and fellowship. Or rather, not lost it, irrevocably, but repressed it: represseion is a kind of losing anyway, not a conscious thrusting away, since it happens below the threshold of consciousnesss. Freud, again in *Civilisation and its Discontents*, put forward the theory that the motive-force behind humanity's social and cultural achievements is the product of its repression, to a great extent, of its sex-instinct; and Wagner, like Freud, regarded *all* love as being rooted in the sex-instinct.

This interpretation of Wotan's sacrifice of an eye as symbolizing his lovelessness is supported by two passages of the text of *The Ring*. The first occurs in Act 2 of *The Valkyrie*, when Wotan confesses to Brünnhilde:

> When youthful love's
> pleasure grew pale,
> my spirit longed for power;
> driven by the fury
> of sudden desire,
> I won myself the world

The 'sublimation' of the sex-instinct (and love-instinct) into cultural (civilization-building) activity could scarcely be more clearly expressed. The second passage occurs in Act 3 of *Siegfried*, when Siegfried muses on Wotan's missing eye and Wotan gives him an amazing explanation:

> S.   But there, one eye is missing!
>   Someone must have
>   knocked it out,
>   because you stubbornly
>   stood in his way . . .
>
> W.   With the very eye
>   that's lacking in me
>   you yourself are looking
>   at the one I still can see with.

Siegfried, Wagner's projection of 'natural man', inspired at this moment entirely by his instinctive need for mutual love and fellowship (which he will soon find in Brünnhilde), has the eye (symbolizing that instinctive need) that Wotan lacks.

Another, more obvious symbol, reinforcing both the symbolism of the spear as Wotan's will to power and that of the sacrificed eye as his repression of love, is the impregnable fortress Valhalla: this is to bring to a climax both Wotan's world-domination and his lovelessness (the latter in that he is prepared to put the love-goddess Freia in pledge for the former). And Wotan is surrounded by further symbols in the shape of the other gods, who are in a sense only aspects of him, reflecting one or other of his own characteristics.

Yet we should not be too abstract in dealing with a living work of art. The other gods are not merely externalized embodiments of characteristics inherent in Wotan; they are at the same time portraits of the kind of people who attach themselves to such a ruler. He who rules through laws, even his own laws, must acquire a conscience about them, a respect for them: this is symbolized by Fricka, who also stands as a typical ruler's wife, the self-righteous guardian of his super-ego ideals, *plus royaliste que le roi*. He must also be very clever in devising these laws, and in cicumventing them when necessary, and this cleverness is symbolized by the Loge of *The Rhinegold* (who has not yet attained his full symbolism as the god of demonic mental inspiration); but he also stands there as the type of cunning, two-faced statesman who aids and abets the ruler with his advice, and sometimes tells him a few home-truths. And if, on occasion, cunning should fail, the ruler must give his aggressive instinct full play: this is symbolized by Donner, who also typifies the kind of 'strong man' on whom rulers rely when violence is the only solution. (But the ruler restrains the 'strong man' in Scene 2 of *The Rhinegold*, where violence is not the only solution, since cunning – Loge – can still find a way out.) The authoritarian ruler inevitably has a greatly impoverished capacity for love, and has lost all the bright hopes and ideals arising from love: this is symbolized by the characterlessness of Freia and Froh, and Wotan's lack of interest in them, but she also stands as the type of lovable woman who is out of place in the ruthless male world of power-politics, and he as the naïvely optimistic type of idealist whom the ruler takes no notice of. This sort of company, or something like it, might have been encountered at the court of any of the famous leaders of history: Alexander, Caesar, Charlemagne, Napoleon . . .

And Hitler? Enough should have been said by now to indicate that this question is a stupid one, but since it is still put forward and answered in the affirmative by people who ought to know better, a digression seems necessary, in order to spell out the truth. (Luckily, this digression will not only serve to defend Wagner from calumny, but will throw further light on the character of Wotan.) Owing to Wagner's intense German patriotism and his eventual racialism and anti-Semitism, he has been labelled a proto-Nazi, and he did have the posthumous misfortune to become Hitler's favourite composer,[7] and (alas!) one of his favourite writers on

[7] So, incidentally, did Bruckner, which seems to indicate that Hitler (not surprisingly) was especially susceptible to the type of Austro-German music dominated by massive and powerful brass sonorities. He might have admired Mahler's second, third, and eighth symphonies, if Mahler had not been a Jew, and if the ostensibly Christian messages of the works had not been anathema to him.

anti-Semitism and 'the purity of the Aryan race'.

We should bewail the fact that Wagner, one of the greatest minds the world has ever known, came eventually to be afflicted by the psychological disease of racialism; but we can surely be more charitable to the creator of those profoundly human dramas *The Ring, Tristan, The Mastersingers,* and *Parsifal,* who was responsible for no one's death, than to the man who produced those wretched daubs and who had six million Jews murdered. And we should be eternally grateful that Wagner, with the supreme artist's infallible intuition, never intruded his racialist theories into his works of art.[8] If we knew as little of Wagner's personal opinions as we know of Bach's or Shakespeare's – which is nothing – we should never guess that he was a racialist at all. The best of the man – and what a best! – went into his art, which is all that matters to us today.

In the case of *The Ring,* the intense Germanness of the plot, the text, and the music should not blind us to the fact that the thinking behind it – the artistic, social, and political thinking set out in *Art and Revolution, The Art-Work of the Future, Art and Climate,* and *Opera and Drama* – is entirely international. Here are four quotations, each completely characteristic, from these four books respectively:

If the Greek art-work embraced the spirit of a fine nation, the art-work of the future must embrace the spirit of free mankind, beyond all the confines of nationality; the national essence in it must be only an ornament, the charm of an individual case amidst a multiplicity, and not a limiting barrier. – *Art and Revolution* (1849).

Two *main stages* in the development of mankind lie clearly before us in history – the *racial-national* and the *unnational-universal.* If we are at present looking to the future for the completion of this second stage, we have in the past the closure of the first stage clearly discernible before our eyes. – *The Art-Work of the Future* (1849).

[8] *Pace* Robert Gutman, who in his book *Wagner: the Man, his Mind and his Music* (1968) uses the most loaded arguments to discover them there. The one possible exception – the allegedly 'Jewish' nature of the squeaky-voice utterances given to Mime – is not proven; though Mahler, who was extremely critical of Jews and of himself as one, accepted Mime as an anti-Semitic caricature, and a legitimate one. 'No doubt with Mime,' he wrote, 'Wagner intended to ridicule the Jews (with all their characteristic traits – petty intelligence and greed – the jargon is textually and musically so cleverly suggested) . . . I know of only one Mime, and that is myself . . . you wouldn't believe what there is in that part, nor what I could make of it.' (Henry-Louis de La Grange, *Mahler,* Vol. 1, 1974, p. 482.) This anecdote shows the unbridgeable gap between pre-Hitler and post-Hitler times.

If we now estimate . . . what is the instinctive impulse of humanity at this present moment of history – if we realize that it can find its redemption only through the recognition of God as the physical actuality of the human race, that its fervent need can only be satisfied by universal human love, and that it must, of infallible necessity, attain this satisfaction – we can rely, with complete certainty, on a future element in life, in which love, extending its need even to the widest circles of all humanity, must create completely undreamt-of works . . . – *Art and Climate* (1850).

We shall have . . . states and religions until we have only *one* religion and *no* state *at all*. But if this religion must of necessity be a universal one, it can be nothing else but the true [instinctive, unconscious] nature of mankind vindicated by consciousness, and every human being must be capable of feeling this unconsciously and of instinctively putting it into practice. – *Opera and Drama* (1850–51).

This 1849–51 internationalism of Wagner's precludes any idea of *The Ring* being written in the spirit of Nazism.

In any case, to argue that Wotan is Hitler is to suffer from the ridiculous illusion that Wagner set out to portray a sympathetic and admirable world-ruler, and in doing so, produced a figure very like the Nazi dictator. In fact, as we have seen, Wagner set out to portray a basically *un*sympathetic and *un*admirable world-ruler, as a symbol of immemorial man-in-supreme-power; and there can be no resemblance to Hitler, since Hitler was something entirely and monstrously new in the history of civilization, which Wagner could not have imagined.

Those who glibly equate Wotan with Hitler either do not know, or have never understood, or have forgotten, the appalling thing that differentiated Hitler from every other tyrant before him. Certainly, he shared several of Wotan's traits – he was avid for power, two-faced, cunning, ruthlessly aggressive, and loveless; but then, so have many other men been who have tried to rule the world. Where Hitler differed from them all was that *he entirely abrogated law, and replaced it with bare-faced lying and brute force* – torture and the threat of torture, murder and the threat of murder; and he had millions of people murdered in cold blood. These things – systematic perversion of the truth, systematic terrorization, systematic slaughter – had never happened on this scale before in recorded history (nothwithstanding Ghengis Khan and Attila); and they are certainly not prefigured in *The Ring*. In fact, if we only think, the whole basis of Nazism – the replacement of law by swindling and brute force – is explicitly repudiated in *The Rhinegold*, at the crucial point in Scene 2 where Donner, the 'strong man', lifts his hammer with the intention of bringing it down on the giants' skulls. Wotan has only to let it fall, and all his problems will be solved: he will be able to keep Freia, and have Valhalla for nothing. But instead, he interposes the spear with its *laws* between Donner and the giants, to enforce the contract; and in doing so he roars out 'Stop, you madman! *Nothing by force!*' – which is the direct antithesis of the Nazi method. And this, as we have seen, was one of Wagner's deliberate contradictions of his source-materials: in the original myth in the *Prose Edda*, the contract is ignored, the hammer falls, and murder is done.[9] So Wagner reveals himself as an explicit *anti*-Nazi before his time.

The truth is that in Wotan we have a realistic, severely critical portrait of the old pre-Nazi type of European ruler, as he had been known up to Wagner's time, and as he has been up to our time too, with the exception of Hitler and some of his European contemporaries, and of one or two others since; all these we may now leave out of the discussion, as *The Ring* was completed long before any of them were born. Wagner himself, in his letter to Röckel on 25 January 1854, offered a contemporary interpretation of Wotan as follows:

> He resembles us to a hair. He is the sum of the intelligence of the present, whereas Siegfried is the man of the future whom we wish for and will to arrive, and yet cannot create – who must create himself by means of our annihilation.

This statement may seem a peculiar one, but we have to remember the context in which it was written. At that time, Wagner had been thinking and writing a great deal about the social and political situation in Europe, and he had been forced into exile through the active part he had played in the Dresden uprising; moreover, he was writing to a fellow-revolutionary who had been unluckier than himself, and who was serving a long term in prison for his revolutionary activities. Furthermore, he was referring to the Wotan of *Siegfried* – the Wanderer, who acts as a mere spectator, unable to influence the course of events; hence the phrase 'He resembles us to a hair', since both Wagner and Röckel had become mere spectators as far as the political future of Europe was concerned – they could only hope that 'the man of the future' would 'create himself'.

But Wotan also, as a symbol of immemorial, historical, and

[9] See p. 177.

contemporary man-in-supreme-power, was for Wagner 'the sum of the intelligence of the present'; and by this he evidently meant, not the scientific, say, or the mathematical or philosophical intelligence of the time, but only the *political* intelligence of the time. Yet this is, after all, the crucial intelligence of any time: whatever advances may be made in any of the various branches of knowledge, society has never advanced any further than the political intelligence of its rulers has permitted. And this intelligence, at its best, has remained rooted in the concept of the will to power by means of law – the concept symbolized by Wotan's spear and the runes engraved on it: the resultant national states may be more brutal, or less brutal, but they are all based on this concept, and thus unfortunately, do not satisfy humanity's instinctive need of mutual love and fellowship.

And here Wagner again shows himself far wiser as an artist than as a political philosopher. For in his writings he inveighs against the law as a curb on man's natural instincts, until one comes to believe that he has no idea of the *necessity* of laws, to restrain humanity's *aggressive* instinct; but in *The Rhinegold* he makes Wotan's conception of law the only decent thing about him. 'Here is Wotan,' he seems to say, 'the type of man who's ruled in Europe since time immemorial. He's greedy for power, hypocritical, dreadfully cunning, brutally aggressive, and practically devoid of love. But there's one good thing about him: he has a noble ideal. Although there's nobody to force him, he rules, not entirely according to his own whims and desires, but to a large extent according to laws. His *own* laws, maybe, but nevertheless laws which have to be *honoured* – even, however deviously, by *himself*. Whatever his disastrous follies and mistakes, he's advanced civilization to a certain point – the point where we are: without him, we might still be savages. He is, in fact, the best we have up to now, even if he's a poor best. But he's been around for a dreadfully long time: can't he change? Or can't some other, finer type of man take over? Let's see, in the rest of the tetralogy, how it *might* happen. Of course, it would need a change in the human heart.'

It is, in fact, that one noble ideal of Wotan's – the ideal of law – that enables us to identify with him in *The Rhinegold*. For we do identify with him, in spite of all his chicanery and brutality: he realizes, as Bernard Shaw has said, that 'it is only by the establishment of a social order founded on common bonds of moral faith that the world can rise from mere savagery'. Nevertheless, there are all the other, far from noble traits in Wotan, which show that he must be replaced, if civilization is to progress. *The Rhinegold* is not for the squeamish: it is a ruthlessly realistic representation of the present state of civilization.

But of course Wotan does not stand alone, in *The Rhinegold*, as a symbol of man in pursuit of power: there is the other main character, Alberich, who contends with him for the mastery of the world, and is far worse than him. What does *he* stand for?

We have seen (p. 159) that Alberich's history runs parallel with Wotan's, but is in direct contrast: with both rulers, the lust for power goes inevitably hand in hand with an inability to love, but the relationship between power and love is different in the two cases. With Wotan, the *satisfaction* of a quest for *knowledge* has resulted in a *creative* pursuit of power based on *law*, resulting *inadvertently* in a severe *weakening* of the capacity for love, which is, however, *not irreversible*. With Alberich, the *frustration* of a quest for *love* has resulted in a *destructive* pursuit of power *without law*, based on a *deliberate rejection* of the capacity for love, which is *total and final*. In both cases, we should remember, another result is the impoverishment of nature (the withering of the Tree of Life caused by the wound made by the cutting of the spear, the darkness in the Rhine caused by the theft of the gold).

So it might seem that Alberich stands simply as the dark, opposite counterpart of Wotan: an entirely negative view of man-in-power set alongside the partly positive one. On the one hand, we might say, man appears great and god-like, seeking knowledge and thereby gaining power through lawful control – even if, regrettably, his exercise of lawful power makes him practically blind to the claims of love; on the other hand, man appears small and dwarf-like, unable to find love, and therefore rejecting love altogether, so as to gain a lawless totalitarian power with which to revenge himself on the whole world for his frustration.

But we cannot take this simple static view of the Wotan-Alberich symbolism, owing to the crucial *dynamic* relationship between the two characters. As we have seen, Wotan symbolizes primordial and historical man-in-power – and Alberich cannot be seen in this light at all: he enters the story only as *a member of the society already built up and controlled by Wotan*. He *challenges* Wotan's rulership of it; but he *never achieves* his ambition of becoming its ruler himself.

And so the parallel-in-contrast between his history and that of
Wotan has to be understood as Wagner's way of distinguishing
between *two different types* of power-seeker at *two different stages* of
human history – the original and still-established type, on the one
hand, and a later, just-emerging rival of that type, on the other.
Wotan, acting on the knowledge brought by consciousness, has
established an ordered society through the exercise of authority
and law, which has unfortunately made it impossible for love to
flower; Alberich eventually appears as one of the underprivileged
in that society, 'predetermined to an unequal share in the means
towards social self-sufficiency'; unable to satisfy his instinctive
need for love in it, he abandons his quest for love altogether in an
attempt to take over that society from Wotan and enslave it by
brute force which acknowledges no law at all. And his means of
doing so is to slave-drive his fellow-creatures, the Nibelungs, into
amassing great wealth for him, with which he hopes to corrupt the
world's existing rulers, the gods, and have their women, the
goddesses, at his own disposal.

At this point we have to turn again to Shaw, who was surely
right in seeing Alberich as 'the sworn plutocrat' – the new,
capitalist type of power-seeker which, from Wagner's viewpoint in
time, had recently arisen with the Industrial Revolution and was
contending with the existing (regal, baronial) type of ruler, represented by Wotan, for the domination of society. Shaw's view of
Nibelheim as a place of sweated labour has already been quoted in
Chapter 1 (p. 15); and his view of Alberich as the big capitalist
boss is no less apposite. In the first place he understood what
Wagner meant by representing Alberich as one of the underprivileged in the society established by Wotan, forced by the
impossibility of finding love in that society to try and revenge
himself on it by becoming its master himself: it symbolizes the
original motivation of capitalism. Commenting on Alberich's rejection by the Rhinemaidens and his forswearing of love in favour of
the Rhinegold, Shaw says:

> It is just as if some poor, rough, vulgar, coarse fellow were to offer to take
> his part in aristocratic society, and be snubbed into the knowledge that only
> as a millionaire could he ever hope to bring that society to his feet and buy
> himself a beautiful and refined wife. His choice is forced on him.

And in his comments on the scene in Nibelheim, Shaw indicates
what terrible consequences arose from this original motivation of
wishing to be a millionaire in order to dominate society:

For his gain, hordes of his fellow-creatures are thenceforth condemned to slave miserably, overground and underground, lashed to their work by the invisible whip of starvation . . . The very wealth they create with their labor becomes an additional force to impoverish them; for as fast as they make it, it slips from their hands into the hands of their master, and makes him mightier than ever. You can see the process for yourself in every civilised country today, where millions of people toil in want and disease to heap up more wealth for our Alberics, laying up nothing for themselves, except sometimes horrible and agonizing disease and the certainty of premature death. All this part of the story is frightfully real, frightfully present, frightfully modern; and its effects on our social life are so ghastly and ruinous that we no longer know enough of happiness to be discomposed by it. It is only the poet, with his vision of what life might be, to whom these things are unendurable. If we were a race of poets we would make an end of them before the end of this miserable century[10] . . . If there were no higher power in the world to work against Alberic, the end of it would be utter destruction . . . The moment the Plutonic power is let loose, and the loveless Alberic comes into the field with his corrupting millions, the gods are face to face with destruction, since Alberic, able with invisible hunger-whip to force the labor of the dwarfs and to buy the services of the giants, can outshine all the temporal shows and splendours of the golden age, and make himself master of the world, unless the gods, with their bigger brains, can capture his gold.

There can be no doubt that Wagner himself saw Alberich in this light. Shaw's interpretation is entirely in harmony with Wagner's own socialist views, expressed in several passages in *The Art-Work of the Future*, which have a direct bearing on the character of Alberich:

Luxury is as heartless, inhuman, insatiable, and egotistic as the need which brought it into being . . . it lives on the unsatisfied hunger of thousands upon thousands of the poor . . . it holds a whole world in iron chains of despotism . . .

And again:

. . . the luxury of the rich continues to exist only through the want of the poor; and it is the very want of the poor that ceaselessly provides new consumer goods for the luxury of the rich; while the poor man, out of the need of nourishment for his vital strength, sacrifices this vital strength of his to the rich.

From this it is clear that Wagner – to whom, in Shaw's words, 'these things were unendurable' because of his poet's 'vision of what life might be' – poured all his detestation of the evils of

[10] Published in 1898.

capitalism into the creation of Alberich, and particularly into the creation of Alberich's actions in the Nibelheim scene in *The Rhinegold* – symbols which could speak so much more powerfully for him than his political prose.

And yet it is impossible to sustain a purely socialist interpretation of the character and behaviour of Alberich as those of the big capitalist boss, with the implication that the remedy for the situation is a political and economic one. It would restrict the range of Wagner's symbolism too severely – and indeed, it was on this point that Shaw's interpretation of *The Ring* finally came to grief: when he reached *The Twilight of the Gods*, in which Wagner's projected remedy turns out to be, not a political or economic, but a metaphysical one, he could only dismiss that final work as a betrayal of all that had gone before. The truth is that beneath Wagner's political and economic symbolism lies a fundamental psychological one, which goes to the heart of the matter. What the Rhinemaidens offer Alberich, in indicating the nature of the Rhinegold, is not wealth and luxury, but 'measureless power' (*masslose Macht*). And Alberich himself makes clear, in his outburst to Wotan in Nibelheim, that what he is after *is* measureless power – mastery of the world: the treasure he amasses, by slave-driving his fellow-Nibelungs, is merely a means to that end (though the slave-driving itself is, of course, already a first satisfaction of his power-lust). The aim of the capitalist, the symbolism tells us, is indistinguishable from that of the pre-capitalist seekers for power. The real goal is not wealth, but domination of society; wealth is simply the means of achieving that domination.

At this point, it becomes evident that Wagner's artistic diagnosis of the ills of human civilization, in *The Rhinegold*, is even more 'frightfully real, frightfully present, frightfully modern' than Shaw imagined. It goes beyond Shaw's analysis of the situation, and is amazingly prophetic, since events in recent times have made ever more obvious the fact that the crucial danger to civilized society – whether that society is pre-capitalist, capitalist, socialist, 'national-socialist' (fascist), or communist – is man's apparently ineradicable lust for power. A modern writer has spoken of the 'revelation' made by George Orwell in *Nineteen Eighty-Four*:

Orwell has picked on the hidden truth which Bakunin once knew and which the Marxists have obscured – that the love of power is stronger and more perverting than any material or economic motive.[11]

[11] George Woodcock, *The Crystal Spirit*, London 1967.

Well, Wagner knew Bakunin, who was one of his fellow-conspirators in the 1849 Dresden uprising, and *The Rhinegold* shows that he also knew what Bakunin knew – and what we have come to know today. If one wanted to adopt the Shavian style of contemporary exegesis, one could say that Alberich, made omnipotent through the invisibility conferred by the Tarnhelm, is a would-be equivalent of Orwell's 'Big Brother'. Hear him speak, in his cloak of invisibility:

> *Nibelungs all,*
> *bow down to Alberich!*
> *He is everywhere,*
> *watching you!*
> *Rest and repose*
> *you've done with now!*
> *You must work for him,*
> *though you cannot see him!*
> *When you don't think he's there,*
> *You'd better expect him!*
> *You're subject to him for ever!*

Or perhaps, in the German context of Wagner's work, one should say that those who want to find Hitler in *The Ring* should look for him in Alberich, the maleficent tyrant of the drama, since although Nazism was not itself a capitalist hegemony, Hitler certainly used the resources of German capitalism in his attempt at world-domination. Except that, as is obvious, Wagner could not believe that such a creature would ever succeed in dominating the world: Alberich never manages to achieve the 'measureless power' he is seeking, even though he keeps trying to the end. Nevertheless, there is enough of unscrupulous power-lust in Wotan himself – especially when he becomes practically indistinguishable from Alberich, as he robs him of the ring by brute force – to indicate that Wagner was fully aware of the dangerous possibility that the world might come to be dominated by a ruler exercising power without any moral principle whatsoever. Wotan's dealings with the labourers who build his impregnable fortress for him, compared with Alberich's dealings with the miners who amass his huge treasure for him, may be controlled by law, to some extent; but when Wotan seizes Alberich's ring, he is presumably prepared to make full use of it – to treat all the members of his society as slaves without rights. This is the old type of ruler at his worst – defeating an evil opponent with that opponent's evil methods, until he becomes just as evil himself. Fortunately, in Wotan's case, his sense of destiny comes to his aid, in the form of Erda, to save him and his society from such a catastrophe. He begins to feel guilty, and to want to change his ways, which is a hopeful sign.

But if Shaw's interpretation overlooks Wagner's central point that the root of all evil is the lust for power,[12] he was certainly right on the more general question of what area of human experience Wagner was dealing with. Writing of *The Ring* as a whole, he referred to 'European history', and said: 'It was in that massive material . . . that Wagner found the stuff for his masterpiece.'[13] And of *The Rhinegold* he said that it contained 'the whole tragedy of human history and the whole horror from which the world is shrinking today'[14] – words which are just as true of it now, if in a different sense from Shaw's. *The Rhinegold* stands as a profound analysis of the loveless, power-ridden world in which Wagner lived, and in which we still live today. Its symbolic meaning can be best summed up in a couple of questions, with their answers. Where, in the political organization of the world, is the place of love? – Nowhere. Where, in the political organization of the world, is the place of power? – Everywhere.

Wagner knew that there could be no political or economic remedy for man's aggressive power-lust: it would need a transformation of human nature. He certainly advocated a revolution, and he took part in one himself, but not in the hope that this or that political party would triumph, or that this or that economic programme would be implemented. He hoped that, if only the revolution could totally destroy the old church-and-state authoritarianism, the 'man of the future' would emerge, and the mass of humanity would be free to satisfy their instinctive need of mutual love and fellowship. And this transformation, he thought, would again be a change *back* to the original, natural state of affairs. To quote from *The Art-Work of the Future* again:

> Man will be what he can and should be, only when his life is a true mirror of nature, a conscious pursuit of the only real necessity, *inner natural necessity* . . . the true man will not appear, therefore, until genuine human nature, and not the arbitrary laws of the state, shape and regulate his life.

[12] Shaw was quite unaware of this, as is shown by his blind admiration for the dictators of the period between the wars – Mussolini, Hitler, Stalin.

[13] Op. cit., Preface to the Third Edition, 1913.

[14] Op. cit., original edition, 1898.

This 'genuine human nature', Wagner thought, would be the opposite of the distorted human nature of the 'absolute egoist' who 'sees in other human beings nothing but the natural means of his own existence, and . . . consumes them, like the fruits and animals of nature . . .'. It would be based on mutual love and fellowship:

> The life-need of man's life-needs is the *need for love* . . . But man satisfies his need for love only through *giving*, through giving *himself* to other men, and at the highest point, to *all humanity*.

And from *Art and Climate:*

> Only through the *highest power of love* can we attain to *true freedom*, for there is no true freedom except *that which is common to all humanity*.

Once again, what Wagner expressed theoretically, in his writings, he symbolized in *The Ring;* and as before, he dropped the 'golden age' element of his theorizing – the idea of a return to a lost state of nature – as irrelevant. For in Act 1 of *The Valkyrie*, the coming together of Siegmund and Sieglinde symbolizes the emergence (not the *re*-emergence, since there is no golden-age humanity in *The Ring*) of the 'need for love' which is 'the life-need of man's life-needs'. And this love is not merely sexual – though it is rooted in sex: it is also compassionate love, and family love. It appears in direct contrast to the world of *The Rhinegold* – Wotan's world of power without love; and it has to struggle, first against Hunding, who is evidently part of Wotan's world, since he has forced Sieglinde to marry him without love; and later against Wotan himself, who is prepared to sacrifice both the lovers to the exigencies of power-politics.

To go further into this matter would be to anticipate. However, it already serves to show that in moving on from *The Rhinegold* to *The Valkyrie*, we shall be obliged to treat Wagner's symbolism from a rather different point of view. The power-versus-love symbolism of *The Rhinegold* continues, of course, but from a different standpoint: whereas *The Rhinegold*, as we have seen, is a realistic representation of the power-dominated world of the past and present, *The Valkyrie* (and *Siegfried* too, for that matter) is an idealistic prognostication of a possible future in which man's aggressive power-lust will gradually give way to mutual love and fellowship. Certain elements in *The Valkyrie* (and even in *Siegfried*) will be referable to the past and present, certainly; but we shall be mainly concerned with the hoped-for future.

And another change is noticeable. Whereas in *The Rhinegold*, Wagner's critical analysis of existing power-politics is acted out on a crowded stage, with the interacting motives of a considerable number of characters, in *The Valkyrie* (and even more in *Siegfried*) his vision of a possible future change in human nature is largely acted out in the hearts of one or two individuals. The emphasis progressively shifts from society to the individual, from the outer world to the inner, so as to concentrate on imagined new types of humanity, exemplifying the way in which the change may come about. If we were to continue with the broad social interpretation necessary for *The Rhinegold*, we should find ourselves faced with unanswerable questions, such as 'Why, if this future is so rosy, does no-one liberate the oppressed Nibelungs?' or at least 'What happened to the Nibelungs when Alberich lost the ring?' *The Rhinegold* shows the world as it is, with the Nibelungs (the workers) oppressed by capitalism; *The Valkyrie* and *Siegfried* switch to a portrayal of possible new human types, motivated by superabundant vitality, courage, and love, who alone could set such a world to rights.

One final word. Love, as Shaw said, is a well-known 'romantic nostrum for all ills', and the reader may well feel discouraged at the thought that this is all that Wagner is going to offer us as a remedy for our power-ridden civilization. However, the love that Wagner envisaged is by no means one of the kinds of love so dear to the romantics as a nostrum – idealized sexual love or a feeling of affectionate benevolence; it is an active *social* force, at once sexual, compassionate, self-sacrificial, and creative. In any case, it is not *all* that Wagner is going to offer us, but only a stage on the way to the final remedy: in *The Twilight of the Gods*, as we have seen, love is swept away with everything else, and the ultimate remedy turns out to be a metaphysical one.

However, the idea of love as a regenerative social force has itself been much derided since the experience of the First World War, and may well seem intolerably naïve today. Yet in terms of this world it remains the only hope for humanity, if humanity is to survive and flourish. It may be apposite to quote in this connection a passage from an article, *The Menace to Freedom*, written in 1935 by E. M. Forster and reprinted in 1951.[15] Forster, who was certainly no starry-eyed Utopian, ended his article:

[15] E. M. Forster: *Two Cheers for Democracy*.

Man has another wish, besides the wish to be free, and that is the wish to love, and perhaps something may be born from the union of the two . . . Love, after a dreadful period of inflation, is perhaps coming back to its proper level, and may steady civilization; up-to-date social workers believe in it. It is difficult not to get mushy as soon as one mentions love, but it is a tendency that must be reckoned with, and it takes as many forms as fear. The desire to devote oneself to another person or persons seems to be as innate as the desire for personal liberty. If the two desires could combine, the menace to freedom from within, the fundamental menace, might disappear, and the political evils now filling all the foreground of our lives would be deprived of the poison which nourishes them. They will not wilt in our time, we can hope for no immediate relief. But it is a good thing, once in a way, to speculate on the remoter future . . . There is the Beloved Republic to dream about and to work for through our dreams; the better polity which once seemed to be approaching on greased wheels; the City of God.

Despite all that has happened since the article was published in 1935, love is still alive, and Forster's words are still relevant.

The Valkyrie

In so far as time can be measured in the timeless world of *The Ring*, at least some twenty years must elapse between the end of *The Rhinegold* and the beginning of *The Valkyrie*, to allow Wotan's semi-human offspring – Siegmund and Sieglinde – to grow to maturity. And during this period a number of important events have happened, six of which should be registered before we examine *The Valkyrie* itself.

First, Loge has abandoned the gods – or, to put it more realistically, he has abandoned Wotan: he was essentially Wotan's helper, and Wotan alone of the gods takes any further part in the stage-action of *The Ring*, except for Fricka, who makes her final devastating appearance in Act 2 of *The Valkyrie*. The relationship between Loge's departure and the departure of Loki in the mythology, together with the significance of this for the symbolism of *The Ring*, has already been discussed at length (pp. 238–44). Two further events are that Fafner has turned himself into a dragon, and is guarding the ring, the tarnhelm, and the treasure in a cave in the forest, and that Alberich has begotten a son on a mortal woman, to be his agent in his attempt to regain the ring; these will be considered when we come to *Siegfried* and *The Twilight of the Gods* respectively.

The other three events are measures taken by Wotan in his own quest to regain the ring. He has ordained that the bravest human heroes shall go to Valhalla after their deaths in battle, to defend it against any possible attack; he has begotten the nine Valkyries upon Erda,[1] to be the inciters of men to heroism, and the choosers of the bravest among the slain; and he has begotten the Volsung twins – Siegmund and Sieglinde – on a mortal woman, with the intention that Siegmund shall be his own agent in his attempt to regain the ring. The begetting of the Valkyries can wait for consideration until we come to Act 2 of *The Valkyrie*, and confront Brünnhilde; but the use of human heroes to defend Valhalla, and

[1] Of the nine Valkyries, only Brünnhilde is described in the text as being the daughter of Wotan and Erda, but the other eight also seem to be, since Wotan refers to them as Brünnhilde's sisters.

the fathering of the Volsung twins, must be dealt with here, before we turn to the action of Act 1.

The former is taken straight from the mythology: the *Prose Edda* tells us that when the gods shall battle against the primordial powers of evil on the last day of the world, the human warriors who have gone to Valholl after their deaths will fight beside them. And similarly with Wotan's begetting of the Volsung twins: the mythical Volsungs traced their ancestry back to Odin, like so many of the historical Teutonic kings.

But although Wagner took these elements straight from the mythology, he gave them a meaning of his own, through the special sense of purpose he infused into them. The Odin of the mythology has done three separate things, which are quite unconnected: he has from the beginning of the world recruited an army of dead heroes in Valholl, to help the gods against the eventual attack by the primordial powers of evil on the last day of the world; he has come into possession of a ring he wanted to keep, used it to pay a ransom, and apparently forgotten all about it after Fafnir has made off with it; and he has begotten the race of Volsungs for no particular purpose, except in so far as they will be an especially powerful reinforcement for the army in Valholl. But Wagner tied these three things together, with the ring as the focal point. Wotan has *not* lost interest in the ring (which is of course a talisman of world-domination, unlike the one in the sources); it is because he is afraid that Alberich may regain it that he recruits the army of heroes to defend Valhalla against the attack that would follow such an eventuality; and it is because he needs to prevent this eventuality that he begets Siegmund to act as his agent – since he himself cannot act in the matter, owing to the contract with Fafner which is engraved on his spear. Siegmund (and later Siegfried) is to be the free hero – free from the laws binding Wotan, that is – who will kill Fafner and regain the ring.

It may be as well to stress this point here immediately, in the case of Siegmund, since the vital link can easily pass unnoticed. What is Siegmund actually there for? What is the essential purpose of this character, in the logically unfolding plot of *The Ring*, and in relation to its central symbol, the ring of world-domination that Wotan needs to prevent Alberich from regaining? The overwhelming impact of the incestuous love between Siegmund and Sieglinde, and its culmination in the tragic death of Siegmund himself, added to the fact that it is Siegfried who eventually functions as the dragon-slayer, all tend to make us overlook that what Siegmund is there for in the first place, from Wotan's point of view, is not to love Sieglinde, beget Siegfried on her, and die, but to kill the dragon and regain the ring. Indeed, the harsh training which has been his whole life, engineered by Wotan, is intended to lead up to this consummation, which fails to materialize only because Wotan's plans have been misconceived: Siegmund, despite his apparent independence, born of his training by Wotan to defy the laws of the gods, is not a free hero at all, as Fricka eventually points out with deadly logic, but simply Wotan's pawn, dependent on the sword which Wotan has provided for him.

All this is evident from some words Wotan addresses to Fricka in Act 2, when defending Siegmund's position, and from what he says to Brünnhilde, after he has yielded to Fricka's logic, and decided to let Siegmund die. To Fricka he says:

> *Our need is a hero*
> *who, free from the gods' protection,*
> *breaks loose from the laws of the gods:*
> > *so that he alone*
> > *may do the deed*
> *which, much as the gods require it,*
> *the god is barred from doing.*

What the 'deed' was to have been becomes quite clear when Wotan tells Brünnhilde of his failure with Siegmund:

> *Anxiously I deliberated*
> *how to snatch the ring from my enemy* [Alberich] . . .
> *I should have to wrest from Fafner*
> *the ring that I paid him as wage:*
> > *but I may not attack him*
> > *with whom I contracted . . .*
> > *Only one could do*
> > *what I may not:*
> > *a hero I never*
> > *stooped to help,*
> > *a stranger to the god,*
> > *free from his favour,*
> > *all unwitting,*
> > *all unbidden,*
> > *of his own need,*
> > *with his own weapon,*
> > *could do the deed*
> > *that I must shun . . .*

Brünnhilde asks:

> But the Volsung, Siegmund,
> Does he not act freely?

And Wotan replies:

> Wild I roamed
> the woods with him;
> against the counsel of the gods
> I incited him to be bold:
> now against the vengeance of the gods
> his only protection is the sword
>   that a god's favour
>   bestowed on him.
>   Why be so clever
>   at defrauding myself?
>   How easily Fricka
>   unravelled my deceit!

These passages make it quite obvious that Siegmund is Wotan's attempt to create a free hero who shall kill Fafner and regain the ring. This fundamental point tends to be lost sight of because the opening of *The Valkyrie* plunges us into a great love-story – though Wagner did give a hint there as to Siegmund's potentiality as a dragon-slayer by making Hunding refer to the sign he bears of this. Comparing Siegmund with Sieglinde, Hunding says:

> How like my wife!
> The glistening serpent
> Shines out of his eyes too.

It was a mythological tradition that all the members of a dragon-slayer's family bore some sign of a dragon in their eyes. And Wagner's conception of Siegmund as a potential dragon-slayer does have a very slight basis in the mythology: as Jacob Grimm pointed out, *Beowulf* (mistakenly) mentions 'Sigemund' as the hero who killed a dragon and thereby won a treasure, and does not mention Siegfried at all.

In approaching *The Valkyrie* then, we must be clear at the start that Siegmund's primary function, in Wotan's mind, is to kill the dragon and regain the ring. His twin-sister Sieglinde, his early separation from her, his reunion with her, and his need to rescue her from a forced and loveless marriage – all these have been destined for him by Wotan, to increase his hardihood and independence before he carries out his main task. And a weapon has been provided too – the sword: it may serve him in dealing with the hated husband, but it is essentially for killing the dragon with. The fact that it is Sieglinde who becomes all-important to Sieg-mund, as an object of love and compassion, and that this does eventually establish his own genuine independence of Wotan, affecting the whole later course of events by converting the Wotan-dominated Brünnhilde to love and compassion, is some-thing that Wotan did not bargain for. But it is time to turn to the action of Act 1.

Act 1

All the events narrated or enacted in Act 1 of *The Valkyrie* are drawn from *Volsunga saga*: there is no other source, except on points of detail. But Wagner's manipulation of this material is so extreme that he comes up with quite a different story from the one told in *Volsunga saga*. The original is far too long to quote entire, so for part of the time it will be necessary to summarize. The beginning of the story – leading up to the birth of the Volsung twins – places four generations between Odin and Sigmund, as follows.

Odin had a son called Sigi, a landowner who killed out of envy a serf who excelled him at hunting: for this he was declared an outlaw, and so 'he could not stay at home with his father'. But when he left his country (unspecified), Odin went with him, and procured him 'a large force of fighting-ships', which enabled him to conquer land for himself; he made an important match, and became King of Hunland and a great warrior. When he grew old, his brothers-in-law murdered him for the kingdom, but his son, Rerir, avenged him and took the kingdom over. Rerir flourished, and became a great warrior, too; he married, but his wife proved barren, and so they prayed to the gods for a child. Frigg heard their prayer and spoke to Odin, who sent a Valkyrie to Rerir with an apple: Rerir[2] ate the apple and his wife soon became pregnant. But she could not give birth: she remained pregnant for six years, during which time Rerir died, and at last she ordered that the child should be cut out of her. And so, as she died, a boy was born, who was called Volsung; and he became an even greater warrior than his father and grandfather before him. He married the Valkyrie who had brought Odin's apple to his father, and they had ten sons and a daughter: the eldest son was Sigmund, and the daughter Signy, his twin sister.

Wagner cut down this genealogy ruthlessly, making Wotan, as Wälse (Volsung),[3] the immediate father of Siegmund, which

[2] Not his wife, as might have been expected.

[3] In old Norse, Volsung is the name of Sigmund's father and also the word for a member of the whole race: in English we follow this, calling Sigmund's father 'Volsung' and a member of the whole race 'a Volsung'. German, however (and the

enabled him to keep Wotan in the centre of the story, as shaper and controller of events. And for once, his manipulation of the source-material coincides exactly with modern theories about the original form of the mythology. Professor Finch puts the matter succinctly:

> Volsi was probably a lesser deity closely associated with Odin in his fertility aspect, or else an hypostasis of that God. That Odin should appear instead of Volsi in [*Volsunga saga*] as founder of the Volsung line is thus understandable – less understandable is the appearance of Volsung as Odin's great-grandson. The name Volsung is a patronymic, as is Wælsing in *Beowulf*, but Wælsing, i.e. son of Wæls (Volsi), is Sigmund himself. It would thus seem that the Sigi and Rerir of [*Volsunga saga*] are later interlopers and that Volsi-Odin's son was originally Sigmund . . .[4]

Wagner, then, was actually 'right', on this occasion, in his manipulation of his source-material – and for another reason too: the story begins in an unspecified country, which is nevertheless clearly identifiable as Scandinavia from the 'force of fighting ships' (Viking ships) which Odin procures for Sigi. It is only with Sigi's settling down as 'King of Hunland' (an old Norse word for Germany) that the story is transferred to Germany, where it belongs. Wagner also tidied up the plot by dispensing with Sigmund's nine brothers (who are in fact not named, and who contribute nothing to the story except their early and ignominious deaths). He left the two twins only – described in *Volsunga saga* as being 'in all respects the finest and best-looking of the children of King Volsung': he gave to Sigmund his true German name of Siegmund, and to Signy the name of Sieglinde (which is that of Siegmund's wife and Siegfried's mother in the *Nibelungenlied* – see p. 84).

Nevertheless, there are three elements in this genealogical introduction which Wagner used for his own purposes: Odin as the head of a homestead (Sigi 'could not stay at home with his father'); Odin in exile with his son, helping him (with the 'force of fighting ships'); and Odin's disappearance from this part of the story, leaving his son to fend for himself. None of these is in the story of Sigmund as told in *Volsunga saga:* Wagner's Siegmund

'Volsungs' were of course originally figures of German myth), calls the father 'Wälse' and a member of his race 'ein Wälsing' (which Wagner altered to 'Wälsung'). Interestingly enough, the words appear in the Anglo-Saxon epic *Beowulf* as Wæls and Wælsing. The earlier Norse word for 'Wälse' was probably Volsi.

[4] R. G. Finch, op. cit. pp. xxxv–xxxvi.

incorporates elements of Sigi.

To return to the story now, from which we may quote an extended passage, revealing, amongst other things, that the character we know as Hunding is called Siggeir in the saga:

> They say that King Volsung had a hall built, strong and stately, and in such a way that an oak-tree stood in the hall and the branches of the tree rose out above the roof of the hall, while the trunk was rooted deep in the hall; and they called this tree Child-Stem.[5]
>
> There was a king called Siggeir, who ruled over Gothland; he was a famous and mighty king. He journeyed to King Volsung, and asked for Signy's hand in marriage. The King received this proposal well, and so did his sons; she herself was unhappy about it, but she asked her father to decide, as he did in all things concerning her. The King was of a mind to see her married, and so she was betrothed to King Siggeir. And when the marriage-meal and the wedding were to take place, Siggeir was to come to King Volsung for the feast.
>
> The King made lavish preparations for the feast . . . and King Volsung's guests and King Siggeir and his sons came on the appointed day . . . And it is said that great fires were made along the hall; and as was mentioned before, the great tree stood there in the middle of the hall.
>
> Now it is told that, as the men were sitting by the fires in the evening, a man stepped into the hall, who was unknown to them. The man was clothed in this way: he wore a spotted cape, he was barefooted, and he had linen breeches bound to his legs; he had a sword in his hand, and he went over to the tree; he had on a deep-brimmed hat; he was very tall, and full of years, and one-eyed.[6] He lifted the sword and thrust it into the tree, so that the sword went in up to the hilt. All the men shrank from greeting him, and then he spoke, and said: 'Whoever pulls this sword out of the tree shall take it from me as a gift, and he shall prove for himself that he never bore a better sword in hand than this one'. Thereupon the old man went out of the hall, and no one knew where he was going.
>
> Now they stood up, and did not delay in going and trying to pull the sword out, and that man thought himself the luckiest who first took hold of it. But there was no one who could pull it out, for it did not move in the slightest when they seized it. Then King Volsung's son Sigmund went up and pulled the sword out of the tree, and it was as if it lay there loose in front of him. The weapon seemed to everyone so good that no one thought he had seen such a fine sword. And King Siggeir offered to give Sigmund its weight in gold for it. But Sigmund said: 'You could have taken this sword no less than I, when it stood there, if it had become you to bear it; but it came into my hand first, and now you shall never have it, even if you

[5] In the old Norse, 'Barnstock' – which is really a proper name: von der Hagen gave the German translation of the word – *Kinderstamm* (Child-Stem).

[6] This whole description would leave the original readers of (or listeners to) *Volsunga saga* in no doubt that the 'man' was none other than Odin in the guise of the Wanderer – the figure we encounter in Wagner's *Siegfried*.

offer me all the gold that you have'. King Siggeir grew angry at these words, thinking that he had been spoken to slightingly; but since he was a malicious man, he made as if he took no notice of the remark. That same evening, however, he thought out a plan which later came to fruition.

From this account of Signy's wedding, Wagner took three things: her reluctance to marry King Siggeir, the main scene of the marriage-feast (as described in Sieglinde's narration), and the fact that Sigmund alone could draw the sword from the tree. But all the rest is different from what is narrated in Act 1 of *The Valkyrie*. The marriage-feast takes place in Volsung's hall; Volsung is there, and he and his sons (including Sigmund, presumably) approve of the marriage, so that it is a superficially happy occasion: although Signy is reluctant to marry King Siggeir, she does so in obedience to her father's wishes; Sigmund draws the sword from the tree immediately, at the marriage-feast; and the character we know as Hunding is called Siggeir.

Let us deal with this last point straightaway. The name Siggeir was impossible for Wagner, since it was old Norse, and even if he could have Germanized it, it would have begun with the syllable *Sieg* (victory), which would have brought it too near to the names Siegmund and Siegfried, even suggesting consanguinity. He needed a strongly contrasting name, such as Hagen is to Siegfried, and he found it in Hunding, the traditional enemy of Sigmund, whose name is appropriately sinister (the English equivalent would be Houndson). As the *Poetic Edda* says (prose introduction to *The Second Lay of Helgi Hundingsbana*):

Hunding was the name of a mighty king . . . He was a great warrior, and had many sons who went with him on his campaigns. There was strife and enmity between King Hunding and King Sigmund, and each slew the other's kinsmen.

And so although, in *Volsunga saga*, Hunding is not involved at all in Signy's wedding and is eventually killed by one of Sigmund's sons called Helgi, and although Sigmund himself is killed by Hunding's sons, Wagner nevertheless took his name, and gave it to the husband of Signy. And so we are left with four characters only: Wotan (Odin) as Wälse (Volsung), Siegmund (Sigmund), Sieglinde (Signy), and Hunding (Siggeir).

But the other four points – why did Wagner make such drastic changes? Chiefly, of course, because of his own symbolic needs, and yet primarily because of the unstageability of the vast mass of material presented by *Volsunga saga*, which develops as a feud between King Siggeir's men and the Volsungs. It will be most convenient to give the rest of the story straightaway, summarizing and quoting by turns: it will take us into Act 2 of *The Valkyrie*, right up to Siegmund's death.

After the marriage-feast, King Siggeir returned home with Signy; and three months later he invited King Volsung and his men – ostensibly for an amicable feast, but actually with the intention of killing them (the aforementioned 'plan' he had thought out). Signy warned her father, on his arrival, of Siggeir's treachery; but he, with a true Nordic care for his reputation, said that the Volsungs, although outnumbered, would not return home, but stand and fight. Battle took place, and ended with the death of King Volsung and the capture of all his sons. The sons were condemned to death; but Signy, hoping to save them, asked her husband that they should not be executed immediately, but put in the stocks instead. This was done, and on nine successive nights, a she-wolf[7] appeared at midnight, and each time she killed and ate one of them, until all were dead except Sigmund. 'And according to some people', the saga says, 'that wolf was King Siggeir's mother, and she had taken on that shape through witchcraft and magic'.

Signy had been powerless to do anything, but now that it came to Sigmund's turn, she managed to send a trusted servant with honey, to smear over his face, and put into his mouth. And when the she-wolf came, it smelt the honey, and licked it from his face, and then thrust its tongue into his mouth. He bit into its tongue, and it jerked violently backwards, putting its feet against the stocks, so that they fell apart. But Sigmund held on so firmly that the she-wolf's tongue was torn out by the roots, and it died; and so he was free. King Siggeir believed that all the Volsungs were now dead; but Signy and Sigmund, meeting in secret, decided that he should build an underground retreat in the forest, and she would provide him with everything he needed, while they awaited their chance of avenging their father and their nine brothers.

Years passed, and then Signy sent to Sigmund her ten-year-old son by King Siggeir, to see whether he could help with the revenge. But the boy showed a lack of courage in refusing to bake bread when Sigmund asked him, because 'there was something

[7] This word, *ylgr*, is wrongly translated in Wagner's source, von der Hagen's German version, as *Elk* (elk).

alive in the flour' (Sigmund had put a poisonous snake in it). Having failed this first test, he was killed by Sigmund, at Signy's bidding – and a year later the same fate befell her second son by King Siggeir. She now decided that any sons she had by King Siggeir would be valueless for her purpose of revenge, and so:

The story goes that one day, when Signy was sitting in her room, a sorceress came to her, who was skilled in magic arts. 'I would like us', said Signy, 'to exchange shapes'. And the sorceress answered: 'It's for you to decide'. Then she worked her magic so that they exchanged shapes, and the sorceress sat in Signy's seat, and went to bed with the king; and he had no idea that it wasn't Signy who was with him.

Now we must tell how Signy [in the shape of the sorceress] went to her brother's retreat, and asked him to give her shelter for the night – 'since I've lost my way in the forest, and don't know where I'm going'. He said she could stay there: he wouldn't deny her shelter, as a woman all on her own, and it seemed to him that she wouldn't repay his granting of her request evilly, by betraying him. So they went into the retreat, and sat down to a meal; he kept looking at her, and she seemed to him an attractive woman. And when they had finished eating, he said he would like them both to share one bed; she raised no objection, and so he lay with her there for three nights. After that, she went back home to the sorceress.[8]

And when the time came, Signy gave birth to a boy, who was called Sinfiotli;[9] and when he grew up, he was both tall and strong. He took after the Volsungs, and when he was scarcely ten years old, Signy sent him to Sigmund's retreat. Before she had sent her other two sons to Sigmund, she had given them a test: she had stitched their coats on to their arms, through skin and flesh, and they had borne it badly, and screamed at the pain. She did the same with Sinfiotli, but he didn't flinch. Then she tore the coat off, so that the skin came away with the sleeves, and asked him whether the wounds hurt him. He said that such wounds could only seem very slight to a Volsung.

Now the boy came to Sigmund. And Sigmund asked him to bake bread for them both, while he himself went to look for firewood: he gave him a sackful of flour and went out into the forest. When he came back, Sinfiotli had finished baking. Then Sigmund asked if he had found anything in the flour. 'I certainly had a suspicion that there was something alive in it, when I first started kneading', he replied, 'but I've kneaded it in, whatever it was'. Sigmund laughed at that, and said: 'I fancy you won't have any of that bread for your supper tonight, since you've kneaded into it the most deadly poisonous snake . . .'

Sigmund, who did not know that Sinfiotli was his own son and a Volsung, but thought he was a son of King Siggeir, was surprised

---

[8] 'and they resumed their own shapes.' Von der Hagen's translation omits this clause.

[9] This is not Siegfried (Sigurd); he is born later. But Sinfiotli is a very Siegfried-like character, and Wagner's Siegfried took over from him the feature of being the offspring of an incestuous union between Sigmund and his sister.

when the boy kept urging him to avenge himself. But he felt that he was still too young to help him, and so:

> . . . he decided to harden him first, by means of severe tests. For some summers[10] they roved through the forest and killed men for booty . . .
>
> Now it happened one day . . . that they came across a lair in the bushes, and some men were sitting inside it . . . These men were escaping temporarily from an evil fate, for wolf-skins were hanging above them, in front of the lair, and they could only throw off the wolf-skins every ten days . . . Sigmund and Sinfiotli got into the skins, and couldn't get out of them again; and they took on the nature of wolves, their lair and their howl, and each understood the other's howling. Now they went raiding through the marshes, each taking his own way; and they first came to an agreement that each would risk fighting up to eight men, but no more, and if he was in difficulties, he was to give a wolf-call . . .

On their separate journeys, Sinfiotli proved an even tougher fighter than Sigmund, once taking on and killing eleven men without howling for help. And when the day came to throw off the wolf-skins, they burnt them; and Sigmund was now certain that Sinfiotli was fully ready to help him take his revenge on King Siggeir.

They went to King Siggeir's hall and hid themselves in some ale-barrels in an outer room; and they decided, with Signy, to have their revenge that night. Signy had by now two more young children by King Siggeir; and one of them, bowling his hoop, came across the two intruders and began running to tell his father. Sinfiotli, at Signy's bidding, killed the two children, but after a desperate struggle with the King's retainers, he and Sigmund were overpowered; they were led away and buried alive, with a great heavy slab of stone on top of the burial-mound. But while the mound was being filled in, Signy contrived to throw into it some pork, wrapped in straw, which contained Sigmund's sword; and with the sword the two men managed to saw through the slab of stone and escape. They went up to King Siggeir's hall at night, and set fire to it, and then:

> Sigmund told his sister to come out and to receive from him all praise and honour, as some kind of recompense for all that she had had to suffer.
>
> She answered: 'You shall hear whether I have kept in memory the murder of King Volsung: I let my children be killed because they were too cowardly to avenge our father; and I came to you in the forest, in the shape of a sorceress, and Sinfiotli is our son. He has such a powerful nature because he is both the son of the son, and of the daughter, of King

---

[10] Again there is a mistranslation by von der Hagen, who has 'One summer'.

Volsung. I have striven in every way to bring death to King Siggeir, I have so striven to achieve vengeance, that I do not wish to live any longer; and I will now gladly die with him whom I was forced to marry'. Then she kissed her brother Sigmund, and Sinfiotli, and bidding them farewell, she leapt into the blazing hall. Thus did Signy meet her death, with King Siggeir and all his court.

Sigmund now returned to Hunland with Sinfiotli, and drove out the king who had established himself there in succession to King Volsung. He took a wife, Borghild, who bore him two sons, Helgi and Hamund: Helgi, a mighty warrior, killed King Hunding and several of his sons, and was helped in other exploits by a Valkyrie, Sigrun, whom he afterwards married. Sinfiotli came to a tragic end: Borghild poisoned him because he had killed her brother in a fight over a woman. And now Odin appears again, revealing his continued interest in the Volsungs:

> Sinfiotli drank, and immediately fell dead to the floor.
> Sigmund started to his feet, almost on the point of dying with grief; he took the body in his arms, and went into the forest, and came to a firth. There he saw a man in a little boat; the man asked if he wanted to be taken across the firth, and he said that he did. The boat was so small, that it would not hold them all, and the body was taken across first, Sigmund walking along the side of the firth. And immediately, both boat and man vanished from Sigmund's sight. After this, Sigmund went home; he banished the queen, and soon afterwards she died. Sigmund now ruled his kingdom as before . . .

This ends the part of the story which Wagner drew on for Act 1 of *The Valkyrie*, but it will be convenient to summarize briefly the remainder, which he used for Act 2, since the interpretation of Act 1 will not make sense without it: it will be dealt with in more detail when we come to Act 2. Sigmund took another wife, Hjordis; but one of King Hunding's sons had also tried to woo her, and he and his remaining brothers decided that the time had come to put an end to the Volsungs once and for all. They went to Hunland with a large army, and engaged the Volsungs in battle. While the battle was in progress, Odin appeared, again in the guise of the Wanderer, and held out his spear in front of Sigmund; Sigmund struck at it with his sword, and the sword snapped into two pieces. Sigmund's luck now promptly changed: the battle was lost, and he and most of his army met their deaths. Sigmund was at first only wounded, and his wife Hjordis went out on to the battlefield where he lay, to see if his wounds could be healed. But he refused to be tended: he told her that she was pregnant with a boy-child and asked her to preserve the pieces of the sword for him; and then she watched over him until he died. The boy-child, of course, was to be Sigurd (Siegfried).

When Wagner adapted this discursive and bloodthirsty narrative to form part of *The Valkyrie*, he had greater difficulty in fashioning a convincing dramatic framework for Act 1 than for any other act of the whole tetralogy. This is shown by the fact that his three successive prose-sketches for it were from the start misconceived in one respect, and the finished text was (luckily) different from all of them.

From the beginning, he decided to start, as usual, *in medias res*, and to make past events clear by means of a back-narration. He started at the point where Sigmund is living in his underground retreat in the forest, and his twin-sister Signy is living with her hated husband King Siggeir. This corresponds broadly to the situation at the start of *The Valkyrie*, where Siegmund is an outlaw in the forest, and his twin-sister Sieglinde is living with her hated husband Hunding. But the situation itself is really a quite different one, because Wagner was obliged to alter every one of the events leading up to this situation, except for Signy's reluctance to marry King Siggeir (Sieglinde had certainly been more than reluctant to marry Hunding). In the saga, the whole reason for the existing situation is the Volsung twins' need to avenge King Siggeir's treacherous killing of their father, King Volsung, and of their nine brothers. Wagner, having dispensed with the nine brothers, also had to dispense with the whole revenge element of the story, since he had made Volsung (Wälse) none other than Wotan in human form, as the progenitor of the Volsung twins, and the killing of Wotan was clearly impossible from every point of view. And so, having put Hunding in place of Siggeir, he had to invent a different crime for him to commit against the Volsungs.

Wagner's own story, as narrated by Siegmund, begins with Wälse (Volsung), who, unknown to his human family, is Wotan: he figures as father and head of a human homestead, with a human wife, and twin offspring, Siegmund and Sieglinde. This idea Wagner took from the genealogical introduction of *Volsunga saga*, in which Odin appears as father and head of a human homestead, with a wife (unmentioned), and a son, Sigi (see p. 282). Wälse takes Siegmund out hunting and fighting in the forest: this feature Wagner derived from Odin's helping of Sigi when he had to leave home and become an outlaw (procuring him 'a force of fighting-ships'); but the detail comes from the account of Sigmund's own bringing-up of his son Sinfiotli. From this Wagner took the whole general atmosphere of the two being outlaws in the forest, the element of the son's hard training by his father for a specific purpose, and even the idea of the two being werewolves: Siegmund, in his narration, calls himself Wölfing (Wolf-Cub), and Wälse, his father, Wolfe; and he says that when Wolfe disappeared and abandoned him to his own devices, he left behind him an empty wolf-skin.

Wotan's disappearance from the scene is again taken from the story of Sigi, from which Odin also disappears, leaving his son to fend for himself. But Wagner added something here: he implied that Wotan, after his departure, remained the controller of Siegmund's destiny, forcing upon him his continued hard life as an outlaw. When Siegmund tells Hunding and Sieglinde how he was pursued after the battle he has just been engaged in, he uses the phrase 'Mich hatzte das wütende Heer' (the furious host hounded me). This phrase Wagner got from Jacob Grimm's *Deutsche Mythologie*: 'das wütende Heer' was an old German superstition that a ferocious horde of demons sometimes went riding through the night, threatening the lonely wayfarer; and Grimm pointed out that the phrase in Middle High German was 'Wüetunges Heer', which indicated that the superstition was a submerged folk-memory of 'Wuotans Heer' (Wotan's Army). Yet although Wagner made Wotan keep hunting Siegmund the solitary outlaw, to harden him further, he also made him first promise his son that he would find a sword in his hour of greatest need.

Why Siegmund and Wotan-Wälse should have become outlaws in the forest is explained by an earlier event – an event which Wagner invented, to replace the killing of King Volsung by King Siggeir, and which made his story entirely different from that of *Volsunga saga*. This event, again told by Siegmund in his narration, is that, when he was still a young boy, he returned home from one of his forays with his father, to find his family home burnt to ashes,[11] his mother dead, and his twin-sister missing, presumed killed. This, no doubt, Wagner adapted from the burning-down of King Siggeir's hall by Sigmund and Sinfiotli, transferring it to the other side of the account. However, he did not lay the burning-

[11] Wagner here mentions the oak-tree around which the Volsung homestead was built.

down of Wälse's house specifically to Hunding's[12] account: the deed was done, as Siegmund tells us, by a race called the Neidings. But, as we learn from Sieglinde's narration, she survived; she was carried off by the Neidings, and they handed her over to Hunding, who forced her to marry him against her will. This is the crime that Hunding has committed against the Volsungs, and which they need to avenge. Wagner thus changed the main motive of the story from revenge of a dead father to rescue of an enslaved sister.

For the scene of the marriage-feast, as narrated by Sieglinde, Wagner drew on the saga's description of the wedding of Signy to King Siggeir (see p. 284), making the appropriate changes. In the first place, with Wälse's home burnt down and Sieglinde abducted, he had to make the marriage take place in Hunding's home, with only Hunding's men present; the Volsungs are represented by the lone Sieglinde, who does not even know where her father and brother are, or even if they are still alive. Next, just as Odin enters in the saga, disguised as the Wanderer, and thrusts a sword into the Volsungs' oak-tree, so does Wagner's Wotan enter, disguised as the Wanderer, and thrust a sword into Hunding's ash-tree; but for Wagner the sword is the weapon for killing the dragon with, the means of regaining the ring for Wotan, and Wotan is Sieglinde's and Siegmund's father. And finally, since Wagner gave Siegmund a quite different history from Sigmund, and therefore made it impossible for him to be at the marriage feast, it followed that the sword would have to remain embedded in the tree, after the unavailing attempts of Hunding and his men to remove it.

This made possible, of course, Wagner's supreme stroke of dramatic genius – the saving up of the withdrawal of the sword by Siegmund for the final, climactic moment of Act 1 of *The Valkyrie*. But he was slow to realize it, because from the beginning he was hypnotized by the idea of presenting visibly on the stage the *whole* business of the sword from the saga – Wotan thrusting it into the tree, and Siegmund more or less immediately pulling it out. And his first rough prose-sketch shows that he even intended this to happen, as in the saga, in Volsung's (Wälse's) home, by making Hunding live there (presumably after Wälse and Siegmund had been driven from it by enemies):

[12] Not in his final text, that is: he did in one of his prose-sketches.

(Hunding is living in Wälse's dwelling: Siegmund appears there as a stranger, hunted from house and home.)

Act I. Siegmund comes (pursued and unarmed) to Hunding; hospitable reception, but secret mistrust on Hunding's part. Siegmund tells of his life, his wild expeditions, his trials and struggles. Sieglind – Hunding's wife – feels love for him, which Siegmund, powerfully moved by her sympathy, passionately returns. During the meal, Wodan has entered as a stranger: he thrusts a sword into the ash-tree: Siegmund pulls it out. Sieglind senses that he must be a Volsung. She steals to him in the night, to find out more about his life: he is inflamed with an even wilder desire; likewise, her sympathy with regard to his fate changes, against her will, into burning love-longing. As he enfolds her in a powerful embrace, he cries out 'I am a Volsung, and Siegmund is your lover'. Horrified and enraptured at the same time, Siegelind [sic] cries 'You are embracing your own sister, Sieglind!' Siegmund: 'Wife and sister, let glow then the Volsung blood!'[13] He embraces her with furious ardour. The curtain falls.

If Act 1 of *The Valkyrie* had been cast on these lines, it could have had no effect comparable with the act as we know it today. But Wagner, having brought Wotan into the action, disguised as the Wanderer, was extremely reluctant to get rid of him again. In his second, more detailed prose-sketch, he firmly set the scene in Hunding's home, and established the present action as far as the end of Siegmund's narration and Hunding's warning to him on going to bed; but he still made Wotan enter with the sword – and this time stay the night and witness the love-scene between his twin offspring! Even in the final, fully-worked-out prose-sketch, although he abandoned the idea of Wotan staying the night, he still brought him on to the stage, with the sword:

Wodan enters in the shape of an old man, with grey hair and beard, one-eyed, with a round hat and a grey cloak . . . He draws out a sword, and thrusts it into the stem of the ash-tree, up to the hilt. As he turns to go, he declares that the sword shall belong to the man who can pull it out of the stem. Hunding tries to, but all his efforts are in vain; he has to give up, and maintains that no man can move it. Siegmund steps up, and pulls the sword out, joyfully hailing it as his own property. Sieglinde is amazed and delighted: Hunding grows pale with rage, and tries to stifle his ill-humour with a strong drink, which Sieglinde has prepared for him. Wodan has disappeared, unnoticed . . .

And inevitably, when Sieglinde comes to Siegmund, later in the night, she is given no narration:

[13] Wagner had already nearly got his 'curtain-line': the German is 'Weib und Schwester, so glühe denn Wälsungenblut!'. The final text, in perfect alliteration, reads 'Braut und Schwester/bist du dem Bruder/so blühe denn Wälsungenblut!'; or, in English, 'Bride and sister/be to your brother/let bloom then the Volsung blood!'.

Then the door of the inner room opens: Sieglinde steps through it. She asks Siegmund if he is asleep. The latter jumps up, with joyful amazement.

Sieglinde has made sure that her husband is in the deepest sleep, having given him a drugged drink. She has come, full of two mingled passions: intense love for Siegmund and – the urge to find out who he is, since she thinks she can only guess that he is her brother. Siegmund ardently moves towards her: he takes this nocturnal visit purely as a token of love. His passion is so violent that, although she tries to control herself, to find the composure necessary for her enquiries, she is carried away. She gives a start – the entrance-door has sprung open: she asks who has gone out. Siegmund indicates the magnificent spring night: no one has gone out; Spring opened the door, and came inside . . .

From Siegmund's Spring Song onwards, the sketch proceeds to the end of the act more or less as we know it today, except of course that Siegmund does not pull the sword from the tree, having already done so.

Wagner could never have been satisfied with the act in this form, with Siegmund's withdrawal of the sword as a non-climactic event in the middle of the action. Later, suddenly, he realized what was by far the most effective way of handling this element, as a hastily-written note in the margin of the above passage shows. After the words 'she has come', at the beginning of the second sentence of the second paragraph above, he inserted a cross, with another cross in the margin and a note reading as follows:

to show him the Wodan-sword. The story of the sword provides the opportunity for her to tell her own story.

And so, at one blow, Wagner reconstructed the act in its present form. He removed Wotan from the action; he restored to the past – to the wedding-feast where it belonged – Wotan's thrusting of the sword into the tree; he provided a narrative for Sieglinde to recount this, together with her own unhappy story; and he transferred to the end of the act Siegmund's withdrawal of the sword, as a climactic piece of action setting the seal on the whole scene of love and recognition.

Apart from perfecting the dramatic shape of Act 1 of *The Valkyrie*, this last-minute reconstruction had other beneficial results, affecting *The Ring* as a whole. The removal of Wotan from the action of Act 1 had the effect that in *The Valkyrie* he appears on the stage entirely in his role of the battle-god, a terrifying figure above and beyond mortal ken. And this aloofness makes his later abandonment of Siegmund and Sieglinde entirely in character, as it would

not have done if he had first appeared before them, in Act 1, in the
benevolent and apparently human shape of the Wanderer. Admittedly, he has, in the past, appeared before them as their human
father, Wälse, and before Sieglinde, at the marriage-feast, as the
Wanderer; but that *was* in the past, which dramatically speaking, is
very different from appearing on the stage. In any case, the Wotan
of *The Valkyrie*, we feel, is not yet ready to *appear* in his benevolent
role of the Wanderer; indeed, his removal from Act 1 of *The Valkyrie*
entailed the saving-up of his appearances in that role for *Siegfried*,
where he features as a grimly genial observer of favourable events
(until Siegfried shatters his spear). This has the effect of clearly
demarcating Wotan's various roles throughout *The Ring*; in *The
Rhinegold* he stands entirely as the chief of the gods; in *The Valkyrie*
entirely as the battle-god; in *Siegfried* entirely as the Wanderer; and
in *The Twilight of the Gods* entirely as the death-desiring god, who,
although he never shows himself, broods over the action in the
narration and the music.

Moreover, the reconstruction greatly improved the *musico*-
dramatic opportunities of Act 1 of *The Valkyrie*; indeed, that must
have been Wagner's main reason for effecting the reconstruction,
since he always drew up his texts in a musico-dramatic shape. In
the first place, the fanfare-phrase attached to the sword (Ex. 63, p.
234) now plays a superb part: first as a latent, mysterious force
(when Siegmund, left alone, sees the hilt gleaming in the firelight,
and later, when Sieglinde tells him how it was thrust into the tree
at the marriage-feast by 'an old man'); and then as a vivid reality at
the climax of the action, when Siegmund withdraws the sword
from the tree. It seems difficult to imagine how the phrase could
have played such a magnificent part if Wagner had merely used it
in connection with his original idea – that of having Wotan thrust
the sword into the tree, in the middle of the action, and Siegmund
pull it out again very shortly afterwards. Also, we should not have
had that great passage where Siegmund, left all alone, cries out for
the sword his father promised him he would find in his hour of
need – '*Ein Schwert verhiess mir der Vater . . . Wälse! Wälse! wo ist dein
Schwert?*' – which refers back decisively to Wotan's music in Scene
4 of *The Rhinegold* at the moment when he was 'struck' by his
'grand idea'. All this heroic music connected with the sword is
absolutely essential, in order to counterbalance the wonderful
love-music evolved from the second part of Freia's theme, and
thereby to keep in the forefront the heroic element of *The Ring*

during this act so overwhelmingly devoted to love.

Perhaps the reason why Wagner was so reluctant to do away with Wotan's appearance on the stage was the fact that it was the only visible link with *The Rhinegold*; without it, this second part of the tetralogy would, at the beginning, be entirely disconnected from the first. Three entirely new characters would be introduced, who had not appeared in *The Rhinegold*; the subject-matter would be a human love-story – something at the opposite pole from the power-politics of *The Rhinegold*; Siegmund, together with his twin-sister Sieglinde, whom he rescues from the clutches of Hunding, might be revealed as the offspring of Wälse (Volsung) – but the identity of Wälse with Wotan could not be made clear in the text, since none of the characters was aware of it. Perhaps Wagner did not yet realize, when he began sketching the text of *The Valkyrie*, quite what a mighty musical weapon he would have in hand when he began putting into practice his so far theoretical notion of continual musical reminiscence. For it is, of course, the *music* which connects to *The Rhinegold* the totally disconnected text of Act 1 of *The Valkyrie*. And indeed, the persistent reminiscences of Wotan's music – Valhalla, the Sword (his 'grand idea'), and even an isolated reference to the Spear – is far more appropriate and effective, in evoking mysteriously his dominating though absent figure, than any stage-appearance could have been.

But we must return to Wagner's story, and examine what other alterations he made to the narrative of *Volsunga saga*. The next one, and a very important one, was the incest element.

Although it may seem that he could have taken the incest element or left it, as he chose, this is not in fact the case. He was more or less obliged to include it, if he wished to make a coherent dramatic plot which should be at least basically faithful to his source-material. He no doubt took as his starting-point the fact that in the German sources, as we have seen, the woman who is Siegmund's only wife and Siegfried's mother (but not Siegmund's sister) has the name Sieglinde. But the Siegmund and Sieglinde of the German sources are no more than names – they have no history of any kind. As we have seen, it was only in this Scandinavian source, *Volsunga saga*, that Wagner could find a detailed history of Siegmund, as Sigmund: he comes into possession of a sword, provided for him by Odin; and when this sword is eventually shattered to pieces by Odin, and he dies in battle, the pieces are preserved by his new wife, Hjordis, who is pregnant, for their unborn son Sigurd (Siegfried).

It is obvious that Hjordis, sympathetic character though she is, and dramatically though she figures in the last tragic hours of Sigmund's life in *Volsunga saga*, could not provide Wagner with the wife-figure for Siegmund that he needed, since she too has no earlier history. But Sigmund's own earlier history in *Volsunga saga* is closely bound up with that of his twin-sister, whose name, Signy, could possibly be regarded as a corrupt Scandinavian form of the German name Sieglinde. She is there when he pulls Odin's sword from the tree, she saves his life, she mates with him, and she allies herself with him in an attempt to take vengeance on her hated husband King Siggeir (whom Wagner preferred to call Hunding). In *The Valkyrie* there was no room for *two*[14] women in Siegmund's life: the most simple plan was to regard his twin-sister Signy as the Scandinavian version of the German Sieglinde, to let Sieglinde live instead of committing suicide like Signy, and to transfer from Hjordis to her the conception of Siegfried (on the analogy of her incestuous conception of Sinfiotli) and the preservation of the pieces of Sigmund's sword. This transfer meant that the incest element in *Volsunga saga* inevitably became part of *The Valkyrie*.

But in taking over the incest element, Wagner altered its character decisively. There is something extremely cold-blooded about this element in *Volsunga saga*: Signy, who knows her brother very well, changes shapes with a sorceress so that she can sleep with him, not because she is sexually attracted to him, but simply in order to conceive by him a pure-strain Volsung son who will alone be courageous enough to help them avenge their father King Volsung on the man responsible for his death. Wagner, with his altered story, in which Volsung is Wotan and has thus not been killed, had no use for this cold-blooded element of the saga (as he had no use for all its cold-blooded cruelties – Signy's testing of her first two children's courage by stitching their coats to their arms, the murder of all four of her children by King Siggeir, and her decision to burn to death with the husband she has so hated). He transformed the incest element into a love-story: when Siegmund arrives at Hunding's home, he and Sieglinde have not seen each

[14] Sigmund, of course, had *three*; but Wagner naturally ignored Borghild and her two sons, Helgi and Hamund, who were anyway Scandinavian accretions on the original German myth.

other since they were children, or early adolescents; indeed, with Siegmund's continual forays in the forest with his father, described in his narration, he hardly even knew, as he says, either his sister or his mother. And so, since he conceals his true identity by calling himself 'Wölfing' the son of 'Wolfe', they meet as strangers,[15] and they fall passionately in love.

Incest is such a strict taboo in civilized communities that its presence in a great work of art used to shock many people. Nowadays, since Freud and Jung, it merely leads to speculation concerning the psychology of an artist who can see fit to go artistically against the taboo, and to psycho-analytical interpretation of the work of art, and the artist, concerned.

We find this kind of thing in Robert Donington's book, in the chapter on *The Valkyrie*. Mentioning the well-known fact that Wagner 'went through a stage of very close emotional attachment to his sisters', he applies the Jungian category of 'incest-fantasies' to the relationship between Siegmund and Sieglinde:

> The purpose of the incest taboo is to prevent our slipping back from our measure of human consciousness and responsibility into an animal state of unconsciousness and irresponsibility . . . unconscious fantasies of incestuous reunion with the mother . . . are among the factors which pull us back from living as courageously, as freely and as consciously as we otherwise might . . . To transfer our main unconscious incest fantasies from the mother to the sister is a normal stage of growth, and prepares us for the later stage of separating our sexual desires from our incest-longings still farther in ordinary mating . . . The retrogression symbolised by incest can lead to a regressive entanglement in escapist infantile fantasies; or it can lead on to a regenerative reliving of infantile situations . . . It may well be counted a prefiguration of rebirth for Siegmund if he can win his manhood under the symbolism of pulling his father's sword out of a tree related, as this tree undoubtedly is related, to the mother-world of nature.

Unfortunately, theorizing like this is strictly irrelevant to the case of Siegmund and Sieglinde, in which, as we have seen, the harmful retrogressive tendencies of incest, mentioned above, cannot possibly be present. These retrogressive tendencies can only operate when a brother and sister fall in love within, or near to, an enduring family circle, in the full knowledge that they are brother and sister. But the family circle of the Volsung twins has been broken up at an early stage; they have long been separated, and have led hard lives amongst strangers; and when they fall in love

[15] Sieglinde later *senses* who Siegmund must be, but this is not at all the same as recognizing a brother who is constantly in and out of one's company.

they have no idea that they are brother and sister. For Siegmund, Sieglinde is a beautiful stranger, who later, almost unbelievably, turns out to be his long-lost sister; likewise, for Sieglinde, Siegmund is a handsome stranger, who later, almost unbelievably, turns out to be her long-lost brother. And being deeply in love by the time of the recognition, they are enraptured rather than disturbed by it; they consummate their love, and Sieglinde conceives a child.

Wagner, in inventing this love-relationship between the long-separated Volsung twins, made it the absolutely central symbol of Act 1 of *The Valkyrie*: it stands there as a great flowering of human love, in opposition to power (Hunding's power, as possessor of the unwilling Sieglinde), after the power-ridden, loveless world of *The Rhinegold*. As a result, incestuous though it was, Wagner had to let the lovers rejoice in it, and condone it himself. And he saw no reason why not. According to conventional ways of thinking, Siegmund and Sieglinde, once they realized that they were brother and sister, should have been horror-stricken,[16] as Oedipus and his mother Jocasta were, in their somewhat similar situation. But in *The Valkyrie*, the only person who is horror-stricken is Fricka (guardian of the law – of conventional ways of thinking). She expostulates with Wotan in Act 2:

> *The brother embraced*
> *his sister as a bride!*
> *Physical love between siblings –*
> *when has it ever been known?*

But Wotan, always on the look-out for something new,[17] replies imperturbably:

> *Today you have known it. Learn then*
> *that things can happen*
> *of their own accord*
> *which have never happened before.*

And later, he adds:

> *That they are in love*
> *is as clear as day,*

[16] Wagner did retain a slight suggestion of this attitude on Sieglinde's part in one of his prose-sketches: when she realized that Siegmund was her brother, she was 'horrified and enraptured at the same time' (see p. 293).

[17] Later in the scene, he has the lines 'Convention is all/that you ever understand;/but what never yet happened/preoccupies my mind'.

> *so listen to some honest advice!*
>   *Since sweet delight*
>   *Shall reward your blessing,*
> *bless then, smiling on love,*
> *Siegmund's and Sieglinde's union!*

Wotan never gives way to Fricka over this matter. The point on which he is defeated in his argument with her in Act 2 is not the incestuous nature of the love between the Volsung twins; it is the fact that Siegmund is not a free hero, as he had intended, but merely his own pawn. He obviously condones and blesses the incestuous love-relationship, and he is clearly speaking for Wagner. In *Opera and Drama*, there is an analysis of the Oedipus myth, in which Wagner deals with the subject of incest. He wrote this (or perhaps refurbished it from an earlier essay) in 1850; two years before, he had drawn up that prose-summary which was to develop into the complete text of *The Ring* – and which included Siegmund and Sieglinde, with their incestuous relationship; and one year later, he was to set down his first prose-sketches of Acts 1 and 2 of *The Valkyrie*. So the Volsung twins must have been very much in his mind when he wrote his vindication of the incestuous relationship between Oedipus and his mother Jocasta.

For that is exactly what it is – a vindication. There is not the slightest anticipation of Freud here, not the faintest suggestion that the two notorious actions of Oedipus – his killing of his father and his marrying of his mother – correspond to something very real in the unconscious of every man. Indeed, Freud's conception of the Oedipus complex would surely have been repellent to Wagner's way of thinking, with his belief in the original virtue of humanity – even though there is a startling foreshadowing of it in his art (in the music-drama *Siegfried*). But if Wagner's analysis of the Oedipus myth can tell us nothing about the Oedipus complex, it can tell us a great deal about his attitude towards the incestuous relationship between the Volsung twins. For it consists of a wholesale attack on the idea that there can be anything harmful about incestuous love when it happens unwittingly between two people who meet one another as strangers. In the first place, it dismisses the notion that incest can be genetically harmful:

Did Oedipus sin against human nature when he married his mother? Most certainly not. Otherwise nature, violated, would surely have revealed the fact by allowing no children to issue from this marriage. But nature, in fact, showed herself entirely willing. Jocasta and Oedipus, who had met as two strangers [*ungewohnte Erscheinungen*], loved each other, and were only disturbed in their love from the moment when it was made known to them from outside that they were mother and son. Oedipus and Jocasta did not know in what social relationship they stood to one another: they had acted unconsciously, according to the natural instinct of the purely human individual. And from their union sprang an enrichment of human society, in the shape of two strong sons and two noble daughters . . .

This mythological argument against the supposed genetic harmfulness of incest is supported by modern knowledge. As Donington says, 'Nature has no more objection to incest than a cattle-breeder or a cat-fancier'; and a clinical psychologist has recently reaffirmed the fact, saying that geneticists 'are generally agreed that incest or inbreeding in itself causes no inherited damage in offspring'.[18]

Secondly, Wagner places the argument where it really belongs – in the social sphere:

In family life – the most natural, but the most confined basis of society – it had become established, quite of itself, that a completely different kind of attachment develops between parents and children, and between the siblings themselves, from that which makes itself known amid the sudden and violent excitation of sexual love. In the family, the natural bonds between the begetters and the begotten become the bonds of familiarity, and again, only from familiarity does a natural attachment develop between the siblings. But the first fascination of sexual love is awakened in the young by someone unfamiliar, someone confronting them newly from outer life; and this stimulus is so overwhelming that it draws them out of the family circle, where they have never encountered it, and impels them towards experience of the unfamiliar. Sexual love is the disruptive influence which breaks the restrictive barriers of family life, so as to enlarge it into the wider world of human society.

This view of the essential cultural value of the incest taboo is similar to Freud's, in *Totem and Taboo*, and again the taboo does not apply to the relationship between the Volsung twins. Siegmund and Sieglinde, like Oedipus and Jocasta, are entirely 'unfamiliar' to each other when they meet, and have long since been in no danger of staying within 'the restrictive barriers of family life', since they are already members of the 'wider world of human society'. Siegmund has long been a lone fighter against the evil customs of that society, Sieglinde a helpless victim of those evil customs; and so when they fall in love, the situation belongs entirely to the

[18] Herbert Maisch: *Incest*. English translation by Colin Bearne, London 1973.

world of 'experience of the unfamiliar' – i.e., to the normal world of adult love.

We must now confront the objections to Wagner's transformation of *Volsunga saga* put forward by Jessie L. Weston.[19] Her reputation as an expert in mythology is such that they cannot be left unanswered; and in answering them, we can gain much insight into Wagner's symbolic intentions. In her book, she maintained that, although the story of Siegmund and Sieglinde (Sigmund and Signy) is 'distinctly repellent to our ideas as told in the saga', it is 'even more so as represented by Wagner'.

The saga regards them . . . as descendants of Odin, and therefore of superhuman nature, and their whole story is cast in a superhuman mould. It must be admitted that such characters lose the more, the more they are euhemerised;[20] to represent them as mortals is to run the risk of making them repulsive; they must be influenced by some force extraneous to themselves, be it Passion or be it Fate, the irresistible power of which we ourselves as spectators acknowledge, before, as men and women, we can cordially accept and sympathise with them. The compiler of the Volsunga-saga seems instinctively to have felt this, when he represented Signy as practically embodied revenge. Considering the sanctity of the tie of blood, *Sippe*, among the Northern nations, and the treachery of which the Volsungs have been the victims, Signy's conduct, even though she sacrificed her womanhood and the natural feelings of a mother to her vengeance, is perfectly intelligible; and the final scene in which, her task accomplished, she chooses death with the husband she has betrayed rather than life with Siegmund, goes far towards mitigating the natural horror we feel for her conduct. Utterly outside all possible conceptions of womanhood, Signy is yet one of the most awful and imposing figures in the whole roll of Helden-saga.

At the same time, the companion of her vengeance, Siegmund, never loses his hold on our sympathy; his conduct is perfectly natural and legitimate throughout, and in the most repulsive feature of the situation he is an unconscious agent. It is Signy's overwhelming passion for revenge which dominates and explains the whole situation; she, in fact, has remained superhuman, while Siegmund has become human.

When, however, we examine the situation in the *Valkyrie*, we find that the whole 'motif' is changed – it is no longer Passion, but Fate, which is the determining factor in the situation; and into this idea of Fate Wagner has introduced a complexity of thought which, unless the actors are able by the force of their own personality to enlist on their side the sympathies of the audience, must, by its very difficulty of comprehension, go near to

[19] Op. cit., pp. 72–8.
[20] Treated as human beings.

wrecking the situation: emphasising, while it fails to explain, the repellent nature of their conduct.

The idea that Siegmund can only carry out the task for which he has been born by being independent of all laws, human and divine, and becoming practically a law unto himself, is undoubtedly a fine conception, but one which, at this early stage of the drama, it is not easy to grasp; and the extremely complex character assigned to Wotan makes it difficult for us to regard him, himself helpless in the grasp of Fate, as being really the operative agent in the conduct of Siegmund and Sieglinde.

With regard to these criticisms, it has first to be pointed out, as it was pointed out in Chapter 1, that Wagner was not trying to dramatize ancient myths purely for the sake of doing so, but to interpret through his art such of their meaning as seemed to him still to have relevance for his own time, and where that meaning was lacking, to supply it himself. He could not have set the revenge-story of *Volsunga saga* in its original form, for two very good reasons. The first, which is purely practical, is that it would not have fitted into the framework of *The Ring*. The second, which is purely personal, is that as an artist Wagner was not interested in primitive tales of revenge for their own sake: if he had been – if he had taken *Volsunga saga* as the basis of an independent opera – he would have been a different kind of musical dramatist, writing a different kind of music-drama altogether, something like Richard Strauss's *Elektra*. Admittedly, his decision to take the old Teutonic mythology as the basis of a tetralogy symbolizing the unhappy past and present of human history, and its possible ameliorated future, made it necessary for him, in this particular case, to transform his source-material almost beyond recognition: not only to make a quite different story out of it, as already mentioned, but to turn the more than Elektra-like figure of Signy and the more than Orestes-like figure of Sigmund into his fierce but compassionately loving Siegmund and Sieglinde. However, the artistic quality of an opera based on existing material – whether a myth, a piece of history, a play, or a novel – is in no way dependent on how far it is faithful to that existing material. Sometimes it will be only 'after' the original, a good way away from it, and yet an original masterpiece in its own right, with a quite different significance. *The Valkyrie* is a great work of art in itself, and part of a greater one: *Volsunga saga* is something else.

Wagner was *forced* to 'euhemerize' Sigmund and Signy because, at this stage of the tetralogy, he wanted to represent the upsurge of human love after the gods' power-dominated world of *The Rhinegold*. In *The Ring*, Siegmund and Sieglinde *are*, in the mythological sense, superhuman, being the twin offspring of the god Wotan; but since even Wagner's Wotan and his gods are treated as symbols of humanity (a fact which Miss Weston seems not to have realized), so, naturally, are Siegmund and Sieglinde. Nevertheless, they are certainly driven by Fate, as Miss Weston admitted; but what is difficult to understand in her argument is the criticism she makes of Wagner's handling of this element. She complains that he 'has introduced a complexity of thought which, unless the actors are able by the force of their own personality to enlist on their side the sympathies of the audience, must, by its very difficulty of comprehension, go near to wrecking the situation: emphasizing, while it fails to explain, the repellent nature of their conduct.' And again that 'the extremely complex character assigned to Wotan makes it difficult for us to regard him, himself helpless in the grasp of Fate, as being really the operative agent in the conduct of Siegmund and Sieglinde'.

There *is* complexity of thought, certainly, in *The Valkyrie*; but it is of a different kind from what Miss Weston, with her mythological expert's preconceptions, supposed, and far less difficult of comprehension. To begin with, Wagner's Wotan is *not* 'helpless in the grasp of Fate', as the Odin of Scandinavian mythology was.[21] As a ruler of the world, he has, in *The Rhinegold*, been prevented by his sense of destiny (symbolized by Erda) from keeping Alberich's ring, and thereby from opting for tyrannical world-power based on a total rejection of the claims of love. And this turning-point in his life has bred in him a sense of guilt for his past follies and misdeeds, which has led him to take certain measures of his own to protect his world against the eventuality of Alberich's regaining the ring from Fafner, and to make it in some ways a better world. He has begotten on Erda nine Valkyries, divine warrior-maidens, who are to recruit an army of the bravest of human heroes, after their deaths in battle, to lead a new life in Valhalla and defend it in the event of an attack by Alberich's Nibelung army. He has begotten twin children on a mortal woman, and brought up the male child to be the greatest hero of all – a fierce opponent of the oppressive laws that Wotan himself has created, and therefore independent of Wotan and able to regain the ring from Fafner.

[21] See pp. 229–31 for the argument that Erda does not symbolize fate.

To none of these measures has Wotan been compelled by fate.

So Wotan is quite clearly 'the operative agent in the conduct of Siegmund and Sieglinde'. The fact that he has engineered their fate – which is that they shall be separated in youth, that Siegmund shall become an outlaw, that Sieglinde shall be married by force to a man she does not love, and that Siegmund shall eventually rescue her from this loveless marriage – does quite definitely 'explain [some of] their conduct'. Admittedly, this *is* an 'early stage of the drama' for these things to be 'easy to grasp'; but they all become clear in Act 2, during Wotan's dialogues with Fricka and Brünnhilde. In any case, our experience of *The Ring* is not confined to a single acquaintance with it: from our second acquaintance onwards, we know the whole story from start to finish, and our real illumination begins to grow.

However, Wotan is not the *only* 'operative agent in the conduct of Siegmund and Sieglinde'. There is one fact concerning these characters which was overlooked, or undervalued, by Miss Weston – and that is the most obvious one. If the fact that they are driven by Fate – the fate that Wotan has engineered for them – is not to be revealed until Act 2, the fact that they are driven by Passion – the passion of love[22] – is evident throughout Act 1; and this does, most powerfully, 'enlist on their side the sympathies of the audience' from the very beginning. Moreover, the passion of love, here, is rooted, not only in sex, but also in compassion. The only evidence we have about Siegmund's previous conduct is what he tells in his narration – that he has been trying to rescue a girl from being forced by her kinsmen to marry a man she does not love; and since, in the action of Act 1, he finds himself faced by the same situation, and adopts the same attitude, we realize that his opposition to Wotan's laws, bred in him by Wotan, has come to take the form of a fierce compassion for the victims of a power-dominated society. Hence his position as an outlaw. Likewise, Sieglinde's own unhappy lot leads her to feel compassion for this outlaw.

This is something that lay outside Wotan's calculations – which is really the whole point of *The Valkyrie*. In begetting his two human children, in giving them their hard fate, and in bringing up Siegmund to be independent, an opponent of his own oppressive laws, he was primarily concerned with preventing Alberich from regaining the ring. With his power-orientated view of things, he

[22] Perhaps Miss Weston did not regard love as a passion.

did not realize that there would arise in his two children, in their distress, that 'life-need of man's life-needs, the need for love'. Nor did he realize that, meeting after long separation, and not recognizing each other, they would *fall* in love. If he *had* intended this to happen, as part of the fate that he had wished on to them, Fricka would certainly have taken him to task for it in Act 2; but in fact she makes no such accusation. She is simply horrified by the fact that Wotan's Volsung children, of their own accord, have committed incest and adultery. And when she asks 'When has it ever been known?', Wotan confirms that he never planned it, by replying 'Learn now that things can happen of their own accord that never happened before'.

Wotan, who is always on the lookout for things that are new and creative, condones and blesses the love between Siegmund and Sieglinde, because he is proud of them for having lived out their fate so staunchly. He loves them, and he sees their love as an extra embellishment setting the seal on their achievement. But his conception of love is still very rudimentary, and his love for his children is essentially paternalistic and authoritarian. Although he has devoted so much time and effort to bringing up his son as a free hero, independent of himself and of his laws, it is merely so that he shall carry out the demands of his father's will – destroy the dragon and regain the ring, which he will then, presumably, be expected to return to his father. (Wotan wants to have it both ways again, but this time he will get it neither way.) He does not realize that Siegmund's falling in love has made him *genuinely* independent: love, compassionate love, and not power, becomes the motivating force in Siegmund's life. This genuine independence of Siegmund will be revealed later, during his death-doomed dialogue with Brünnhilde, when he refuses to go to Valhalla, because Sieglinde cannot accompany him to that exclusively male paradise. And by his refusal, Siegmund does achieve something after all, in spite of Wotan's abandoning of him – something invaluable. He sets Brünnhilde thinking, and – when he threatens to kill Sieglinde and her unborn child rather than leave them defenceless in a power-dominated society – he converts her from a mere dispassionate agent of Wotan into a compassionate and loving woman.

And there is another thing that Wotan, hypnotized by his own power, does not realize: that this compassionate love between Siegmund and Sieglinde, if allowed to flourish and to influence other human beings, will eventually eat away his repressive laws and his tyrannical control of the world, so that humanity will supersede the gods altogether. When Fricka points this out to him, telling him that he is crazy to allow mere human beings to bring about the gods' downfall – and that this first 'free' man, Siegmund, is in fact only an extension of his own power, a puppet, entirely dependent on the invincible sword he has provided for him – Wotan reveals the authoritarianism of his love for his children. He sacrifices them – in great anguish, certainly, but with absolute conviction – to the exigencies of the gods' power-politics.

All this is the 'complexity of thought' that Wagner introduced into his adaptation of *Volsunga saga*, and the 'extremely complex character' that he assigned to Wotan – but in a different sense from Miss Weston's. It has its own magnificent logic, if we keep in mind the power-versus-love symbolism in *The Rhinegold*, and still keep applying it in *The Valkyrie*.

Miss Weston also enlarged on her statement about the 'repellent nature' of the conduct of Wagner's Siegmund and Sieglinde:

> Not only do we find that Sieglinde is in dramatic interest distinctly inferior to her prototype Signy, but we also feel that the wrongs inflicted upon her by Hunding are not in themselves of a nature to justify her conduct. True, he has purchased her from robbers and married her against her will, but in those primitive times such conduct was hardly exceptional, much less unforgiveable; and there is a certain rough chivalry in Hunding's treatment of Siegmund and observance of *Gast-recht* [guest-rights], which makes the latters flight with the wife of his host bear a disagreeably treacherous aspect. One is not surprised at Hunding's pursuit of the pair, and it certainly rather destroys sympathy with the hero, and sorrow at his fate, to have a lurking feeling that, after all, he deserved it.

It should not really be necessary to answer 'moral' strictures of this outmoded kind, except that some people accept them, and go beyond them, even today, owing to a failure to examine Wagner's text with sufficient care. (In recent years, in a review of a performance, a critic described Siegmund as 'the most contemptible of all Wagner's heroes'.) Miss Weston's views, only too obviously, belong to a time – the eighteen-nineties – when the rights of women were as yet hardly thought of; when adultery, especially by a woman, was regarded as a disgrace; and when incest between brother and sister – even if they met as strangers – was something quite unmentionable.

Wagner, of course, was dramatizing a revolutionary condemnation of these hidebound Victorian ideas. Even without taking into consideration his complex symbolism, the mere story-line of Act 1 of *The Valkyrie* condemns such ideas outright. Sieglinde, as a child, has seen her home burnt down and her mother killed by the Neidings, who then carried her off; later, robbers or murderers (*Schächer*) – presumably the Neidings, who had murdered her mother – gave her, against her will, as a wife to the grim warrior Hunding, for whom she felt no love. Conduct like this may have been 'hardly exceptional' in 'those primitive times', but it was surely unforgiveable, even in those times, by any woman of spirit. Sieglinde seems to belong to any time (even, perhaps, the Victorian period) when she says to Siegmund:

> *All that I have suffered*
> *in raging sorrow,*
> *all that made me smart*
> *with dishonour and shame,*
> *sweetest revenge*
> *would pay for it all!*

Small wonder that a man like Siegmund, full of compassion for the victims of a barbarous society, should feel bound to rescue such an unfortunate woman, especially when he discovers that she is his sister and they have fallen in love with each other. Can there be anything 'treacherous' in such an attitude, just because Hunding, observing the customs of his society, grants Siegmund 'guest-rights' – shelter and a night's sleep?

Miss Weston, like others since, was misled by Wagner's habit of making his villains, not mere 'baddies', but real characters in their own right, with integral personalities of their own (cf. Alberich, Mime, and Hagen). Hunding, when he arrives home and finds Siegmund there, behaves with stern correctness, according to the lights of his society. He introduces himself, offers his guest shelter, and asks his identity. Siegmund, of course, has to conceal his identity, because 'Siegmund the Volsung' is a known and hated outlaw. While he tells his story, Hunding comments that, since he is obviously the victim of an unlucky fate, no man can be happy to meet him, when he comes as a stranger asking for hospitality. Then, when Siegmund tells how he has been trying to rescue the girl who was being forced by her kinsmen to marry against her will, Hunding realizes that he and Siegmund are enemies. These people are his own kinsmen, and he was called out to support them in the fight, to take vengeance on Siegmund for those he had killed; he arrived too late, but coming home, he finds the enemy himself there. He tells Siegmund this; he cannot strike him dead there and then, because he has offered him guest-rights – a shelter for the night – but he tells him that, weaponless though he is, he must be ready to fight in the morning. Not much 'chivalry', even of a 'rough' kind, here; imagine a man with a spear killing a weaponless opponent!

Nevertheless, Hunding's conduct is perfectly correct, according to the laws of his warrior society, and he is a very impressive figure. He and Siegmund are enemies, and he believes himself to be in the right: it is entirely lawful for a man to force an unwilling woman to live with him as a wife, even when, as with Sieglinde, she apparently has no male relatives to protect her; anyone who fights against this law of possession-by-force is just a criminal. Hunding has his enemy at his mercy, and, after observing the law of guest-rights, he intends to exact full vengeance by killing him. Siegmund would seem, actually, not to be at Hunding's mercy, since the main door is secured inside only by a simple wooden bolt: all he needs to do is to pull the bolt back and make good his escape. But he naturally will not abandon the wife, with whom he has fallen in love; and he is hoping against hope that the sword his father promised him will materialize, since this is certainly his hour of greatest need.

But Hunding's granting of guest-rights lays no obligation on Siegmund to respect Hunding's possession of Sieglinde. Hunding is now clearly Siegmund's enemy, and Siegmund, too, believes himself to be in the right: in spite of the customs of society, no man has the right to *force* a woman to live with him as his wife. Sieglinde believes so as well: Hunding is to her a hated enemy, and all she desires is to escape from him, which she cannot do, as a defenceless woman, without the aid and protection of a man. So when Siegmund draws the sword from the tree, he is entirely within his rights, as he sees them (and as Wagner saw them), to rescue Sieglinde from her loveless marriage, and to take her away with him.

But would it not have been more honourable (or perhaps much sweeter!) for Siegmund to have waited for the morning, surprised Hunding by having a sword, and fought it out there and then? (That is what the Sigmund of *Volsunga saga* would surely have done.) No, because Siegmund is not at all like Hunding: Hunding thinks only of revenge and killing, Siegmund thinks only of love and life. Although Sieglinde spoke of 'sweetest revenge', she meant no more than escape: the two lovers are not interested in causing Hunding's death, but only in getting away from him and living their own life of love together. (Siegmund would remain a warrior, undoubtedly, but in the service of the defenceless, as before.) Actually of course, Wagner could not, owing to the exigencies of building a coherent drama, have made Siegmund wait for the morning and fight it out immediately with Hunding: the fight had to take place at the end of Act 2, so as to allow for Fricka's annihilation of Wotan's plans, Wotan's change of mind about Siegmund, and Brünnhilde's defiance of Wotan's final orders. But, as we have seen before, Wagner's practical plot-building and his symbolic intentions invariably fit one another like a glove.

It is of course Wagner's symbolism, in Act 1 of *The Valkyrie*, that makes perfect sense of the story, and finally vindicates his transformation of the events of *Volsunga saga* against the criticisms of Miss Weston. It fits with beautiful logic into the symbolism already established by *The Rhinegold*. The symbolism there is one of power-versus-love, with power having almost entirely the upper hand. Now, in *The Valkyrie*, Wagner wanted to symbolize the growth and flowering of human love, in opposition to that power, which is why he turned the family-feud-and-revenge story of *Volsunga saga* into a story about a woman who is forced to marry a man she does not love and is rescued from her loveless marriage by her brother, who becomes her lover. For Hunding stands as a characteristic member of the society which follows Wotan's repressive laws: he lives entirely by power, and has no time for love. In some lines which Wagner gave to Fricka and Wotan in Act 2 and later discarded (though he had them printed as footnotes in the publication of the final text of *The Ring*), Fricka makes this very point. She begins her plea for Hunding's rights as a husband with a reference to 'the holy oath of marriage', and Wotan replies:

> *Unholy*
> *I regard the oath*
> *that binds those not in love.*

This is from the text as set. In the unset lines, Wotan continues:

> *The woman's case*
> *weighs light with you,*

if you consecrate the force
with which Hunding married his wife!

This is, of course, special pleading by Wotan on Sieglinde's behalf. Generally, he is still not at all averse to force, and Fricka replies:

If brute force,
  obstinately savage,
lays the world in ruins,
  who bears the guilt
  alone for the harm
but the raging one, Wotan, you?
The weak you never protected,
You only stand by the strong;
  the anger of men
  with their harsh spirit,
  their murder and pillage,
  are your mighty work.

This was made even clearer in Wagner's final extended prose-sketch for Act 2, where Fricka says to Wotan: 'If anyone can be accused in this matter, it is Wotan alone: who lets men do as they like – use force? . . . If Hunding was violent and predatory, the guilt was yours, since you could have stopped him.' It seems a pity that Wagner did not carry this idea over into his final text, to make the vital connection between Wotan's philosophy of power and Hunding's consequently lawful use of power; but he was worried by the inordinate length of the Wotan-Fricka and Wotan-Brünnhilde scenes taken together, and something had to go. There is an over-compression in the text here.

Fricka, in the discarded lines of the text, could hardly have made a more accurate description, and condemnation, of the human society fostered by Wotan: a society dominated by people like Hunding, with his possession of Sieglinde by force; like Hunding's kinsmen, who are ready to compel one of their young women-folk to undergo an unwanted marriage; and like the Neidings, who burn the Volsungs' home to ashes, in the absence of the male Volsungs, kill the mother, and abduct the girl. This society is a human extension of the power-motivated, loveless world of Wotan in *The Rhinegold*, and is governed likewise by Wotan's laws. And Wagner once again showed his genius for dramatic compression, evoking this society vividly by means of a single character on the stage – Hunding – and two passages of the narration he gave to Siegmund: he was thus able to provide a whole social context against which to set the flowering of the love between Siegmund and Sieglinde. As said before, his vision of a change in human nature, from the love of power to the power of love, is represented progressively, in *The Valkyrie* (and even more in *Siegfried*), as taking place in the hearts of one or two individuals; but in Act 1 of *The Valkyrie*, at least, we see the power of love acting as a dynamic social force, just as we saw the love of power acting as a dynamic social force in *The Rhinegold*. For both Siegmund and Sieglinde, the attachment between them is no mere personal love-affair, but is born of a deep compassion for the victims of their power-dominated society, a compassion itself born of the *need* of love aroused in them by their hard fate.

Even the naming of the sword – the last symbol left unexplained – underlines this fact. In *Volsunga saga* Sigmund's sword has no name; but when he is dying, and gives the pieces of it to Hjordis to preserve for their unborn son Sigurd, he says that 'a good weapon will be made from them, that will be called Gram'.[23] In the Scandinavian sources, Sigurd's sword is in fact called Gram, and in the German sources Balmung.[24] But Wagner made Siegmund, in drawing the sword from the tree, christen it Nothung (Need), and explain the name beforehand, in first laying hands on the hilt, by invoking 'Holiest love's deepest need'. The natural human instinct for love has been reduced to deepest need by the way it has been rejected in *The Rhinegold*, and is still being rejected in *The Valkyrie*.

Now, with the aid of Siegmund's sword, it seems, the need for love is about to begin to be satisfied. A pity that, in Act 2, the sword is going to be smashed, and Siegmund killed, to suit the exigencies of Wotan's power-politics (surely Siegmund is the most *contemptibly betrayed* of all Wagner's heroes). But love itself will not be destroyed: thanks to Siegmund's love-inspired revolt against the pathetic fate allotted him by Wotan, it will live on in Brünnhilde.

[23] An old Teutonic word meaning 'wrath'. Modern German 'Gram' means 'grief' – so that Wagner could not use this name anyway.

[24] An old German word meaning 'destruction'; Wagner began by using this name, in his prose sketches for *The Valkyrie*, but eventually discarded it.

Act 2

As we have seen, Wagner, in fashioning the plot of Act 1 of *The Valkyrie*, had at his disposal a plethora of source-material in *Volsunga saga*, from which he could select only a few elements; but when he came to fashion the plot of Acts 2 and 3, he had very little to go on. The plot of these two acts, in fact, is based on nothing more than four short passages of narrative. The first two, also from the saga, tell of the end of Sigmund's life, in the battle with the sons of Hunding:

When the fighting had lasted for some time, a man came on to the battlefield, wearing a low hat over his eyes and a blue cloak; he was one-eyed, and had a spear in his hand.[1] This man advanced towards King Sigmund, and lifted the spear up against him, and when Sigmund struck at it forcefully, his sword hit against the spear, and snapped into two pieces. After that, the fortune of battle changed, and King Sigmund's luck deserted him . . . The king did not spare himself, but there's a saying that 'few against many can't prevail'. In this battle, King Sigmund fell . . . together with the greater part of his army . . .

Before this battle, as said earlier, Sigmund had taken a new wife, Hjordis, and she features in the second passage:

Hjordis, the night after the battle, went out to the scene of carnage: she came to where King Sigmund lay, and asked if his wounds could be healed. He replied: 'Many have been cured when there was little hope; but my luck has deserted me, and so I do not want to be made well. Odin does not wish me to draw my sword any longer, since it lies here broken: I have endured battles as long as it was his pleasure . . .

You are pregnant with a boy-child; tend him well, and with great care, and this boy will be the most famous and the most splendid of our race. Preserve well the pieces of the sword: a good weapon will be made from them, that will be called Gram, and our son will bear it, and perform with it many heroic deeds, which will never be forgotten as long as the world lasts. Comfort yourself with that; but my wounds are wearying me, and I shall soon be joining my kinsmen who have gone before'.

Hjordis sat watching over him until he died; and then the day began to break . . .

The unborn son is of course Sigurd (Siegfried).

[1] Odin again, of course, in the guise of the Wanderer.

With regard to the first passage, it has to be realized that the Sigmund of *Volsunga saga* was an old man by the time of his death. If, at the time of Signy's marriage to King Siggeir, one supposes him – as the eldest of ten brothers, all old enough to fight – to have been at least twenty-four, and if one then adds on the time for his three marriages, and for all King Siggeir's and his own sons (except Sigurd) to grow up, then he must have lived to an age of seventy or more. So that Odin's motive, in breaking Sigmund's sword, is simply that, after such a long and heroic life, it is now time for him to die an honourable death fighting against odds, and to receive his reward of going to Valhalla – a fate which Sigmund accepts as all in the natural course of things.

But Wagner's Siegmund is young when he dies (which he does, of course, not in battle, but in single combat with Hunding); and Wotan's motive in breaking his sword is to preserve the power of the gods – his own power – against this young rebel, who (as he has been convinced by Fricka) is after all nothing but his own pawn. Also Siegmund revolts against his fate, refusing to go to Valhalla because he will not see his beloved Sieglinde there. In addition Wagner, as well as providing these motivations for the two characters, preferred to present Wotan here, with the inimical attitude he invented for him, not in his guise as the Wanderer, but in his basic role in Teutonic mythology – *Heervater*, the battle-god, with his attendant Valkyries. This decision, of course, fitted in with his desire to leave Wotan's appearance as the Wanderer until *Siegfried*, where he acts almost entirely as a benevolent observer of events, rather than as a ruthless controller of them.

It is in his basic role of battle-god that Wotan-Odin appears in the third passage of narrative that Wagner drew on. This also appears in *Volsunga saga*; but the version there is an adaptation of a prose-link in the *Ballad of the Victory-Bringer* in the *Poetic Edda*, which is given here because it is slightly fuller. It is a piece of narrative telling the history of the sleeping Brynhild (called in this poem Sigrdrifa – the Victory-Bringer), when Sigurd has awoken her:

> She gave her name as Sigrdrifa, and she was a Valkyrie. She told how two kings warred with each other: one was called Hjalmgunnar, an old man and a great warrior, and Odin had promised him the victory; the other was Agnar, the brother of Auda – there was no one willing to shield him. Sigrdrifa slew Hjalmgunnar in the battle; but Odin, as a punishment for this, pricked her with a sleep-thorn, and said that from then on she should

never again win victory in battle, but should be married. 'But I said to him that I had made a vow never to marry a man who could be afraid'.

The fourth passage, expanding this, is from another lay in the *Poetic Edda*, called *Helreith Brynhildar* (Brynhild's Ride to Hel). This poem tells how Brynhild, after being burned on a funeral pyre, journeys on the hearse to Hel, the cold and misty land of the dead, and how her way is barred by a giantess, who arraigns her for the harm she has done. Brynhild tries to justify her deeds by telling her story: she narrates the same events as in the passage from the *Ballad of the Victory-Bringer* just quoted, but adds a verse telling how Odin surrounded her in her sleep with fire, to keep away every man except the one who did not know the meaning of fear. And she makes clear that Odin realized this man would be Sigurd (Siegfried):

> I killed Hjalmgunnar · the ancient King,
> sent him down · to the depths of Hel;
> made Agnar the victor · Auda's brother:
> then grim was Odin's · anger against me.
>
> With shields he enclosed me · in Skatalund,
> red and white · their rims overlapping;
> then he willed · that I should be woken
> by him who fearless · was ever found.
>
> He set round my hall · that faced the south
> the foe of the branches[2] · blazing high,
> and decreed that one · alone should cross it –
> he who would give me · Fafnir's gold.

It was in these last two passages that Wagner found the opportunity of making the crucial link he needed. Nowhere in the mythology does Brünnhilde appear except in conjunction with Siegfried; but Wagner, by replacing the anonymous Hjalmgunnar and Agnar[3] with Hunding and Siegmund, was able to connect Brünnhilde with Siegfried's parents. As Jessie L. Weston said, this 'cannot be considered otherwise than as a dramatic gain': by means of it, Wagner was able to construct the continuous, taut, coherent plot he needed. And he filled out this plot, and enriched his symbolism greatly, by devising scenes which have no exact equivalents in the mythology, but are based on the mythology's general ideas: Odin as battle-god telling a Valkyrie which side to take in a combat between two warriors; Odin (and Wotan) as battle-gods

---

[2] 'foe of the branches' is a 'kenning' (poetical periphrasis) for 'fire'.

[3] Nothing is known of them except the information in these two passages.

being worsted in arguments with their wives; a Valkyrie becoming involved in the life and death of a hero. Finally, there was the tying-up of two loose ends. The preservation of the pieces of Siegmund's sword for his unborn son, carried out in *Volsunga saga* by Hjordis, had obviously to be transferred to Sieglinde (with Brünnhilde assisting); and the saving of the life of Sieglinde, who is in an even more perilous situation than Hjordis (she is at the mercy of Wotan), would obviously have to be effected by Brünnhilde. All this plot-work, and the symbolism which Wagner imposed on it, must now be examined in detail; and it will be most convenient to start at the beginning of Act 2, with the battle-god and the Valkyrie.

As said in the section on Scene 2 of *The Rhinegold*, Odin-Wotan, with his spear, was, as a matter of historical fact, the primeval battle-god of the ancient Teutons (Wotenaz), with all the gruesome characteristics which that implies. But Wagner's Wotan, in *The Rhinegold*, does not figure as battle-god at all. He appears there as chief of the gods, ruler of the world with a basically civilizing mission, symbolized by his spear, which Wagner transformed into an instrument of law; and at the same time he is an astute and devious tyrant. In *The Valkyrie*, however, we see the other aspect of the spear, and the other side of Wotan too: the battle-god appears, with the spear as an instrument of war, dealing death to those whom he does not favour. As usual, Wagner managed to have it both ways. The spear which he turned into an instrument of law and civilization is still the instrument of war that it was in the mythology: the type of man who rises to rule and roughly civilize the world, by giving it laws, nevertheless gains or maintains his power by force of arms, by the maxim 'Might is Right'.

Throughout the *Poetic Edda* there appear, as periphrases for the name of Odin, the names *Valfadir, Herfadir,* and *Sigfödr*, which are all titles for him as battle-god: *Valfadir* means 'Father of the Slain' (as Valholl means 'Hall of the Slain'); *Herfadir* means 'Father of Hosts' (i.e. of armies); and *Sigfödr* means 'Father of Victory'. And in Acts 2 and 3 of *The Valkyrie* Wagner used the German equivalents – *Walvater, Heervater,* and *Siegvater*: all three are merely etymological transformations of the old Norse names, though one German legend about Wotan has survived which does represent him as the god who dispenses victory (summarized on p. 128). In *The Valkyrie*, we do not see Wagner's Wotan on the stage as Father of Hosts;[4] but he certainly figures as Father of the Slain and Father of Victory, and he appears in these roles immediately at the beginning of Act 2, with his Valkyrie, Brünnhilde.

The word 'Valkyrie' (Old Norse *valkyrja,* modern German *Walküre,* Anglo-Saxon *wælcyrge*) means 'chooser of the slain' – of those whom Odin decided should die in battle and go to Valholl; and the Valkyries, acting under the orders of the Father of the Slain, saw to it that they did die, and escorted them there. Moreover, under the orders of the Father of Victory, they made sure that those whom he favoured were victorious; and they also served the drinks in Valholl. (See p. 144 for the *Prose Edda's* summary of their activities.)

As with Odin-Wotan, the original Valkyries, as a matter of historical fact, were a terrifying part of the primitive Teutonic war-cult: they were the priestesses of the battle-god – grisly old women who officiated at the sacrificial rites when prisoners were put to death ('given to Odin') – and who sometimes did the killing themselves, which often involved use of the ritual spear. As H. R. Ellis Davidson[5] says:

It would hardly be surprising if strange legends grew up about such women, who must have been kept apart from their kind for these gruesome duties. Since it was often decided by lot which prisoners should be killed, the idea that the god 'chose' his victims, through the instrument of the priestesses, must have been a familiar one, apart from the obvious assumption that some were chosen to fall in war.

By the time of the *Poetic Edda*, these 'strange legends' had transformed the gruesome old 'Valkyries' of historical fact into supernatural warrior-women who took an active part in battles, and decided, according to Odin's orders, who should win and who should die. But there are two different conceptions of the nature of Valkyries in the *Poetic Edda*. On the one hand – in the lays of the gods – they seem to be supernatural creatures, of no known parentage, who belong entirely to the gods' world. The *volva*, in *The Wise-Woman's Prophecy*, tells Odin:

---

[4] Nevertheless, the fact that in Act 3 two of the Valkyries, Helmwige and Ortlinde, are carrying on their saddles dead heroes – Sintolt the Hegeling and Wittig the Irming – suggests this wider range of Wotan's activities; and Wotan admits to Fricka in Act 2 that 'wherever bold forces spring up, I openly encourage warfare'.

[5] Op. cit.

> Valkyries I saw · from afar assemble,
> ready to ride · to the ranks of the gods:
> Skuld held the shield · Skogul came after,
> Gunn, Hild, Gondul · and Geirskogul.
> You have heard the names · of Herjan's[6] maidens
> who as Valkyries ride · around the world.

Odin himself, in *The Ballad of Grimnir*, gives another, almost
entirely different list of the Valkyries who serve the drinks in
Valholl:

> Hrist and Mist · hand me the horn,
>   Skeggjold and Skogul;
> Hild and Thrud · Hlok and Herfjotr,
>   Gol and Geironul.
> Randgrid and Radgrid · and Reginleif
>   Bring the heroes beer.

All these Valkyries, of whom we hear nothing else anywhere in the
mythology, seem to be envisaged as formidable other-wordly
beings, with no human attributes at all. The names 'Skogul',
'Hlok', and 'Gol', for example, mean respectively 'Raging', 'Shriek-
ing', and 'Screaming'.

On the other hand, in the lays of the heroes, where alone we
find bands of Valkyries taking part in battle, only the leader is
given a name; and she invariably turns out to be a *human*
warrior-woman, the beautiful young daughter of a king, a kind of
romantic heroine, though also possessed of supernatural powers.
The only three occasions on which this happens are in the three
lays concerning Helgi: he was in fact a Danish hero, but the
Icelandic bards eventually wove him into the story of the Volsungs
by making him the son of Sigmund by Borghild (see p. 289). In the
first lay, a prose-link tells us:

Helgi was once sitting on a hill, when he saw nine Valkyries riding; one
of them was the most lovely. She said . . .

One of the things she said was how Helgi could obtain a wonderful
sword:

> Swords I know lying · in Sigarsholm,
> just four less · than five times ten.
> One of them · is the best of all,
> the destroyer of shields · trimmed with gold.

---

[6] Another periphrasis for Odin: 'Leader of Hosts'.

And then, in the next prose-link, we discover who she was:

There was a king called Eylimi, whose daughter was Svava; she was a Valkyrie and rode through the air and on the sea. She often sheltered Helgi in battles after this.

Helgi obtained the sword that Svava had told him of, and she protected his fleet from disaster in an ensuing naval engagement. And we learn from a further prose-link:

King Helgi came to King Eylimi and asked for the hand of his daughter Svava. Helgi and Svava were betrothed, and loved each other famously. Svava remained at home with her father, but Helgi went out on expeditions. Svava was still a Valkyrie, as before.

In the second and third lays, the name of the leader of the Valkyrie band is Sigrun, who is the daughter of King Hogni.[7] In a prose-link in the third lay, we read:

There was a king called Hogni, whose daughter was Sigrun. She was a Valkyrie and rode through the air and across the sea.

She fell in love with Helgi; and when her father wanted her to marry another warrior, Hodbrodd, she turned for help to Helgi, who was away fighting:

When she heard this, she rode away with the Valkyries across air and sea to find Helgi . . .

> Sigrun the joyful · victor sought;
> Helgi's hand · she pressed to her heart;
> she greeted the king · 'neath his helm she kissed him.
>
> The king was moved · by the maiden's acts:
> long with all · her heart she had loved
> Sigmund's son · before she had seen him.
>
> *Sigrun says:*
> 'They betrothed me to Hodbrodd · before the host;
> but I want to marry · another man.
> Yet King, I fear · the wrath of my friends:
> it will foil an ancient · wish of my father.'
>
> *Helgi says:*
> 'Have no fear · of Hogni's anger,
> nor the unkindness · of your kin.
> You shall, maiden · with me now live:
> your noble birth · I know full well.

[7] Not the same Hogni who is the Scandinavian equivalent of the German Hagen.

Helgi set out with a fleet to do battle with Hodbrodd, and again the Valkyrie protected the ships:

> On the sea, a man-killing storm overtook them. Lightning flashed above them and strokes of it struck the ship. Then they saw in the air nine Valkyries riding, and recognized Sigrun. And immediately the storm subsided, and they came safely to land.

Helgi's army defeated Hodbrodd's, and Hodbrodd was killed. So was Sigrun's father, Hogni, by Helgi himself; nevertheless, she married Helgi, and bore him sons. But Sigrun's brother, Dag, killed Helgi to avenge his father; and after that, 'Sigrun, through grief and sorrow, did not live much longer'.

Neither of these Valkyries, Svava nor Sigrun, is represented as acting *under orders from Odin* in protecting Helgi, making him victorious, and seeing that his enemies come to grief. Yet there is a strong implication that they must be, since Odin also figures in the story: in the third lay, he gives Sigrun's brother Dag his own spear to kill Helgi with, and when Helgi arrives in Valholl he appoints him to rule over everything with himself. Since Helgi is represented as a Volsung, the son of Sigmund, Odin is his great-great-great-grandfather; and he is shown here ending Helgi's life much as he ended Sigmund's, through the agency of his spear, and receiving him into Valholl. Therefore, until Odin decided it was Helgi's time to die, Svava and Sigrun must, as Valkyries, have been commanded by him to see that Helgi was continually victorious.

If we now turn to Brynhild, we find that she is another of these human Valkyries. Admittedly, when we first meet her, in the passage in the *Ballad of the Victory-Bringer*, where she is awoken by Sigurd and tells the story of Hjalmgunnar and Agnar, she seems to be a supernatural figure, since she is simply described as a Valkyrie named Sigrdrifa (Victory-Bringer), and no parentage is given for her (see p. 314). However, the fact that Odin has decreed that she shall be a Valkyrie no more, but shall be married, implies that she is a human Valkyrie, since there is no case in the mythology of a supernatural creature being turned into a human being. Also, in the equivalent passage in *Volsunga saga*, her name is given as Brynhild, and Sigurd says: 'I have heard that you are the daughter of a rich king'. She does not take up this point, but later on in the saga, before Sigurd goes to the Giukungs (Gibichungs), we find that she has *returned home* and Sigurd revisits her there, to renew their troth. And now she is revealed as being the daughter of King Budli: she has a sister called Bekkhild, who 'had stayed at home and learnt weaving, while Brynhild wore helmet and armour, and went to war'.[8] Brynhild, then, is a human Valkyrie, like Svava and Sigrun; and although she is not represented in the mythology as leading a band of Valkyries in action like them, it is nevertheless clear, from what she tells Sigurd in retrospect about Hjalmgunnar and Agnar, that she has been engaged in Valkyrie activities *under the orders of Odin*, since she says that she disobeyed those orders, and was punished for it.

Wagner, however, wanted it both ways once more, since he needed to represent the change in Brünnhilde's character from a non-human agent of Wotan to a compassionate woman. And certain scholars' views of the mythology offered him some justification. They held that, in the earlier, perhaps unwritten mythology, there must have been *two* Valkyries connected with Sigurd – Sigrdrifa, the superhuman Valkyrie that he awakened on the mountain, and in another source altogether Brynhild, the human Valkyrie that he met in her home – and that the two figures became unified into one person by the time of the *Poetic Edda* and *Volsunga saga*. And so in Act 2 of *The Valkyrie*, as far as the moment when Brünnhilde changes her mind and decides to help Siegmund, Wagner makes her a supernatural Valkyrie, entirely subservient to Wotan; but from that moment onwards, he represents her as a human Valkyrie, defiant of him. Even so, Wagner made her from the beginning, and throughout, the daughter of Wotan, thereby defying the fact that in the mythology no supernatural creature becomes a human being.

Wagner, of course, *needed* to make Brünnhilde the daughter of Wotan, so as to keep Wotan at the very centre of events, as the progenitor of all the characters who are engaged in rebelling against him, or rather in bringing to pass what the better part of him dimly envisages as the only hope for his power-dominated world. And in doing so, he found some justification in one of Jacob Grimm's more dubious speculations in *Deutsche Mythologie*. Grimm, in his chapter on Wodan, points out that in the Scandinavian sources, one of Odin's names is Oski (Wish), and Odin's Valkyries are sometimes referred to as 'Oskmeyar' (Wishmaidens). By Grimm's own phonetic law, the contemporary Old

[8] 'Bekkhild' means 'Bench-Woman', and 'Brynhild' means 'Coat-of-Mail Woman'.

High German equivalent of the Old Norse word 'Oski' should have been 'Wunsco', or 'Wunscjo', but he could not find such a word in the German literature surviving from that period. He did find, however, in *Middle* High German poetry and prose, its equivalent, the word 'Wunsch' (which even today is the German word for 'wish'), used to denote a god-like being who dispensed 'the sum total of well-being and blessedness'. He gives some fifty examples of its use, including two of 'des Wunsches kint' (Wish's child), and one of 'ein Wunschkint' (a Wish-child). The implication is that these were later German usages, akin to the Old Norse usage 'Oskmeyar' (Wish-maidens) for Odin's Valkyries, and therefore, since 'Oski' was Odin, 'Wunsch' had originally been Wotan. Wagner no doubt assumed, on the analogy of 'Wunschkint' (Wish-child), that the Norse 'Oskmeyar' (Wish-maidens) were really 'Wish-daughters' – i.e. 'daughters of Odin'. And so he made his Valkyries the daughters of Wotan. That this was his chain of reasoning is evident from Brünnhilde's use, in her scene with Siegmund, of the word 'Wunschmädchen' to refer to the Valkyries who serve the drinks in Valhalla, and Siegmund's use, in the same scene, of the word 'Wotanskind' in addressing Brünnhilde. These formations Wagner could not have derived from anyone but Grimm.

So Wagner made his Valkyries, and even Brünnhilde at the beginning of Act 2, supernatural beings, the daughters of Wotan (by the earth-goddess Erda, who is not in the mythology – see p. 226). But for the details of their activities, he had to rely on the accounts of the human Valkyries, Svava and Sigrun: in these accounts, as will have been noticed, the number of Valkyries is usually given as nine, which Wagner accepted, and one of them is either described as the fairest or identified as the leader, and this one became for him Brünnhilde. She acts as a supernatural Valkyrie in the early stages of Act 2 of *The Valkyrie*, accepting Wotan's orders, first to give victory to Siegmund, and then (unwillingly) to Hunding; but later she takes upon herself the status of a human Valkyrie, defying Wotan's orders, championing the Volsungs, and later becoming involved in the life and death of Siegfried. It should be noticed, in passing, that Wagner took two other points from the account of the Valkyrie Sigrun and the hero Helgi. Brünnhilde says, in Act 3 of *Siegfried* –

> O *Siegfried! Siegfried!* . . .
> *If you only knew, delight of the world,*
> *how I always loved you!*
> *I fostered you,*
> *before you were born* . . .

– which clearly derives from the description of Sigrun's love for Helgi:

> Long with all · her heart she had loved
> Sigmund's son · before she had seen him.

And the *name* Sigrun – Germanized as Siegrune – Wagner gave to one of his own Valkyries.

However, for the moment, we see Brünnhilde acting out the bit of pre-history that Wagner invented for her. In fact we see a dramatization of a situation often implied in the mythology but never represented as actually taking place – a Valkyrie gladly receiving orders from the Father of Victory to see that his favourite triumphs in the forthcoming fight.

Wotan's plans with regard to Siegmund are now almost accomplished, and at the beginning of Act 2 he stands at the top of a mountain-gorge, giving Brünnhilde her orders. She is to see that Siegmund is victorious over Hunding, and after that, he will, as Wotan sees it, be ready to kill the dragon Fafner and regain the ring for his father.

But Brünnhilde, after receiving her orders, sees the angry Fricka approaching in her ram-drawn chariot. She seems to have had some experience of the marital strife between Wotan and Fricka, since she chaffs Wotan about Fricka's arrival: she says that, much as she relishes combats between heroes, the prospect of husband-and-wife combat does not appeal to her, and she quickly gets out of the way. By this brief bit of business, Wagner deftly indicated that he intended Fricka, Wotan's wife, the goddess of marriage, champion of convention and the laws established by him, and Brünnhilde, his Valkyrie daughter, champion of his new plans against his own laws, to be at opposite poles: to embody, in fact, *the* two opposite poles of Wotan's own character. But Brünnhilde, the Valkyrie under orders, does not as yet understand all the issues involved, and is amused by the whole thing; she has no idea that a catastrophe is looming. Wotan, on the other hand, is well aware of all the issues involved, and is extremely uneasy, as is shown by his words:

> *The old storm,*
> *the old trouble!*
> *Yet here I must make a stand!*

This particular altercation between Wotan and Fricka has no actual equivalent in the mythology: it is based on the mythology's general idea of strife between the chief of the gods and his wife. In the *Ballad of Grimnir*, in the *Poetic Edda*, Odin and Frigg argue about the merits of two human heroes, their respective favourites (the passage is quoted on p. 150); and Jacob Grimm, in his *Deutsche Mythologie*, referred to a passage in a Latin work by an eighth-century Christian writer – the *History of the Goths*, by Paulus Diaconus – which narrates a 'ridiculous fable' of the ancient Germans about contention between Wôdan and his wife over two warring tribes, again their respective favourites (the passage is summarized on p. 128). And in both cases, the outcome of the argument is the wife's outwitting of the husband, who is then forced to abandon his own favourite, and support the favourite of his wife.

These two marital quarrels, as can be seen, strike us as quite unimportant, since they have no wider implications. But the quarrel between Wotan and Fricka, in Act 2 of *The Valkyrie*, is provided with the most concentrated tragic content. In spite of the slyly humorous picture Wagner draws of the great battle-god – Father of Hosts, Father of the Slain, and Father of Victory – being given a sound drubbing by his jealous and righteously indignant wife (no doubt based on his own personal experience with his first wife, Minna), the issue at stake is no less than the life or death of the love-inspired 'free hero' Siegmund, and probably of his beloved Sieglinde. It is not that Fricka 'outwits' Wotan: she defeats him fairly in argument because she appeals to that side of his character which originally led him to make her his wife – the old, conservative, power-dominated side responsible for his creation of his authoritarian world with its immutable laws. Although he does not realize it, this side is still far stronger than his new, progressive side, committed to circumventing these laws through his children the Volsungs, since his new side has as yet no real appreciation of the value of love. So once Fricka points out that his pursuit of his new ideas will inevitably result in the destruction of the world of the gods he created with his old ideas – and further, that he is in fact only battling against himself, since Siegmund is no more than his own pawn – he can only give in. Fricka awakens scant sympathy – rather hostility – from a modern audience, since she stands against progress, and against the triumph of love; but Wagner, giving the character, as always, its own integrity, makes it clear that – with Wotan's precarious imbalance between the two sides of his character – Fricka is right. Perhaps it is because she is *so* right that she receives such little sympathy.

In a sense, she is simply an *alter ego* of Wotan; but we must preserve the separate identity of Wagner's characters, if we are not to find the scene on the stage confusing. She stands there as Wotan's wife, who embodies all Wotan's old ideas – the power of the gods, the immutable laws by which it was created, the stability it has always known. Enough has already been said in advance about the symbolic significance of this scene, and so it will suffice to summarize it as clearly as possible. Fricka, suppressing her jealous anger, approaches Wotan with all the calm majesty of the ruler's consort, goddess of marriage and of the rights of marriage – although she implies disdainfully that he has been trying to evade this confrontation. And she puts forward her plea, based on one of the 'immutable' laws established by Wotan: the Volsung twins have wronged Hunding by adulterously breaking up his marriage; Hunding has prayed to her, as the goddess of marriage, for vengeance; and she has promised him that punishment will be forthcoming. The old Wotan would have administered the punishment without question; but the new Wotan, who is the Volsungs' father, asks – irresponsibly from Fricka's point of view – what harm the pair have done, since they were motivated by love.

Fricka brings him back to the 'holy vow of marriage'. Wotan objects calmly that the 'vow' cannot be 'holy' which unites two people who are not in love – in other words, Hunding *forced* marriage on Sieglinde. This is again the new Wotan, offering special pleading on behalf of his daughter Sieglinde; the old Wotan, who had no objection at all to force, would never have put forward such an argument. Fricka then points out that the adulterous union between the Volsung pair is also incestuous: rooted in convention, she asks, with horror, when such a thing was ever heard of. The new Wotan, who has no use at all for convention, but is always looking for something new, is unperturbed: he replies that it has been heard of now – things can happen of their own accord which never happened before.

Then suddenly Fricka, motivated by insecurity, adopts a different argument, and presses it with great anger. Is it then to be the end of the gods, she asks: their rule is based on the immutable laws that Wotan has established, but Wotan himself is destroying those laws in favouring the Volsung twins. This further mention of the Volsung twins reminds her that they are the product of Wotan's own adultery with a mortal woman; and she pours out all her sexual jealousy and her contempt for mere human beings, whom she sees as nothing compared with the gods. Here she brings her argument as the goddess of marriage home to her own husband: Wotan himself has been unfaithful and deserves to be punished, or at least to be forced to make restitution of conjugal rights, according to his own laws. But the new Wotan still remains unimpressed. Quietly, he points out that the gods are in a tight corner, and that what they need is a free human hero, untrammelled by the gods' laws who will be able to do the deed which those laws prevent himself from doing. This 'free human hero', of course, is Siegmund, and the 'deed' is the regaining of the ring from Fafner.

Fricka simply asks what men can do that the gods cannot; they can only do anything by the favour of the gods. And when Wotan asks in his turn if she takes no account of their own courage, she again asks who gave them that courage. Men are only strong, she insists, with Wotan's help, and in Siegmund, his son, she only finds Wotan all over again. Wotan, moved, replies that Siegmund grew up by himself in fierce suffering, and that he never protected him. Whereupon Fricka answers:

> *Then do not protect him today!*
> *Take back the sword*
> *you gave to him.*

At Fricka's mention of the sword (how accusingly the sword's arpeggio-figure flashes across the musical texture!), everything changes. Wotan is suddenly on the defensive: he shouts angrily that Siegmund gained the sword in his hour of need, but then listens with apprehension as Fricka tells him what he knows is only the truth – 'you created the need for him'. He is perfectly aware, of course, that he has created Siegmund's whole destiny for him – his terrible hardships, his hour of need, and his finding of the sword. Siegmund is in fact, as Fricka insists, no free hero, but a pawn, a slave; and she demands his death, so that her own power, and that of the gods, shall remain unchallenged. Wotan, overcome with impotent fury, can only admit that she is right: he agrees to abandon Siegmund, and to let him die.

Brünnhilde returns, and Fricka addresses to her a parting shot of crushing irony, using one of the grandiose titles of Wotan the battle-god:

> *The Father of Hosts*
> *is waiting for you;*
> *let him tell you*
> *What course he has chosen.*

The only basis in the mythology for the scene between Wotan and Brünnhilde which follows now is that Odin is said to have ordered Brynhild to give victory to Hjalmgunnar and that she was unwilling to obey these orders. But Wotan, in ordering Brünnhilde to give victory to Hunding, is telling her to see to it that Siegmund – his own son and her human half-brother, and therefore, although she has never come into contact with him, someone of great importance to her – is killed. And this makes her disobedience a crucial matter of principle, whereas Brynhild's disobedience in the myth seems to be motivated purely by a passing sympathy for the underdog, Agnar – 'there was no one willing to shield him'. Also Wagner presents Wotan as acting in a way quite foreign to Odin, making his decision unfree and equivocal, and letting him first pour out to Brünnhilde his guilt and shame at being powerless to act as he wishes. The partial sense of guilt which he super-imposed on the mythological character towards the end of *The Rhinegold* is here intensified to the point of great vulnerability, and eventually raised to a self-destructive level.

Brünnhilde, who has only ever encountered the optimistic new Wotan before, now finds herself faced by the old Wotan in a mood of utter despair; and she realizes that something has gone appallingly wrong. When she asks him what is the matter, all she receives in reply is a violent release of the pent-up rage within him – a desperate cry that shame and misery have come upon the gods, and that he is the least free and the most wretched of all living beings. Terrified, she throws down her shield, spear, and helmet, and kneels by his side, asking him to tell her all about it; but he answers that if he were to confide in her, he would lose his firm grip on his will. She then reminds him that *she* is his will: what else *is* she, if *not* his will? And she is speaking the truth – as far as the new Wotan is concerned: the old Wotan exerted his will through the repressive laws engraved on his spear, and through the militant upholder of those laws, his wife Fricka; the new Wotan, who has been concerned with circumventing those laws by means of his agent, the 'free hero' Siegmund, has begun to exert his will through his Valkyrie daughter Brünnhilde. On the other hand, the new Wotan has been changed back into the old Wotan again, and the old Wotan is perfectly right in declaring that, if he confides in Brünnhilde, he will lose his firm grip on his will: when he actually does confide in her, a few moments later, the result is that he can no longer control her – she rebels against him. Since she is his daughter by Erda – who, as was stated in the chapter on *The Rhinegold*, represents Wotan's sense of his own destiny – she is the product of his communing with that sense of destiny, and of the new ideals born of that communing, which are concerned with trying to make something better of the power-dominated world he has built up. And as such, she will eventually act as an independent will, furthering the ideals of the new Wotan in spite of the old Wotan.

So once again we have an *alter ego* situation – and once again we must insist on retaining the separate identity of Wagner's characters, if the scene on the stage is not to become confusing. Looking at the symbolism schematically, there is only one character in the Fricka and Brünnhilde scene in Act 2 of *The Valkyrie*, and that is Wotan, with his dreadful conflict between his old and new selves, of which Fricka and Brünnhilde are merely the embodiments. But just as we must still see Fricka in her own right, as the jealous goddess of marriage who brings her husband back to 'a right way of thinking', so we must see Brünnhilde as the rebellious daughter who tries to do 'what she knows her father really wants', in spite of his wife-dominated decision. (But here, for the moment, we must see her as the subservient daughter, the disciplined Valkyrie, ready to obey his orders without argument – except that, in her evident affection for her father, we may sense a foreshadowing of the compassionate woman she will have become, through her disobedience, by the end of the act.)

The new Wotan momentarily takes over from the old, as he agrees that, in confiding in her, he is confiding in himself. And as he confides in her – or rather, *confesses* to her – all his troubles and problems come flooding out. Long ago – he begins – when youthful love lost its interest for him, he began to long for power. Aided and abetted by Loge, who afterwards deserted him, he attained and exerted power over the whole world by repressive laws, which he did not realize were latently evil; yet even in the midst of his power, he still yearned for love. Alberich, however, renounced love altogether, so as to steal the Rhinegold and make from it a ring that would confer on him power unlimited; he, Wotan, robbed Alberich of his ring, but instead of returning it to the Rhinemaidens he used it to pay for Valhalla, the castle which the giants built for him, and from which he rules the world. He had wanted to keep the ring for himself, and to make use of the tyrannical power it would confer; but the wisest of all wise-women, the earth-goddess Erda, had warned him to give it up, and had also foretold that the gods must eventually pass away.

Here, of course, Wotan is acquainting Brünnhilde with the events of *The Rhinegold,* of which she naturally has no knowledge, since she was born after those events; and at the same time Wagner is reminding the audience of those events to indicate that Wotan's present dilemma is the inevitable outcome of them. But Wagner has often been criticized for this – chiefly by the naïve type of opera-goer who has not done sufficient 'homework' on the German text, and the anti-Wagnerian type of critic whose knowledge of the text covers only its main outlines, and not its detail. Here, they have said, is one of the unnecessary *longeurs* of *The Ring*. Why should Wotan recount the events of *The Rhinegold*, with a consequent repetititon of music from that work, they have asked, when *The Rhinegold* itself has already presented these events on the stage, together with their appropriate themes? Luckily, since performances of *The Ring* in English have been given regularly in London, this uninformed criticism has largely ceased: once the text is understood in detail – as Wagner naturally intended it should be – the spectator realizes that Wotan's monologue is by no means a simple re-telling of the events of *The Rhinegold*. He is for the first time expressing his own anxious reflections on those events, and these reflections are of the utmost symbolical and psychological importance. They finally make clear – as has been argued in this interpretation – that *The Rhinegold* can only be properly understood on the basis of a conflict between political power and the claims of love; and at the same time they reveal that Wotan is overwhelmed by his own guilt in having rejected love in favour of power. As for the return of musical material from *The Rhinegold*, it is – far from being simply restated – merely hinted at in this dark new context, as if in a dream. What is more, from this point onwards – that is, for by far the greater part of the monologue – Wotan goes on to impart information about events which have taken place since the end of *The Rhinegold*, and have not yet been mentioned in *The Valkyrie*. So the supposed *longeur* – the reference to what happened in *The Rhinegold* – lasts, in the theatre, a whole eternity of two and a half minutes. Rather than criticize Wagner's prolixity, we should marvel at his powers of compression.[9]

Wotan now goes on to deal with the events which have taken place since the end of *The Rhinegold*. On hearing Erda foretell the end of the gods, he had lost all his equanimity, and had longed to find out more about it. He had descended into the bowels of the earth, overpowered Erda by the magic of love, and begotten Brünnhilde upon her. And to avert the end of the gods, he had brought up Brünnhilde with her eight sisters, to incite men – whom the gods had hitherto treated as slaves – to do battle with one another, and to bring the bravest of those killed in battle to Valhalla, to form a protective army, so that his enemies should find him prepared. And at this point Wagner used a rather desperate device, also used by Shakespeare, to remove the danger of monotony inherent in a long monologue. Just as Miranda, in *The Tempest*, is made to interject an occasional passive remark during Prospero's long opening speech, to preserve a faint illusion that the monologue is really a dialogue, so now does Brünnhilde interrupt Wotan for the same purpose. Her interposition is just as passive as Miranda's, contributing nothing to the content of the monologue: 'We have completely filled your hall – I have myself brought many heroes to you: Why are you so troubled, if we have not failed you?' Yet Wagner is able to be more successful than Shakespeare, owing to the extra dimension of music: Brünnhilde's interjection sweeps into Wotan's monologue with a natural continuity guaranteed by its coming in the middle of an orchestral development of the Valhalla theme.

And at least this interjection leads Wotan on to his next point, which is that, while he and his army of heroes could easily defeat Alberich and his army of Nibelungs, they could not do so if Alberich were to regain the ring from Fafner. With the ring – or rather, with the new stock of gold that the ring would enable him

[9] It should be said that Wagner himself had some qualms about the length of this scene, especially since it followed the none-too-short Wotan-Fricka altercation. However, after completing it, he went through both scenes in his head, at the right tempo, with a view to possible cutting, and came to the conclusion that the length was necessary for the sake of clarity. In any case they would, he said, make a tremendous impression in the theatre – which of course they always do, given a first-rate performance.

to pile up – Alberich would be able to entice Wotan's heroes away from him, and turn them against him.[10] Wotan goes on to tell Brünnhilde that he himself cannot regain the ring from Fafner by force, owing to the contract he made with Fafner to pay for Valhalla, which is engraved on his spear. Therefore he needs a free hero, independent of the laws of the gods, who will do what he himself is barred from doing – but how can he find such a hero? Any man he chooses for that task, and stimulates to perform it, cannot really be independent at all, but only an extension of himself, a pawn, a puppet.

Brünnhilde now makes her second interjection, and it is much more to the point than her first, since Wotan has begun to deal with a matter which concerns her deeply – the fate of her unknown, but nevertheless cherished, human half-brother. 'But the Volsung, Siegmund,' she asks, 'does he not act of his own accord?' The old Wotan now reappears, remembering his altercation with Fricka, and his bitter defeat by her: 'Against the counsel of the gods,' he replies, 'I incited him to be bold; but now, against the *vengeance* of the gods, his only protection is the sword – which a god's favour bestowed on him.' And he laments his stupidity in so naïvely deceiving himself – how easy it had been for Fricka to unravel the deceit! But now Brünnhilde is beginning to be really alarmed: 'So you are going to take victory away from Siegmund?'

This simple statement of the terrible decision which has been forced on Wotan, with his own agreement, intensifies his guilt to the point of self-annihilation. He reflects that, in robbing Alberich of his ring and his gold – and in spite of the fact that he soon parted with them – he has come under Alberich's curse: he must abandon the man he loves, murder the man he cherishes, and betray the man who trusts him. Then, his expression changing from one of frightful suffering to one of despair, he rises to the full height of tragic grandeur. The pomp and magnificence of the world he has created, he cries, shall fall into ruins: he will abandon his work, since the only thing he now longs for is the end which Erda

[10] The ring, we must remember, gave Alberich *immediate* power only over his fellow-Nibelungs; it is the wealth that the ring would bring him – wealth discovered in the earth by using the ring as a gold-diviner – that would enable him to exert power over everyone else, through bribery and corruption (see p. 207f). We naturally tend to think of Wotan's heroes as duplications of Siegmund, and therefore incorruptible, but Siegmund is of course an exception: Wotan's heroes are recruited from the normal world of men dominated by his own laws, which have encouraged them to seek personal power above all else, and therefore made them vulnerable to bribery.

foretold him. Then he reflects that Alberich, too, is working towards that same end. One of the things that Erda has prophesied was that 'When the dark enemy of love shall out of anger beget a son, the end of the gods will not be long delayed'. And he had since heard a rumour that Alberich had begotten a son on a woman whom he had enticed with gold: this miracle had graced the man who had renounced love, while he, Wotan, who had begotten his son with love, could not create the free hero he needed. With bitter fury, he confers his blessing on Alberich's son, when he shall be born, and bequeathes to him the glittering nothingness of the world of the gods, for him to glut his hate on. Brünnhilde, now terrified, asks Wotan what she must do. 'Fight for Fricka', he replies, 'protect marriage and its vows: since my own will is of no use for the purpose of creating a free hero, her decision is my decision too'. She pleads with him to take back his word – he loves Siegmund, she urges, and she must protect him. But Wotan is adamant: she must kill Siegmund and give victory to Hunding – and she must call on all her courage, since Siegmund will be wielding a conquering sword, and will hardly die a coward.

And now Brünnhilde, without the slightest reflection, takes her first step towards disobedience. She reminds Wotan that it is he who has always taught her to love Siegmund, and that Siegmund's noble virtues are dear to his own heart; and then she bursts out with a refusal to obey what she calls his 'two-faced command'. Wotan, who by now of course is entirely the old Wotan, is enraged to encounter what he has never encountered before – defiance from a subordinate; and his rage is intensified on the one hand by his anguish at having to abandon Siegmund in spite of his heart's wishes, and on the other by his sense that he has demeaned himself by having confessed his guilt and shame to this very subordinate. He reminds Brünnhilde that she is nothing else but the blind instrument of his will, cows her with threats of exercising the crushing destructive force of the all-powerful chief of the gods, repeats his command to her to kill Siegmund, and strides furiously away, forgetting that Brünnhilde is the instrument of his new will, not of his old one.

There is a tremendous dramatic irony in this dialogue. Wotan, confiding in Brünnhilde, has asked where on earth he can find a free hero – a hero independent of his own laws, who will not be a mere extension of himself, a pawn, a puppet. Whereupon Brünnhilde, unwittingly, straightaway reveals herself as just such a free hero, by defying his orders: in doing so, she shows that she is potentially independent of his laws, and the very opposite of a pawn or a puppet. Of course it was the new Wotan who confided in Brünnhilde, and it is the old Wotan who is confronted by her defiance. But in any case, it is evident that both Wotans are blind to the fact that the first condition of a free hero is that this free hero shall either disobey Wotan, as Brünnhilde will do, or be unaware of his existence, as Siegfried will be: in other words, that Wotan must give up his own power. Of course, the fact that Brünnhilde is a woman makes it quite impossible for him to realize that she is just the free hero he is looking for, since, as the ruler of the old European man-dominated civilization, he has the utmost contempt for women, even when, as in Fricka's case, one of them is able to dominate him.[11] Wagner himself of course, as we can see from his characterization of Sieglinde, and even more of Brünnhilde, was not bounded by such limitations. In one of his letters to Röckel (25 January 1854), he wrote: 'Siegfried alone (man alone) is not the complete "human being"; he is merely the half; only together with Brünnhilde does he become the redeemer.' And before Siegfried's birth – here, in *The Valkyrie* – Brünnhilde is to make it possible, by her lone defiance, for them both to become redeemers.

But for the moment, she still feels it her duty, as a Valkyrie, to obey Wotan's orders. She stands there a long time, shocked and dazed, reflecting that she has never seen her father in such a state before. Putting on her armour again, she feels it weighing unwontedly heavy upon her: she laments that she must betray Siegmund, and goes into the cave where she has left her horse, to wait.

Siegmund and Sieglinde now appear, she striding ahead of him breathlessly, he trying to restrain her. This scene has no basis of any kind in the mythology, not even in the characters of the two prototypes: the distraught and self-accusing Sieglinde is at the opposite pole from the hard and implacably revengeful Signy; Siegmund is full of fierce courage, certainly, but he exhibits a compassion that is quite foreign to the character of Sigmund. Grasping Sieglinde gently but firmly, he manages to persuade her to rest for a while; from his words we gather that, after their night

[11] We may remember that the crafty plan to get Valhalla built by the giants, without paying them their stipulated wage, was worked out in secret by the male gods without consulting the goddesses, as Fricka reminds Wotan in Scene 2 of *The Rhinegold*.

of love in Hunding's dwelling, she started up and ran away so fast through the forest, and across the rocky hills, that Siegmund could hardly keep up with her. He tries to calm her, and asks her to tell him what is the matter.

She embraces him lovingly, but then springs up in horror, crying that she is unworthy of him. Her body, which has been continually used by a husband who had no love for her, has died, and all that she can offer Siegmund is her corpse. Though she found the most ecstatic joy in his embrace, when he gave all his love to her, and she gave all her love to him, she is a completely dishonoured creature. She can never belong to him: she would only bring him shame and disgrace. Siegmund replies that the shame and disgrace she has suffered shall be expiated by Hunding's blood, when Nothung pierces his heart. But Sieglinde is beyond consolation – she is now simply terrified, and is visited by hallucinations. She thinks she hears the horns of Hunding and his kinsmen, and the howling of their dogs, crying to heaven about the broken marriage-vow. She stares in front of her, as if insane: 'Where are you, Siegmund? Do I still see you? Let the stars of your eyes shine on me once again: do not avoid the kiss of your abject wife!' She throws herself sobbing on his breast for a moment, but then springs up again in panic. She is certain now that she can hear Hunding's horn: Siegmund's sword will be useless against the dogs – he had better throw it away. She has a final prophetic hallucination of Siegmund's sword being shattered, and then, with a last cry of his name, she faints in his arms. Siegmund listens to her breathing to make sure that she is still alive; then, as he sits down, he draws her down with him, so that her head is in his lap. Overcome by compassion, he leans over her and tenderly kisses her on the forehead.

We should be absolutely clear that it is in no way remorse for adultery or incest that has brought Sieglinde to this pitiable state. She is certainly terrified that, in breaking the marriage-vow, she and Siegmund will be subject to the vengeance of Hunding; and she has a prophetic intuition that Siegmund will be killed and his sword shattered. But what has really driven her to distraction and near-madness is the weight of the years she has spent as the unloved wife but sexual slave of Hunding. Wagner emphasizes Sieglinde's sexual degradation – 'my body, dishonoured and disgraced, had died' – so as to emphasize what the 'rejection of love in favour of power' really means, in terms of the relationship between woman and man. And of course, this makes nonsense of Miss Weston's Victorian statement that although Hunding has 'married her against her will', nevertheless 'in those primitive times such conduct was hardly exceptional, much less unforgivable'. In this brief, swift, deeply moving scene, Wagner was concerned to stress once more the desperate plight of love in a world entirely given over to the pursuit of power. Just as, in the first act, he was careful to keep clearly in view the political theme of *The Ring*, amidst the overwhelming impact of the love of Siegmund and Sieglinde, so here, in a second act almost entirely concerned with the political theme, he was careful to keep clearly in view the love and compassion – and total vulnerability – of the Volsung twins, in Wotan's power-dominated world. The position of love, in relation to power, is scarcely more hopeful now than it was in *The Rhinegold*.

Now Brünnhilde steps out of the cave, dressed in full armour, and approaches Siegmund, to tell him that he is to die. Nowhere in the mythology is there a model for such a scene, nor is it even said as a general statement that a hero who actually saw a supernatural Valkyrie was already 'fey' – doomed to death. The scene, like Scene 1 of *The Rhinegold*, is some measure of Wagner's total absorption in the mythology and his ability to contribute entirely original ideas to it, which carry complete conviction as being a natural part of it. It can be said that, if the mythology had contained this idea, no one would have been in the least surprised.

Brünnhilde, having decided that she must obey her father's orders, is now once more the dispassionate, unquestioning executor of those orders. From her point of view, in any case, Siegmund, although he may be momentarily overcome by the fact that he is to be robbed of his victory over Hunding, will eventually be proud and glad to be going to Valhalla, the warriors' paradise. There is no indecision in her manner – though there is potentially, unknown to her, in her heart – as she tells him that he must shortly follow her. The scene continues as one of Wagner's great question-and-answer dialogues, corresponding to many such in the *Poetic Edda*, whereby the factual basis of some aspect of the mythology is expounded. The aspect expounded here is the function of a Valkyrie and the life of the chosen warriors in Valhalla – but as always with Wagner, the question-and-answer dialogue does not merely give facts: it is full of dramatic irony, and it leads to a tremendous dramatic culmination, of a far-reaching kind not to be found in the sources.

Siegmund first asks Brünnhilde who she is, so beautiful and so stern. She informs him that any warrior who becomes aware of her presence is one who is doomed to die by her choice. 'And where will you lead me?', he asks. 'To Walvater,' [Father of the Slain] she replies, 'in Valhalla'. Siegmund, no doubt, knows all about Valhalla, but he asks Brünnhilde about it to savour the bitter irony of his fate – that he is not only to be betrayed, and to die, but to be eternally separated from Sieglinde. 'Will he only meet Walvater in Valhalla?', he asks. 'And all the fallen heroes there, who will embrace and welcome you' is the answer. Will he meet his father Volsung there? – yes. Will he be greeted gladly by a woman there? – yes, by the wish-maidens; Wotan's daughter [Brünnhilde herself] will offer him drink. Siegmund now asks his all-important question, the answer to which he already knows. He grants that she seems godlike, and that he recognizes her as a holy *Wotanskind* [child of Wotan] – there is just one thing he wants to know: will his bride and sister, Sieglinde, accompany him there? The answer of course is 'no', since Valhalla is a purely male paradise, for warriors only.

This negative answer brings about the tremendous moment when Siegmund – who has been Wotan's pawn and is now to be Wotan's victim – reveals himself as nobody's anything, but simply himself (which he has believed himself to be all along, of course). He bends tenderly over Sieglinde, gently kisses her forehead, and then turns calmly to Brünnhilde. With the greatest deliberation he utters the momentous refusal: 'Then greet Valhalla for me, greet Wotan, greet Volsung and all the heroes, greet also the lovely wish-maidens; to them I will not follow you.'

Here Wagner parts company with his sources altogether. Although, as a matter of historical fact, later Norse heroes came to feel that Odin was an untrustworthy god, who might at any time abandon and even kill one of his devoted followers, no man could possibly have defied him in this way by refusing to go to Valhalla when chosen to do so. And this purely Wagnerian moment is really the decisive one in the whole of *The Ring*. In the long struggle between power and love, begun in *The Rhinegold*, love has always – despite its apparent triumph in Act 1 of *The Valkyrie* – been totally on the losing side; but now that it has its back to the wall, and seems certain to be extinguished, it makes a tremendous come-back, through Siegmund's love-motivated act of rebellion against the highest manifestation of power. From now on, owing to the effect of this act of rebellion on Brünnhilde, which makes her finally defy Wotan in her turn, love, after a dreadful struggle, will be in the ascendant. Siegmund's wretched life, deliberately engineered for him by Wotan, has finally brought him to the point where the warrior's virtues of courage and skill in combat – though he has both of them in full measure – seem as nothing to him in comparison with Sieglinde and his love for her. And this is something that the old Wotan never conceived of, and the new Wotan is still quite ignorant of – though it is the essence of that total independence of the laws of the old Wotan that the new Wotan has been seeking in his conception of a free hero. But by being transmitted to Brünnhilde, it will dissolve the power-complex of the old Wotan, and make it easier for the new Wotan – through his agents Brünnhilde and Siegfried – to take over entirely.

But there is a long way to go before this takes place. Brünnhilde, at first, regards Siegmund's defiance as senseless. She tells him that he has seen the Valkyrie's searing glance, and so he has no choice but to go with her. He replies that wherever Sieglinde is, he must be: Brünnhilde's glance does not frighten him, nor can it force him to abandon Sieglinde. Brünnhilde becomes impatient at his apparent refusal to face facts: 'So long as you are alive', she points out, 'nothing can force you; but it is death, you fool, that is going to force you, and that is what I have come to tell you'. Siegmund now decides to find out how he has been betrayed. He asks Brünnhilde the name of the hero who is going to kill him; and she tells him that it is Hunding. He replies that it is he who is going to kill Hunding; but she insists that he, Siegmund, is the one who has been chosen to die. Siegmund then asks her if she knows the sword he is bearing: the one who provided it for him decreed that he would win victory with it. But she answers, with great emphasis, that the one who provided it for him has now decreed his death, and will take away the power from the sword.

Since Siegmund has realized that she is a *Wotanskind*, carrying out Wotan's orders in choosing him as the one who is to die, it may be questioned at this point whether he becomes aware that his father Volsung, who provided the sword for him, is none other than Wotan himself. This never becomes clear, but it hardly matters, since Siegmund is prepared to defy everyone, whether

Volsung, Brünnhilde, or Wotan. He tells Brünnhilde to make less noise, or she will awaken the sleeping Sieglinde. And at this point, Wagner again created a culminating image for the love-versus-power symbolism, as he had done in *The Rhinegold*. There, when Fasolt found the last chink in the pile of gold heaped up in front of Freia, and caught sight of her glance, the shining eyes of the goddess of love were set in direct opposition to the gleaming gold of the 'accursed ring' of tyrannical world-domination. Here Siegmund bends tenderly over Sieglinde, with the words

> *Alas! Alas!*
> *Sweetest wife!*
> *Unhappiest of faithful women!*
> *Against you rages*
> *The world in arms . . .*

Again, one helpless woman, representing love, is set in direct opposition to a world of men avid for power. Siegmund goes on to call down shame on the one who provided the sword for him, for decreeing disgrace for him instead of victory, and declares that if he has to die, he will go, not to Valhalla, but to Hel – the Norse equivalent of the Greek Hades, reserved for all those except the warriors chosen for Valhalla.

Brünnhilde is completely shaken by this: she begins to under-stand Siegmund's unheard-of standard of values. She asks him if he sets such little store by everlasting bliss, and if this poor woman, weary and sorrowful, hanging exhausted from his lap, means everything to him. Siegmund looks at her bitterly, and tells her that, though she looks young and beautiful and radiant, he knows how cold and hard she is; if she can only gloat over his misery, then she will have to, but she must not tell him about the frigid delights of Valhalla. Brünnhilde now begins to be sympathe-tic towards his sufferings: with growing emotion, she asks him to leave his wife in her protection. He replies that he and no other shall protect her while she is alive; if he must die, he will kill her first. Brünnhilde, deeply moved, asks him once more to leave Sieglinde in her care, for the sake of the child in her womb. Thus it is she who acquaints him with the fact that his wife is pregnant, whereas in *Volsunga saga* it was Sigmund who acquainted his wife with the fact. Siegmund is by now beside himself – how much this Valkyrie knows about him that he does not know about himself! Since his sword, he cries – which was provided for him by a betrayer, and will now betray him like a coward – cannot serve him

The Valkyrie 339

against his enemy, he will use it to kill both his wife and her unborn son; and he makes a movement to do so.

Brünnhilde cries out to him to stop. She is now completely won over by the helpless plight of her human half-brother, his sister-wife, and her unborn son. She tells him that he shall live, and Sieglinde with him – his sword will be true to him, and she will protect him; and she rushes away through the mountains. For good or ill now, Siegmund's defiance has fortified her will to disobey Wotan, and to put all her strength on the side of love in its struggle against power. We may remember that she is the new Wotan's 'love-child' by Erda, his sense of destiny, and that the new Wotan overpowered Erda with 'the magic of love'. In communing with his sense of destiny, in order to find some way of setting the wrongs of his world to rights, he did so in a spirit of love – the love that he longed for in the midst of his power. The result was his plan concerning the Volsung twins – whom he begot, with love, by a mortal woman, and who themselves fell in love – and Brünnhilde, who, as his 'love-child' by Erda, became the embodiment of his new will to set his world to rights. But since the new Wotan's plans concerned with the Volsungs had been misconceived, so that when he was faced with Fricka he had been forced by her logic to abandon those plans and to decree the death of the son he loved, he became the old Wotan again, wedded to nothing but power. Brünnhilde, however, moved by Siegmund's distress, and spurred by his defiance, has become independent of Wotan, and is now trying to fulfil the love-inspired demands of his new will, which the old Wotan is unable to do. It is Brünnhilde's love-inspired begetting that explains how, having been brought up to be the impassive executor of Wotan's battle-orders, she can take compassion on Siegmund, and throw herself behind him, in the name of love.

In the final scene of the act, we shall see the old Wotan exerting his power-motivated will – through its symbol, the spear – in the most destructive way possible, to annihilate the love that is in revolt against it. But for the moment, as a calm before the storm, we are given one final glimpse of Siegmund's love and compassion for Sieglinde. Leaning over her again, he realizes that she is now in a deep sleep, smiling in her dreams; and deciding to let her sleep on peacefully while the battle takes place, he gets up, lays her down gently, and kisses her tenderly. Then, hearing Hunding's horn, he draws his sword and goes away to look for his enemy.

At this point we encounter one of those unexpected strokes of genius that are so characteristic of Wagner. On the empty stage, Sieglinde's happy dream turns into a nightmare: she is back in her old home, waiting for her father and her brother to return. She sees some strange men approaching: frightened, she calls out to her mother that they seem none too friendly, and then realizes that they are setting fire to the house. She feels the flames licking around her, and as she cries for help to the absent Siegmund, she wakes up with a start, to find a storm raging and to hear the voices of Siegmund and Hunding in the distance, shouting defiance at one another. As we watch her live through again the traumatic event of the Neidings' raid on her childhood home, it is finally impressed on us what a terrible, love-deprived life has been allotted to her by her father Wotan, from that moment until this present one, when she knows intuitively that her would-be rescuer, Siegmund, is about to be taken from her. In this way, Wagner gives us one final, devastating image of love at its most defenceless in a power-dominated world. For by now we can have no hope that Wotan will allow his will to be thwarted by Brünnhilde. As Siegmund and Hunding close with one another – Siegmund taunting Hunding with the fact that he now has the sword that he pulled from his house-tree – Sieglinde rushes towards them, calling with all her might to them to stop, or to kill her first. But she is turned aside by a dazzling light as Brünnhilde appears, telling Siegmund to trust to his sword, and covering him with her shield. Then, as Siegmund thrusts at Hunding, Wotan arrives through the clouds and stands over Hunding, holding his spear out crossways at Siegmund. Brünnhilde, terrified at finding herself engaged in combat with her own father – the Father of Hosts – falls back; Siegmund's sword shatters on Wotan's spear; Hunding thrusts his spear into Siegmund's breast; and Siegmund falls dead to the ground. Sieglinde, hearing his death-sigh, collapses with a cry, as if lifeless.

This incident – the shattering of the sword on the spear – is, of course, the only basis in the mythology for this final scene of the second act. But how far Wagner has come from *Volsunga saga*! There, we encounter a more or less friendly Odin, taking one of his great-great-grandsons, a hero full of years, to the Valholl he will accept as his natural reward; but Wagner presents us with the appalling spectacle of Wotan ensuring the death of his young son, whom he has loved, and admired, and regarded as his only hope of the betterment of his power-dominated world. It is of course the old Wotan, not the new, who has done this; and the new Wotan will only reappear, through the agency of Brünnhilde, near the end of the third and final act of *The Valkyrie*, by which time it will be too late to revoke his destruction of Siegmund – not that he shows any concern about that. Where does Siegmund in fact go? To Valhalla, to swell Wotan's army of heroes, or to Hel, where he said he would go, to be with Sieglinde? It may seem an idle question, but Siegmund is such a sympathetic character that we feel impelled to ask it. Wagner offers no answer – presumably because the end of the world is not far off (twenty years?), when the gods and the heroes are to be consumed in elemental fire.

Brünnhilde now reveals that, in spite of her terror when faced by Wotan as the Lord of Hosts, she is nevertheless still against him, and totally committed to the cause of the Volsungs. She turns to the unconscious Sieglinde, lifts her on to her horse, and slips away with her. Wotan is left towering over Hunding, who is pulling his spear out of Siegmund's breast. He looks sorrowfully at Siegmund's corpse, and tells Hunding, with terrible irony, to go and kneel before Fricka, and inform her that Wotan's spear has avenged what has caused her shame. 'Go!', he murmurs, with suppressed fury, and again, 'Go!' The second time, he makes a contemptuous sign with his hand, and Hunding falls dead. Ernest Newman, rather too punctiliously, criticized Wagner for this moment: he pointed out that, in his final prose-sketch, Wotan does not have the words 'Go! Go!', and Hunding is left alive; and he asked, in relation to the text as it stands, how a dead Hunding could go and kneel before a living Fricka.[12] One would have thought that, since Fricka is a goddess, a supernatural being, Hunding, whether alive or dead (if dead, he would at least go to Hel), could still have conveyed Wotan's message to her; but this is in any case beside the point. What Wagner surely intended us to understand is that Wotan, who is beside himself, vents his furious irony on Fricka and Hunding together, and then, overcome with revulsion from Hunding (Fricka's slave, as she had said that Siegmund was Wotan's 'slave'), strikes him dead.

Wotan's thoughts now turn to Brünnhilde, and he bursts into a

[12] *Wagner Nights*, p. 467.

terrible rage: when he overtakes her, she shall regret her crime, and suffer the most dreadful punishment. He disappears in thunder and lightning.

Act 3

The third act begins with the famous Ride of the Valkyries, and it might seem that, on the face of it, no interpretation of this vivid scene is necessary. Wagner is obviously in his element portraying one of the most picturesque features of the mythology – or rather of the mythology as made explicit by him. He pictures the nine Valkyries in full armour, riding through the air on horseback (without their leader for the moment) – equivalent to the nine that Helgi saw, led by Svava, and again, led by Sigrun. He gives them names of his own (though taking in Sigrun as Siegrune), and he lets them make horse-laugh jokes about the fancy one's stallion has taken for another's mare, and then about the strife between their horses caused by the former strife between the dead heroes they carry on their saddles.[1] They have come to their 'assembly area' on a mountain peak, prior to riding in a band to Valhalla with their catch for the day.

However, the Ride does at the same time reinforce the symbolism from two points of view. In the first place, it emphasizes Wotan's role as Father of Hosts – his total control of the world as battle-god: the dead heroes that four of the Valkyries have brought with them are just a few representing the countless numbers that the whole band have collected from the carnage that has been going on perpetually everywhere, stimulated by them according to Wotan's orders. Secondly, the portrayal of these eight warrior-maidens offers a normal standard of Valkyrie conduct against which to set Brünnhilde's unique act of disobedience. The only indication of what Brünnhilde was like before her early objection to Wotan's 'two-faced command' is the short scene at the beginning of Act 2, where she gladly accepts his orders to award victory to Siegmund. There, in fact, Wagner provides her with a very brief 'Ride of the Valkyries' of her own, to indicate her Valkyrie nature,

[1] Eric Blom once described the *Walkürenritt* as 'the most tasteless piece of music ever written'. What could have been the use of a *tasteful* 'Ride of the Valkyries'? In any case, the melodic and harmonic substance is something amazingly new. (Further, Eric Blom was probably referring not to this scene but to the concert version, which was much altered. Wagner never called the scene *Walkürenritt*.)

but the actual Ride reveals this nature much more clearly. The Valkyries, we can see, are cold, hard, inhuman instruments of Wotan guided only by military discipline, who regard human suffering and death as a joke, and are utterly devoid of softer and tenderer feelings. Brünnhilde has differed from them only in that Wotan has taught her to love his son and favourite Siegmund, who was her half-human brother; but in any case this 'love' was entirely at a distance, and was from Wotan's point of view paternalistic and authoritarian, as he has just shown by sacrificing Siegmund to political necessity. Nevertheless, this seed of love has grown in Brünnhilde, and come to full flower since she actually encountered Siegmund and witnessed his terrible distress. She is now more woman than Valkyrie, as Wotan will shortly be pointing out.

The eight Valkyries are waiting for Brünnhilde; and as she approaches, the contrast between them and her is emphasized still further. She is riding at an extraordinary speed, as if she were in flight; the other figure on her saddle is not a male warrior, but a woman; and when she arrives, she asks them to protect and help her in her great distress, since she is fleeing from the Father of Hosts. These actions and words are diametrically opposed to the character of a normal Valkyrie, and her eight sisters ask her if she is out of her mind, to have given the Father of Hosts cause to hunt her down. She tells them briefly what has happened with regard to Siegmund, and again they call her mad to have disobeyed the orders of the Father of Hosts. She asks six of them in turn to lend her their horses, so that she may rescue Sieglinde from Wotan's wrath, but they all refuse. Unquestioning obedience to the battle-god, and total dedication to their allotted task of carrying dead warriors to Valhalla, is all they can understand.

Sieglinde now intervenes, declaring that she has no desire to be saved. Once Siegmund was killed, all she wanted was to be killed as well, by Hunding; and she asks Brünnhilde to strike her dead then and there. But Brünnhilde tells her that she has a duty to live, on account of the boy that she bears in her womb – at which news Sieglinde's whole attitude changes entirely. Her face lights up with exalted joy, and she now begs Brünnhilde and the other Valkyries to save her and her child. Brünnhilde decides that, since none of the Valkyries will lend her a horse, Sieglinde had better escape alone, while she (Brünnhilde) stays and faces Wotan's vengeance. The Valkyries decide that Sieglinde's best course is to make for the east, for the forest where Fafner the dragon lies in his lair, guarding the Nibelung hoard. A sinister place for a helpless woman, objects one of them – but a safe refuge, Brünnhilde counters, since Wotan shuns that place like the plague. All this time, Wotan has been drawing nearer, on the crest of a storm, and Brünnhilde now gives Sieglinde last-minute instructions (based on the instructions given in *Volsunga saga* by the dying Sigmund to Hjordis). She must be brave, laugh at any dangers and tribulations she may encounter, and hold to one thought alone: that the child she bears in her womb will one day be the noblest hero in the world. She must preserve for him the pieces of his father's shattered sword, since one day he will reforge them and wield the sword anew; and Brünnhilde then gives him the name of Siegfried. Sieglinde, enraptured by what she regards as a miracle, undertakes to save her child, pours out her gratitude to Brünnhilde, and hurries away towards the east.

Wotan approaches, and his voice can be heard through the storm calling to Brünnhilde to stop. She is now overcome with fear, and the Valkyries so far go against their own natures, out of loyalty to her, as to hide her amongst them, as they turn to face the furious Wotan.

Here Wagner again parts company with his sources altogether. Although, in the mythology, Brynhild's disobedience of Odin is mentioned, presumably as an isolated instance, wholesale insubordination of this kind – mild and ineffectual as it turns out to be – is unthinkable where the Valkyries of Odin are concerned. Wagner's Valkyries beg Wotan to control his fury against Brünnhilde, but all they receive for their pains is a scathing dressing-down, beginning with a phrase which further stresses his contempt for the female sex – *Weichherziges Weibergezücht* (soft-hearted brood of women). Have they inherited this weakness from him, he asks? Did he bring them up to ride bravely into battle, did he make their hearts hard and harsh, so that they would weep and whine the moment he furiously punished disloyalty amongst them? Are they aware that Brünnhilde, who understood the innermost workings of his will, has defied that will, and turned her arms against him? Wotan uses the time-honoured argument of a father faced by a rebellious child – does she realize that she owes her very existence to him? Let her step forth, and not hide away in fear of her punishment.

Brünnhilde steps forth, humbly but firmly, and asks Wotan to pronounce his punishment. He tells her that it is not he who is punishing her – she has brought the punishment upon herself. She was the instrument of his will – that was the only reason for her existence – and she has turned that will against him; she has been a Valkyrie – one of the immortals – but she can be one no more. And here Wagner, who has been superimposing his own symbolism on his sources, links up with them once more, as he lets Wotan decree for Brünnhilde the shameful fate that Odin decreed for Brynhild. She shall be sunk into a deep sleep, and lie here on the mountain; and she shall become nothing more than a defenceless woman, the prey and chattel of any man who happens to pass this way and wake her. Brünnhilde's Valkyrie sisters, appalled by the fate that Wotan is allotting her, are again moved to expostulate with him, and beg him to rescind his terrible judgement. But Wotan quells them instantly. Brünnhilde has been banished from their company, he tells them, and shall become a mere submissive wife of a mortal man, spinning by the fireside, a butt for the mockery of men – at which contemptuous dismissal she utters a cry and falls to the ground. The other Valkyries, horrified, draw away from her, and Wotan tells them to abandon her: if any one of them shows any sympathy for her, she shall suffer the same dreadful fate. Completely cowed, they run to their horses, with cries of woe, and ride away, amid thunder-clouds and flashes of lightning. The storm soon subsides, and the weather turns calm again, as Wotan and Brünnhilde remain alone on the stage.

Here, once again, Wagner reveals his sure dramatic instinct. He has made Wotan pronounce his cruel punishment of Brünnhilde in front of the Valkyries for two reasons. First, so as to allow him to reassert his absolute authority over them as battle-god; second, and more important, so as to leave free the long final scene of the drama for the argument between Wotan and Brünnhilde about the rights and wrongs of what she has done – the argument in which she eventually induces him to become the new Wotan again – and more than that, the *real* new Wotan – by showing him the way to achieve this.

The mythological basis for this scene, as stated earlier, consists of two brief statements in the *Poetic Edda*. The first occurs in a prose-link in the *Ballad of the Victory-Bringer:*

Odin, as a punishment, . . . pricked [Brynhild] with a sleep-thorn, and said that from then on she should never again win victory in battle, but should be married. 'But I said to him [Brynhild speaking] that I had made a vow never to marry a man who could be afraid.'

Here, of course, Brynhild is a human Valkyrie who is being made to give up arms in favour of marriage, whereas Wagner's Brünnhilde suffers the far greater degradation (never suffered by anyone in the mythology) of being turned from a supernatural Valkyrie into a mortal wife. Degradation, that is, in the eyes of Wotan and her sister Valkyries, and in her own eyes at first; but there can be no doubt that Wagner saw the metamorphosis of the cold, Wotan-dominated Valkyrie into a warm, compassionate, and rebellious woman as a great step forward in humanity's quest for a world based on fellowship and love.

The second passage is given to Brynhild, in the poem *Brynhild's Ride to Hel*, after she has been burnt on a funeral pyre, and is confronted by an accusing giantess on the way to Hel. She says of Odin:

> He set round my hall · that faced the south
> the foe of the branches [fire] · blazing high,
> and decreed that one · alone should cross it –
> he who would give me · Fafnir's gold.

Why Odin should have decreed that only Sigurd should wake the sleeping Brynhild is not stated; but Wagner accepted this element, giving it his own motivation. And the motivation he gave it is this. The Wotan who is punishing Brünnhilde – for turning, as the instrument of his will, against him – is the old Wotan, dominated by Fricka, and thus still concerned entirely with the power of the gods; whereas Brünnhilde, in so far as she is the instrument of Wotan's will, is the instrument of the will of the new Wotan, who has been ranged on the side of his children the Volsungs, and particularly on the side of Siegmund, the son he has reared to defy the laws of the gods. Herein lies Wotan's illogical position; and Brünnhilde argues against it for all she is worth, advocating the cause of the Volsungs by emphasizing the existence of their unborn son, Siegfried, and the possibility of her joining forces with him, when he grows up. But so entrenched is Wotan in the character of his old self that it takes her a long time to convince him.

From this moment onwards, *The Ring* moves on to a different plane: that of a change in human nature taking place in the hearts of one or two individuals. Hunding is gone, and so are the Neidings, the representatives of Wotan's power-dominated world of men; in Act 3 of *The Valkyrie*, and in the whole of *Siegfried*, human society disappears from the scene, only to return, completely unchanged, as the Gibichungs in *The Twilight of the Gods*. What has happened to the oppressed Nibelungs of *The Rhinegold*? – Wagner does not tell us. What has happened to the ring – the instrument of total world domination? Wagner at least has told us this: its power is suspended, as it were, since it is being guarded in a cave in the forest by the dragon Fafner, who has neither the will nor the intelligence to make use of it. And Wagner has also told us what has happened to Alberich, the creator of the ring: he has begotten a human son to act as his agent in his quest to regain it from Fafner. Thus everything is in abeyance for the time being: a new generation is in process of coming to maturity – Brünnhilde, Siegfried, and Hagen; and until they have reached maturity, the question 'Who is going to rule the world, and for what purpose?' remains open. Power of the old Wotan type continues, naturally, in the world of men, as will be evident from the behaviour of Gunther and Gutrune in *The Twilight of the Gods*; but whether that power is eventually going to involve the slavery of all but a few, or be abrogated in favour of the reign of human fellowship and love, who can say? Brünnhilde, and later Siegfried, are to be the champions of fellowship and love; and in the last scene of *The Valkyrie*, we see Brünnhilde, face to face with the high-handed protagonist of power – her own father – winning her own victory, and thereby achieving her independence, her maturity.

She begins by trying to get Wotan to argue instead of castigate. Still lying on the ground, she lifts her head and asks him, timidly but reproachfully, whether what she did was so shameful that it deserved so shameful a punishment; then, raising herself to a kneeling position, she pleads with him to lay aside his anger, look her in the eyes, and explain clearly the nature of her guilt. Wotan's fury has burnt itself out, and subsided into deep gloom: gravely, and without moving, he suggests that she considers what she has done – the nature of her guilt is explained clearly enough by that. Now that discussion is possible, she continues by exploiting the division between his old and new selves: she tells him that she only tried to carry out his orders. These were, of course, the orders of the new Wotan, but it is the old Wotan who replies, asking her if he gave her orders to fight for Siegmund. When she answers that he did, he reminds her that he rescinded these orders; but she replies that he only did so when Fricka had made him a stranger to his original intention, an enemy to himself. This brings a bitter rebuke from the old Wotan: she must have thought him cowardly and stupid, but if it were not for her treachery, he would hardly have punished her for that, since she would have been too insignificant a target for his anger.

He is moving back to anger again, but Brünnhilde tactfully brings him back to the main argument, by stressing her unworthiness and then going straight to the point at issue – the conflict within him. She is not wise, she tells him, but she knew one thing – that he loved Siegmund; and she also understood the other thing which forced him – painful though the decision was – to withdraw his protection from the one he loved. But she kept her eyes on the one thing only, and she saw what he could not see, since she had to see Siegmund, to warn him of his death. What she saw was his dire distress – his great love turned to terrible suffering, and his desperate defiance. It made her feel ashamed, and she began to think how she could be of use to him: the only thing that seemed possible was to share either victory or death with him. All this stirred the love in her heart – the very love that Wotan himself had implanted there.

Wotan now seriously begins to defend himself. He stresses the dreadful anguish he had to endure, when his concern for the world which he had built up, and which he loved, compelled him to stifle his love for Siegmund in his heart – and afterwards to try to bury his grief beneath the ruins of that world (he is referring to his words to Brünnhilde in Act 2, when he despairingly envisaged letting that world fall into ruins). All this is certainly true; but now he spoils his argument by belittling the value of the love that Brünnhilde has been referring to. While he was suffering in this way, he continues, she was consoling herself with sweet pleasure, laughing as she drank the blissful draught of love. These are extraordinary phrases with which to describe Brünnhilde's intense life-and-death involvement in Siegmund's fate: they reveal that love – real love, including compassion, acting as a dynamic social force – still has no value for Wotan, because he does not understand it. He apparently has not even taken in Brünnhilde's statement that she was prepared to share death with Siegmund – destruction at Wotan's hands. With this incomprehension of love, he tells her that she must follow her own 'light mind', which has caused her to sever herself from him: she can no longer take part in his councils.

Brünnhilde keeps to the point – that her love was at one with his own love for his son. She could not understand his second command; all that she understood was that she must love the one that he loved. Then she takes her stand on the fact that she is, as his will, an essential part of him, indeed a half of him. Surely, she insists, he cannot want to dishonour this half of him in a way that would dishonour himself: if she is to become a butt for the mockery of men, he too will be disgraced. But Wotan retorts with a brutal remark which shows him to be still the old Wotan, who has supported enforced marriage without love: 'You followed blissfully the power of love – now follow the man that you will have to love'. Faced by this refusal to admit her stature as half of himself, she begs him that, if she must become the wife of a domineering man, that man shall be no cowardly boaster, but someone fully worthy of her. But Wotan merely replies that he cannot choose for her – she has severed herself from him and his decisions. Brünnhilde's last remark shows that she has Siegfried in mind, and now she murmurs confidentially to Wotan, telling him three things about the Volsungs that he does not yet know: that the greatest of all heroes will one day be born of the Volsung race that he has begotten; that Sieglinde will bear this child, in sorrow and suffering; and that she has in her possession the sword that he provided for Siegmund. To the first two pieces of information, Wotan simply replies that he has abandoned the Volsungs, and will do nothing to protect the wife; but when she mentions the sword, he becomes angry, and shouts that it was shattered to pieces by him. She must not try to disturb his spirit, he continues more quietly: he must carry out the punishment now – sink her in a deep sleep, for the first passer-by to awaken and claim as his wife – and leave her.

During the foregoing, Brünnhilde has risen to her feet, but now she falls on her knees again, and implores Wotan, if he will not rescind her punishment, to surround her in her sleep with something terrifying, so that only a fearless hero will be able to find her and awaken her. But Wotan still will not relent: she asks too great a favour, he replies. Whereupon she clasps his knees, and makes her final plea: rather than inflict such a shameful punishment on her, she begs, let Wotan wipe her out of existence with his spear. Then she is struck by a sudden flash of wild inspiration: let the 'something terrifying', that she has asked to be surrounded with, be a great fire, which will destroy any coward who tries to cross it. At this, Wotan is suddenly overcome and deeply moved, and yields at last, turning back, as if by magic, into the new Wotan again. He turns to Brünnhilde ardently, lifts her to her feet, and gazes with emotion into her eyes. He now reveals that he really does love his daughter, who has so bravely disobeyed him in his own best interests, and that she is in fact the pride of his heart. He becomes as warmly loving as he had been coldly dismissive before, bidding her a long, passionate, regretful farewell. For he has to part from her – but he will set such a bridal fire blazing for her as never blazed for any other bride; and through it only the one fearless hero shall come, who will be freer than Wotan, the god. He lays her down, kisses her godhood away, and puts her to sleep; then, thrusting his spear out and thus exerting the force of his will, he commands Loge to set his fire blazing around the mountain peak. As the flames arise, and encircle the peak, he sets his seal on the situation with a final edict: 'The man who fears the point of my spear shall never cross the fire!' Then, with one last sad look at the sleeping Brünnhilde, he vanishes through the fire.

Brünnhilde's courage, pertinacity, and inspiration have finally brought Wotan to recognize the truth. She is no 'light-minded' rebel, 'consoling herself with sweet pleasure', but, as she told him, 'half of himself' – the better half of himself, it can be said, who has understood what he, blinded by his obsession with power, has been incapable of understanding. She has in fact restored him from the old Wotan, in despair, to the new Wotan, with great hopes for the future of his world, by solving for him his apparently insoluble problem of finding a free hero, totally independent of himself. Not that this solving of the problem is the sole reason for his affection for Brünnhilde: he loves her for what she has done for him, certainly, but it is for what she is that he loves her as well, now that he can see clearly what that is. Also, he evidently loves her dearly for herself, since he is deeply grieved at having to part with her. In his farewell, he thinks of all the happy times they have spent together; he rhapsodizes about her eyes and her voice, and kisses her tenderly; and he thinks with envy of the 'happier man' on whom, one day, her eyes will shine, as they will shine no more on him. And when she is asleep, he gazes at her sadly, and he does so again as he strides away to conjure up the fire, and again when he finally vanishes through the flames. Here, in this last scene of *The Valkyrie*, Wagner has woven into his great social and political vision a profoundly moving element of father- and-daughter love, just as in the first act he wove in a profoundly moving element of brother-and-sister and man-and-woman love.

Of course, the two things are in no way separate, since Wagner's social and political vision is concerned with the struggle of love against power. The value of love is in fact what Wotan has been forced to recognize. The old Wotan longed for love, but in fact he was contemptuous of love, and of women, too; the new Wotan found pleasure in a paternalistic and authoritarian love for his children – though he was prepared to sacrifice them in the interests of his own power. But the *real* new Wotan who has emerged from his conflict with Brünnhilde has come to recognize exactly what love is – not as an abstract intellectual idea (no one can recognize what love is from that point of view) – but in the shape of a loving woman. For he has been made to understand, through the self-sacrificing love of Brünnhilde (his better self) for Siegmund, that he must sacrifice his own power, and let his world be taken over by the power of love. This is not made explicit in the text, but it is implicit in the solution, which Brünnhilde has provided for him, of his problem of finding a free hero. Siegfried (Wotan does not mention his name, since he does not know that Brünnhilde has given him a name) can grow up without even knowing who Wotan is, can kill the dragon of his own accord, regain the ring, keep it for himself, and – when he awakens Brünnhilde – give it to her as a love-token, learn Wotan's new love-inspired wisdom from her, and take over Wotan's world with her, in the name of love. In so far as Wotan will not give any assistance to Siegfried, he will be obliged to bequeath the future of the world to him; and in so far as Siegfried will inherit the love between his father and his mother, that future will belong to love. Whether or not Wagner intended us to assume that Wotan had it all worked out in his mind like this, we cannot tell. Probably, with his instinct for ending each of the dramas of *The Ring* with a strong sense of 'to be continued in our next instalment', he intended Wotan to be 'struck by a grand idea', as at the end of *The Rhinegold*, which comes to detailed fruition in the succeeding drama of the tetralogy. (Actually, of course, it was Brünnhilde's idea, but she is, after all, his better self, and he has now accepted her as such.)

Strangely enough, what has finally convinced Wotan is Brünnhilde's 'inspired' idea that she should be surrounded by fire. But if we remember the symbolism of *The Rhinegold*, fire means Loge, and Loge is the god of demonic mental inspiration.[2] And so

[2] See pp. 167–75.

Brünnhilde's 'inspired' idea of the fire, which is immediately accepted by Wotan as if it were his own, is the sudden demonic mental inspiration which comes to her, and then immediately to him, and makes him realize how the power-dominated world he has created can be redeemed. Bernard Shaw used all his intellectual subtlety to interpret the fire of Loge as 'the Lie' – the false truths of Christianity, enforced by the Church, which would deter anyone but the most fearless thinker from penetrating to the actual truth about the future of humanity. But as we have seen, Loge, in *The Rhinegold*, is practically the god of truth, the one character who continually tells Wotan the simple facts that he does not want to face. Also, Shaw's view is too abstract for Wagner; and in any case, he rigidly continued to interpret *The Ring* according to the political symbolism of *The Rhinegold*, without realizing that Act 3 of *The Valkyrie* has moved on to the new level of a change in human nature taking place in the hearts of one or two individuals.

The point is that this second 'grand idea' which has struck Wotan will be as fruitful as the first was fruitless, because it is a *real* idea, born of the demonic mental inspiration symbolized by Loge's fire. If we think of the Wotan of Scene 4 of *The Rhinegold*, lifting the sword and hailing Valhalla with it, envisaging the army of human heroes who shall defend that mighty fortress – and further, a semi-human son who shall be the greatest hero of all, a 'free hero' independent of himself (yet dependent on the sword which Wotan will provide for him) – we must realize the difference between this unreal 'grand idea' and the real one at the end of *The Valkyrie*. The first, although it was born of a desire to better the world, was still attached to the absolute power of Wotan – and therefore Wagner did not accompany it with the music of Loge, who afterwards, in fact, stood on the stage apart from the gods, wondering whether he should not leave them to their own grandiose devices. So Wotan's first grand idea, still attached to his obsession with power, fell into ruins, crushed by the logic of the equally power-obsessed Fricka. But out of those ruins arose his second grand idea – forced on him by Brünnhilde, symbolized by the fire of Loge, and born of a decision to give up his power and recognize the claims of love; and this will be far more successful. How successful, we can only find out when we turn to *Siegfried*.

Bibliography

This bibliography is intended only as an easy reference to the main books referred to in the present volume. A more comprehensive bibliography is contained in Robert Gutman's *Richard Wagner: the Man, his Mind and his Music*.

Gerald Abraham: *A Hundred Years of Music*, London, 1938.

Aylmer Buesst: *The Nibelung's Ring*, London, 1932.

Robert Donington: *Wagner's 'Ring' and its Symbols*, Faber and Faber, 1963, 1969, 1974.

W. Ashton Ellis: *The Prose Works of Richard Wagner*, London, 1892–9.

Robert W. Gutman: *Richard Wagner: the Man, his Mind and his Music*, Secker and Warburg, 1968, Pelican Books, 1971.

Alfred Lorenz: *Das Geheimnis der Form bei Richard Wagner*, Berlin, 1924–33. 4 volumes.

Ernest Newman: *The Life of Richard Wagner*, London, 1933–47. 4 volumes.

Ernest Newman: *Wagner Nights*, London, 1949.

Kurt Overhoff: *Die Musikdramen Richard Wagners*, Salzburg, 1967.

George Bernard Shaw: *The Perfect Wagnerite: A Commentary on the Nibelung's Ring*, London, 1898.

Richard Wagner an August Röckel, Breitkopf & Härtel, 1912.

Richard Wagner's Letters to August Roeckel, translated by Eleanor C. Sellar, Bristol, 1897.

Richard Wagner: Skizzen und Entwürfe zur Ring-Dichtung, edited Otto Strobel, Munich, 1930.

Curt von Westernhagen: *Richard Wagners Dresdener Bibliothek 1842 bis 1849*, Wiesbaden, 1966.

Jessie L. Weston: *Legends of the Wagner Dramas*, London, 1896.

Baron Hans Paul von Wolzogen: *Führer durch die Musik zu Richard Wagners Der Ring des Nibelungen*, Leipzig, 1878.

Volsunga saga oder Sigurd der Fafnirstodter und die Niflungen, German translation by Friedrich Heinrich von der Hagen, Breslau, 1815.

The Saga of the Volsungs, Nelson, London and Edinburgh, 1965. (Edited and translated with Introduction, Notes and Appendices, by R. G. Finch.)

Christian Friedrich Rühs: *Die Edda, nebst einer Einleitung über nordische Poesie und Mythologie*, Berlin, 1812.

Lieder der älteren oder Sämundischen Edda, herausgegeben zum erstenmal durch Friedrich Heinrich von der Hagen, Berlin, 1812.

Friedrich Majer: *Mythologische Dichtungen und Lieder der Skandinavier*, Leipzig, 1818.

Karl Simrock: *Die Edda die ältere und jüngere*, Stuttgart, 1851.

Henry Adams Bellows: *The Poetic Edda*, New York, 1923.

Paul B. Taylor and W. H. Auden: *The Elder Edda*, a selection, London, 1969.

Arthur Gilchrist Brodeur: *The Prose Edda*, New York and London, 1916.

Jean Isobel Young: *The Prose Edda of Snorri Sturluson*, Cambridge University Press, 1954.

Karl Lachmann: *Kritik der Sage von den Nibelungen*, an essay published as an appendix to Lachmann's edition of the *Nibelungenlied: Zu den Nibelungen und zur Klage: Anmerkungen*, Berlin, 1836.

The Nibelungenlied, Penguin Books, 1965. (Foreword and translation by A. T. Hatto.)

Das Lied vom hürnen Seyfrid, Critical Edition with Introduction and Notes by K. C. King, Manchester University Press, 1958.

Wilkina- und Niflunga-saga, oder Dietrich von Bern und die Nibelungen, German translation by Friedrich Heinrich von der Hagen, Breslau, 1814.

Jacob Grimm: *Deutsche Mythologie*, Göttingen, 1835. Enlarged second edition 1844.

J. S. Stallybrass: *Jacob Grimm's Teutonic Mythology*, London, 1883–8. Re-issued by Dover Edition, New York, 1966.

Wilhelm Grimm: *Die deutsche Heldensage*, Göttingen, 1829.

H. R. Ellis Davidson: *Gods and Myths of Northern Europe*, Penguin Books, 1964.

Brian Branston: *The Lost Gods of England*, Thames and Hudson, London, 1957.

Index

(For the characters in *The Ring*, only principal references are given)